SIDREA Series in Accounting and Business Administration

This is the official book series of SIDREA - the Italian Society of Accounting and Business Administration. This book series is provided with a wide Scientific Committee composed of Academics by SIDREA. It publishes contributions (monographs, edited volumes and proceedings) as a result of the double blind review process by the SIDREA's thematic research groups, operating at the national and international levels. Particularly, the series aims to disseminate specialized findings on several topics – classical and cutting-edge alike – that are currently being discussed by the accounting and business administration communities. The series authors are respected researchers and professors in the fields of business valuation; governance and internal control; financial accounting; public accounting; management control; gender; turnaround predictive models; non-financial disclosure; intellectual capital, smart technologies, and digitalization; and university governance and performance measurement. This book series is indexed in Scopus.

Marisa Agostini • Valentina Beretta
Maria Chiara Demartini • Alessandro Ghio
Sara Trucco
Editors

Diversity and Equity in Accounting

Emerging Issues, Challenges and Opportunities

Springer

Editors
Marisa Agostini
Sustainability Lab
Venice School of Management, Ca' Foscari University
Venice, Italy

Valentina Beretta
Dipartimento di Scienze Economiche e Aziendali
Università degli Studi di Pavia
Pavia, Italy

Maria Chiara Demartini
Dipartimento di Scienze Economiche e Aziendali
Università degli Studi di Pavia
Pavia, Italy

Alessandro Ghio
ESCP Business School
Paris, France

Sara Trucco
Università degli Studi Internazionali di Roma
Rome, Italy

ISSN 2662-9879 ISSN 2662-9887 (electronic)
SIDREA Series in Accounting and Business Administration
ISBN 978-3-031-78246-6 ISBN 978-3-031-78247-3 (eBook)
https://doi.org/10.1007/978-3-031-78247-3

This Springer imprint is published by the registered company Springer Nature Switzerland AG
The registered company address is: Gewerbestrasse 11, 6330 Cham, Switzerland

Preface

This volume is promoted by the Italian Association of Scholars in Accounting and Business Administration (SIDREA). It is the outcome of the collaborative study on equity and inclusion in accounting, management control, governance, and auditing promoted by the EIREA research group composed of more than 60 scholars. Such a research group was established in 2023 with the intention of disseminating and promoting the development of research, teaching, and third mission engagement on equity and inclusion in accounting, management control, governance, and auditing, topics that are increasingly present and relevant in national and international debates.

This thematic group of SIDREA brings together researchers from various Italian and international institutions and different levels of seniority, aware of the growing need for a space to highlight more voices in business administration. In doing so, it creates a community of researchers around the themes of equity and inclusion.

The group analyzes issues surrounding the concept of equity, understood as the pursuit of social justice. This involves taking deliberate actions to remove systemic, group, and individual barriers and obstacles that hinder opportunities and compromise well-being. Equity is achieved by identifying and eliminating policies, practices, attitudes, and cultural messages that create and reinforce unjust outcomes. It is important to highlight the difference between equality and equity. While both promote social justice, equality is achieved by treating everyone the same regardless of needs and circumstances. Equity is achieved by treating people differently based on needs and circumstances, considering historical and systemic inequalities.

Additionally, the group focuses on the concept of inclusion and studies its multiple facets in light of various definitions proposed in literature and professional practice. In particular, it refers to the following definitions of inclusion proposed by internationally recognized bodies, which identify the multiple socioeconomic challenges, including at the corporate level, related to social inclusion, such as "the process of improving the conditions of participation in social life for disadvantaged people due to age, disability, race, ethnicity, origin, gender, religion, or economic status or other, through greater opportunities, access to resources, voice, and respect for rights. Social inclusion is recognized as both a process and a goal" (United

Nations, 2016). It includes enhancing the circumstances for individuals and groups to actively engage in social activities and improving the abilities, opportunities, and dignity of marginalized individuals based on their identity, to participate in social interactions. Additionally, it ensures that those at risk of poverty and social exclusion can access the opportunities and resources necessary to fully engage in economic, social, political, and cultural life, maintaining a standard of living deemed normal by their society. This also promotes greater involvement in decision-making processes that affect their lives and ensures access to their fundamental rights.

Furthermore, the range of topics addressed allows for the examination of intersectionality, that is, how the multiple heterogeneous dimensions of managing inclusion, typically underrepresented in the accounting profession and governance systems, influence and relate to each other. This allows for the identification of synergies that can be created between the typically underrepresented dimensions in companies and how these, through an equitable and inclusive environment, can contribute to the creation of a new organizational and cultural model for businesses.

The thematic group thus analyzes recent literature trends that advocate for valuing the themes of equity and inclusion as fundamental elements of corporate culture and determining factors of the business growth model, even in an increasingly international and multicultural context. Once the topic is framed theoretically, the thematic group aims to conduct field analyses by collecting both secondary and, especially, primary data through qualitative and quantitative research methodologies, such as interviews, surveys, case study analyses, and document analyses on corporate practices undertaken by companies to promote equity and inclusion within their operations and in the social context in which they operate, and to understand the potential positive impacts of such practices on society.

Finally, this thematic group fits into a global context where there are numerous initiatives on equity and inclusion and business economics, such as those recently promoted by the American Accounting Association and the European Accounting Association, but all in English and more influenced by the Anglo-Saxon environment. Therefore, to promote similar initiatives in a different cultural context, this thematic group specifically focuses on the Italian context with the aim of promoting research, teaching, and third mission engagement on equity and inclusion in business economics in the Italian landscape.

The goal of this edited book is to identify and discuss issues concerning equity and diversity in accounting. This volume specifically attempts to develop a collective book that presents stories of commitment to equity and inclusion by researchers and professionals in the field of business economics. This type of publication would be an important documentation of the actions taken and the challenges faced by individuals from marginalized communities while working in accounting, management control, governance, and auditing.

Summary Section

This book offers further evidence on Diversity, Equity, and Inclusion (DEI) within corporate environments, exploring its impacts and implications across various sectors and settings. It begins with a review of the state of DEI in accounting and its intersection with corporate social responsibility. The subsequent sections present empirical case studies examining DEI disclosures in sustainability reports.

The chapters cover a wide array of topics related to DEI, encompassing literature reviews, empirical studies, case studies, and explorations of DEI in diverse organizational contexts (corporate, nonprofit, family firms, local governments, universities). This comprehensive scope facilitates a deeper understanding of DEI adoption and its implications across sectors, offering a holistic view of challenges and opportunities in promoting diversity and inclusion.

Furthermore, the chapters contribute to identifying research gaps and proposing future directions. For instance, they highlight gaps in the literature concerning the impact of disability management on firm performance, the intersection of gender diversity and AI in accounting, and the effectiveness of DEI policies in family firms. These gaps underscore the need for further research to better understand how DEI practices translate into organizational outcomes.

The book employs a variety of research methodologies, including bibliometric analysis, systematic literature reviews, qualitative case studies, and empirical studies using regression models. This methodological diversity enhances the robustness of findings and provides a broader understanding of DEI issues from multiple perspectives. It reflects the complexity of DEI research, necessitating interdisciplinary and varied approaches to capture its full implications.

Moreover, the book acknowledges the significance of contextual factors such as cultural traditions, regulatory frameworks, and industry dynamics in shaping DEI practices and outcomes. This contextual sensitivity is crucial for understanding why DEI initiatives may succeed or fail in different organizational and geographical settings. It underscores the importance of tailored approaches to DEI that account for local specificities and challenges faced by diverse groups.

While the text provides a rich exploration of DEI issues, it also identifies limitations that suggest avenues for further research. These include the predominance of studies from specific geographical regions (e.g., Europe and Italy) and sectors (e.g., corporate and academic institutions) over others. Future research could benefit from more global perspectives and a broader representation of organizational contexts to enhance the generalizability of findings.

In conclusion, the insights from the chapters of this book serve as a valuable resource for academics, practitioners, and policymakers interested in advancing DEI agendas within accounting and related fields. Its comprehensive coverage, methodological rigor, identification of research gaps, and practical implications significantly contribute to the ongoing dialogue on DEI in organizational settings.

Part I

Part I investigates the state of the art of Diversity and Equity in Accounting.

Chapter 1, titled "Corporate diversity, equity and inclusion: A bibliometric literature review," conducts a bibliometric analysis of existing literature on corporate DEI, discussing the current state and emerging trends. This review delves into the evolving DEI landscape within the accounting profession and its impact on corporate social responsibility (CSR) practices. By integrating insights from multiple sources, the study offers valuable perspectives for scholars, practitioners, and policymakers aiming to promote DEI in corporate settings and identifies potential research directions for academics.

Chapter 2, titled "Diversity as determinant of firm performance: A literature review," systematically reviews the current knowledge on the relationship between diversity (age, culture, abilities, ethnicity, gender, etc.) and firm performance (economic, environmental, social, innovative, etc.). Using the MySLR platform, two main research topics were identified: "gender diversity and performance" and "other diversities (ethnic, cultural, age, disabilities) and performance." The chapter interprets these topics within the input-mediator-outcome (IMO) framework and highlights literature gaps, suggesting future research directions. Notably, the diversity-performance relationship in public administrations, disability management's impact on firm performance, and the effect of migrant employees on firm-level performance require further study.

Chapter 3, titled "The reporting of diversity, equity, and inclusion by nonprofit organizations. First evidence from the literature," aims at analyzing the connections between DEI, nonprofit organizations (NPOs), and reporting in scholarly literature. The chapter discusses issues that could influence the scientific discussion on DEI in the nonprofit context, with a special focus on the reporting system. This preliminary analysis aims to assist researchers interested in DEI in nonprofit reporting by highlighting the main research gaps identified in the literature.

Finally, Chap. 4, titled "Diversity, equity, and inclusion practices in family firms: A review of the literature," offers an in-depth overview of current DEI practices in family firms and suggests areas for future research to enhance awareness of these beneficial practices. Utilizing a systematic literature review on the Scopus database, the analysis identifies key contributors, major journals, and emerging topics in the field. The findings highlight main research clusters and recent trends, outlining the evolution of academic interest in DEI within family businesses. Each cluster includes proposed future research directions. The study identifies significant gaps in existing literature, providing a research agenda for scholars. Practically, it serves as a valuable resource for family firms to recognize the importance of DEI and to implement relevant policies in their operations.

Part II

Part II investigates the trends related to the reporting and the disclosure of diversity and equity practices adopted by firms. In particular, this section is composed of 5 contributions.

Chapter 5, titled "Diversity, equity, and inclusion disclosure in corporate reporting," aims to analyze the extent to which companies report on their DEI practices and achievements in the literature. It emphasizes that non-financial reports should address the challenges companies face in managing diversity, show the representation levels of various minority groups, and report on different perceptions of diversity. The introduction of specific regulations and the use of non-financial statements are expected to enhance diversity reporting. However, the literature review conducted found very few relevant articles, indicating that the topic of DEI in corporate reporting is only recently gaining attention and is still limited.

Chapter 6, titled "Diversity, equity, and inclusion in environmental social and governance disclosure," investigated the quality of DEI disclosures in sustainability reports and identifies the factors influencing these disclosures, thus contributing to the adoption of agency theory in analyzing DEI disclosures and providing practical implications for corporate governance and policymaking. By using a regression model on 157 global companies, the study constructs a DEI disclosure index and performs a content analysis of sustainability reports. According to the results, board gender diversity, board independence, and board size positively affect DEI disclosure quality.

Chapter 7, titled "Are the European sustainability reporting standards effective to fight modern slavery risk," examines the role of reporting and disclosure in supporting companies in combating modern slavery, through the adherence to reporting frameworks, such as GRI standards and the ESRS. While accounting standards can address modern slavery, the analysis identifies their limitations. In particular, results of this study suggest the adoption of the Corporate Sustainability Due Diligence Directive and collaborative approaches to enhance reporting effectiveness and provide insights for future regulatory and stakeholder engagement.

Chapter 8, titled "Social equity reporting and practices in local governments," focuses the analysis on local governments by exploring how social equity policies are communicated and translated into practices that impact social equity. It adopts an exploratory case study to examine the disclosure and implementation of social equity policies, highlighting their effects on social equity. The study provides insights for policymakers on how to improve the regulation of local government disclosure processes and calls for further research on the influence of various actors in public administration.

Finally, Chap. 9, titled "Assessing Italian B-Corps commitment to diversity and inclusion and its linkage with financial performance," investigates the relationship between DEI policies and financial performance in Italian B-Corps. The study examines how DEI policies may enhance business profitability and contributes to the debate on DEI by discussing B Lab's approach to DEI measurement and scoring. In particular, results of this study underline a gap in standards and practices for measuring DEI impacts. The findings aim to draw regulators' attention to the importance of DEI in business and provide evidence of its linkage with financial performance.

Part III

Part III investigates the organizational challenges on diversity and equity. In particular, this section is composed of 5 contributions.

Chapter 10, titled "Diversity in accounting: Implications for environmental sustainability," provides a systematic literature review on studies that combine accounting research on diversity and environmental sustainability. Through descriptive and content analyses, the review provides an overview of trends, systematizes key contributions, and outlines implications for future research. The review reveals that most articles focus on the role of gender diversity on corporate boards and its impact on corporate environmental sustainability. The findings show that board gender diversity positively influences corporate environmental disclosure and performance. Additionally, contextual factors such as cultural traditions, industry dynamics, regulatory frameworks, and corporate governance mechanisms are crucial in understanding the relationship between board gender diversity and environmental sustainability outcomes.

Chapter 11, titled "Queer dimensions and other diversities: Valorization and positive language within organizations," examines the mandate programs of mayors from a sample of Italian municipalities, covering over 20% of the Italian population, to analyze references to LGBTQ+ and fluid dimensions. The language is studied from a pragmalinguistic perspective, considering it as a system designed by the actor for its audience, which provides crucial context. The findings reveal common approaches to diversity and help define a framework for actions that promote inclusive attitudes and language within organizations.

Chapter 12, titled "Female leadership," explores themes of resilience, innovation, and empowerment, emphasizing the importance of historical context. It traces the evolution of women's leadership roles from ancient matriarchal societies to the suffragette movement, highlighting the progress made and the barriers that still exist. Understanding this history is crucial for appreciating current advancements and addressing ongoing challenges. It provides examples of exemplary leadership journeys, such as the one of Indra Nooyi, Mary Barra, and Gail Kelly, which highlight common traits that have driven their success: resilience, innovation, and empowerment. These leaders have overcome obstacles and broken barriers in traditionally male-dominated industries. They have redefined leadership paradigms with their commitment to excellence, integrity, and inclusivity, inspiring aspiring female leaders globally. Their legacies demonstrate that resilience, innovation, and empowerment are essential for effective and impactful leadership.

Chapter 13, titled "How do cultural and personnel controls influence inclusive workplace climate for people with disability? Insights from the Italian context," aims at analyzing how cultural and personnel controls impact the inclusive workplace climate (IWC) for people with disability (PwD), as perceived by non-managerial public employees. A survey conducted among subordinate employees in Italian municipalities, tested with a regression model, revealed that cultural and personnel controls positively influence perceptions of IWC for PwD through organizational identification. These findings contribute to research on integrating management controls with public employees' social responsibility and CSR drivers in public organizations. Public managers and policymakers should emphasize informal controls to enhance collaboration with human resource management and promote meaningful inclusion of PwD in the workplace.

Chapter 14, titled "Exploring gender disparities in the era of AI," examines the impact of artificial intelligence (AI) on gender disparities in the accounting profession. The rapid advancement of AI and automation has transformed job structures, locations, schedules, and career paths, raising concerns about job displacement across skill levels. This research focuses on how AI affects gender disparities in accounting, using qualitative methods and in-depth interviews to analyze risks and opportunities for women versus men. The study reveals that while AI can enhance efficiency and productivity, it also poses risks like job displacement and work insecurity, with gender disparities in STEM education exacerbating these issues. Women are underrepresented in crucial AI-related fields, underscoring the need for equitable training and resources. The chapter highlights the importance of targeted educational programs and inclusive policies to mitigate AI's adverse effects and promote gender equality in the evolving job market.

Finally, Chap. 15, titled "Do women behave more ethically than men? Evidence from the impact of female CEO on the level of earnings management," investigates the influence of women CEOs on earnings management. Based on gender socialization theory (Gilligan, 1982), which suggests that women have stricter ethical judgments, the study hypothesizes and finds a negative relationship between the presence of women CEOs and the level of earnings management. The findings indicate that having women in corporate governance can enhance corporate accountability, attributed to female-specific traits such as stricter ethical standards and a lower tendency toward opportunistic behavior.

Part IV

Part IV investigates DEI from an empirical corporate case viewpoint.

Chapter 16, titled "Equity and inclusion from a historical organizational perspective: The case of the FIAT Group," examines FIAT's (Fabbrica Italiana Automobili Torino) longstanding commitment to equity and inclusion for its employees, tracing its efforts from the company's early years. Through content analysis of FIAT's reports and disclosures, the chapter reveals the company's early initiatives such as housing, education, healthcare, retirement assistance, and company canteens aimed at enhancing worker inclusion and support. This historical perspective highlights FIAT's dedication to social issues and employee inclusion. The research contributes to the equity and inclusion debate, offering insights into the evolving role of large companies in their communities and guiding managers on past and future actions for promoting these values.

Chapter 17, titled "Drivers, barriers, and enablers of gender equality certification system: Insights from a case study," uses a qualitative approach and case study method to explore the drivers, barriers, enablers, and benefits of gender equality certification systems under the UNI/PdR 125:2022 practice. Given the tool's recent introduction, research on this topic is limited. This pilot case study aims to lay the groundwork for further research, whether qualitative or quantitative, to examine these factors in larger samples of companies. The study also discusses practical implications for businesses and policymakers.

Chapter 18, titled "The integration of diversity, inclusion, and equity in management control systems: The multiutility experience," investigates how management control systems (MCSs) can foster DEI. To achieve this, a case study of an Italian multi-utility company was conducted. The qualitative study highlights the complexities involved in adopting and adapting new management tools. Both primary data, gathered through semi-structured interviews with managers, and secondary data, such as sustainability reports, were analyzed. The study examines the efforts of managers in an Italian organization recognized for its DEI initiatives. The findings suggest that MCSs and their key performance indicators (KPIs) can promote DEI at various organizational levels.

Part V

Part V investigates the trend related to diversity and equity in university governance and education. The section is composed of 5 contributions.

Chapter 19, titled "Action and perception of gender equality in higher education institutions: The case study of the University of Trieste," explores the evolution of gender equality at the University of Trieste, focusing on the role of the Comitato Unico di Garanzia (CUG). Using case study methodology, it analyzes documents from the university and semi-structured interviews with CUG members. The findings highlight the actions taken to promote gender equality and the members' perceptions of these efforts. It underscores the importance of collaboration among university stakeholders to enhance dialogue.

Chapter 20, titled "The determinants of gender equality in the academic world: An empirical analysis in international universities," explores factors influencing gender equality in higher education, focusing on university size, complexity, internationalization, and age. Analyzing 96 international universities, the findings show that complexity positively impacts gender equality, while age negatively affects it.

Chapter 21, titled "Gender equality as public value: An empirical analysis of gender equality plans in Italian higher education institutions," investigates how higher education institutions (HEIs) develop strategies to promote gender equality (GE) and their contribution to public value (PV). A content analysis of GEPs from public Italian HEIs identifies common paths and recurring patterns, by highlighting the need to regulate leadership access and address vertical staff segregation, while also fostering a GE culture and integrating GE objectives into overall strategies.

Chapter 22, titled "Disability disclosure in the sustainability reports of universities: An exploratory study in Italy," analyzes the current state of sustainability reporting on disability by Italian universities in the Network of Universities for Sustainable Development. Through content analysis, it examines the presence and type of disability-related information in these reports, identifying accountability gaps. Findings reveal that while some reports mention disability actions, many only describe legally required actions or basic data, with few taking a comprehensive view across teaching, research, and third mission.

Chapter 23, titled "Diversity in sustainability accounting education: The role of formative assessment to promote inclusion," seeks to encourage contemplation regarding inclusive teaching and learning methods in sustainability accounting education by employing a case study based on implementation of assessment for learning (AfL) strategies in an Italian university. The study demonstrates how this approach fosters inclusive learner engagement, allowing students to apply their knowledge to real-world challenges. Through collaborative assessment criteria development and peer review activities, aligned with sustainable assessment principles, students deepen their understanding of sustainability accounting and stakeholder engagement policies.

Venice, Italy — Marisa Agostini
Pavia, Italy — Valentina Beretta
Pavia, Italy — Maria Chiara Demartini
Paris, France — Alessandro Ghio
Rome, Italy — Sara Trucco

Contents

Part V Diversity and Equity in University Governance and Education

Contributors

Marisa Agostini Sustainability Lab, Venice School of Management, Ca' Foscari University, Venice, Italy

Selena Aureli Department of Management, Bologna University, Bologna, Italy

Mariasole Bannò Department of Mechanical Engineering, University of Brescia, Brescia, Italy

Monica Bartolini Department of Management, Bologna University, Bologna, Italy

Laura Berardi Department of Economic Studies, G. d'Annunzio University of Chieti-Pescara, Pescara, Italy

Valentina Beretta Dipartimento di Scienze Economiche e Aziendali, Università degli Studi di Pavia, Pavia, Italy

Laura Broccardo Department of Management "Valter Cantino", University of Turin, Torino, Italy

Eleonora Cardillo Department of Economics and Business, University of Catania, Catania, Italy

Francesca Maria Cesaroni Department of Economics, Society and Politics, University of Urbino Carlo Bo, Urbino, Italy

Ericka Costa University of Trento, Trento, Italy

Grazia Garlatti Costa Università degli Studi di Trieste, Dipartimento di Scienze Economiche, Aziendali, Matematiche e Statistiche, Trieste, Italy

Maria Chiara Demartini Dipartimento di Scienze Economiche e Aziendali, Università degli Studi di Pavia, Pavia, Italy

Paola Demartini Department of Business Studies, Roma Tre University, Rome, Italy

Tommaso Fornasari Department of Economics and Management, University of Brescia, Brescia, Italy

Claudia Frisenna Department of Economics and Business, University of Catania, Catania, Italy

G. Galizzi Department of Management, University of Bergamo, Bergamo, Italy

Isabel María García-Sánchez Economics and Business Administration, IME-Instituto Multidisciplinar de Empresa, University of Salamanca, Salamanca, Spain

Alessandro Ghio ESCP Business School, Paris, France

Katia Giusepponi Department of Education, Cultural Heritage and Tourism, University of Macerata, Macerata, Italy

Carmela Gulluscio "UnitelmaSapienza" University, Rome, Italy

Vitiana L'Abate Department of Management, Finance and Technology, LUM University, Casamassima, Italy

Antonio Leotta Department of Economics and Business, University of Catania, Catania, Italy

Barbara Sveva Magnanelli Department of Business Administration, John Cabot University, Rome, Italy

Arcangelo Marrone Department of Management, Finance and Technology, LUM University, Casamassima, Italy

Eleonora Masiero Università degli Studi di Trieste, Dipartimento di Scienze Economiche, Aziendali, Matematiche e Statistiche, Trieste, Italy

Sara Giovanna Mauro University of Modena and Reggio Emilia, Modena, Italy

Valentina Minutiello Accounting, School of Economics and Management, Carlo Cattaneo University – LIUC, Castellanza, Italy

Maria Lucia Monaco Department of Economic Studies, G. d'Annunzio University of Chieti-Pescara, Pescara, Italy

Laurie Mook School of Community Resources and Development, Arizona State University Downtown Phoenix Campus, Phoenix, AZ, USA

Giorgia Moschini Department of Management, Bologna University, Bologna, Italy

Alessio Maria Musella Università degli Studi di Napoli "Federico II", Dipartimento di Scienze Economiche e Statistiche, Naples, Italy

Zeila Occhipinti University of Pisa, Pisa, Italy

Lara Oliva Department of Biosciences and Territory, University of Molise, Campobasso, Italy

C. Oppi Department of Management, University of Bergamo, Bergamo, Italy

Federica Palazzi Department of Economics, Society and Politics, University of Urbino Carlo Bo, Urbino, Italy

Manuela Paolini Department of Economics, University of Studies G. d'Annunzio Chieti-Pescara, Chieti, Italy

Federica Picasso University of Trento, Trento, Italy

Vincenzo Pontrelli Department of Management, Finance and Technology, LUM University, Casamassima, Italy

Pina Puntillo Università della Calabria, Arcavacata, Italy

Nicola Raimo Department of Management, Finance and Technology, LUM University, Casamassima, Italy

Elisa Raoli Department of Scienze dell'Economia e della Gestione Aziendale (SEGESTA), Catholic University of the Sacred Heart, Milan, Italy

Domenico Raucci Department of Economics, University of Studies G. d'Annunzio Chieti-Pescara, Chieti, Italy

Carmela Rizza Department of Economics and Business, University of Catania, Catania, Italy

Davide Rizzotti Department of Economics and Business, University of Catania, Catania, Italy

Daniela Ruggeri Department of Economics and Business, University of Catania, Catania, Italy

Annalisa Sentuti Department of Economics, Society and Politics, University of Urbino Carlo Bo, Urbino, Italy

Anna Serbati University of Trento, Trento, Italy

Silvia Soriano Department of Business Studies, Roma Tre University, Rome, Italy

Salvatore Tallarico University of Pisa, Pisa, Italy

Patrizia Tettamanzi International Financial Reporting and Analysis, School of Economics and Management, Carlo Cattaneo University– LIUC, Castellanza, Italy

Silvia Tommaso Department of Business Administration and Law, University of Calabria, Rende, Italy

Elisa Truant Department of Management "Valter Cantino", University of Turin, Torino, Italy

Sara Trucco Università degli Studi Internazionali di Roma, Rome, Italy

Roberto Verona University of Pisa, Pisa, Italy

Filippo Vitolla Department of Management, Finance and Technology, LUM University, Casamassima, Italy

Part I
Diversity and Equity in Accounting: State of the Art

Corporate Diversity, Equity, and Inclusion: A Bibliometric Literature Review

Valentina Beretta, Maria Chiara Demartini, and Sara Trucco

1 Introduction

In contemporary debate, the concepts of inclusion, diversity, and equity (IDE) have garnered significant attention, particularly within the context of corporate social responsibility (CSR). Despite the increasing spread of ESG (Environmental, Social, and Governance) topics at the corporate level, a significant portion of the research and commitment in the field of CSR focuses on the environmental aspect of sustainability rather than its social dimension (Sharma & Ruud, 2003). In terms of social performance, for a long time, the accounting profession has been perceived as "an environment dominated by white men from the middle class" (Anderson-Gough et al., 2005, p. 480). Indeed, groups of people who deviate from this norm often face substantial barriers when trying to enter and/or advance in the accounting profession (Agrizzi et al., 2021; Annisette & Trivedi, 2013; Dambrin & Lambert, 2006, 2008; Hammond et al., 2009; Rumens, 2016). Furthermore, it is recognized that accounting practices and governance systems reinforce patriarchal systems and heteronormative practices (Broadbent, 1998; Rumens, 2017). In recent years, IDE concerns have gained traction as a "corporate imperative" particularly within studies on accountants and corporate auditing, notably among major firms like the Big4 (Lehman, 2019). However, despite these efforts, instances of discrimination persist in contemporary contexts (Bujaki et al., 2021; Kokot-Blamey, 2021; Lassou et al., 2021; Leiby & Madsen, 2017).

V. Beretta · M. C. Demartini
Dipartimento di Scienze Economiche e Aziendali, Università degli Studi di Pavia, Pavia, Italy
e-mail: valentina.beretta@unipv.it; mariachiara.demartini@unipv.it

S. Trucco (✉)
Università degli Studi Internazionali di Roma, Rome, Italy
e-mail: sara.trucco@unint.eu

M. Agostini et al. (eds.), *Diversity and Equity in Accounting*, SIDREA Series in Accounting and Business Administration,
https://doi.org/10.1007/978-3-031-78247-3_1

This study presents a bibliometric analysis of the previous literature related to corporate IDE and it provides a discussion of the state of the art and emerging trends. The definitions of the IDE concepts have recently been widely debated by academics, practitioners, and institutions and they have been analyzed from different perspectives, including the intersectionality of identities and the role of corporate governance in shaping inclusive practices. This literature review explores the evolving landscape of IDE within the accounting profession and its implications for CSR practices. By synthesizing insights from diverse sources, this study provides insights for scholars, practitioners, and policymakers seeking to advance the agenda of IDE within corporate environments and it suggests avenues for further research for academics.

The remainder of this chapter is organized as follows: Sect. 2 explores the state of the art of the IDE concepts; Sect. 3 explores IDE in the accounting profession, Sect. 4 presents the research methodology and Sect. 5 presents the results, while Sect. 6 discusses conclusions and future research directions.

2 Inclusion, Diversity, and Equity: A State of the Art

The definitions of the concepts of IDE have recently been widely debated by academics, practitioners, and institutions. In analyzing these concepts, we took into account some definitions provided by the World Bank, the Commission of the European Communities, and the Agenda 2030 and we compared them with the few definitions provided by the literature to provide a comprehensive framework of analysis.

First, in accordance with the World Bank, 2013, the social inclusion can be defined as follows: "*The process of improving the terms for individuals and groups to take part in society*" and "*The process of improving the ability, opportunity, and dignity of people, disadvantaged on the basis of their identity, to take part in society*" (World Bank, 2013, pp. 3–4). In a similar vein, the Commission of the European Communities, 2003, provided the following definition of social inclusion: "*Social inclusion is a process which ensures that those at risk of poverty and social exclusion gain the opportunities and resources necessary to participate fully in economic, social, political and cultural life and to enjoy a standard of living that is considered normal in the society in which they live. It ensures that they have greater participation in decision making which affects their lives and access to their fundamental rights*" (The Commission of the European Communities, 2003, p. 10). The definition of social inclusion provided in the report explicitly pertains to individuals facing disadvantage due to factors such as age, gender, disability, race, ethnicity, background, or socio-economic status, for two specific reasons. Overall, inclusion is a core aspiration of the 2030 Agenda and in general, it is underlined that there is a requirement for both theoretical and practical efforts to define inclusion comprehensively, alongside endeavors to enhance the accessibility of data. These aims are especially captured in the 17 Sustainable Development Goals that are aimed at diminishing poverty and hunger, while also striving to guarantee various essentials such as good health, education access, modern energy, and information availability. Thus, it is possible to conclude that social inclusion is both a process and a goal and it can be considered as a multidimensional phenomenon and a process of improving the terms of participation in society, particularly for those people who are disadvantaged, through enhancing opportunities, access to resources, voice, and respect for rights.

Fostering social inclusion involves overcoming obstacles that prevent people from fully participating in society. It aims to incorporate all individuals, promoting equity and acceptance. However, promoting social inclusion does not always guarantee harmonious coexistence, as some groups may still face exclusion. It is important to differentiate social inclusion from social integration, but both are essential for enhancing societal cohesion.

Furthermore, according to Molefi and colleagues, *"Diversity refers to the variety of similarities and differences among people, often called diversity dimensions, including, but not limited to: gender, sex, gender identity and expression, ethnicity, race, native or indigenous identity/origin, age, generation, disability, sexual orientation, culture, religion, belief system, marital status, parental status, pregnancy, socio-economic status/caste, appearance, language and accent, mental health, education, geography, nationality, work style, work experience, job role and function, thinking style, and personality type. Representation of various diversity dimensions within organizations may vary by geography, time, or organization*" (Molefi et al., 2021, p. 22). Hence, the concept of diversity pertains to the presence of a range of different attributes within a group of individuals. These attributes encompass various aspects that contribute to our uniqueness, including cognitive abilities, personality traits, and factors influencing our identity. Discrimination is closely associated with diversity in the workplace. Prejudice and unfair employment methods bar individuals with particular characteristics, posing challenges for organizations striving to establish and uphold diversity.

The Global Diversity, Equity, and Inclusion Benchmarks (GDEIB) is designed to guide organizations to achieve the best practices for firms. In doing so, GDEIB refers to the term intersectionality. In accordance with GDEIB, intersectionality describes the different manner in which individuals simultaneously belong to multiple marginalized groups. These identities can merge, coincide, or intersect within an individual or community, leading to various interconnected systems of discrimination or oppression (such as a black woman, an impoverished Indigenous individual, or a gay person with a disability). Consequently, the collective intersectional experience of a person or group exceeds the mere accumulation of individual instances of discrimination or disadvantage. The term intersectionality was coined by Kimberlé Crenshaw in 1989 and it describes the way in which different types of discrimination (it means unfair treatment because of a person's sex, race, etc.) are connected to and affect each other (Crenshaw, 1989, 2021, 2013). Therefore, IDE strategies are encouraged to be multifaceted, taking into consideration the different aspects that characterize the concept.

3 Inclusion, Diversity, and Equity in the Accounting Profession

After the definition of the general concepts of IDE, we studied these concepts among the literature in the accounting field.

In the last two decades, an increasing number of studies have highlighted the importance of CSR as a strategic business tool to meet the interests of different stakeholders, beyond the financial interest (Aguinis & Glavas, 2019; Turker, 2009). Furthermore, a lot of articles have highlighted a positive link between ESG issues and the creation of value in the firm (Signori et al., 2021). Indeed, while ESG issues are becoming more prevalent in the corporate debate, a considerable portion of research within the field of CSR emphasizes environmental sustainability rather than its social counterpart (Sharma & Ruud, 2003). In the field of social performance, the accounting profession has long been perceived as predominantly inhabited by white men from middle-class backgrounds (Anderson-Gough et al., 2005, p. 480). Undoubtedly, individuals or groups diverging from this norm often face significant barriers when seeking entry into or advancement within the accounting sector (Agrizzi et al., 2021; Annisette & Trivedi, 2013; Dambrin & Lambert, 2006; Hammond et al., 2009; Rumens, 2017). Moreover, it is acknowledged that accounting practices and governance structures perpetuate patriarchal norms and heteronormative standards (Broadbent, 1998; Rumens, 2017). In recent times, there has been a growing recognition of inclusion and equity concerns as essential aspects of corporate governance, particularly in studies concerning accountants and corporate auditing, with larger firms like the Big4 leading this charge (Lehman, 2019). Nevertheless, discrimination remains prevalent in the industry today (Bujaki et al., 2021; Kokot-Blamey, 2021; Lassou et al., 2021; Leiby & Madsen, 2017). Within this framework, several studies have been conducted in order to explore the dimensions of the gender diversity, in order to understand the link between the board gender diversity and the firm performance (Brahma et al., 2021; Solakoglu & Demir, 2016), the link between gender diversity and innovation (Sastre, 2015), and, in general, the connection between gender diversity and accounting quality (García-Sánchez et al., 2017). The concepts of IDE are not solely linked to gender, thus necessitating a comprehensive overview of the literature to identify the most/least studied aspects. However, limited studies have been conducted to consider the other dimensions of diversity and equity within the firms. Thus, the aim of this study is to conduct a comprehensive review of existing literature related to corporate IDE and its CSR implications and to provide an overview of the state of the art and emerging trends. Additionally, the study aims to identify emerging trends and gaps in the literature, providing insights and recommendations for future research directions. The novelty of this study lies in its comprehensive exploration of studies within the field of IDE beyond the traditional scope of gender. While previous research has primarily focused on gender-related aspects, this study seeks to broaden the examination to encompass a wider array of dimensions of diversity and equity within firms. By delving into these less-studied areas, the research aims to uncover new insights and perspectives that have been overlooked in existing literature. Therefore, the study not only fills a crucial gap in the current understanding of IDE but also opens up avenues for exploring the intersectionality of diversity and equity within organizational contexts.

4 Methodology

This study adopts a bibliometric analysis, defined as "*a popular and rigorous method for exploring and analyzing large volumes of scientific data*" (Donthu et al., 2021, p. 285). Following the structure provided by Donthu and colleagues, this methodology is structured in four different steps.

First, the authors have to define the aims and scope of the study (Donthu et al., 2021). As previously mentioned, this study aims to present the state of the art and emerging trends in the literature on corporate equity, diversity, and inclusion. In particular, a bibliometric analysis is the most effective tool for achieving research objectives when there is the need to evaluate a sizable volume of literature and summarize large quantities of data (Donthu et al., 2021; Grant & Booth, 2009; Macpherson & Jones, 2010). The purpose of this study is to present the state of the art and emerging trends in the literature on corporate IDE.

Second, the authors have to choose the techniques (Donthu et al., 2021). In this analysis, two different approaches are adopted.

The first approach, the performance analysis, examines the contributions of research constituents to a given field (Cobo et al., 2011; Ramos-Rodríguez & Ruíz-Navarro, 2004). Performance analysis evaluates the contributions of research elements within a specific field (Cobo et al., 2011; Ramos-Rodríguez & Ruíz-Navarro, 2004). This type of analysis, characterized by its descriptive nature, is a key aspect of bibliometric studies (Donthu et al., 2021). It is commonly integrated into reviews, even those not involved in science mapping, as it is a standard practice to showcase the performance of various research elements (such as authors, institutions, countries, and journals) in the field.

The second approach, the science mapping, examines the relationship between research constituents (Baker et al., 2020; Cobo et al., 2011; Ramos-Rodríguez & Ruíz-Navarro, 2004). Science mapping explores the connections between research elements (Baker et al., 2020; Cobo et al., 2011; Ramos-Rodríguez & Ruíz-Navarro, 2004), emphasizing intellectual interactions and structural relationships. Various techniques, including citation analysis, co-citation analysis, bibliographic coupling, co-word analysis, and co-authorship analysis, can be employed for science mapping. When integrated with network analysis, these techniques effectively reveal both the bibliometric and intellectual structure of the research field (Baker et al., 2020; Tunger & Eulerich, 2018). As part of this study, we investigate the intellectual linkages between publications by identifying the main clusters of papers (Appio et al., 2014; Minutiello & Tettamanzi, 2022; Van Eck & Waltman, 2014).

Third, authors have to define the data collection methods (Donthu et al., 2021). In this study, the following inclusion criteria are adopted. Consistently with previous research (Demartini & Beretta, 2020; Massaro et al., 2016), to maximize journal coverage and thus ensure that all relevant articles within the conceptual boundaries of the research were included, different databases, namely Scopus, EBSCOhost, and Web of Science, were considered. More specifically, the search was focused on the business and management discipline to detect articles that are most relevant to the purposes of the research. Title, Keywords, and Abstract fields were searched using Boolean operators. The keywords used were carefully selected to ensure inclusion of all relevant articles. For the purposes of this research and in line with previous research (e.g., Brottman et al., 2020; Khatib et al., 2020; Yeo & Jeon, 2023), the following keywords, and related acronyms, were used: "inclusion"; "diversity"; "equity"; "Corporate governance"; and "corporate social responsibility." The time period investigated ranges until April 2023. Books, working papers, and conference proceedings were excluded because of the insufficient peer review process. Thus, this choice was driven by the increased accessibility, dissemination, and impact of academic journal articles compared with other output types. Subsequently, titles and abstracts have been manually reviewed by authors in order to control for the alignment of the topic of the paper to the accounting field. The database search retrieved 3520 articles, of which the following were excluded:

- 237 duplications
- 7 errors in the record
- 1508 titles out of scope
- 458 abstract out of scope.

The final sample is composed of 1310 articles.

The data analysis proceeded with the use of the network visualization analysis software VOSviewer and with the computer-assisted qualitative data analysis software (CAQDAS), namely NVivo12 for the keywords frequency analysis.

Finally, as part of the fourth step, the bibliometric analysis is run and the findings are reported (Donthu et al., 2021).

5 Findings

In terms of ***publication year***, results show that there are 24 active years of publication, with the first article appearing in 1970. As shown in Fig. 1, the academic interest in the topic registered a sharp increase in the last years. In particular, publications starting from 2016 represent more than 80% of the total publications considered in the sample (Table 1).

In terms of ***publication titles***, results show that the articles included in the sample are published in 373 different academic journals. However, the first 19 journals, as shown in Fig. 2, are contributing with almost the 44% of the publications and the first 29 journals are contributing with the 50% of the publications (Table 2). The

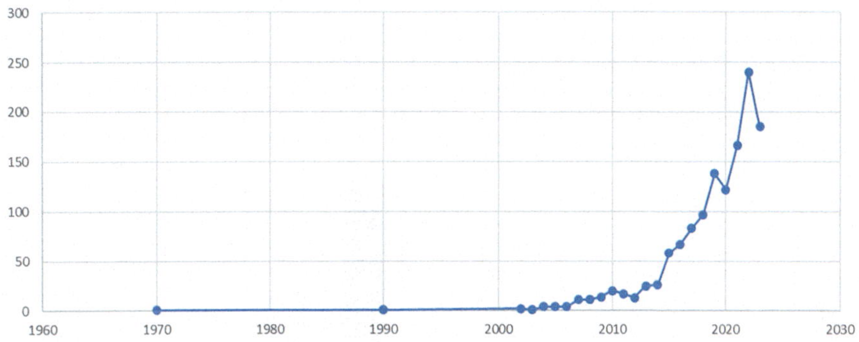

Fig. 1 Number of publications per year

Table 1 Cumulative percentage of publications per year

Year	Publications %	Cumulative publications %
1970	0.08%	0.08%
1990	0.08%	0.16%
2002	0.15%	0.31%
2003	0.08%	0.39%
2004	0.31%	0.70%
2005	0.31%	1.01%
2006	0.31%	1.32%
2007	0.84%	2.16%
2008	0.84%	3.00%
2009	1.07%	4.07%
2010	1.53%	5.60%
2011	1.30%	6.90%
2012	0.99%	7.89%
2013	1.91%	9.80%
2014	1.98%	11.78%
2015	4.43%	16.21%
2016	5.11%	21.32%
2017	6.34%	27.66%
2018	7.40%	35.06%
2019	10.53%	45.59%
2020	9.31%	54.90%
2021	12.67%	67.57%
2022	18.32%	85.89%
2023	14.12%	100%

leading journal in the field is represented by the Journal of Business Ethics with 100 publications related to the topics of this research.

From the results emerging from the science mapping analysis, it is possible to identify four main different clusters, as presented in Fig. 3, emerging from the bibliographic coupling analysis.

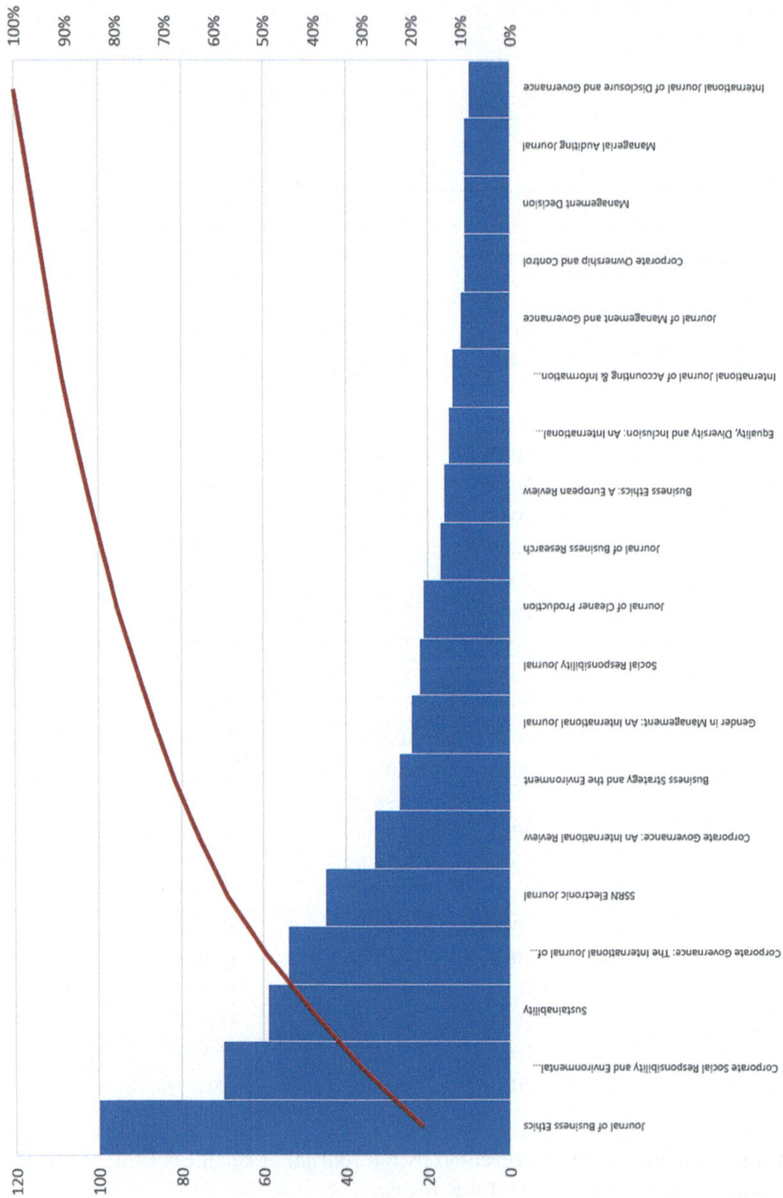

Fig. 2 Number of publications per journals

Table 2 Cumulative percentage of publications per journal

Journal	No. of publications	Cumulative publications %
Journal of Business Ethics	100	7.69%
Corporate Social Responsibility and Environmental Management	70	13.07%
Sustainability	59	17.60%
Corporate Governance: The International Journal of Business in Society	54	21.75%
SSRN Electronic Journal	45	25.21%
Corporate Governance: An International Review	33	27.75%
Business Strategy and the Environment	27	29.82%
Gender in Management: An International Journal	24	31.67%
Social Responsibility Journal	22	33.36%
Journal of Cleaner Production	21	34.97%
Journal of Business Research	17	36.28%
Business Ethics: A European Review	16	37.51%
Equality, Diversity and Inclusion: An International Journal	15	38.66%
International Journal of Accounting & Information Management	14	39.74%
Journal of Management and Governance	12	40.66%
Managerial Auditing Journal	11	41.51%
Management Decision	11	42.35%
Corporate Ownership and Control	11	43.20%
International Journal of Disclosure and Governance	10	43.97%
Meditari Accountancy Research	9	44.66%
Journal of Risk and Financial Management	9	45.35%
Journal of Management & Governance	9	46.04%
Journal of Financial Reporting and Accounting	9	46.73%
Journal of Corporate Finance	9	47.43%
Journal of Accounting in Emerging Economies	9	48.12%
Accounting & Finance	9	48.81%
Journal of Applied Accounting Research	8	49.42%
Frontiers in Psychology	8	50.04%
European Management Journal	8	50,65%

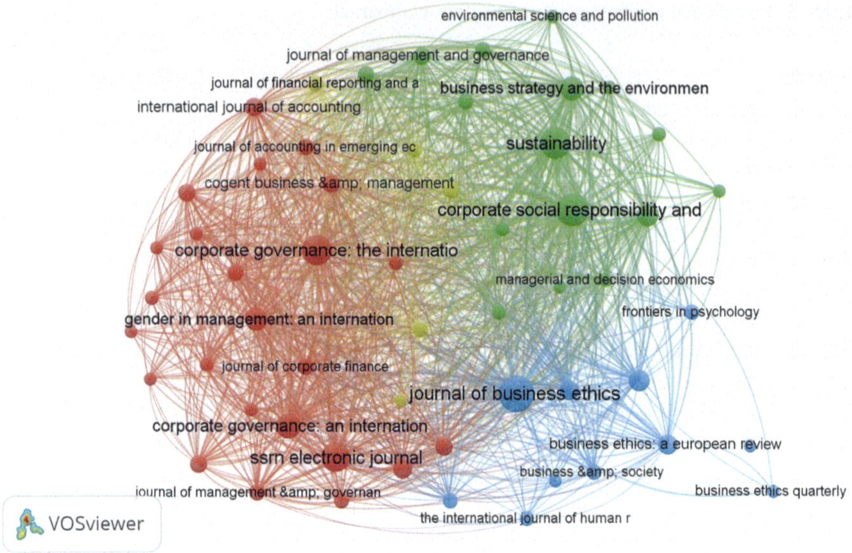

Fig. 3 Bibliographic coupling network of publication titles

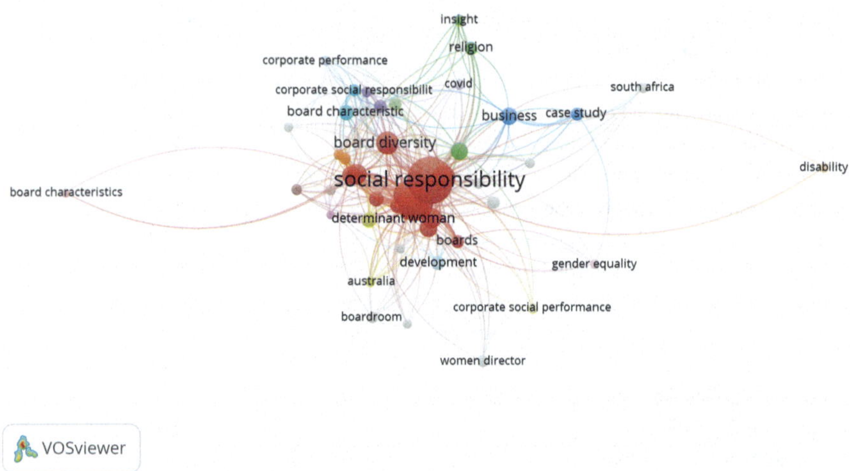

Fig. 4 Bibliographic coupling network of keywords

Finally, in terms of topics, bibliographic coupling network formed different clusters, as provided in Figs. 4 and 5. In particular, 27 clusters are identified.

Additionally, results from the keywords frequency show that, while the mostly investigated topics are related to diversity, in general, and gender diversity, in particular, other topics are highly represented, such as those represented in Table 3.

Fig. 5 Word cloud of most recurring keywords in titles and abstract

Table 3 Title and/or abstract frequency of keywords

Keyword	Frequency
Diversity	3381
Genders	2839
Cultural	489
Equality	269
Ethnic	213
Inclusion	211
Religious	159
Disabilities	104
Discrimination	85
Race	33
Sexual	32

6 Discussion and Conclusion

In contemporary CSR discussions, IDE has gained attention and it is now considered a corporate imperative. Despite ESG's focus on environmental sustainability, CSR often prioritizes the environment over social aspects (Sharma & Ruud, 2003). IDE concepts, debated by academics and practitioners, include intersectionality and corporate governance's role in shaping inclusive practices, which are currently underinvestigated (Sadler & Wessels, 2019). This study conducts a bibliometric analysis of corporate IDE literature, discussing current trends. The review explores IDE in the accounting profession and its CSR implications.

The analysis of publication trends reveals interesting insights into the evolution of research in the field of IDE. Over the span of 24 active years, dating back to the first work in 1970, scholars have made significant contributions to the academic literature, with a diverse array of topics explored across 373 different academic journals. The identification of four main clusters of publication trends underscores the multifaceted nature of research in this domain, reflecting the diverse perspectives and methodologies employed by scholars to investigate issues of IDE. This segmentation highlights the complexity of the subject matter and the various lenses through which it is examined, ranging from organizational dynamics to societal norms and individual experiences. Furthermore, the analysis of keyword frequency provides valuable insights into the prevailing themes and areas of focus within the literature. While diversity emerges as a central theme, gender diversity gained particular attention, reflecting the growing recognition of gender-related disparities and the imperative to address them within organizational contexts. Overall, these findings offer a comprehensive snapshot of the current landscape of research on IDE, highlighting both the progress made and the ongoing challenges that need further exploration.

This study contributes to the literature of IDE in the accounting profession, by providing a comprehensive analysis of publication trends and thematic clusters within the field, highlighting that gender is only a dimension of IDE and more and more studies are nowadays focusing on the other dimensions of IDE (Brown-Liburd et al., 2024; Egan, 2021; Gould et al., 2020) and their intersections (Ruiz Castro & Holvino, 2016; Tiron-Tudor & Faragalla, 2022).

Drawing from academic literature, institutional frameworks, and global agendas, the study analyzes IDE definitions, dimensions, and challenges, providing guidance for advancing IDE in corporate settings and suggesting research avenues. In particular, future studies can be conducted in the areas identified below:

- *Understanding structural, relational, and individual challenges:* This involves conducting a comprehensive analysis of the structural challenges, which encompasses organizational policies and practices that may inadvertently perpetuate inequity.
- *Examining benefits of inclusive corporate organizations:* This involves assessing the advantages of having inclusive and equitable corporate organizations, including enhanced employee engagement, improved decision-making processes, and increased innovation.
- *Identifying empowerment tools for inclusion and equity:* This requires identifying and implementing new empowerment tools designed to address inclusion and equity within companies.
- *Mapping performance indicators and remuneration policies:* This involves mapping performance indicators related to inclusion and equity and understanding their potential implications in remuneration policies.
- *Understanding impact of inclusion networks:* This entails understanding the impact of inclusion networks for marginalized groups within companies on corporate performance.
- *Understanding role of invisible disabilities:* This involves recognizing and understanding the role of invisible disabilities, such as neurodiversity and chronic illnesses, in the accounting profession and corporate governance.

- *Analyzing intersectionality challenges:* This requires recognizing and analyzing the challenges related to intersectionality in the accounting profession, management control, corporate governance, and auditing.
- *Exploring social issues in ESG reporting:* This involves exploring social issues related to IDE in ESG reporting and non-financial documentation of companies.

Funding Funding for this chapter is provided by Progetto PRIN 2022 "Non-Financial disclosure and Audit Quality: Future perspectives in Italy and Europe (n-FAQ)"—Codice progetto 2022YALETF—CUP F53D23003200006—Finanziamento dell'Unione Europea—NextGenerationEU—missione 4, componente 2, investimento 1.1.

References

Agrizzi, D., Soobaroyen, T., & Alsalloom, A. (2021). Spatiality and accounting: The case of female segregation in audit firms. *Accounting, Organizations and Society, 93*, 101238.

Aguinis, H., & Glavas, A. (2019). On corporate social responsibility, sensemaking, and the search for meaningfulness through work. *Journal of Management, 45*(3), 1057–1086.

Anderson-Gough, F., Grey, C., & Robson, K. (2005). "Helping them to forget": The organizational embedding of gender relations in public audit firms. *Accounting, Organizations and Society, 30*(5), 469–490.

Annisette, M., & Trivedi, V. U. (2013). Globalization, paradox and the (un) making of identities: Immigrant chartered accountants of India in Canada. *Accounting, Organizations and Society, 38*(1), 1–29.

Appio, F. P., Cesaroni, F., & Di Minin, A. (2014). Visualizing the structure and bridges of the intellectual property management and strategy literature: A document co-citation analysis. *Scientometrics, 101*, 623–661.

Baker, R., Freeman, G. K., Haggerty, J. L., Bankart, M. J., & Nockels, K. H. (2020). Primary medical care continuity and patient mortality: A systematic review. *British Journal of General Practice, 70*(698), e600–e611.

Brahma, S., Nwafor, C., & Boateng, A. (2021). Board gender diversity and firm performance: The UK evidence. *International Journal of Finance & Economics, 26*(4), 5704–5719.

Broadbent, J. (1998). Civil Society in Japan: Through an environmental lens.

Brottman, M. R., Char, D. M., Hattori, R. A., Heeb, R., & Taff, S. D. (2020). Toward cultural competency in health care: A scoping review of the diversity and inclusion education literature. *Academic Medicine, 95*(5), 803–813.

Brown-Liburd, H. L., Ghio, A., & Roberts, A. A. (2024). Diversity, equity, inclusion and belonging: Practice problems of real consequence. *Accounting Horizons, 38*(1), 1–5.

Bujaki, M. L., Durocher, S., Brouard, F., & Neilson, L. C. (2021). Conflicting accounts of inclusiveness in accounting firm recruitment website photographs. *European Accounting Review, 30*(3), 473–501.

Cobo, M. J., López-Herrera, A. G., Herrera-Viedma, E., & Herrera, F. (2011). Science mapping software tools: Review, analysis, and cooperative study among tools. *Journal of the American Society for Information Science and Technology, 62*(7), 1382–1402.

Crenshaw, K. (1989). Demarginalizing the intersection of race and sex: A black feminist critique of antidiscrimination doctrine, feminist theory and antiracist policies. *University of Chicago Legal Forum, 1989*(1), 139–167.

Crenshaw, K. (2021). Demarginalizing the intersection of race and sex: A black feminist critique of antidiscrimination doctrine, feminist theory and antiracist politics. *Droit et Société, 108*, 465.

Crenshaw, K. W. (2013). Mapping the margins: Intersectionality, identity politics, and violence against women of color. In *The public nature of private violence* (pp. 93–118). Routledge.

Dambrin, C., & Lambert, C. (2006). Le deuxième sexe dans la profession comptable: Réflexions théoriques et méthodologiques. *Comptabilité-Contrôle-Audit, 12*(3), 101–138.

Dambrin, C., & Lambert, C. (2008). Mothering or auditing? The case of two big four in France. *Accounting, Auditing & Accountability Journal, 21*(4), 474–506.

Demartini, M. C., & Beretta, V. (2020). Intellectual capital and SMEs' performance: A structured literature review. *Journal of Small Business Management, 58*(2), 288–332.

Donthu, N., Kumar, S., Mukherjee, D., Pandey, N., & Lim, W. M. (2021). How to conduct a bibliometric analysis: An overview and guidelines. *Journal of Business Research, 133*, 285–296.

Egan, M. (2021). Diversity, inclusion, and the opportunities for accounting research. *Social and Environmental Accountability Journal, 41*(3), 201–207.

García-Sánchez, I.-M., Martínez-Ferrero, J., & García-Meca, E. (2017). Gender diversity, financial expertise and its effects on accounting quality. *Management Decision, 55*(2), 347–382. https://doi.org/10.1108/MD-02-2016-0090

Gould, R., Harris, S. P., Mullin, C., & Jones, R. (2020). Disability, diversity, and corporate social responsibility: Learning from recognized leaders in inclusion. *Journal of Vocational Rehabilitation, 52*(1), 29–42.

Grant, M. J., & Booth, A. (2009). A typology of reviews: An analysis of 14 review types and associated methodologies. *Health Information & Libraries Journal, 26*(2), 91–108.

Hammond, T., Clayton, B. M., & Arnold, P. J. (2009). South Africa's transition from apartheid: The role of professional closure in the experiences of black chartered accountants. *Accounting, Organizations and Society, 34*(6–7), 705–721.

Khatib, S. F. A., Abdullah, D. F., Elamer, A. A., & Abueid, R. (2020). Nudging toward diversity in the boardroom: A systematic literature review of board diversity of financial institutions. *SSRN Electronic Journal*. https://doi.org/10.2139/ssrn.3706162

Kokot-Blamey, P. (2021). Mothering in accounting: Feminism, motherhood, and making partnership in accountancy in Germany and the UK. *Accounting, Organizations and Society, 93*, 101255.

Lassou, P. J., Hopper, T., & Ntim, C. (2021). Accounting and development in Africa. *Critical Perspectives on Accounting, 78*, 102280.

Lehman, C. R. (2019). Reflecting on now more than ever: Feminism in accounting. *Critical Perspectives on Accounting, 65*, 102080.

Leiby, J., & Madsen, P. E. (2017). Margin of safety: Life history strategies and the effects of socioeconomic status on self-selection into accounting. *Accounting, Organizations and Society, 60*, 21–36.

Macpherson, A., & Jones, O. (2010). Strategies for the development of International Journal of Management Reviews. *International Journal of Management Reviews, 12*(2), 107–113.

Massaro, M., Dumay, J., & Guthrie, J. (2016). On the shoulders of giants: Undertaking a structured literature review in accounting. *Accounting, Auditing & Accountability Journal, 29*(5), 767–801.

Minutiello, V., & Tettamanzi, P. (2022). The quality of nonfinancial voluntary disclosure: A systematic literature network analysis on sustainability reporting and integrated reporting. *Corporate Social Responsibility and Environmental Management, 29*(1), 1–18.

Molefi, N., O'Mara, J., & Richter, A. (2021). Global diversity, equity and inclusion benchmarks—Standards for organizations around the world.

Ramos-Rodríguez, A., & Ruíz-Navarro, J. (2004). Changes in the intellectual structure of strategic management research: A bibliometric study of the Strategic Management Journal, 1980–2000. *Strategic Management Journal, 25*(10), 981–1004.

Ruiz Castro, M., & Holvino, E. (2016). Applying intersectionality in organizations: Inequality markers, cultural scripts and advancement practices in a professional service firm. *Gender, Work and Organization, 23*(3), 328–347. https://doi.org/10.1111/gwao.12129

Rumens, N. (2016). Sexualities and accounting: A queer theory perspective. *Critical Perspectives on Accounting, 35*, 111–120.

Rumens, N. (2017). Postfeminism, men, masculinities and work: A research agenda for gender and organization studies scholars. *Gender, Work and Organization, 24*(3), 245–259.

Sadler, E., & Wessels, J. S. (2019). *Transformation of the accounting profession* (Vol. 27, p. 448).

Sastre, J. F. (2015). The impact of R&D teams' gender diversity on innovation outputs. *International Journal of Entrepreneurship and Small Business, 24*(1), 142–162.

Sharma, S., & Ruud, A. (2003). On the path to sustainability: Integrating social dimensions into the research and practice of environmental management. *Business Strategy and the Environment, 12*(4), 205–214.

Signori, S., San-Jose, L., Retolaza, J. L., & Rusconi, G. (2021). Stakeholder value creation: Comparing ESG and value added in European companies. *Sustainability, 13*(3), 1392.

Solakoglu, M. N., & Demir, N. (2016). The role of firm characteristics on the relationship between gender diversity and firm performance. *Management Decision, 54*(6), 1407–1419.

The Commission of the European Communities. (2003). *Joint report on social inclusion*. Office for Official Publications of the European Communities.

Tiron-Tudor, A., & Faragalla, W. A. (2022). Intersections of women's identities in professional accountancy careers. *Qualitative Research in Accounting & Management, 19*(5), 564–603. https://doi.org/10.1108/QRAM-02-2021-0038

Tunger, D., & Eulerich, M. (2018). Bibliometric analysis of corporate governance research in German-speaking countries: Applying bibliometrics to business research using a custom-made database. *Scientometrics, 117*, 2041–2059.

Turker, D. (2009). Measuring corporate social responsibility: A scale development study. *Journal of Business Ethics, 85*, 411–427.

Van Eck, N. J., & Waltman, L. (2014). Visualizing bibliometric networks. In *Measuring scholarly impact: Methods and practice* (pp. 285–320). Springer.

World Bank. (2013). What do we mean by social inclusion? In *Inclusion matters: The foundation for shared prosperity* (pp. 49–65). World Bank. https://doi.org/10.1596/978-1-4648-0010-8_ch1

Yeo, J., & Jeon, S. H. (2023). Diversity, equity, inclusion, and accessibility in recent public administration research: A systematic review of the literature since George Floyd. *Journal of Policy Studies, 38*(2), 33–54.

Diversity as Determinant of Firm Performance: A Literature Review

Silvia Tommaso

1 Introduction and Aim of the Chapter

Nowadays, diversity and inclusion represent a highly topical subject; in the business context diversity matters and the ability to include can represent a competitive advantage (Saxena, 2014; Kalargyrou, 2014; Urbancová et al., 2020; Richard & Miller, 2013). Diversity in business, for instance in the workforce or in the board of directors, represents a growing phenomenon (Roberge & van Dick, 2010) that can determine advantages such as an increase of innovative performance (Richard, 2000; van Dijk et al., 2012), financial performance (Arora, 2022; Richard et al., 2013), and environmental and social performance (Orazalin & Baydauletov, 2020).

This chapter focuses on the benefits that the so-called diverse companies (Hunt et al., 2015), organizations that embrace diversity and inclusion, can achieve. Diverse companies are those that foster a diverse and inclusive workplace. The topic of diversity in organizations has been addressed by several scholars over the years in its different meanings; diversity in organizations can be represented by several socio-demographic dimensions: for instance, age, gender, and ethnicity (Ciocirlan & Pettersson, 2012).

To paraphrase Saxena (2014), a diverse company could be defined as an organization characterized by similarities and differences among directors, managers, and/or employees in terms of age, cultural background, physical abilities and disabilities, ethnicity, religion, gender, and sexual orientation.

The purpose of this study is to investigate the current state of knowledge on the relationship between diversity (and, consequently, inclusion) and firm performance.

S. Tommaso (✉)
Department of Business Administration and Law, University of Calabria, Rende, Italy
e-mail: silvia.tommaso@unical.it

M. Agostini et al. (eds.), *Diversity and Equity in Accounting*, SIDREA Series in Accounting and Business Administration,
https://doi.org/10.1007/978-3-031-78247-3_2

To achieve the objective of the study, the chosen research methodology is the systematic literature review (Torraco, 2005; Tranfield et al., 2003; Denyer & Tranfield, 2009). The proposed review has two original features.

Firstly, different meanings of diversity and different meanings of performance are considered. While many studies on diversity and performance have looked at gender diversity and business performance, in this chapter diversity and performance are understood in a broad sense. Diversity is not only gender diversity but also ethnic, age, cultural, etc., and performance is not only economic but also environmental, social, innovative, etc.

Secondly, a digital platform has been used to conduct systematic literature reviews. This platform is named MySLR and supports reviews in the organization and management field of study (Ammirato et al., 2023). Particularly, MySLR supports researchers in classifying the contributions and discovering research topics.

After this brief introduction, the chapter outlines the research methodology (Sect. 2), presents descriptive results of the analysis (Sect. 3), describes the main topics identified in the literature (Sect. 4) and interprets the relationship between diversities and performances within the input–mediator–outcome framework (Sect. 5). Finally, limitations, academic and practical implications, and future directions of research on this topic are described in the conclusions.

2 Methodology

A systematic literature review is conducted to verify the state of knowledge about the topic and to identify research gaps as well as to establish new directions of research. For the systematic literature review, MySLR (Ammirato et al., 2023), a software platform, is used.

The steps of the literature review are the following. In the first phase, documents have been selected. In the second phase, an analysis of the selected papers has been conducted. The third phase has been dedicated describing, through the analysis of the content of the papers, the results of the analysis.

2.1 Documents Selection

The documents on which the analysis was carried out were extracted from Web of Science database and selected according to Preferred Reporting Items for Systematic Reviews and Meta-Analyses (PRISMA) Statement (Page et al., 2021; Fig. 1).

Documents have been extracted using research query as follow:

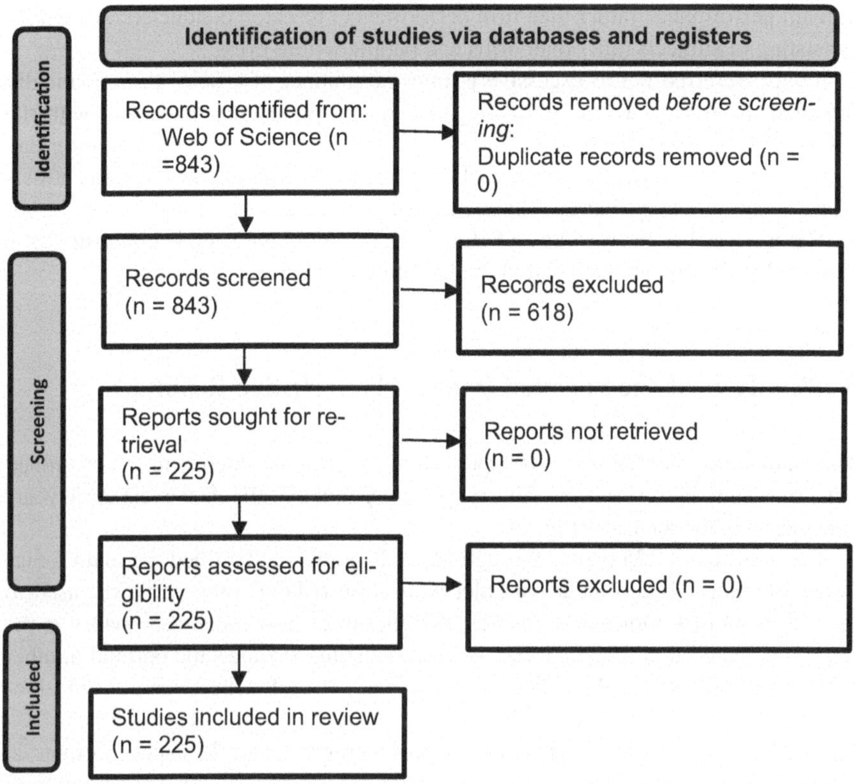

Fig. 1 Documents selection (PRISMA 2020 flow diagram). Source: Our Elaboration from Page et al. (2021)

(performance) AND ((racial diversit*) or (cultural diversit*) or (ethnic diversit*) or (disabilit* diversit*) or (demographic diversit*) or (age diversit*) or (gender diversit*) or (neurodivergent diversit*) or diversit*) AND (firm* or enterprise* or business* or compan* or public admi

nistration*)

The results have been refined by language (English), Web of Science categories (Management), Document Types (Article), and Publication Years (until 2023). A total of 843 documents were identified.

No duplicates were found, so 843 papers were screened by reading the title, the authors key words, the Web of Science keywords and the abstracts to ensure consistency with the research objectives. Inconsistent with the research objectives were considered: papers whose object of analysis is networks and thus examining diversity (i.e., knowledge diversity) among partner firms; papers that consider individual or team performance rather than firm performance; research conducted on samples consisting of subjects other than firms and people within firms.

It was preferred not to excessively limit the number of articles to be manually screened in order to avoid eliminating documents potentially consistent with the purpose of the research. Indeed, limiting the sample too greatly is a warning flag that affects both the depth and rigor of the review, and it could have serious effects on its results and contributions (Snyder, 2019).

The process has been adjusted before selecting the final sample consisting of a total of 225 documents included in the literature review.

3 Analysis of the Selected Papers: Descriptive Results

The analysis of the 225 selected papers shows a growing interest in the examined topic over time by researchers. This increase particularly affects the last three years considered in the analysis (Fig. 2).

The analysis of 225 papers through MySLR platform identified the main topics in the literature. The "Latent Dirichlet Allocation (LDA)" procedure was used to identify a set of k topics and a matrix that measures how much each paper in the sample is linked to a specific topic. LDA curve (Fig. 3) shows the optimal number of topics ($k = 2$) where the coherence value was -1.61 for the Gensim LDA algorithm and ensures the coherence of the topics (Chen & Liu, 2014).

The LDA technique assigned 151 papers to topic 1 and 74 papers to topic 2. Figure 4 highlights the intertopic distance map and suggests a strong polarization of the papers on each topic.

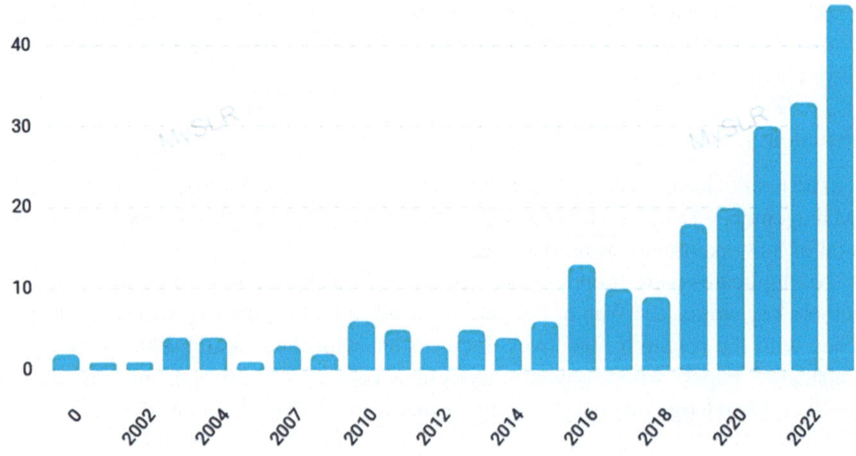

Fig. 2 Papers publication over time

Fig. 3 Coherence values

Gender diversity is present in both topics but with a different focus: in topic one, the focus is mainly on the top management team, while in topic two, it is on the workforce.

4 Main Topics

This section is devoted to a description of the two topics. The description is developed on the basis of the main concepts of the papers assigned to each topic. Based on the analysis developed in the previous paragraph, topic one could be called "Gender diversity and performances" while topic two could be called "Other diversities and performances."

The word clouds in Fig. 5 summarize and visualize these definitions.

The manual review of the content of the papers allowed for a better description of the two topics as well as the aims and results of the studies published to date.

Due to space constraints, the complete dataset is not included in the chapter but it is available at Supplementary Data. The list of references at the end of the chapter includes only contributions explicitly mentioned in the text as being most significant or explanatory.

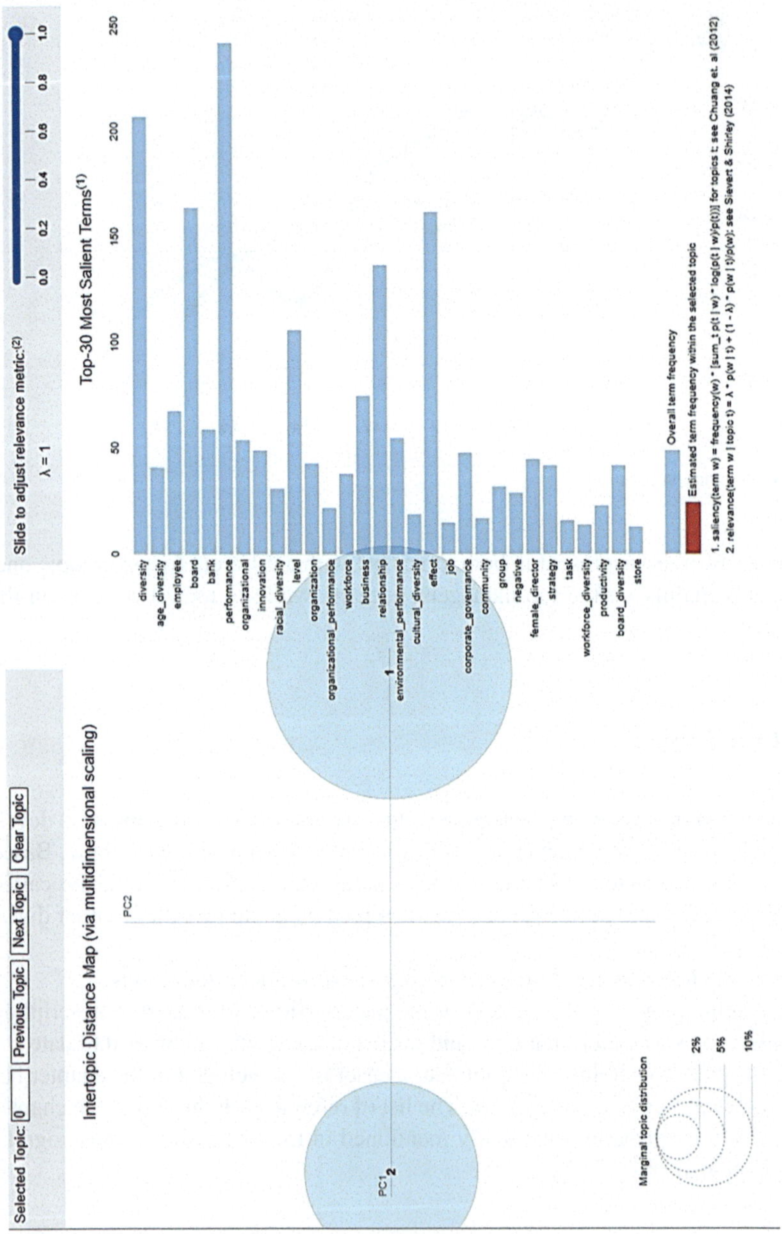

Fig. 4 Intertopic distance map

Fig. 5 Words clouds

4.1 Topic One "Gender Diversity and Performances"

Topic one is dominated by studies that have aimed to investigate the link between gender diversity and firm performance. In most of the studies under this topic, gender diversity is understood as the relationship between men and women and does not include people of non-binary gender.

Many studies have investigated the relationship between gender diversity on the board of directors (or in the management team) and financial performance (Tran et al., 2023; Hassan & Marimuthu, 2018; Kagzi & Guha, 2018). In most cases (Solakoglu & Demir, 2016; Singhania et al., 2022; Arora, 2022), financial performance was measured both through accounting-based performance indicators and market-based performance indicators.

Many studies have shown a positive relationship between gender diversity and financial performance. Among others, Terjesen et al. (2016) found that firms with more female directors have higher firm performance by market (Tobin's Q) and accounting (return on assets) measures. In other papers, a negative relationship has been shown. Yang et al. (2019), for instance, found a negative effect of mandated female representation on firm performance and on firm risk. Other researchers do not find a significant relationship between the gender diversity of the board and financial performance (Carter et al., 2010; Khan et al., 2023).

Other studies have verified the link between board gender diversity and environmental performance. In this regard, the study of Orazalin and Baydauletov (2020) shows, for European listed companies over the period 2009–2016, that board gender diversity is positively associated with environmental and social performance. Galletta et al. (2022) analyzed the impact of female directors and managers on sustainability performance in the banking sector finding that increasing the percentage of female directors improves environmental and financial performances.

The findings of Glass et al. (2016) suggest that firms characterized by gender-diverse leadership teams are more effective than other firms in pursuing environmentally friendly strategies.

With reference to environmental performance, other papers investigate how gender diversity on boards acts in combination with other factors. Cordeiro et al. (2020)

studied the relationship between ownership control and female board diversity in influencing corporate environmental performance in the U.S. context; the results show that majority family owners and dual-class owners are likely to choose female directors to help advance corporate environmental social responsibility, and, in fact, these two types of majority ownership interact with board gender diversity to positively influence corporate environmental performance.

Other studies investigated the linkage between:

- Gender-diverse boards and intellectual capital performance, finding a positive relationship (Arora & Tiwari, 2023; Smriti & Das, 2022);
- Gender diversity in the top management team or in the board of directors and organizational innovation, showing a positive gender diversity interaction effect on innovation (Wu et al., 2022).

There are few studies on the presence of LGBT-supportive policies for employees and their impact on financial performance (Pichler et al., 2018; Shan et al., 2017). In this regard, Pichler et al. (2018) found interesting results: the business value and profitability benefits associated with LGBT-supportive policies are greater for companies engaged in research and development (R&D); and the business value and profitability benefits of LGBT-supportive policies persist in the presence of state anti-discrimination laws.

4.2 *Topic Two "Other Diversities and Performances"*

Topic two focuses on the impact that diversities in age, culture, ethnicity, etc., have on firm performance.

Only a few articles dealing with gender diversity are included in this topic. Articles dealing with gender diversity focus on workforce rather than board and top management (included in topic 1). The study by Wikhamn and Wikhamn (2020), for instance, investigated the relationship between gender diversity in R&D units and innovation-related employee productivity for a sample of firms from Sweden; their results support the idea that diverse workforce is beneficial for firm success. Studies by Ali et al. (2011) and by Hsu and Lawler (2019) indicate a curvilinear relationship between gender diversity in the workforce and organizational performance. Particularly, Ali et al. (2011) investigated the link between gender diversity and organizational performance in publicly listed Australian firms while Hsu and Lawler (2019) tested their hypothesis for manufacturing companies in Taiwan. In both cases, the results show that different proportions of gender diversity have different effects on performance.

Several authors examine the relationship between ethnic diversity and firm performance. Andrevski et al. (2014) found that ethnically diverse management groups compete more intensively and increase performance (measured by market share gain and average stock return). Results of the study by Richard et al. (2003) suggest that an ethnically diverse workforce provides firms a competitive advantage when it is in conjunction with an innovation-focused business strategy. Roberson and Park (2007) get different results: firm performance declines with increases in the representation of ethnic minorities in leadership up to a point, but exceed a certain percentage further increases in diversity are associated with increases in performance.

Ethnic diversity is associated with cultural diversity. Bouncken et al. (2016) verified a high potential of creativity and innovativeness in firms with cross-cultural teams.

Concerning age-diverse workforces, research by Li et al. (2021) sheds light on how age-diverse workforces may create value through cultivating knowledge-based organizational resources. Lee and Kim (2020), also, show a positive effect of workforce age diversity on financial performance in the Asian context. Instead, Kunze et al. (2011) found that age diversity is related to the emergence of an age-discrimination climate in firms, which negatively impacts overall firm performance.

Other researches show a relationship between similarity to firm stakeholders and firm performance. The study by Gonzalez (2012) demonstrates that managerial demographic similarity to firm internal and external stakeholders is related to greater expertise to access diverse markets. For retail stores, Leonard et al. (2004) found that similarity between employees and customers increases sales in the case of Asian employees when many nearby residents are Asian immigrants who do not speak English, but this relationship was not found in other cases.

Finally, the study by Coll and Mignonac (2023) demonstrates that an adequate management system of disabilities in firms contributes to the job performance of employees with disabilities and the research by Oware and Mallikarjunappa (2021) shows that employee disability associated with technology innovation has a positive influence on financial performance (return on assets and return on equity) of firms.

5 An Interpretation of the Results within the Input–Mediator–Outcome (IMO) Framework

This section is devoted explaining the results of the literature review according to the input–mediator–outcome (IMO) framework. The input–mediator–outcome (IMO) framework (Paul et al., 2023; Ilgen et al., 2005) allows us to identify how the relationship between inputs and outcomes is transmitted through mediational influences (Yu et al., 2017).

With the understanding that the research needs to be expanded (see the next section in which the limitations of the research are highlighted), the initial results of this analysis highlight that diversity in top management and board of directors generally influences the different types of performance considered (often positively; more rarely negatively): environmental, social, financial, innovative, and intellectual capital. For instance, and in addition to what is stated in the section devoted to the description of the two topics, Gavana et al. (2023) analyze the effect of structural and demographic board diversity on French, German, Italian, Spanish, and Portuguese nonfinancial listed family firms' corporate social performance. Findings show that corporate social performance benefits from having female directors in family firms.

It could be argued that individual differences among top managers or among directors generally lead to the adoption of strategies that are more effective at achieving performance goals (not only financial, but also environmental, social, etc.). Interaction among different cultures, knowledge, experiences, and sensitivities guides in adopting better performance-oriented strategies.

Figure 6 summarizes this relationship.

When diversity affects the workforce, however, it impacts financial and innovative performance but not others.

This influence is detected when:

- The diversity of the front-office staff tracks the diversity of community (for instance, Richard et al., 2017)
- The company adopts effective diversity management mechanisms and inclusion policies (for instance, Lee & Kim, 2020)
- The company's external and internal environment is characterized by acceptance of diversity in the workplace and combating discrimination including through state anti-discrimination laws (for instance, Pichler et al., 2018)

6 Conclusions, Limitations, and Future Research Directions

Despite the literature review presented in this chapter could be expanded with the inclusion of "grey" literature such as policy and industry reports identified from websites and the inclusion of other papers from other databases such as Scopus, results are useful to provide some thoughts in order to identify gaps in the literature and, consequently, academic implications for future research directions.

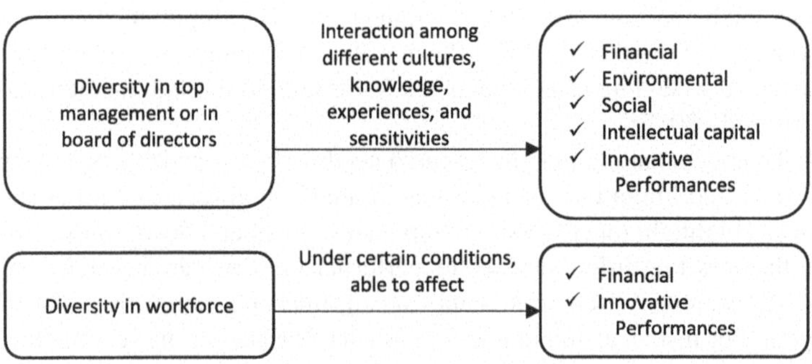

Fig. 6 Relationship among input, mediators, and output: an IMO framework-based proposal

Diversity in workforce composition in firms is increasing (WEF, 2023; McKinsey & Company, 2023) and, consequently, there is an increase in studies investigating the link between diversity in organizations and firm performance. The literature review revealed the prevalence of studies investigating diversity from a gender perspective by assessing its impact mainly at the level of financial or environmental performance. However, not many studies investigate gender diversity in workforce, focusing rather on gender diversity at the board of directors or top management level.

A growing research attention there is on the organizational consequences of age-diverse workforces as well as of ethnic diversity and this is associated with the global trend of increasing workplace age and ethnic diversity.

Studies investigating the linkage between diversity and performance measure diversity mainly through numbers (e.g., number of workers by age group) and ratios (e.g., ratio of men to women). Only few studies, however, investigate the link between diversity management system and firm performance. The article by Armstrong et al. (2010) demonstrates that a diversity and equality management system can contribute to firm performance, suggesting to investigate this link for different diversities.

The relationship between diversity and performance has not been given serious attention in the context of public administrations; this context is also worthy of further study.

Greater attention in research should be deserved to disability and to understanding how disability management and inclusion systems in the firms can impact different types of performance (financial, innovative, environmental, social, etc.). In this regard, the paper by Whelpley and Perrault (2021) explains the firm's ability to gain a competitive advantage by hiring and managing autistic individuals.

Only a few papers take into account migrant employees. Among these, Laursen et al. (2020) investigated, in the Dutch context, whether businesses' recruitment of high-skilled migrants contributes to enhance the firm-level innovation. Particularly, the results show that the hiring of migrants who increase the cultural diversity of the company contributes to raising the innovation performance of the company; furthermore, firms with a high integration capacity based on previous experience in employing highly qualified migrants derive greater innovation-related benefits from hiring migrants compared to firms with a low integration capacity.

Finally, further research direction is indicated by the papers excluded from this analysis and concerns the impact that diversity (in its different meanings) among partner firms (both in the top management component and in the workforce) has on the performance of the business network itself.

References

Ali, M., Kulik, C. T., & Metz, I. (2011). The gender diversity–performance relationship in services and manufacturing organizations. *The International Journal of Human Resource Management, 22*(07), 1464–1485.

Ammirato, S., Felicetti, A. M., Rogano, D., Linzalone, R., & Corvello, V. (2023). Digitalising the systematic literature review process: The MySLR platform. *Knowledge Management Research & Practice, 21*(4), 777–794.
Andrevski, G., Richard, O. C., Shaw, J. D., & Ferrier, W. J. (2014). Racial diversity and firm performance: The mediating role of competitive intensity. *Journal of Management, 40*(3), 820–844.
Armstrong, C., Flood, P. C., Guthrie, J. P., Liu, W., MacCurtain, S., & Mkamwa, T. (2010). The impact of diversity and equality management on firm performance: Beyond high performance work systems. *Human Resource Management, 49*(6), 977–998.
Arora, A. (2022). Gender diversity in boardroom and its impact on firm performance. *Journal of Management and Governance, 26*(3), 735–755.
Arora, A., & Tiwari, R. (2023). Using gender diversity to improve intellectual capital performance: An Indian investigation. *International Journal of Disclosure and Governance, 21*, 1–16.
Bouncken, R., Brem, A., & Kraus, S. (2016). Multi-cultural teams as sources for creativity and innovation: The role of cultural diversity on team performance. *International Journal of Innovation Management, 20*(01), 1650012.
Carter, D. A., D'Souza, F., Simkins, B. J., & Simpson, W. G. (2010). The gender and ethnic diversity of US boards and board committees and firm financial performance. *Corporate Governance: An International Review, 18*(5), 396–414.
Chen, Z., & Liu, B. (2014, June). Topic modeling using topics from many domains, lifelong learning and big data. In *International conference on machine learning* (pp. 703–711). PMLR.
Ciocirlan, C., & Pettersson, C. (2012). Does workforce diversity matter in the fight against climate change? An analysis of fortune 500 companies. *Corporate Social Responsibility and Environmental Management, 19*(1), 47–62.
Coll, C., & Mignonac, K. (2023). Perceived organizational support and task performance of employees with disabilities: A need satisfaction and social identity perspectives. *The International Journal of Human Resource Management, 34*(10), 2039–2073.
Cordeiro, J. J., Profumo, G., & Tutore, I. (2020). Board gender diversity and corporate environmental performance: The moderating role of family and dual-class majority ownership structures. *Business Strategy and the Environment, 29*(3), 1127–1144.
Denyer, D., & Tranfield, D. (2009). Producing a systematic review. In D. Buchanan & A. Bryman (Eds.), *The SAGE handbook of organizational research methods*. Sage.
Galletta, S., Mazzù, S., Naciti, V., & Vermiglio, C. (2022). Gender diversity and sustainability performance in the banking industry. *Corporate Social Responsibility and Environmental Management, 29*(1), 161–174.
Gavana, G., Gottardo, P., & Moisello, A. M. (2023). The effect of board diversity and tenure on environmental performance. Evidence from family and non-family firms. *Journal of Family Business Management*, (ahead-of-print).
Glass, C., Cook, A., & Ingersoll, A. R. (2016). Do women leaders promote sustainability? Analyzing the effect of corporate governance composition on environmental performance. *Business Strategy and the Environment, 25*(7), 495–511.
Gonzalez, J. A. (2012). Relational demography between managers and stakeholders and business unit performance. *Journal of Leadership & Organizational Studies, 19*(4), 450–461.
Hassan, R., & Marimuthu, M. (2018). Contextualizing comprehensive board diversity and firm financial performance: Integrating market, management and shareholder's perspective. *Journal of Management & Organization, 24*(5), 634–678.
Hsu, I. C., & Lawler, J. J. (2019). An investigation of the relationship between gender composition and organizational performance in Taiwan—The role of task complexity. *Asia Pacific Journal of Management, 36*, 275–304.
Hunt, V., Layton, D., & Prince, S. (2015). Diversity matters. *McKinsey & Company, 1*(1), 15–29.
Ilgen, D. R., Hollenbeck, J. R., Johnson, M., & Jundt, D. (2005). Teams in organizations: From input-process-output models to IMOI models. *Annual Review of Psychology, 56*(1), 517–543.

Kagzi, M., & Guha, M. (2018). Does board demographic diversity influence firm performance? Evidence from Indian-knowledge intensive firms. *Benchmarking: An International Journal, 25*(3), 1028–1058.

Kalargyrou, V. (2014). Gaining a competitive advantage with disability inclusion initiatives. *Journal of Human Resources in Hospitality & Tourism, 13*(2), 120–145.

Khan, I., Khan, I., Khan, I. U., Suleman, S., & Ali, S. (2023). Board diversity on firm performance from resource-based view perspective: new evidence from Pakistan. *International Journal of Productivity and Performance Management.*

Kunze, F., Boehm, S. A., & Bruch, H. (2011). Age diversity, age discrimination climate and performance consequences—A cross organizational study. *Journal of Organizational Behavior, 32*(2), 264–290.

Laursen, K., Leten, B., Nguyen, N. H., & Vancauteren, M. (2020). Mounting corporate innovation performance: The effects of high-skilled migrant hires and integration capacity. *Research Policy, 49*(9), 104034.

Lee, H. W., & Kim, E. (2020). Workforce diversity and firm performance: Relational coordination as a mediator and structural empowerment and multisource feedback as moderators. *Human Resource Management, 59*(1), 5–23.

Leonard, J. S., Levine, D. I., & Joshi, A. (2004). Do birds of a feather shop together? The effects on performance of employees' similarity with one another and with customers. *Journal of Organizational Behavior: The International Journal of Industrial, Occupational and Organizational Psychology and Behavior, 25*(6), 731–754.

Li, Y., Gong, Y., Burmeister, A., Wang, M., Alterman, V., Alonso, A., & Robinson, S. (2021). Leveraging age diversity for organizational performance: An intellectual capital perspective. *Journal of Applied Psychology, 106*(1), 71.

McKinsey & Company (2023). Listen to the report: Diversity matters even more: The case for holistic impact, December 2023.

Orazalin, N., & Baydauletov, M. (2020). Corporate social responsibility strategy and corporate environmental and social performance: The moderating role of board gender diversity. *Corporate Social Responsibility and Environmental Management, 27*(4), 1664–1676.

Oware, K. M., & Mallikarjunappa, T. (2021). Disability employment and financial performance: The effect of technological innovation of listed firms in India. *Social Responsibility Journal, 17*(3), 384–398.

Page, M. J., McKenzie, J. E., Bossuyt, P. M., Boutron, I., Hoffmann, T. C., Mulrow, C. D., et al. (2021). The PRISMA 2020 statement: An updated guideline for reporting systematic reviews. *International Journal of Surgery, 88*, 105906.

Paul, J., Khatri, P., & Kaur Duggal, H. (2023). Frameworks for developing impactful systematic literature reviews and theory building: What, why and how? *Journal of Decision Systems*, 1–14.

Pichler, S., Blazovich, J. L., Cook, K. A., Huston, J. M., & Strawser, W. R. (2018). Do LGBT-supportive corporate policies enhance firm performance? *Human Resource Management, 57*(1), 263–278.

Richard, O., McMillan, A., Chadwick, K., & Dwyer, S. (2003). Employing an innovation strategy in racially diverse workforces: Effects on firm performance. *Group & Organization Management, 28*(1), 107–126.

Richard, O. C. (2000). Racial diversity, business strategy, and firm performance: A resource-based view. *Academy of Management Journal, 43*(2), 164–177.

Richard, O. C., & Miller, C. D. (2013). Considering diversity as a source of competitive advantage in organizations. In Q. M. Roberson (Ed.), *The Oxford handbook of diversity and work.* Oxford University Press.

Richard, O. C., Kirby, S. L., & Chadwick, K. (2013). The impact of racial and gender diversity in management on financial performance: How participative strategy making features can unleash a diversity advantage. *The International Journal of Human Resource Management, 24*(13), 2571–2582.

Richard, O. C., Stewart, M. M., McKay, P. F., & Sackett, T. W. (2017). The impact of store-unit–community racial diversity congruence on store-unit sales performance. *Journal of Management, 43*(7), 2386–2403.

Roberge, M. É., & Van Dick, R. (2010). Recognizing the benefits of diversity: When and how does diversity increase group performance? *Human Resource Management Review, 20*(4), 295–308.

Roberson, Q. M., & Park, H. J. (2007). Examining the link between diversity and firm performance: The effects of diversity reputation and leader racial diversity. *Group & Organization Management, 32*(5), 548–568.

Saxena, A. (2014). Workforce diversity: A key to improve productivity. *Procedia Economics and Finance, 11*, 76–85.

Shan, L., Fu, S., & Zheng, L. (2017). Corporate sexual equality and firm performance. *Strategic Management Journal, 38*(9), 1812–1826.

Singhania, S., Singh, J., & Aggrawal, D. (2022). Board committees and financial performance: Exploring the effects of gender diversity in the emerging economy of India. *International Journal of Emerging Markets*.

Smriti, N., & Das, N. (2022). Do female directors drive intellectual capital performance? Evidence from Indian listed firms. *Journal of Intellectual Capital, 23*(5), 1052–1080.

Snyder, H. (2019). Literature review as a research methodology: An overview and guidelines. *Journal of Business Research, 104*, 333–339.

Solakoglu, M. N., & Demir, N. (2016). The role of firm characteristics on the relationship between gender diversity and firm performance. *Management Decision, 54*(6), 1407–1419.

Terjesen, S., Couto, E. B., & Francisco, P. M. (2016). Does the presence of independent and female directors impact firm performance? A multi-country study of board diversity. *Journal of Management & Governance, 20*, 447–483.

Torraco, R. J. (2005). Writing integrative literature reviews: Guidelines and examples. *Human Resource Development Review, 4*(3), 356–367.

Tran, N. M., Ngo, Q. G., & Tran, Q. T. (2023). Top management team gender diversity and the financial performance of Vietnamese SMEs: Family and non-family owned firms. *Gender in Management: An International Journal, 38*(3), 394–411.

Tranfield, D., Denyer, D., & Smart, P. (2003). Towards a methodology for developing evidence-informed management knowledge by means of systematic review. *British Journal of Management, 14*(3), 207–222.

Urbancová, H., Hudáková, M., & Fajčíková, A. (2020). Diversity management as a tool of sustainability of competitive advantage. *Sustainability, 12*(12), 5020.

Van Dijk, H., Van Engen, M. L., & Van Knippenberg, D. (2012). Defying conventional wisdom: A meta-analytical examination of the differences between demographic and job-related diversity relationships with performance. *Organizational Behavior and Human Decision Processes, 119*(1), 38–53.

WEF. (2023). *Diversity, equity and inclusion lighthouses 2024*. World Economic Forum (WEF).

Whelpley, C. E., & Perrault, E. (2021). Autism at work: How internal and external factors influence employee outcomes and firm performance. *Journal of General Management, 46*(3), 210–219.

Wikhamn, W., & Wikhamn, B. R. (2020). Gender diversity and innovation performance: Evidence from R&D workforce in Sweden. *International Journal of Innovation Management, 24*(07), 2050061.

Wu, J., Richard, O. C., Triana, M. D. C., & Zhang, X. (2022). The performance impact of gender diversity in the top management team and board of directors: A multiteam systems approach. *Human Resource Management, 61*(2), 157–180.

Yang, P., Riepe, J., Moser, K., Pull, K., & Terjesen, S. (2019). Women directors, firm performance, and firm risk: A causal perspective. *The Leadership Quarterly, 30*(5), 101297.

Yu, A., Matta, F. K., & Cornfield, B. (2017). Is leader–member exchange differentiation beneficial or detrimental for group effectiveness? A meta-analytic investigation and theoretical integration. *Academy of Management Journal, 61*(3), 1158–1188.

The Reporting of Diversity, Equity, and Inclusion by Nonprofit Organizations. First Evidence from the Literature

Laura Berardi, Laurie Mook, and Maria Lucia Monaco

1 Introduction

Nonprofit organizations[1] (NPOs) serve as critical agents of social and environmental change, and their performance and impact are measured and communicated through their reporting systems. Diversity, equity, and inclusion (DEI) have gained prominence as a crucial aspect of organizational functioning, influencing various "sectors," including nonprofit, third, and social economy sectors (Walker, 2019; Bernstein & Salipante, 2023; Castillo, 2018; Weisinger et al., 2016; Buse et al., 2016; Mumford, 2022). This chapter explores the existing literature to understand how DEI is addressed in the reporting and related issues of nonprofit organizations such as measuring and assessing organizational performance; accounting and accountability; and transparency. Therefore, we aim to investigate the state of the art in the literature on the topic of DEI as reported by NPOs.

Several research studies analyze DEI issues in business companies as part of non-financial reporting information, but less studied are the same issues related to nonprofit organizations (Ghio et al., 2024; Taylor et al., 2019). We aim to fill this gap starting from debates already developed in the literature, especially in management, accounting, and social science studies.

[1] Also known as third sector, social economy, or charitable organizations.

L. Berardi (✉) · M. L. Monaco
Department of Economic Studies, G. d'Annunzio University of Chieti-Pescara, Pescara, Italy
e-mail: laura.berardi@unich.it

L. Mook
School of Community Resources and Development, Arizona State University Downtown Phoenix Campus, Phoenix, AZ, USA

M. Agostini et al. (eds.), *Diversity and Equity in Accounting*, SIDREA Series in Accounting and Business Administration,
https://doi.org/10.1007/978-3-031-78247-3_3

Our overarching research question asks, "what is known about connections between DEI, NPOs and reporting in the scholarly literature?" We break this down into two sub-questions, one that seeks to quantify the extent of academic literature on the confluence of DEI, NPOs, and reporting, and the other to identify the prominent keywords and thematic aspects within this literature:

- **Question 1.** How prevalent is the academic literature on the intersection of DEI, NPOs, and reporting (or accounting, or transparency)?
- **Question 2.** What are the main keywords and issues associated in this literature?

We introduce next some issues that could influence the scientific discussion on the topic of DEI applied to the nonprofit context with a special focus on the reporting system. This is followed by sections on methods and findings, and a conclusion that includes areas for further research.

2 Background

2.1 DEI Definition in Nonprofit Literature

In the literature focused on nonprofit organizations, DEI is defined with particular attention to how these aspects impact organizational effectiveness, governance, and leadership (Creary et al., 2019), organizational strategy (Zemsky & Mann, 2008), stakeholder engagement, and service delivery.

"Diversity" is viewed not just as the presence of varied physical and social characteristics among individuals (such as race, ethnicity, gender, age, etc.) (Jehn et al., 1999), but also includes cognitive diversity (Reynolds & Lewis, 2017), such as differences in perspectives, problem-solving abilities, and information processing styles. Scientific studies often investigate how these diverse characteristics contribute to innovation, resilience, and problem-solving within nonprofits.

"Equity" refers to the deliberate process of providing different levels of support based on an individual's or group's needs to achieve fairness in treatment and outcomes (Gilliland & Chan, 2001). In scientific literature, equity is often analyzed through the lens of access to resources, opportunities, and participation in programs. This involves identifying structural barriers that might prevent certain groups from benefiting equally and designing interventions to dismantle such barriers.

"Inclusion" is defined as the practice of actively involving all diverse members in decision-making processes and ensuring that each person's contributions are valued, and their needs are considered in the development of policies and practices. Scientific research on inclusion in nonprofits often focuses on measuring the sense of belonging and engagement among staff and beneficiaries, and how this affects organizational performance and mission fulfillment (Randel, 2023).

2.2 Significance of DEI for Nonprofits

Literature in this field generally stresses that DEI is not just a moral or ethical issue but also a strategic one. Effective implementation of DEI principles is linked to improved organizational outcomes, including higher employee satisfaction, better client service, more innovative problem-solving, and enhanced credibility and appeal to funders and supporters.

Many nonprofits aim to serve diverse communities with varied needs. Implementing DEI principles ensures that these organizations can effectively understand and serve these communities better. By aligning their operations and strategies with DEI principles, nonprofits can enhance their service delivery to be more culturally responsive and equitable. Nonprofits rely on the trust and support of their stakeholders, including clients, donors, volunteers, and local communities. A strong commitment to DEI can increase engagement and trust among these groups, thereby strengthening the organization's base of support and increasing its impact.

Funders are increasingly emphasizing DEI in their grant-making criteria. Nonprofits that demonstrate a genuine commitment to DEI are more likely to attract and retain funding. Additionally, demonstrating progress in DEI can enhance an organization's credibility and reputation, which are crucial for long-term sustainability.

Diverse teams are shown to be more innovative (Hewlett et al., 2013) and effective, bringing a variety of perspectives and solutions to the table. Inclusion ensures that all employees feel valued and empowered to contribute their best work. Equity in policies and practices helps attract diverse talent and retain staff, which is essential in maintaining a resilient and adaptable workforce.

In many regions, there are legal requirements related to non-discrimination that nonprofits must adhere to. Beyond compliance, embracing DEI helps organizations go beyond the minimum standards to become leaders in promoting fairness and justice (Melaku & Winkler, 2022).

As global demographics change and societal awareness of DEI issues grows, nonprofits need to adapt to remain relevant and effective (Ferraro et al., 2023). Embracing DEI helps ensure that an organization remains connected to the current and emerging needs of the communities it serves.

Inclusion in decision-making processes leads to better outcomes by incorporating a wide range of experiences and viewpoints. This is especially critical in nonprofits, where the consequences of decisions can significantly impact many lives.

Nonprofits are uniquely positioned to model DEI not only internally but also in their broader interactions with communities, setting a standard for other sectors. The challenge for many organizations lies in moving from a nominal commitment to effective implementation, which involves ongoing training, assessment, and adaptation of DEI strategies.

2.3 DEI in Reporting Frameworks from the Literature

DEI in the context of reporting and accounting involve several important considerations and practices that can enhance transparency, fairness, and accountability in financial operations and reporting. The key themes related to DEI and Reporting, *DEI metrics; integrated reporting and DEI; GRI and DEI; inclusive reporting standard; CSR and DEI; transparency in DEI reporting; stakeholder engagement.*

Organizations can include "*DEI metrics*" in their financial reporting, such as spending on diversity programs, the demographic breakdown of grant recipients, or investments in minority-owned businesses. Metrics are quantitative and qualitative measures used by organizations to assess progress in DEI. These metrics often include demographic data, retention rates, promotion rates, and employee satisfaction surveys among others (Kalev et al., 2006). The Reporting on these metrics can hold organizations accountable to their DEI goals and can also highlight the financial impact of DEI initiatives.

By integrating DEI into reporting, organizations not only enhance their transparency and accountability but also promote fairness and inclusion, which can lead to better financial health and more sustainable operations. Social and non-financial reporting is mainly influenced by some frameworks, such as ESG, GRI, Integrated Reporting, CSR (Crane et al., 2014), and UN SDGS 2030. DEI is included in these important frameworks, so social reporting system should consider DEI issues as crucial.

"*Transparency in DEI*" refers to the openness and clarity with which organizations report their DEI metrics and initiatives, helping stakeholders assess the authenticity and seriousness of their efforts. Bohnet (2016) discussed transparency as a mechanism to improve gender equality, applicable to broader DEI effort.

"*Engaging a diverse group of stakeholders*" in discussions about financial planning and reporting can ensure that the needs and perspectives of all community members are considered. This may involve seeking feedback on financial reports or involving stakeholders in discussions about budget priorities.[2]

3 Methods

The study was carried out following the Scoping Review method. Scoping reviews are conducted to provide a broad and systematic review of a body of emerging literature. They are "exploratory projects that systematically map the literature available on a topic, identifying key concepts, theories, sources of evidence and gaps in the research" (Grimshaw, 2010, 34) and inform future research (Peters et al., 2020). They answer research questions such as, "What is known about this concept" (Tricco et al., 2018, 8).

A scoping review consists of multiple steps (Levac et al., 2010, 3). First a research question is identified, which is broad in nature in line with the objectives of a

[2] Freeman published (1984) the foundational text on stakeholder theory also relevant in the context of DEI.

scoping review. Then a plan is put together to set the boundaries of the initial search, for instance, "where to search, which terms to use, which sources are to be searched, time span, and language" (Levac et al., 2010, 3). Sources of data include databases, reference lists, and hand searching of key journals. The next stage is selecting articles and reviewing their titles, abstracts, and keywords by two or more independent reviewers for inclusion and exclusion criteria. Those that are left are then fully screened by at least two reviewers for the final selection. Data are then extracted and charted, and the last step is collating, summarizing, and reporting the results.

As noted by Levac et al. (2010, 5), "A strength of scoping studies includes the breadth and depth, or comprehensiveness, of evidence covered in a given field. However, practical issues related to time, funding, and access to resources often require researchers to consider the balance between feasibility, breadth, and comprehensiveness."

Starting from our research questions, we determined the parameters of the bibliographic search on the Scopus and Web of Science databases, the largest databases of peer-reviewed literature, used by many scholars to perform a bibliometric analysis. To ensure the quality of our analysis, we considered only articles, book chapters, conference papers, and reviews. All selected documents were from the Business (management and accounting) and social sciences subject area, and all were written in English. The search was performed in February 2024 and all years were included, with the earliest article published in 1997.

The search string for the Scopus database was: TITLE-ABS-KEY (diversity OR equity OR inclusion) AND TITLE-ABS-KEY (nonprofit OR "social economy" OR "non profit" OR "third sector" OR "social enterprise" OR "social cooperative" OR "charit*" OR "not for profit") AND TITLE-ABS-KEY (report* OR account* OR transparen*) AND (LIMIT-TO (DOCTYPE, "ar") OR LIMIT-TO (DOCTYPE, "re") OR LIMIT-TO (DOCTYPE, "ch") OR LIMIT-TO (DOCTYPE, "cp")) AND (LIMIT-TO (SUBJAREA, "SOCI") OR LIMIT-TO (SUBJAREA, "BUSI")) AND (LIMIT-TO (LANGUAGE, "English")).

We then reviewed the keyword list that was generated through this search and included in the search keywords with direct connection to the intersection of these areas. An example of included and excluded keywords is shown in Appendix.

The three top journals in the field of nonprofit studies were then hand searched for relevant articles that might have been missed. The journals were *Nonprofit and Voluntary Sector Quarterly*, *Nonprofit Management and Leadership,* and *Voluntas: An International Journal of Voluntary and Nonprofit Organizations*.

Using Rayyan.ai, we integrated the 180 documents retrieved from Scopus with 79 documents from Web of Science, based on the same search string used in Scopus. We also reviewed the top three nonprofit journals which added 23 documents to the review. In total, we started with 282 documents. We then eliminated 30 duplicate documents, leaving 252 documents. The abstracts were then analyzed for the inclusion of a focus on the reporting of DEI by nonprofit organizations. After an abstract review by three reviewers, 146 documents not focused on the topics of this chapter were excluded. This left 106 documents to screen fully. Through the analysis of the full paper of these 106 documents, 61 documents were excluded for not being related to the intersection of DEI reporting by nonprofit organizations, leaving 45 articles to analyze (Fig. 1).

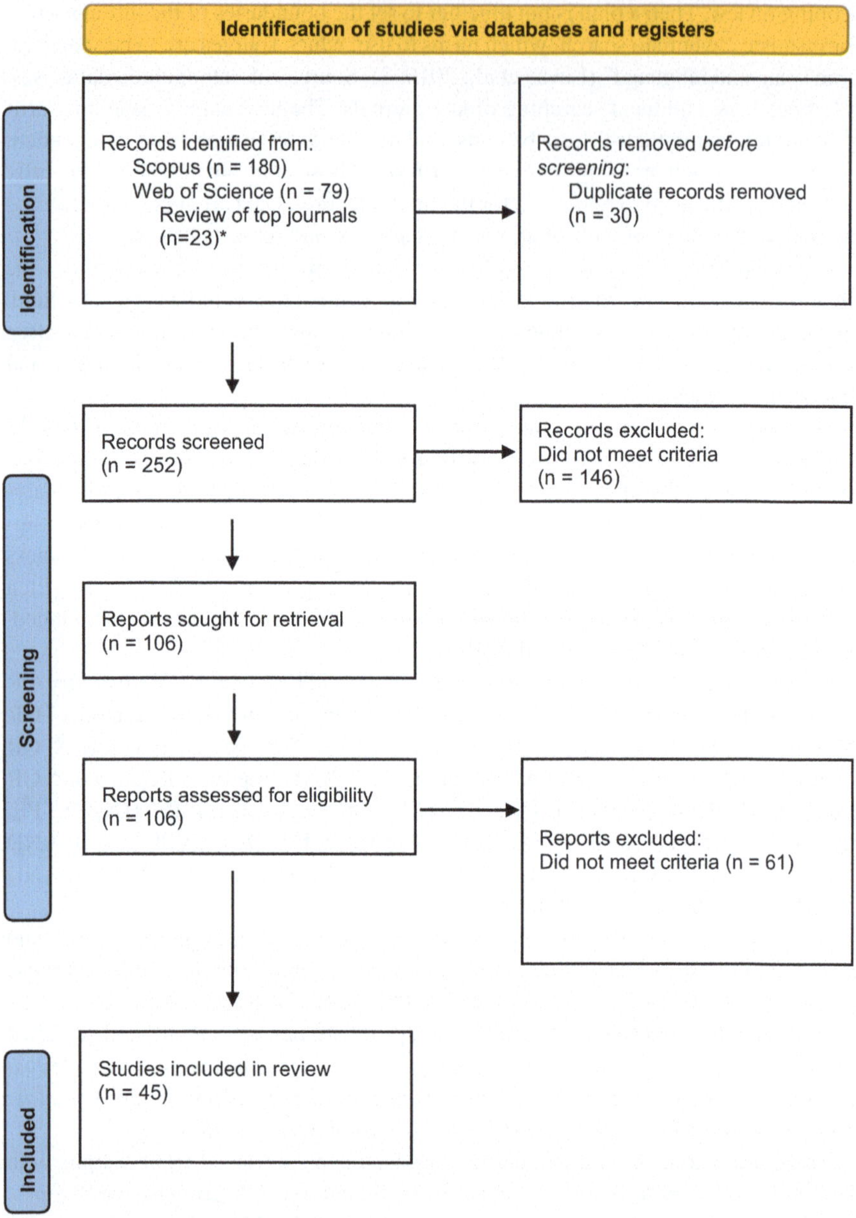

Fig. 1 PRISMA flow diagram for the scoping review. (*) *Nonprofit and Voluntary Sector Quarterly, Nonprofit Management and Leadership, and Voluntas: International Journal of Voluntary and Nonprofit Organization. From*: Page et al. (2021)

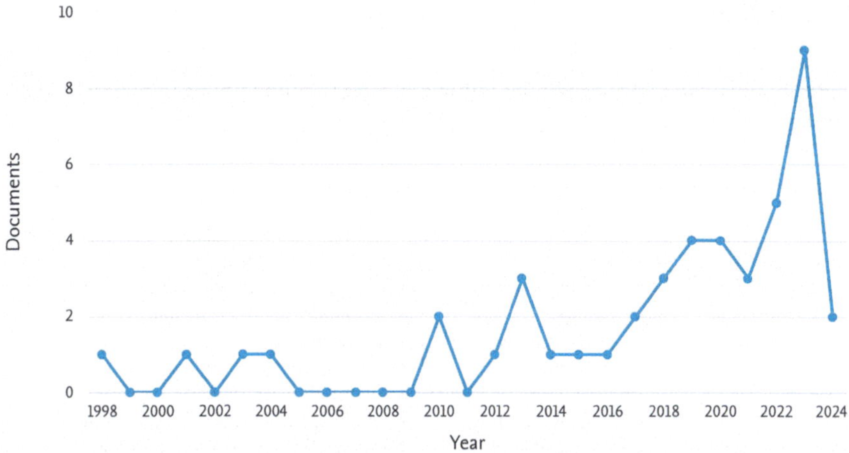

Fig. 2 Documents by year*. *2024 represents only those documents published to mid-February

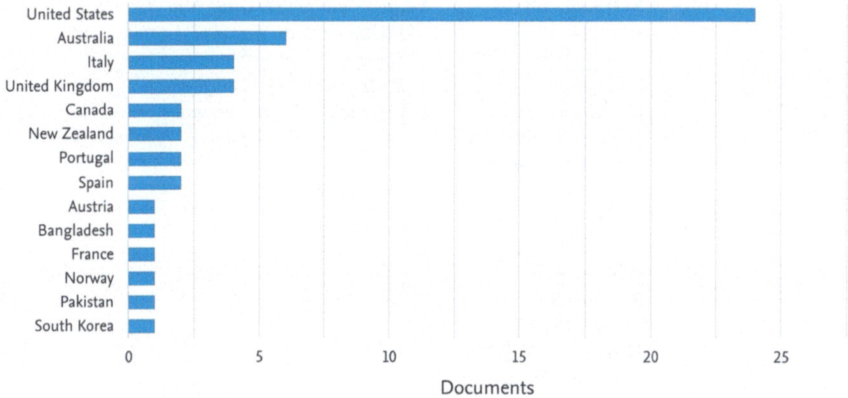

Fig. 3 Documents by country

The 45 documents by year are shown in Fig. 2. There is a noticeable increase of publications from 2019 onward, indicating a growing interest in the topic.

The authors of these publications cover a wide geographical area, including North America, Europe, Oceania, and Asia. However, authors in the United States dominate the publications (Fig. 3).

4 Findings

In the 45 documents, we found the following main trending topics linked to the DEI definition (Table 1):

Table 1 45 Documents on DEI and NPO reporting system

DEI issues		NP types	Reporting system issues
DIVERSITY *(board, CEO, leadership, management, workforce, clients)* *(gender, ethno-racial, ethnocultural, knowledge, demographic)*	**30**	**NPOs** *(nonprofit organizations,* i.e. *foundations, associations, charities, volunteering organizations, 501(c)(3) organizations)* in different fields *(Arts, sports, environmental, health, member-serving)* **SOEs** *(social enterprises, cooperatives, microfinance institutions, social finance organizations)* **B-CORP** *(benefit corporations)* **CSOs** *(civil society organizations)* **NGOs** *(non-governmental organizations)* **Other** *(Child Welfare Agencies, Local organization, Financial Cooperatives/Credit Unions/mutual cooperative societies)*	**M/A/E** *(Measurement/Assessment/Evaluation of impact, social impact, value creation, performance, social performance, social value added, indicators)* **R/A/A** *(Reporting, Accounting and Accountability,* e.g. *financial performance accounting, contribution to public interest accountability, GRI sustainability reporting, social impact reporting, accounting standardization, MFIs reporting data)* **T** *(Transparency and Accountability,* e.g. *web and social media, GuideStar database)* **O** *(Other issues,* e.g. *social capital, cultural competence, governance and board effectiveness, board performance, innovation, diversity disclosure, volunteer recruiting, volunteer program management, marketing, communication, social network, donation and fundraising, big data)*
EQUITY *(gender-lens investing, gender equity, health equity)*	4	**NPOs** *(nonprofit organizations,* e.g. *foundations, hospitals/ healthcare Organizations)* **NGOs** *(non-governmental organizations)* **SEs** *(social enterprises)* **SEOs** *(social economy organizations)*	**M/A/E** *(Monitoring/Assessment/Evaluation of impact, indicators,* e.g. *segregation and social justice indicators)* **O** (Other issues, e.g. strategic plans)

Table 1 (continued)

DEI issues		NP types	Reporting system issues
INCLUSION *(ethnicity, minorities at work, gender segregation, inclusive innovation, participation)*	11	**NPOs** (*nonprofit organizations*, e.g. *membership associations)* **SOEs** (*social enterprises, cooperatives*, e.g. *Empresas recuperadas)* **CSOs** (*civil society organizations*) **Other** *(local government organizations, international development program, Nonprofit groups)*	**M/A/E** (*Measurement/Assessment/Evaluation*, e.g. *measure of climate for inclusion, impact, performance*) **R/A/A** (*Reporting, Accounting, and Accountability*, e.g. *Social Economy Satellite Account*) **T** (*Transparency)* **O** (*Other issues*, e.g. *social audit*)

- Diversity (**D**), i.e. *ethnicity, minorities at work, client gender, board gender composition, women participation, gender-mix, gender-lens investigating, board ethnocultural diversity, female leaders, workforce diversity, diversity management, board composition, knowledge diversity, board ethno-racial diversity, board diversity, women at senior level positions, demographic diversity, diversity monitoring statistics, women CEOs, gender gap, board racial diversity, data feminist framework, CEO gender, CEO race, diversity data.*
- Equity (**E**), i.e. *equitable diversity, inequality, health equity initiatives.*
- Inclusion (**I**), i.e. *inclusive innovation, inclusion, integration, gender segregation, inclusion and exclusion, local participation, participatory approach.*

These topics referred to the following nonprofit organizations with various names and fields of activities:

- Nonprofit organizations (**NPOs**), Social Economy organizations (**SEOs**), Civil society organizations (**CSOs**), non-governmental organizations (**NGOs**), Local NPOs.
- Social enterprises (**SEs**), B-Corporations (**B-CORP**), Charities, Cooperatives, Foundations, 501(c)(3) organizations, membership associations.
- Arts organizations, Human services organizations, Hospitals, Environmental organizations, Microfinance Institutions (**MFIs**).
- Other entities, i.e. Child Welfare Agencies, Local government organizations (**LGO**s).

The identified issues related to the nonprofit reporting systems linked to DEI were:

- Measuring/Evaluation/Assessment (**M/E/A**), i.e. *impact, social impact, value, performance, social performance, climate for inclusion, value creation, monitor-*

ing, and evaluation (M&E), measure of Social Added Value, segregation indicators, social justice indicators, transformative innovation potential.

- Reporting/Accounting/Accountability (**R/A/A**), i.e. *financial performance, contribution to public interests, GRI Sustainability Reporting, social impact reporting, accounting standardization, MFIs reporting data, social economy Satellite Account, downward accountability; reporting to researchers, reporting to large databases.*
- Transparency (**T**), i.e. *DEI disclosure, web transparency, social media, social network; communication, GuideStar's database (Candid).*
- Other related issues (**O**), i.e. *social capital, board effectiveness, governance effectiveness, innovation, diversity disclosure, cultural competence, volunteer recruitment, volunteer program manager, marketing, donations/fundraising, board performance, big data, strategic plans, social audit, communication.*

"*Diversity*" is considered in two-thirds of the documents analyzed in general or considering the organizational level and stakeholder categories:

- Board diversity (Jaskyte, 2018; Steane & Christie, 2001; Hinna & Monteduro, 2017; Fredette & Sessler Bernstein, 2021; Bradshaw & Fredette, 2013; Reddy et al., 2013; De Andrés-Alonso et al., 2010; Lee, 2021; Benito-Esteban et al., 2024).
- CEO, leadership, and management diversity (Taylor et al., 2019; Lee, 2023; Brown & Harris, 2023; Dula et al., 2020; Lall, 2019; Lee, 2019).
- Workforce diversity (Cho et al., 2017).
- Clients gender diversity (Beisland et al., 2021).

"*Diversity*" also specifically refers to race/ethnicity/cultural (Fredette & Sessler Bernstein, 2021; Bradshaw & Fredette, 2013; Lee, 2021; Taylor et al., 2019; Lee, 2023; Nybell & Gray, 2004), demographic (Laryea et al., 2022), knowledge (De Andrés-Alonso et al., 2010).

"*Equity*" (4% of documents) is studied also in general (Rogers & Malla, 2019) or referred to specific aspects, such as gender-lens investing (Bolinson & Allan, 2022); gender disparity (Parente & Martinho, 2018); health equity initiatives (Singh & Conley, 2023).

"*Inclusion*" (24% of documents) is mainly associated with the concepts of ethnicity (Bryer, 2012; Adamovic et al., 2023), gender (Monteiro, 2022), and innovation (Calderini et al., 2023). Inclusion could also be referred to different subjects, for instance to the leadership of a membership association (Solebello et al., 2016), or to international development program (Dawson, 1998); local participation in civil society organizations (Williamson et al., 2022), and nonprofit groups (Citroni, 2020).

Several publications (13) on DEI are dedicated to issues of *measuring, monitoring, assessment, and evaluation of nonprofit performance* (value creation, social performance, social impact, and social added value) (Hinna & Monteduro, 2017; Beisland et al., 2021; Khan et al., 2003; Mannarini et al., 2018; Lee et al., 2023; Lall, 2019; Cho et al., 2017; Rogers & Malla, 2019; Bolinson & Allan, 2022; Parente & Martinho, 2018; Adamovic et al., 2023; Chowdhury et al., 2014; Calderini et al., 2023).

Thirteen papers discuss *reporting* (Reddy et al., 2013; Traxler et al., 2020; Adams et al., 2021; Bezboruah & Pillai, 2015), *accounting* (Bryer, 2012; Citroni, 2020), and *accountability* (Lee, 2021; Steane & Christie, 2001; De Andrés-Alonso et al., 2010; Laryea et al., 2022; Solebello et al., 2016; Bernstein & Salipante, 2023; Williamson et al., 2022) issues. One paper refers directly to the *GRI Sustainability Reporting standards* (Traxler et al., 2020). Another nine papers are dedicated to the topic of *Transparency* (Lee, 2019; Taylor et al., 2019; Lee, 2023; Taylor, 2022; Lepkowska-White et al., 2022; Mastracci & Herring, 2010; Benito-Esteban et al., 2024; Lee, 2019; Brandtner et al., 2024), with a specific focus on *DEI disclosure* (Taylor et al., 2019); *GuideStar* (Candid) data (Taylor, 2022; Lee, 2019); *web and social media* presence (Lepkowska-White et al., 2022; Benito-Esteban et al., 2024).

Other related topics treated in the DEI NP literature are social capital and effectiveness (Jaskyte, 2018; Fredette & Sessler Bernstein, 2021); diversity information disclosure (Bradshaw & Fredette, 2013); Cultural competence (Nybell & Gray, 2004); Donations and Fundraising (Brown & Harris, 2023); Board performance (Dula et al., 2020); Big Data (Sandberg et al., 2023); Strategic plans (Singh & Conley, 2023); Social audit (Dawson, 1998), and Volunteer Recruitment (Wymer Jr & Starnes, 2001).

5 Conclusions

This review provides a preliminary understanding of the literature on the intersection of DEI and reporting of nonprofit organizations. Our overarching research question asked, "what is known about the connections between diversity, equity and inclusion, nonprofit organizations and reporting in the scholarly literature?" We broke this down into two sub-questions: how prevalent is the academic literature on the intersection of diversity, equity, and inclusion, nonprofit (or third sector, or social economy, or charitable) organizations and reporting (or accounting, or transparency), and what are the main keywords and issues associated in this literature?

The review analyzed 45 relevant publications from peer-reviewed journals, chapters in books, and conference proceedings found in searches of the social science and business literature of two databases, as well the hand searching of top journals. The reviewed literature indicates that DEI in nonprofit reporting is often linked to themes such as governance—i.e., board diversity and composition (Jaskyte, 2018; Steane & Christie, 2001; Hinna & Monteduro, 2017; Fredette & Sessler Bernstein, 2021; Bradshaw & Fredette, 2013; Reddy et al., 2013; De Andrés-Alonso et al., 2010; Lee, 2021; Benito-Esteban et al., 2024), and leadership or CEO characteristics (Taylor et al., 2019; Lee, 2023); accountability mechanisms (Steane & Christie, 2001; De Andrés-Alonso et al., 2010; Laryea et al., 2022; Solebello et al., 2016; Bernstein & Salipante, 2023; Lee, 2021), impact evaluation methodologies (Adams et al., 2021; Lall, 2019; Bolinson & Allan, 2022; Chowdhury et al., 2014), value creation (Hinna & Monteduro, 2017; Mannarini et al., 2018;), social capital (Jaskyte,

2018; Fredette & Sessler Bernstein, 2021), performance measurement frameworks (Beisland et al., 2021; Lee et al., 2023; Cho et al., 2017; Calderini et al., 2023), etc.

This preliminary analysis could help researchers interested in DEI in nonprofit reporting to focus on the principal research gaps identified in the literature. To build on this study, further empirical analysis on primary data—e.g. evidence from annual reports and social (or sustainability) reports and secondary data—e.g. statistical data or data retrieved from public databases, such as GuideStar, etc., (Lee, 2019; Taylor, 2022), could be conducted for analyses of the issue in different contexts. There is a need for further research on how nonprofit organizations integrate DEI principles into their reporting principles, and the associated challenges and benefits. Future studies can adopt different methodologies such as case studies and content analyses of nonprofit reports. Additionally, as technology evolves, the role of digitalization in these processes could be explored.

Appendix

Keywords included in search strategy:

AND LIMIT-TO (EXACTKEYWORD "xxx") OR

Accountability, Accounting, Board Diversity, Charities, Civil Society, Cooperatives, Cultural Diversity, Disability, Diversity, Diversity and Equity, Diversity Management, Equity, Ethnicity, Female, Foundations, Gender, Inclusion, Inequality, Male, Nonprofit Hospital, Non-Profit Organization, Non-profit Organizations, Nongovernmental Organizations, Nonprofit, Nonprofit governance, Nonprofit Organization, Nonprofit Organizations, Nonprofits, Not-for-profit, Organization, Philanthropy, Race, Social Economy, Social Enterprise, Social Enterprises, Social Entrepreneurship, Social impact, Social Inclusion, Transparency, Third Sector, Value creation, Women.

References

Adamovic, M., Sojo, V., Schachtman, R., & Vargas, A. (2023). Explaining the relationship between ethnicity and depressive symptoms: The roles of climate for inclusion, job self-efficacy, and job demands. *Asia Pacific Journal of Management, 403*, 903–928.

Adams, S., Tweedie, D., & Muir, K. (2021). Social impact reporting in the public interest: The case of accounting standardisation. *Qualitative Research in Accounting & Management, 18*(3), 390–416.

Beisland, L. A., Djan, K. O., Mersland, R., & Randøy, T. (2021). Measuring social performance in social enterprises: A global study of microfinance institutions. *Journal of Business Ethics, 171*, 51–71.

Benito-Esteban, C. I., Elvira-Lorilla, T., Garcia-Rodriguez, I., & Romero-Merino, M. E. (2024). The complex relationship between the board and web transparency in nonprofit organizations. *Voluntas: International Journal of Voluntary and Nonprofit Organizations, 35*(1), 48–60.

Bernstein, R. S., & Salipante, P. (2023). Embedding inclusive, equitable diversity practices in nonprofit organizations: Developing policy to account for system dynamics. In *Nonprofit policy forum*. De Gruyter.

Bezboruah, K. C., & Pillai, V. (2015). Exploring the participation of women in financial cooperatives and credit unions in developing countries. *Voluntas: International Journal of Voluntary and Nonprofit Organizations, 26*, 913–940.

Bohnet, I. (2016). *What works: Gender equality by design*. Belknap Press.

Bolinson, C., & Allan, L. (2022). The field-building and grantee experimentation role of foundations in impact investing as illustrated by a gender-lens investing case example. *The Foundation Review, 14*(4), 6.

Bradshaw, P., & Fredette, C. (2013). Determinants of the range of ethnocultural diversity on nonprofit boards: A study of large Canadian nonprofit organizations. *Nonprofit and Voluntary Sector Quarterly, 42*(6), 1111–1133.

Brandtner, C., Powell, W. W., & Horvath, A. (2024). From iron cage to glass house: Repurposing of bureaucratic management and the turn to openness. *Organization Studies, 45*(2), 193–221.

Brown, V. L., & Harris, E. E. (2023). The Association of Female Leaders with donations and operating margin in nonprofit organizations. *Journal of Business Ethics, 185*(1), 223–243.

Bryer, A. R. (2012). The politics of the social economy: A case study of the Argentinean empresas recuperadas. *Dialectical Anthropology, 36*, 21–49.

Buse, K., Bernstein, R. S., & Bilimoria, D. (2016). The influence of board diversity, board diversity policies and practices, and board inclusion behaviors on nonprofit governance practices. *Journal of Business Ethics, 133*, 179–191.

Calderini, M., Fia, M., & Gerli, F. (2023). Organizing for transformative innovation policies: The role of social enterprises. Theoretical insights and evidence from Italy. *Research Policy, 52*(7), 104818.

Castillo, E. A. (2018). Why are we still struggling with diversity, equity, and inclusion in nonprofit governance. *NonProfit Quarterly*.

Cho, S., Kim, A., & Mor Barak, M. E. (2017). Does diversity matter? Exploring workforce diversity, diversity management, and organizational performance in social enterprises. *Asian Social Work and Policy Review, 11*(3), 193–204.

Chowdhury, A. M. R., Jenkins, A., & Nandita, M. M. (2014). Measuring the effects of interventions in BRAC, and how this has driven 'development'. *Journal of Development Effectiveness, 6*(4), 407–424.

Citroni, S. (2020). Civil society events: Ambiguities and the exertion of cultural power. *European Journal of Cultural and Political Sociology, 7*(2), 150–171.

Crane, A., Matten, D., & Spence, L. (Eds.). (2014). *Corporate social responsibility: Readings and cases in a global context*. Routledge.

Creary, S. J., McDonnell, M. H., Ghai, S., & Scruggs, J. (2019). When and why diversity improves your board's performance. *Harvard Business Review, 27*, 2–6.

Dawson, E. (1998). The relevance of social audit for Oxfam GB. *Journal of Business Ethics, 17*, 1457–1469.

De Andrés-Alonso, P., Azofra-Palenzuela, V., & Romero-Merino, M. E. (2010). Beyond the disciplinary role of governance: How boards add value to Spanish foundations. *British Journal of Management, 21*(1), 100–114.

Dula, L., Nicholson-Crotty, J., & Gazley, B. (2020). Female leaders and board performance in member-serving nonprofit organizations. *Nonprofit Management and Leadership, 30*(4), 655–676.

Ferraro, C., Hemsley, A., & Sands, S. (2023). Embracing diversity, equity, and inclusion (DEI): Considerations and opportunities for brand managers. *Business Horizons, 66*(4), 463–479.

Fredette, C., & Sessler Bernstein, R. (2021). Governance effectiveness: The interaction of ethnoracial diversity and social capital. *Nonprofit and Voluntary Sector Quarterly, 50*(4), 816–841.

Freeman, R. E. (1984). *Strategic management: A stakeholder approach*. Pitman.

Ghio, A., Occhipinti, Z., & Verona, R. (2024). The consideration of diversity in the accounting literature: A systematic literature review. *European Accounting Review, 33*(5), 1–25.
Gilliland, S. W., & Chan, D. (2001). Justice in organizations: Theory, methods, and applications. In N. Anderson, D. S. Ones, H. K. Sinangil, & C. Viswesvaran (Eds.), *Handbook of industrial, work and organizational psychology* (Vol. 2, pp. 143–165). Sage.
Grimshaw, J. (2010). *A knowledge synthesis chapter*. Canadian Institute of Health Research.
Hewlett, S. A., Marshall, M., & Sherbin, L. (2013). How diversity can drive innovation. *Harvard Business Review, 91*(12), 30–30.
Hinna, A., & Monteduro, F. (2017). Boards, governance and value creation in grant-giving foundations. *Journal of Management and Governance, 21*(4), 935–961.
Jaskyte, K. (2018). Board attributes and processes, board effectiveness, and organizational innovation: Evidence from nonprofit organizations. *Voluntas: International Journal of Voluntary and Nonprofit Organizations, 29*(5), 1098–1111.
Jehn, K. A., Northcraft, G. B., & Neale, M. A. (1999). Why differences make a difference: A field study of diversity, conflict and performance in workgroups. *Administrative Science Quarterly, 44*(4), 741–763.
Kalev, A., Dobbin, F., & Kelly, E. (2006). Best practices or best guesses? Assessing the efficacy of corporate affirmative action and diversity policies. *American Sociological Review, 71*(4), 589–617.
Khan, K., Waheed, A., Iqbal, S., & Khan, A. H. (2003). Monitoring and evaluation: Civil society organisations' competitive edge in effective poverty alleviation [with comments]. *The Pakistan Development Review*, 909–924.
Lall, S. A. (2019). From legitimacy to learning: How impact measurement perceptions and practices evolve in social enterprise–social finance organization relationships. *Voluntas: International Journal of Voluntary and Nonprofit Organizations, 30*(3), 562–577.
Laryea, K., Zhao, Y., & Powell, W. W. (2022). San Francisco Bay Area: A left coast Metropolis grapples with technocracy and inequality. *Global Perspectives, 3*(1), 36212.
Lee, B., Sejas-Portillo, R., & Fraser, I. (2023). Balancing perspectives on performance: "Measurement from the inside" and "measurement from the outside". *Nonprofit Management and Leadership, 34*(1), 13–34.
Lee, Y. J. (2019). Scarce as hen's teeth: Women CEOs in large nonprofit organizations. *Nonprofit Management and Leadership, 29*(4), 601–610.
Lee, Y. J. (2021). Nonprofit arts organizations' pursuit of public interests: The role of board diversity. *Nonprofit Policy Forum, 12*(4), 563–587.
Lee, Y. J. (2023). The color of nonprofit leadership: Nonprofits with a CEO of color. *Nonprofit Management and Leadership, 33*(4), 865–878.
Lepkowska-White, E., Parsons, A. L., Wong, B., & White, A. M. (2022). Building a socially responsible global community? Communicating B corps on social media. *Corporate Communications: An International Journal, 28*(1), 86–102.
Levac, D., Colquhoun, H., & O'Brien, K. K. (2010). Scoping studies: Advancing the methodology. *Implementation Science, 5*, 1–9.
Mannarini, T., Talo, C., D'Aprile, G., & Ingusci, E. (2018). A psychosocial measure of social added value in non-profit and voluntary organizations: Findings from a study in the south of Italy. *Voluntas: International Journal of Voluntary and Nonprofit Organizations, 29*, 1315–1329.
Mastracci, S. H., & Herring, C. (2010). Nonprofit management practices and work processes to promote gender diversity. *Nonprofit Management and Leadership, 21*(2), 155–175.
Melaku, T. M., & Winkler, C. (2022). Are your organization's DEI efforts superficial or structural. *Harvard Business Review*.
Monteiro, A. A. (2022). The social economy in Portugal: Legal regime and socio-economic characterization. *CIRIEC-España, revista de economía pública, social y cooperativa, 106*.
Mumford, S. (2022). Doing more with less: Racial diversity in nonprofit leadership and organizational resilience. *Journal of Public and Nonprofit Affairs, 8*(1), 29–57.

Nybell, L. M., & Gray, S. S. (2004). Race, place, space: Meanings of cultural competence in three child welfare agencies. *Social Work, 49*(1), 17–26.

Page, M. J., McKenzie, J. E., Bossuyt, P. M., Boutron, I., Hoffmann, T. C., Mulrow, C. D., et al. (2021). The PRISMA 2020 statement: An updated guideline for reporting systematic reviews. *BMJ, 372*(71), 1–9.

Parente, C., & Martinho, A. L. (2018). The "places and non-places" held by women in social economy organizations. *Voluntas: International Journal of Voluntary and Nonprofit Organizations, 29*(6), 1274–1282.

Peters, M. D., Marnie, C., Tricco, A. C., Pollock, D., Munn, Z., Alexander, L., et al. (2020). Updated methodological guidance for the conduct of scoping reviews. *JBI Evidence Synthesis, 18*(10), 2119–2126.

Randel, A. E. (2023). Inclusion in the workplace: A review and research agenda. *Group & Organization Management*. https://doi.org/10.1177/10596011231175578

Reddy, K., Locke, S., & Fauzi, F. (2013). Relevance of corporate governance practices in charitable organisations: A case study of registered charities. *New Zealand International Journal of Managerial Finance, 9*(2), 110–132.

Reynolds, A., & Lewis, D. (2017). Teams solve problems faster when they're more cognitively diverse. *Harvard Business Review, 30*, 1–8.

Rogers, A., & Malla, C. (2019). Knowledge translation to enhance evaluation use: A case example. *The Foundation Review, 11*(1), 8.

Sandberg, B., Hand, L. C., & Russo, A. (2023). Re-envisioning the role of "big data" in the nonprofit sector: A data feminist perspective. *Voluntas: International Journal of Voluntary and Nonprofit Organizations, 34*(5), 1094–1105.

Singh, S. R., & Conley, C. (2023). Inclusion of health equity initiatives in hospitals' strategic plans. *Health Equity, 7*(1), 753–760.

Solebello, N., Tschirhart, M., & Leiter, J. (2016). The paradox of inclusion and exclusion in membership associations. *Human Relations, 69*(2), 439–460.

Steane, P. D., & Christie, M. (2001). Nonprofit boards in Australia: A distinctive governance approach. *Corporate Governance: An International Review, 9*(19), 48–58.

Taylor, D. E. (2022). The transparency challenge in environmental organizations: Factors influencing whether institutions collect and reveal diversity data. *American Behavioral Scientist, 66*(7), 812–855.

Taylor, D. E., Paul, S., & McCoy, E. (2019). Diversity, equity, and inclusion and the salience of publicly disclosing demographic data in American environmental nonprofits. *Sustainability, 11*(19), 5491.

Traxler, A. A., Greiling, D., & Hebesberger, H. (2020). GRI sustainability reporting by INGOs: A way forward for improving accountability? VOLUNTAS. *International Journal of Voluntary and Nonprofit Organizations, 31*, 1294–1310.

Tricco, A. C., Lillie, E., Zarin, W., O'Brien, K. K., Colquhoun, H., Levac, D., et al. (2018). PRISMA extension for scoping reviews (PRISMA-ScR): Checklist and explanation. *Annals of Internal Medicine, 169*(7), 467–473.

Walker, V. (2019). The road to nonprofit diversity and inclusion. *The Journal of Infectious Diseases, 220*(Supplement_2), S86–S90.

Weisinger, J. Y., Borges-Méndez, R., & Milofsky, C. (2016). Diversity in the nonprofit and voluntary sector. *Nonprofit and Voluntary Sector Quarterly, 45*(1_suppl), 3S–27S.

Williamson, A. K., Kingston, K. L., & Bennison, L. (2022). Similar or different? Downward accountability across civil society organisational forms. *Voluntas: International Journal of Voluntary and Nonprofit Organizations, 33*(5), 1002–1014.

Wymer, W. W., Jr., & Starnes, B. J. (2001). Conceptual foundations and practical guidelines for recruiting volunteers to serve in local nonprofit organizations: Part I. *Journal of Nonprofit & Public Sector Marketing, 9*(1–2), 63–96.

Zemsky, B., & Mann, D. (2008). Building organizations in a movement moment. *Social Policy, 38*(3), 9–17.

Diversity, Equity, and Inclusion Practices in Family Firms: A Review of the Literature

Valentina Minutiello, Isabel María García-Sánchez, and Patrizia Tettamanzi

1 Introduction

That family businesses play a crucial role in the world economy is now beyond discussion (Gavrić & Braje, 2024). To cite some data, considering the European continent alone, approximately 50% of operating businesses are family businesses (Rotaru & Mihai, 2020). Their work stands out from traditional businesses due to the interaction of two souls: that of the business and that of the family. Over the years, the academy has studied their main dynamics and peculiarities. Recently, one of the topics explored concerns the diversity, equity, and inclusion practices envisaged at the corporate governance level (Anderson & Reeb, 2003; Ducassy & Prevot, 2010). These practices may involve the establishment of management bodies with members who differ, for example, in education, race, gender, and age. They imply that every person has access to the same resources and opportunities, removing barriers to accessing experiences and opportunities that can lead to equitable performance and outcomes.

V. Minutiello (✉)
Accounting, School of Economics and Management, Carlo Cattaneo University – LIUC, Castellanza, Italy
e-mail: vminutiello@liuc.it

I. M. García-Sánchez
Economics and Business Administration, IME-Instituto Multidisciplinar de Empresa, University of Salamanca, Salamanca, Spain
e-mail: lajefa@usal.es

P. Tettamanzi
International Financial Reporting and Analysis, School of Economics and Management, Carlo Cattaneo University– LIUC, Castellanza, Italy
e-mail: ptettamanzi@liuc.it

M. Agostini et al. (eds.), *Diversity and Equity in Accounting*, SIDREA Series in Accounting and Business Administration,
https://doi.org/10.1007/978-3-031-78247-3_4

Although these factors apply to all types of organizations, they are especially relevant in the field of family businesses. Especially concerning gender diversity, family businesses would be good vehicles to support female aspirations since they can focus on encouraging women who decide to undertake, direct, or grow a business project (Maseda et al., 2022). Statistics from various countries[1] show that there is a greater number of women between 20 and 50 years old who are already fully immersed in family businesses, sometimes even showing greater integration and commitment to driving growth than men, who tend to show a greater preference for undertaking careers and businesses other than the family. Although the current boards of directors of these companies are made up of members over 60 years of age and the presence of women is unusual, in the near future, if female talent is given the opportunities to develop and grow, these gender disparities will eventually disappear. For example, women who are almost 40 years old today will, in the next ten years, be those who will begin to gain greater relevance within corporate governance bodies.

In addition to the above, the culture of equity and inclusion in family businesses has an important weight in the commitment and loyalty toward their collaborators. It is a determining factor in their quality of life, representing a part of their identity, mainly due to the influence on family values and culture within the business (Brun de Pontet et al., 2020).

Family characteristics can be a challenge or obstacle to achieving an inclusive culture. On the positive side, family businesses are known for treating their employees and other stakeholders like family, which creates a strong environment of care and inclusion. The family cultures and values focus on the long term and doing the right thing, which can facilitate effective inclusion policies, programs, and initiatives. However, the "fixed" values of family businesses and established cultures can lead to diverse points of view not being considered and a lack of opportunities for those who think differently or who come from another type of culture or origin. It is human nature to lean on the familiar, rather than looking outward or to divergent points of view.

As a consequence, the topic is relevant for its practical implications in terms of the success and survival of family businesses over time. However, this line of research has so far been fragmented and not very extensive.

The aim of the chapter is thus twofold. Firstly, according to the current state of literature, it aims to provide a comprehensive view of current practices on diversity, equity, and inclusion in family firms. Secondly, it tries to develop some suggestions for future research to improve the awareness of the importance of these virtuous practices. It answers two research questions:

RQ1. *What is the current state of the art of literature, in terms of topics debated and types of research conducted, on diversity, equity, and inclusion practices in family firms?*

---

[1] For example, see the annual Global Family Business Survey from the STEP Project Global Consortium in collaboration with KPMG Private Enterprise.

RQ2. *What would be interesting future issues to be investigated in this research area, and what should be the future development of research?*

To answer the proposed research questions, a bibliometric literature review is conducted on the Scopus database.

2 Methodology

2.1 *Bibliometric Literature Review: The Search Protocol*

To conduct the literature review, we adopted a bibliometric approach based on a rigid protocol that can also be replicated by other scholars (Kraus et al., 2020). The objective is to ensure that all relevant contributions on the topic of diversity, equity, and inclusion practices in family firms present in the literature are taken into consideration. The steps adopted aim to reduce the level of subjectivity of the analysis, limiting the freedom of choice in the paper selection process.

We chose to use Scopus, as it represents a larger database compared with Web of Science. For this reason, it has often been used to conduct literature reviews (Zhao & Strotmann, 2015; Strozzi et al., 2017).

The research was conducted in January 2024. The first step concerns the definition of the search string, developed on the basis of the keywords most used by previous studies on the topic. It should not be composed of keywords that are too generic in order to avoid selecting papers outside the scope of the literature review nor of keywords that are too specific which could lead to the exclusion of relevant contributions.

The search string used for the selection of papers and applied to the title, abstract, and keywords is the following:

$$\left(\textit{diversity OR equity OR inclusion}\right) \textit{AND} \begin{pmatrix} \left(\textit{family AND firm}^{*}\right) \\ \textit{OR}\left(\textit{family AND business}\right) \end{pmatrix}$$

By applying the search string, we selected 397 papers.

Table 1 shows the inclusion or exclusion criteria subsequently adopted. No time limits have been set to have the possibility of analyzing the entire state of the art of this research area.

A manual screening process based on the reading of title, abstract, and keywords was then adopted for this first selection of papers, aimed at keeping exclusively those papers relating to the topic under investigation. In some cases, in fact, the words "*diversity*," "*equity*," or "*inclusion*" were used with different meanings; for example, the term "*equity*" was often used with reference to the balance sheet of companies.

Table 1 Search protocol

Database	Scopus
Topic lab	Title, Abstract, and Keywords
Keywords	(diversity OR equity OR inclusion) AND ((family AND firm*) OR (family AND business))
Time period	Without limits
Document types	Article or Review
Language	English
Categories	Business, Management, and Accounting

The final sample of papers used to conduct the literature review amounted to 39 articles.

2.2 The Subsequent Steps of the Analysis

A subsequent analysis was then conducted on the previously selected sample of papers aimed at identifying any trends in the number of publications over time and the authors and journals that published the most contributions.

An analysis of the number of citations of the different papers was performed, thanks to the use of the global citation score (GCS) taken from the Scopus database. It is a useful tool for selecting the most relevant papers in the sample (Strozzi et al., 2017).

Finally, a keyword network analysis (KNA) was carried out using the VOSviewer software (http://www.vosviewer.com/). The keywords are representative of the content of the papers, and for this reason, they allow us to identify the topics explored in the research area and understand which topics have been studied most recently (Ding et al., 2001; Strozzi et al., 2017). Thanks to this step, it is possible to divide the sample of papers into different clusters and select the most influential keywords based on the number of occurrences of their use, also including those papers which, for various reasons, may not be characterized by a high number of citations (Van Eck and Waltman 2010).

3 Results

3.1 Publication Trends

Figure 1 represents the trend over time of the publications on the topic of the literature review.

The contributions are included in the period 2012–2024. The attention of scholars over the years seems to remain constant but reaches a peak in 2023 with 14 papers. This aspect implies that the topic has been the subject of greater attention

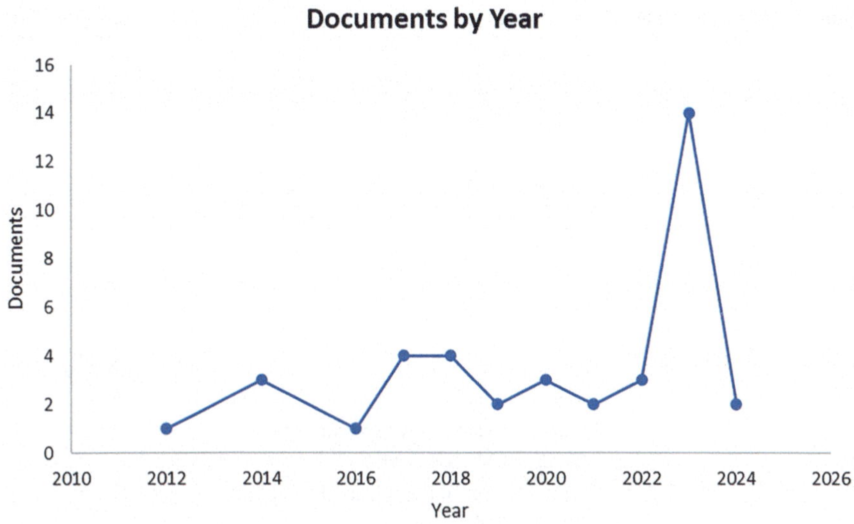

Fig. 1 No. of documents by year

recently. Its newness suggests the presence of numerous gaps in the literature that could be interesting to explore further in the future. Finally, in 2024, there seems to be a declining trend, but this can be justified by the fact that the year is still at the beginning.

3.2 *Authors*

According to our sample, 39 papers were authored by 93 Authors. Of these, 91% published only one paper on the topic, confirming the presence of a high level of dispersion of authorship. This situation is typical of emerging research areas.

Table 2 shows the Authors with more than one paper and the number of citations received overall by each author on publications relating to the topic of diversity, equity, and inclusion in family firms.

The two most influential Authors in the field appear to be Saeed, A. with 44 citations and Sciascia, S. with 28 citations.

3.3 *Journals*

The papers are published in different journals, not necessarily specialized in family business. This confirms the relevance of the topic on a broader and more general level, which also goes beyond the analysis of the dynamics concerning family businesses.

Table 3 shows the list of journals in decreasing order of productivity.

Table 2 Influential Authors

Author	No. of papers	No. of citations on Scopus
Saeed, A.	2	44
Sciascia, S.	3	28
Gjergji, R.	2	4
Vena, L.	2	4
Cortesi, A.	2	4
Gavana, G.	2	2
Gottardo, P.	2	2
Moisello, A. M.	2	2

Table 3 List of journals

Journal	N. of papers
Journal of Family Business Management	5
Journal of Family Business Strategy	3
Gender in Management	2
Corporate Social Responsibility and Environmental Management	2
Corporate Governance (Bingley)	2
Journal of Accounting and Organizational Change	1
Administrative Sciences	1
Business Ethics, the Environment and Responsibility	1
International Journal of Managerial Finance	1
Management Decision	1
Journal of Business Research	1
International Journal of Emerging Markets	1
International Journal of Entrepreneurship and Small Business	1
Strategic Entrepreneurship Journal	1
FIIB Business Review	1
International Entrepreneurship and Management Journal	1
Journal of Small Business and Entrepreneurship	1
British Journal of Management	1
Journal of Risk and Financial Management	1
Journal of International Accounting Research	1
Indian Journal of Corporate Governance	1
International Journal of Gender and Entrepreneurship	1
Journal of Management and Governance	1
Entrepreneurial Business and Economics Review	1
International Journal of Wine Business Research	1
Cross Cultural and Strategic Management	1
Corporate Governance: An International Review	1
Journal of Small Business Management	1
Afro-Asian Journal of Finance and Accounting	1

The first two journals (*Journal of Family Business Management* and *Journal of Family Business Strategy*) are specialized in studies on family businesses and are followed by journals dealing with corporate governance (*Corporate Governance—Bingley*), gender studies (*Gender in Management*), or sustainability (*Corporate Social Responsibility and Environmental Management*). The selection of journals that have dealt with the topic already provides a first suggestion on possible clusters within the research area, confirmed, as we will see, by the subsequent analysis.

In total 29 journals dealt with the topic, although approximately 83% published only one contribution. This data confirms the fragmented nature of the research field.

3.4 Citation Analysis

The number of citations of a paper can be representative of its relevance in a research area (Knoke and Yang 2008). However, it should also be borne in mind that a study normally begins to be cited some time after its publication. There may, therefore, be some recent studies that, although relevant, are not yet characterized by a high number of citations. From another perspective, however, a high number of citations of a paper does not necessarily equate to a high quality of the study (Dawson et al., 2014).

The papers included in the analyzed sample have an average number of citations equal to 21.05 times. Seven papers have not yet been cited, and 20 contributions are cited less than ten times. It is not surprising that most of these studies are among the most recent in date: two are from 2024 and 14 from 2023.

Table 4 reports the top five studies by number of citations in decreasing order. By analyzing the content of these papers, it is possible to distinguish two

Table 4 Global citation score (GCS) of the five most cited papers, together with title, authors, journals, and years of publication

Rank	Title	Authors	Journal	Year	GCS
1	Family firm heterogeneity and governance: A configuration approach	Nordqvist, M., Sharma, P., & Chirico, F.	Journal of Small Business Management	2014	206
2	The causes of gender diversity in Malaysian large firms	Abdullah, S. N.	Journal of Management and Governance	2014	87
3	Women leaders and firm performance in family businesses: An examination of financial and nonfinancial outcomes	Chadwick, I. C., & Dawson, A.	Journal of Family Business Strategy	2018	72
4	Board of directors characteristics and performance in family firms and under the crisis	Vieira, E. S	Corporate Governance (Bingley)	2018	56
5	Are All Non-Family Managers (NFMs) Equal? The Impact of NFM Characteristics and Diversity on Family Firm Performance	Binacci, M., Peruffo, E., Oriani, R., & Minichilli, A.	Corporate Governance: An International Review	2016	54

macro-categories of topics: three studies, in fact, focus on the dynamics of diversity at the corporate governance level of family businesses (Nordqvist et al., 2014; Vieira, 2018; Binacci et al., 2016), while two address the issue of gender disparities and the role of women in the managerial levels of family businesses (Abdullah, 2014; Chadwick & Dawson, 2018).

In particular, the study by Nordqvist et al. (2014) focused on corporate governance mechanisms that allow for maximizing performance in family businesses depending on the different degrees of involvement of family members in ownership and management. Vieira (2018) analyzed the relationship between the characteristics of the board of directors (BoD) and performance in family businesses. In terms of board composition, it emerged that family businesses are characterized by a lower number of independent members and a greater presence of gender diversity compared to non-family businesses. Furthermore, their performance is positively associated with ownership concentration and gender diversity. Binacci et al. (2016) explored the role of non-family managers in relation to company performance, demonstrating how the presence of non-family managers can improve company performance.

As regards the role of women in family businesses, Abdullah (2014) examined in depth the elements that determine the inclusion of women within the boards of large Malaysian firms, distinguishing between family and non-family businesses. The results demonstrated how a greater number of women on the board is positively associated with the presence of family members on the board. This could mean that women's participation is anchored primarily in mechanisms of family ties. Chadwick and Dawson (2018) explored the relationship between the inclusion of women at the managerial level and financial and non-financial performance, distinguishing between different types of companies. It emerged that the presence of women in top roles (such as that of CEO and/or CFO) is positively associated with non-financial performance in the case of family businesses and with financial performance only in the case of non-family businesses.

3.5 Keywords

Studying the use of keywords in a research area is a useful tool for understanding the evolution of Authors' attention to the topics covered over time (Ding et al., 2001). The keywords in fact can be considered an approximation of the content of the papers.

The analysis of the keywords highlights how the topic of diversity, equity, and inclusion practices in family firms has been studied from different points of view.

In this analysis, keywords are represented by nodes and links, whose weight indicates how many times certain keywords have been used together. The representation of all nodes and links provides the co-occurrence network (Callon et al., 1991). To avoid the exclusion of very recent keywords, but also the inclusion of irrelevant topics, a minimum number of co-occurrences was set at three (Strozzi et al., 2017).

Figure 2 shows the result of the keyword network analysis (KNA). As the size of the nodes increases, the frequency of use of the keywords increases. Keywords with the same color belong to the same cluster and identify a specific search topic.

Table 5 reports a list of the keywords used with the number of occurrences, divided by cluster.

The most used keyword is "*family business*."It is followed by "*firm performance*," "*corporate governance*," "*female directors*," and "*board of directors*." The reference to corporate performance shows in what context the presence of diversity within family businesses is usually studied, while the last three keywords present

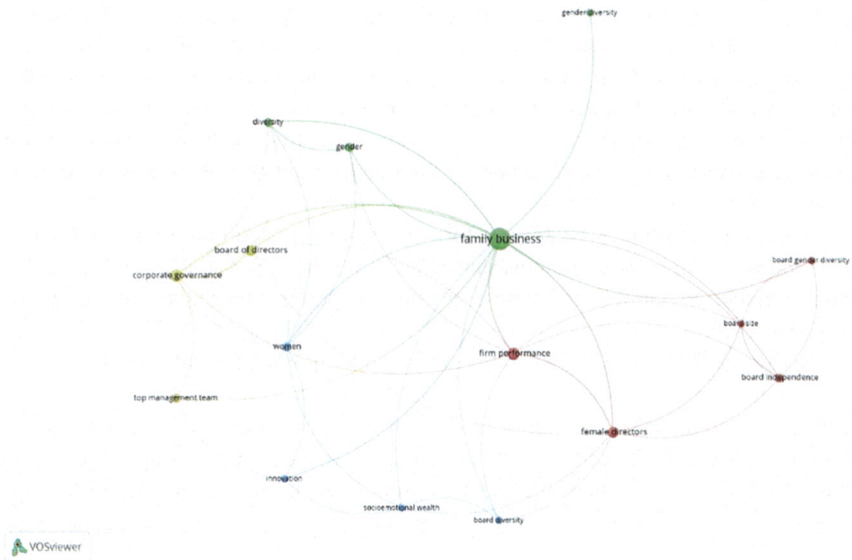

Fig. 2 Keyword network analysis

Table 5 Clusters based on keyword analysis

Cluster 1 (red)		**Cluster 3** (blue)	
Keywords	*Occurrences*	*Keywords*	*Occurrences*
Board gender diversity	3	Board diversity	3
Board independence	4	Innovation	3
Board size	3	Socio-emotional wealth	3
Female directors	6	Women	4
Firm performance	7		
Cluster 2 (green)		**Cluster 4** (yellow)	
Keywords	*Occurrences*	*Keywords*	*Occurrences*
Diversity	4	Board of directors	6
Family business	23	Corporate governance	7
Gender	4	Top management team	4
Gender diversity	3		

three different perspectives for addressing diversity, equity, and inclusion practices in family businesses, i.e., at the level of corporate governance in general, the composition of the board of directors and/or gender diversity.

The KNA also allows us to identify four different clusters, corresponding to four different research areas. The first cluster addresses the topic in terms of the structure and composition of the board of directors (in particular, taking into consideration the presence of women, independent members, and the size of the board) and studies the impacts of the presence of a greater or lesser level of diversity on company performance. The second cluster focuses on the topic of gender diversity in family businesses and explores the role of women within this type of business. The third cluster addresses the issue of diversity by relating it to some peculiarities of family businesses, such as the impact of socio-emotional wealth and the strong propensity for innovation. Also, in this case, the composition of the BoD and the role of women are taken into consideration. Finally, the last cluster focuses on the impacts of diversity on the corporate governance structure, with particular attention to the characteristics of the members of the board of directors and those of the top management team.

In general, therefore, we can state that the topic is studied mainly with reference to the impacts at the corporate governance level, verifying any implications on some characteristics of family businesses, in terms of performance, innovation, and/or corporate culture.

Finally, the KNA also allows us to carry out a temporal analysis of the keywords, thus tracing the chronological evolution of the search area (see Fig. 3). The keywords characterized by the light green color are those used most recently, while those represented in dark blue are those used most in the past. Looking at the figure, it is possible to notice how the most recently used keywords are the following: "*diversity*," "*board gender diversity*," and "*board diversity*." This confirms once

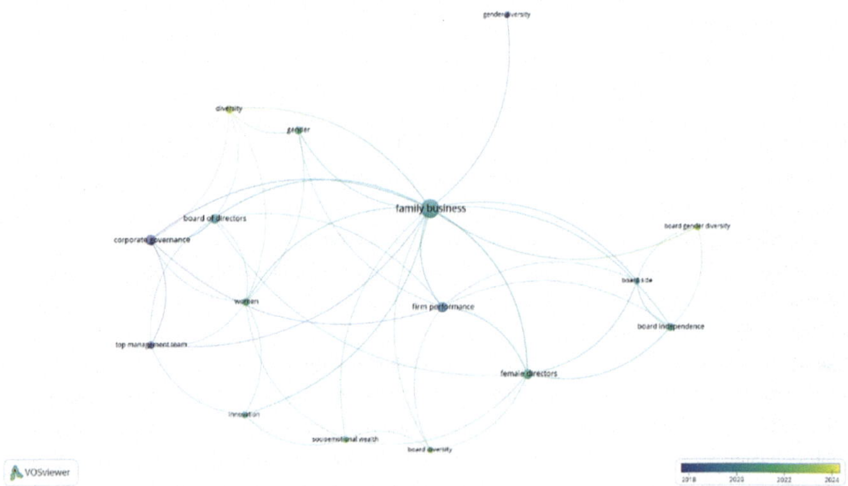

Fig. 3 Keyword temporal analysis

again how the research area has recently focused more on the dynamics of corporate governance and, in particular, on the composition of the board of directors.

3.6 Content Analysis of the Papers and Framework of the Research Area

Proceeding with the analysis of the content of the papers, it is possible to make a distinction between contributions aimed at developing an empirical analysis (37 papers) and theoretical contributions (two papers). The topic, therefore, is studied mainly from a practical perspective. In turn, if we take into consideration only the empirical studies, we notice a prevalence of quantitative techniques (35 papers) compared to qualitative ones (four). Quantitative techniques involve, for example, the application of different types of regressions and the carrying out of panel analyses, while qualitative techniques include the carrying out of interviews, the administration of questionnaires, and the development of case studies.

By reading the papers, the clusters in the literature already identified thanks to the analysis of the keywords are confirmed, but new themes are added to these (see Table 6).

The first cluster refers to the integration of diversity practices at the corporate governance level of family businesses, in terms of size and composition of the board of directors or top management. The second cluster studies the impacts of diversity on the financial performance of family businesses; this group of studies compares the different results between family and non-family businesses. The third cluster did not emerge through the analysis of keywords and focuses on the relationship between diversity practices and ESG disclosure or performance; attention toward sustainability, in fact, is an element often present in family businesses, and

Table 6 Main clusters in the literature on diversity, equity, and inclusion practices in family firms

Topic	Papers
Corporate governance	Galavotti and D'Este (2022); Sfeir (2023); Zhang and Luo (2021); Röd (2019); Nordqvist et al. (2014)
Firms' performance	Xu et al. (2023); Islam et al. (2023); Fėlix and David (2019); Vieira (2018); Rubino et al. (2017); Binacci et al. (2016); Wellalage et al. (2012)
ESG disclosure and/or performance	Arayssi and Jizi (2024); Padungsaksawasdi and Treepongkaruna (2023); Maggi et al. (2023); Gavana et al. (2023a); Gavana et al. (2023b)
Gender diversity	Maseda et al. (2023); Samara and Lapeira (2022); Wang et al. (2023); Wagner et al. (2023); Gjergji et al. (2023); Shukla and Teraiya (2022); Soost and Moog (2021); Mustafa et al. (2020); Magnanelli et al. (2020); Chadwick and Dawson (2018); Mittal and Lavina. (2018); Moreno-Gómez and Calleja-Blanco (2018); D'Amato (2017); Abdullah (2014); Remery et al. (2014)
Family businesses' peculiarities	Gavrić and Braje (2024); Zona et al. (2023); Das (2022); Bauweraerts et al. (2022); Hillebrand et al. (2020); Wąsowska (2017); Saeed et al. (2017)

numerous authors have tried to identify the factors that increase attention toward ESG issues. The fourth cluster focuses exclusively on gender diversity practices within family businesses. Finally, the last cluster takes into consideration some peculiarities and dynamics specific to family businesses, such as the presence of conflicts within the family, socio-emotional wealth, the internationalization process, and the propensity for innovation.

3.6.1 Limitations of the Sample Analyzed and Suggestions for Future Research

Reading previous studies helps to identify some limitations and gaps in the literature, which could be interesting to fill with new studies in the future. Therefore, suggestions for future research are proposed below.

In general, all studies take into consideration a single country or a few countries and are conducted over a single year or a short period of time. For this reason, in the future, conducting cross-sectional and/or longitudinal studies that take into consideration multiple countries simultaneously and longer time periods is recommended. Regarding studies that consider diversity in terms of the composition of the board of directors, it could be interesting to take into account new characteristics that express diversity such as age, experience, education, race, and compensation of its members. Due to the greater availability of data and information, studies analyzed the phenomenon in listed firms, but family businesses are often smaller in size. For this reason, it would be necessary to also take unlisted companies into consideration in future studies. Moreover, a further limitation of the studies on the topic concerns the fact that the heterogeneity of family businesses is not considered in terms, for example, of the percentage of family ownership, number of members involved in the BoD, and generations of the family involved in management.

With reference to Cluster 2 (*Firms' performance*), it would be interesting to conduct analyses that take into consideration the influence on the result of the presence of family businesses at different stages of life, from new foundations to companies already stable on the market. Furthermore, the relationship between diversity and firms' performance could be studied with reference to other internal corporate governance mechanisms, such as board size, independence, or the role of the CEO.

For Cluster 3 (*ESG disclosure and/or performance*), it would be interesting to consider some moderating variables that can influence diversity, such as gender equality at a country level and the impact of specific regulations. Currently, the studies of this cluster only take developed countries into consideration, thus neglecting to analyze the relationship in the case of developing countries. Future research should also study the presence of any differences between the generations of the family involved within the company and also investigate the influence of national culture.

Moving on to Cluster 4 (*Gender diversity*), future research should look for those factors that can make family businesses more inclined to favor the presence of women on the board of directors or in top management and explore the role of a possible female CEO, distinguishing between female family members or not. The women belonging to the family, in fact, should share the same values and objectives, not only of an economic nature. In the future, it is also appropriate to illustrate the different processes of women becoming members of the BoD and verify whether their presence is purely symbolic or has an actual impact on the decision-making process. With reference to gender diversity, it would also be interesting to delve deeper into the role of women in startup companies, characterized by a business with greater risk and a strong drive for innovation.

In Cluster 5 (*Family businesses' peculiarities*) studies should be conducted to understand whether female CEOs in family businesses feel more or less supported in undertaking risky activities and to understand whether the relationship between the presence of female directors on the BoD and changes in R&D intensity depends on the role the board plays.

4 Conclusions

This chapter conducted a systematic literature review on the topic of diversity, equity, and inclusion practices in family firms with the aim of providing a snapshot of the current state of contributions on the topic and proposing useful suggestions for developing research in the future.

The results highlight the novelty of the research area and, therefore, the presence of numerous gaps that can be filled in the future by new studies.

To the best of our knowledge, this literature review represents one of the first attempts at systematizing the contributions in the above-mentioned research field. It aims to provide a holistic view of the research topics on diversity and inclusion in the family firm context. The present work has some interesting implications for both academics and practitioners. Firstly, it depicts the main topics and issues concerning diversity and inclusion practices within family firms, and it allows the main gaps in previous literature to be identified through the definition of an agenda that is useful for scholars to develop new studies in this research area. From a practical perspective, it could be a useful starting point for increasing the awareness on the part of family firms of the relevance of these practices and thus improving the adoption of diversity and inclusion policies in their daily operations. These reflections may be considered by practitioners in their hiring policies and by politicians for introducing incentives for companies and supporting these decisions.

However, the analysis is not without limitations. First, we only used the Scopus database. In the future, it may be interesting to integrate multiple databases to conduct the analysis. Furthermore, we only considered articles and reviews, excluding books and other types of publications. Finally, the paper selection process, although systematic, remains subject to a certain level of subjectivity.

References

Abdullah, S. N. (2014). The causes of gender diversity in Malaysian large firms. *Journal of Management & Governance, 18*, 1137–1159.

Anderson, R. C., & Reeb, D. M. (2003). Founding-family ownership and firm performance: Evidence from the S&P 500. *The Journal of Finance, 58*(3), 1301–1327. https://doi.org/10.1111/1540-6261.00567

Arayssi, M., & Jizi, M. (2024). Royal family board directors and the level of ESG disclosures in GCC listed firms. *Journal of Accounting & Organizational Change, 20*(1), 58–83.

Bauweraerts, J., Rondi, E., Rovelli, P., De Massis, A., & Sciascia, S. (2022). Are family female directors catalysts of innovation in family small and medium enterprises? *Strategic Entrepreneurship Journal, 16*(2), 314–354.

Binacci, M., Peruffo, E., Oriani, R., & Minichilli, A. (2016). Are all non-family managers (NFMs) equal? The impact of NFM characteristics and diversity on family firm performance. *Corporate Governance: An International Review, 24*(6), 569–583.

Brun de Pontet, S., Pendergast, J. & Schuman, A. (2020). *Diversity and inclusion in family enterprise: What, why, and how*. Special Report from *The Family Business Consulting Group*. Available at https://www.thefbcg.com/resource/special-report-diversity-and-inclusion-in-family-enterprise-what-why-and-how/.

Callon, M., Courtial, J. P., & Laville, F. (1991). Co-word analysis as a tool for describing the network of interactions between basic and technological research: The case of polymer chemistry. *Scientometrics, 22*, 155–205. https://doi.org/10.1007/BF02019280

Chadwick, I. C., & Dawson, A. (2018). Women leaders and firm performance in family businesses: An examination of financial and nonfinancial outcomes. *Journal of Family Business Strategy, 9*(4), 238–249.

D'Amato, A. (2017). Do women perform better in family firms? Exploring the moderating role of family firm status. *International Journal of Wine Business Research, 29*(3), 299–315.

Das, A. (2022). Promoting organizational diversity and preserving socioemotional wealth: Can family businesses balance the two? *Journal of Family Business Management, 12*(4), 653–678.

Dawson, S., Gašević, D., Siemens, G., & Joksimovic, S. (2014). Current state and future trends: A citation network analysis of the learning analytics field. In S. Teasley & A. Pardo (Eds.), *LAK 2014: 4th international conference on learning analytics and knowledge* (pp. 231–240). Association for Computing Machinery (ACM). https://doi.org/10.1145/2567574.2567585

Ding, Y., Chowdhury, G. G., & Foo, S. (2001). Bibliometric cartography of information retrieval research by using co-word analysis. *Information Processing and Management, 37*(6), 817–842.

Ducassy, I., & Prevot, F. (2010). The effects of family dynamics on diversification strategy: Empirical evidence from French companies. *Journal of Family Business Strategy, 1*(4), 224–235. https://doi.org/10.1016/j.jfbs.2010.10.001

Fèlix, E. G. S., & David, D. S. T. (2019). Performance of family-owned firms: The impact of gender at the management level. *Journal of Family Business Management, 9*(2), 228–250.

Galavotti, I., & D'Este, C. (2022). The corporate governance-diversification link: Exploring the heterogeneity of family firms. *Corporate Governance: The International Journal of Business in Society, 23*(3), 441–457. https://doi.org/10.1108/CG-01-2022-0043

Gavana, G., Gottardo, P., & Moisello, A. M. (2023a). The effect of board diversity and tenure on environmental performance. Evidence from family and non-family firms. *Journal of Family Business Management, 14*(3), 534–561.

Gavana, G., Gottardo, P., & Moisello, A. M. (2023b). Board diversity and corporate social performance in family firms. The moderating effect of the institutional and business environment. *Corporate Social Responsibility and Environmental Management, 30*(5), 2194–2218.

Gavrić, T., & Braje, I. N. (2024). Managing cultural diversity and conflict in family businesses: An organizational perspective. *Administrative Sciences, 14*(1), 13.

Gjergji, R., Vena, L., Campopiano, G., Sciascia, S., & Cortesi, A. (2023). Strategy disclosure and cost of capital: The key role of women directors for family firms. *Journal of Family Business Strategy, 15*(2), 100570.

Hillebrand, S., Teichert, T., & Steeger, J. (2020). Innovation in family firms: An agency and resource-based lens on contingencies of generation and management diversity. *British Journal of Management, 31*(4), 792–810.

Islam, M. T., Saha, S., & Rahman, M. (2023). Diversity–performance nexus in an emerging economy: An investigation of family and non-family firms. *International Journal of Emerging Markets*. https://doi.org/10.1108/IJOEM-04-2022-0727

Knoke, D., & Yang, S. (2008). *Social network analysis* 154. Sage.

Kraus, S., Breier, M., & Dasí-Rodríguez, S. (2020). The art of crafting a systematic literature review in entrepreneurship research. *International Entrepreneurship and Management Journal, 16*, 1023–1042.

Maggi, B., Gjergji, R., Vena, L., Sciascia, S., & Cortesi, A. (2023). Family firm status and environmental disclosure: The moderating effect of board gender diversity. *Business Ethics, the Environment & Responsibility, 32*(4), 1334–1351.

Magnanelli, B. S., Nasta, L., & Raoli, E. (2020). Do female directors on corporate boards make a difference in family owned businesses? *Journal of International Accounting Research, 19*(1), 85–102.

Maseda, A., Iturralde, T., Cooper, S., & Aparicio, G. (2022). Mapping women's involvement in family firms: A review based on bibliographic coupling analysis. *International Journal of Management Reviews, 24*, 279–305. https://doi.org/10.1111/ijmr.12278

Maseda, A., Iturralde, T., Aparicio, G., & Cooper, S. Y. (2023). Building bridges between gender and family business literature to advance women's empowerment. *Gender in Management: An International Journal, 38*(8), 1029–1074. https://doi.org/10.1108/GM-02-2022-0056

Mittal, S., & Lavina. (2018). Females' representation in the boardroom and their impact on financial distress: An evidence from family businesses in India. *Indian Journal of Corporate Governance, 11*(1), 35–44.

Moreno-Gómez, J., & Calleja-Blanco, J. (2018). The relationship between women's presence in corporate positions and firm performance: The case of Colombia. *International Journal of Gender and Entrepreneurship, 10*(1), 83–100.

Mustafa, A., Saeed, A., Awais, M., & Aziz, S. (2020). Board-gender diversity, family ownership, and dividend announcement: Evidence from Asian emerging economies. *Journal of Risk and Financial Management, 13*(4), 62.

Nordqvist, M., Sharma, P., & Chirico, F. (2014). Family firm heterogeneity and governance: A configuration approach. *Journal of Small Business Management, 52*(2), 192–209.

Padungsaksawasdi, C., & Treepongkaruna, S. (2023). Corporate social responsibility, board characteristics, and family business in Thailand. *Corporate Social Responsibility and Environmental Management, 31*(2), 1340–1353. https://doi.org/10.1002/csr.2636

Remery, C., Matser, I., & Hans Flören, R. (2014). Successors in Dutch family businesses: Gender differences. *Journal of Family Business Management, 4*(1), 79–91.

Röd, I. (2019). TMT diversity and innovation ambidexterity in family firms: The mediating role of open innovation breadth. *Journal of Family Business Management, 9*(4), 377–392.

Rotaru, V., Mihai, L., & Ogarcă, R. (2020). Succesion management in Romanian SMEs. *Management & Marketing Journal, 18*, 135–150.

Rubino, F. E., Tenuta, P., & Cambrea, D. R. (2017). Board characteristics effects on performance in family and non-family business: A multi-theoretical approach. *Journal of Management & Governance, 21*, 623–658.

Saeed, A., Yousaf, A., & Alharbi, J. (2017). Family and state ownership, internationalization and corporate board-gender diversity: Evidence from China and India. *Cross Cultural & Strategic Management, 24*(2), 251–270.

Samara, G., & Lapeira, M. (2022). Women in Latin American family businesses: An institutional logics perspective. *Management Decision, 61*(3), 720–745.

Sfeir, S. E. H. (2023). Who I am affects what I do: How does director diversity influence board roles in medium-sized family firms? *International Journal of Entrepreneurship and Small Business, 48*(2), 128–157.

Shukla, H., & Teraiya, V. (2022). Influence of gender diversity in boards on family and non-family businesses towards innovation and creativity. *FIIB Business Review*. https://doi.org/10.1177/23197145211068603

Soost, C., & Moog, P. (2021). Gender and organizational performance in business succession. *Journal of Small Business & Entrepreneurship, 33*(1), 93–122.

Strozzi, F., Colicchia, C., Creazza, A., & Noè, C. (2017). Literature review on the 'smart factory' concept using bibliometric tools. *International Journal of Production Research, 55*, 6572–6591. https://doi.org/10.1080/00207543.2017.1326643

Van Eck, N. J., & Waltman, L. (2010). Software survey: VOSviewer, a computer program for bibliometric mapping. *Scientometrics, 84*(2), 523–538. https://doi.org/10.1007/s11192-009-0146-3

Vieira, E. S. (2018). Board of directors characteristics and performance in family firms and under the crisis. *Corporate Governance: The International Journal of Business in Society, 18*(1), 119–142.

Wagner, E., Pernsteiner, H., & Riaz, A. (2023). Blood is thicker than water: An analysis of women's presence on Pakistani boards. *Gender in Management: An International Journal, 39*(4), 516–533. https://doi.org/10.1108/GM-04-2022-0139

Wang, J. C., Zhao, Y., Sun, S. L., & Zhu, J. (2023). Female-friendly boards in family firms. *Journal of Business Research, 157*, 113552.

Wąsowska, A. (2017). The internationalisation of family firms: The role of the ownership structure and the composition of top management team. *Entrepreneurial Business and Economics Review, 5*(1), 169–185.

Wellalage, N. H., Locke, S., & Scrimgeour, F. (2012). Does one size fit all? An empirical investigation of board structure on family firms' financial performance. *Afro-Asian Journal of Finance and Accounting, 3*(2), 182–194.

Xu, E. G., Yang, J. W., Shan, Y. G., & Graves, C. (2023). The influence of corporate governance on the performance of family-controlled firms: Exploring the effects of legal jurisdiction. *International Journal of Managerial Finance, 19*(3), 615–644.

Zhang, C., & Luo, L. (2021). Board diversity and risk-taking of family firms: Evidence from China. *International Entrepreneurship and Management Journal, 17*, 1569–1590.

Zhao, D., & Strotmann, A. (2015). Analysis and visualization of citation networks. *Synthesis Lectures on Information Concepts, Retrieval, and Services, 7*, 1–207. https://doi.org/10.2200/S00624ED1V01Y201501ICR039

Zona, F., Pesci, C., & Zamarian, M. (2023). CEO risk preferences in family firms: Combining socioemotional wealth and gender identity perspectives. *Journal of Family Business Strategy, 15*(2), 100553. https://doi.org/10.1016/j.jfbs.2023.100553

Part II
Reporting and Disclosing Diversity and Equity Practices

Diversity, Equity and Inclusion Disclosure in Corporate Reporting

Marisa Agostini

1 Corporate Diversity, Equity and Inclusion: Benefits and Challenges to Account for

Diversity can be intended in various ways. It exists in terms of gender, race, sexual orientation, religion and age, and these are just some examples of the types of diversity that have traditionally been considered. The importance of protecting different forms of diversity is often stated, at least formally. The goal of a more open, tolerant and peaceful society also emerges clearly from the 2030 Agenda (United Nations, 2015) that consists of 17 Sustainable Development Goals (SDGs). Among the 17 SDGs, those that focus most on the issue of diversity are the fifth and tenth, respectively called 'Gender Equality' and 'Reducing Inequalities'. The marked social orientation of these two SDGs is evident. However, a recent report (United Nations, 2021) showed that progress towards the SDGs is slow and has been severely disrupted by the COVID-19 pandemic. Very few countries are committed and to some extent successful in ensuring a truly discrimination-free society and specific contexts, such as inclusive working environments. Companies should increasingly seek to take decisions and actions to remove obstacles and/or barriers that prevent equal opportunities and social welfare. To this purpose, they should both disincentivise negative patterns of behaviour that would reinforce practices contrary to the equity perspective (WBCSD, 2022) and encourage inclusion, embracing diversity and making every employee perceive him/herself as an important part of the organisation (GDEIB, 2021). Equity is perceived as the 'intermediate' mechanism through which the relationship between diversity and inclusion is created and promoted

M. Agostini (✉)
Sustainability Lab, Venice School of Management, Ca' Foscari University, Venice, Italy
e-mail: marisa.agostini@unive.it

M. Agostini et al. (eds.), *Diversity and Equity in Accounting*, SIDREA Series in Accounting and Business Administration,
https://doi.org/10.1007/978-3-031-78247-3_5

(Roberson & Scott, 2022). The literature (Russen & Dawson, 2023) has also highlighted the possibility of a circular, rather than linear, relationship between these three dimensions, considering inclusion as the 'starting point' and the value base on which the organisation is built. If the company creates an inclusive environment internally, it will attract an increasing number of diverse individuals, who will have a greater incentive to stay longer in the organisation (Sakr et al., 2023). The principle of fairness then takes over, the perception of which outside the company will drive people to apply in even greater numbers. Usually, inclusive policies elicit confidence, involvement, appreciation and a perceived sense of participation in the decision-making process. Inclusion, however, can also lead to negative effects, such as the creation of hierarchies. It is for this reason that inclusion must result from practices that reflect a real organisational restructuring in order to incorporate the concept of diversity into the corporate mission (Adamson et al., 2021). The issue of welcoming diversity, also enhancing equity and inclusion, has also given rise to the so-called 'Diversity Management'. This defines the way in which a company seeks to introduce policies aimed at valuing diversity, in order to create an environment where people's needs are met in a diverse, effective, efficient and fair manner. Corporate policies based on diversity, equity and inclusion (hereafter also referred to as DEI) can have different impacts on organisational activities and processes. On the one hand, they may combine with some already existing practices, generating additional and advanced processes (e.g. networking). On the other hand, they do not seem to alter some pre-existing organisational activities (e.g. audit procedures). This evidence highlights how dependencies and co-existences may arise from diversity, business and professional logic within different organisations (Anderson-Gough et al., 2022). In order to monitor the effective implementation of their DEI policies, organisations can implement different tools, including corporate reporting, which primarily serves to communicate the promoted initiatives to external stakeholders. Traditionally, corporate social reporting has represented '*the process of communicating the social and environmental effects of organizations' economic actions to particular interest groups within society and to society at large. As such it involves extending the accountability of organizations (particularly companies), beyond the traditional role of providing a financial account to the owners of capital, in particular, shareholders. Such an extension is predicated upon the assumption that companies do have wider responsibilities than simply to make money for their shareholders*' (Gray et al., 1987, p. ix). Social reporting highlights the impact that the company has on its community, primarily on workers' rights and ethics. It has been one of the tools traditionally adopted to disclose and monitor corporate social responsibility. It has historically been a voluntary form of reporting, while a regulatory evolution is underway to make non-financial disclosure (also concerning diversity) progressively more mandatory (NFRD, 2014; CSRD, 2022). DEI policies represent an increasingly important issue to be considered and monitored for both better corporate performance and cost evaluation, as explained in the following. Several reasons seem to support the link between DEI policies and the achievement of better business performance (Dixon-Fyle et al., 2020), particularly those related to corporate motivation, reputation and innovation. First, organisational diversity can lead to increased productivity. Indeed, the welcoming of diversity can develop a greater sense of belonging in the employee, who, feeling more involved, will carry out (his or her) activities reducing waste and mistakes. By acting on employee involvement and increasing employee motivation, costs can be reduced while also gaining an economic advantage. Furthermore, the company capable of effectively managing diversity can achieve an improvement in its reputation, which can be evaluated positively by shareholders and other key stakeholders. Finally, the company able to embrace diverse competences and implement diversity management strategies can count on the promotion of innovative ideas that can in turn provide an improvement in the company's market positioning (Hunt et al., 2015).

However, diversity entails costs related to both the promotion of inclusion policies and diversity management. Firstly, organisational costs relate to the reformulation and subsequent implementation of the company's diversity strategy and programmes. For instance, they refer to costs for staff recruitment, selection and training to orient employees towards inclusion. Other costs that the company may run into are related to cultural changes: adaptation to the new strategy pursued may take a long time to settle down due to individual resistance to change. In the adoption of DEI policies, the identity of individuals plays a key role (Gardenswartz & Rowe, 1994, 2003). Specifically, identity demarcation refers to the way in which organisational actors avoid switching from one logic to another or hybridising identities within certain organisational practices (Anderson-Gough et al., 2022). In addition, there may also be costs related to internal conflict management arising from difficulties in cooperation or communication between employees. The company must also account for the legal costs incurred in implementing legislative obligations (European Commission, 2003).

Diversity management is therefore an essential and challenging part of the manager's task as it relates to the degree and ways in which organisations generate opportunities to exploit diversity-related potential. The predominance of shareholder value maximisation as the main corporate objective has been successfully displaced in favour of the consideration of a broader set of interests (Amis et al., 2020). The company has to make careful analyses and assessments in this regard: despite the costs mentioned, the benefits can be significant, leading to a radical improvement for the company and society as a whole.

Based on these premises, the chapter aims to systematically review the literature on corporate reporting on diversity, equity and inclusion. Accounting, reporting and control systems have the important task of balancing multiple logics in the presence of increasingly heterogeneous corporate objectives and pressures requiring both flexibility and fairness (Agarwal et al., 2024). In particular, DEI corporate reporting, also in light of ongoing recent regulatory evolution (NFRD, 2014; CSRD, 2022), should account for the impacts, risks and opportunities addressed by companies in managing diversity, equity and inclusion. As highlighted by the following literature review, this chapter is one of the first and few contributions focusing precisely on corporate reporting on diversity, equity and inclusion.

2 Methodology, Analysis and Results

The literature analysis presented in this section was elaborated using the documents reported on the databases Scopus and Web of Science, two of the main databases for searching bibliographic references (Mongeon & Paul-Hus, 2016). In order to examine how the literature has dealt with the topic of DEI in corporate reporting, a systematic literature review was conducted based on two different search strings in two databases and following a consecutive-step approach (Littell et al., 2008; Massaro et al., 2016; Sivarajah et al., 2017).

A first very specific search adopted the following string of words: diversit* AND equit* AND inclus* AND 'corporate AND reporting'. The results obtained up to the year 2023 (included) without entering any other search filter were only three (Jang & Ardichvili, 2020; Khan et al., 2019; Torres et al., 2023). Considering the very limited number of papers retrieved through a string of very specific words, a second much broader search was implemented, which started by considering the three fundamental concepts analysed here (diversity, equity and inclusion) and then gradually refined the search to focus on corporate reporting. In this way, thanks also to the comparison of the results of the two implemented searches, the aim was to highlight the most developed DEI issues in the literature and which research strands still require further development. For both databases (i.e. Scopus and Web of Science), the second search focused on using the following keywords: diversit* (which stands for diversity), equit* (which stands for equity) and inclus* (which stands for inclusion), within titles, abstracts and keywords. In this way, 4310 results were found on Scopus and 3878 on Web of Science. In order to refine the search and focus it on relevant contributions, the following filters were then applied: (Table 1): 'article' (as a type of document) was selected, reducing the results to 2598 on Scopus and 2691 on Web of Science, and 'journal' (as a type of resource) was selected and further reduced the results to 2575 on Scopus. On Web of Science, this filter was not present, so the number of papers remained unchanged. The results were limited to

Table 1 Steps of the second systematic literature review

Step number	Option type	Step description
1	Keywords Input	Specific keywords search criteria: *diversit* AND equit* AND inclus**
2	Document Type	Articles
3	Source Type	Printed or already accepted (for print) by scientific journals
4	Language	English
5	Year	Until 2023 (included)
6	Subject Area	'Business, management and accounting' in Scopus and its equivalent 'Business Economics' in Web of Science
7	Abstract	Relevant articles by reading the abstracts
8	Final sample of articles to be analysed	

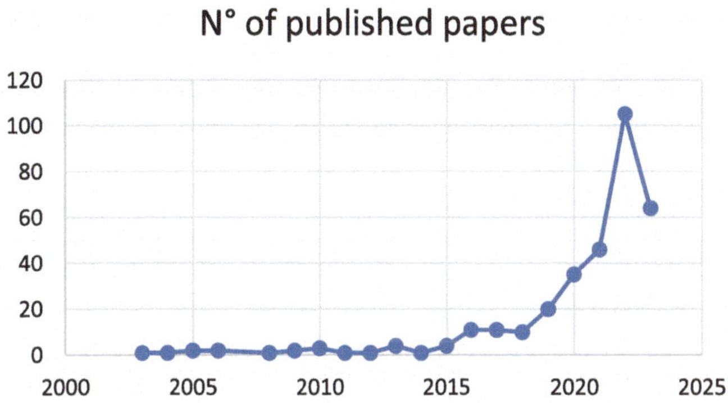

Fig. 1 Articles retrieved from Scopus and Web of Science by year of publication

articles published in English (as the only language), reducing the results to 2521 papers on Scopus and 2603 on Web of Science. Selecting the relevant (search) area of 'Business, management and accounting' in Scopus and its equivalent 'Business Economics' in Web of Science, the final set included 234 results from Scopus and 201 from Web of Science. Finally, the results of the two databases were merged, eliminating the Web of Science papers that were also present in Scopus. In this way, the results to be analysed were reduced to 325 documents.

These 325 results have been edited in 201 different journals, 58 of which have published more than one article on this subject (Appendix 1). In particular, these 58 journals have a total of 182 contributions out of 325, while the other 143 journals contain only one article. It is also noticeable that of the 58 journals listed, only one journal is relevant to accounting, three journals to business and twenty to management. Therefore, most of the articles analysed were not published in journals that traditionally deal with 'business, management and accounting'.

Considering the temporal perspective (Fig. 1), the articles were published in the last twenty years (2003 to 2023) and most of the articles are very recent. Indeed, 302 out of 325 articles have been written since 2016. It is only in recent years that DEI issues have been taken into consideration.

3 Discussion

The analysis of the title, abstract and keywords led to the exclusion of most of the articles previously selected for various reasons (e.g. topic not relevant, context not corporate, focus on customer behaviour), creating a final sample of only 38 articles considered relevant (Appendix 2). The complete reading of such articles led to grouping them according to four different perspectives of analysis:

- General overview of DEI policies. These articles analyse DEI programmes, illustrating the advantages and disadvantages gained by companies adopting them, especially with regard to the (actual and perceived) impact among the various stakeholders.

- Issues related to the integration of disabled people in the organisation and potential improvements of the challenges identified. These papers discuss the concerns of employers in the integration of this category of workers and the policies introduced in this regard.
- Corporate policies in favour of women. These contributions illustrate how the corporate role of women has improved recently, thanks to their introduction also on boards of directors.
- DEI policy reporting. These works describe how companies give stakeholders an insight into their actions in pursuit of DEI goals, thus their level of monitoring and control of inclusive policy developments.

Most of the retrieved literature results deal with the general topic of DEI policies, while some address the specific topics of disability and gender diversity. Combining the results of two implemented search strings in the systematic literature review, only five articles (Bellringer, 2022; Gagnon et al., 2022; Jang & Ardichvili, 2020; Khan et al., 2019; Torres et al., 2023) analyse the main topic of this chapter on corporate reporting and the tools used by companies to disclose DEI policies and actions. These few contributions from the literature are very recent, as are the corresponding regulatory developments concerning corporate reporting. Directive 2014/95/EU (NFRD, 2014) not only made the preparation of the non-financial statement mandatory for some companies, but it directly mentioned diversity, stating that the following must be disclosed: '*a description of the diversity policy applied in relation to the undertaking's administrative, management and supervisory bodies with regard to aspects such as, for instance, age, gender, or educational and professional backgrounds, the objectives of that diversity policy, how it has been implemented and the results in the reporting period. If no such policy is applied, the statement shall contain an explanation as to why this is the case*' (NFRD, 2014, Article 19a, par. 2a). Expressly referring to the workplace, the diversity section of the corporate reports seeks to illustrate the levels of representation of minority groups within the company and to assess employees' DEI perceptions. These represent numerical assessments that can be made: diversity can therefore be measured, and its results can be represented through reporting (Gagnon et al., 2022). Therefore, companies are now called upon to properly account for their DEI practices and to show progress in achieving their DEI goals. Non-financial statements are certainly also instrumental in understanding and communicating the challenges each company faces regarding diversity and the actions it intends to pursue. Despite the significant changes implied by the NFRD (2014), some relevant critical issues still remain, such as the low mandatory preparation of non-financial statements (only for European entities with an average of 500 or more employees per year) and the lack of specificity in the required information. Indeed, according to the NFRD (2014), in the drafting of the non-financial statement, each organisation was allowed to adopt its own reporting methodology and to apply national or international standards and frameworks. In this regard, Khan et al. (2019) focus on the issue of disability and show that 25% of UK-sampled companies do not consider diversity as an important issue worthy of protection, reporting inaccurate information about disability within non-financial statements. Furthermore, less than half of such sampled companies provide information on the disabled workforce or the strategies adopted to enhance them. Therefore, organisations can still select the information to be reported to stakeholders, highlighting some positive information (e.g. policies implemented for the inclusion of disabled people), but omitting to describe other relevant information (e.g. the roles played in the company by disabled people and quantitative information useful to concretely evaluate the actions implemented). Hence, few companies still report on diversity (i.e. low volume of disclosure on the subject), and if they do, the scope of disclosure is not always clearly stated (i.e. low relevance of the information provided). In order to highlight the importance of the disclosure of such non-financial information, there have been many organisations, such as the UN Global Compact and the Organisation for Economic Co-operation and Development (OECD), which have drawn up guidelines in particular to support multinational companies (Jang & Ardichvili, 2020). Specifically, the Global Reporting Initiative (GRI) has instructed companies to also understand the business value of disability, offering examples on how to effectively report critical data on this DEI dimension. This confirms the GRI as a prime promoter of the disclosure and reporting of non-financial information. Through the application of guidelines, companies should be able to generate reliable, material and standardised information with which to assess the situation and implement more informed decision-making (Jang & Ardichvili, 2020). Despite their wide dissemination and application, GRI Standards remain voluntary and are expected to be progressively superseded by the European Sustainability Reporting Standards (ESRS). These are the reporting principles developed by the European Financial Reporting Advisory Group (EFRAG) according to the Corporate Sustainability Reporting Directive (CSRD, 2022). This directive replaces the previous NFRD (2014) with the aim of overcoming its critical shortcomings, first and foremost by broadening the range of companies obliged to report. In addition, the CSRD (2022) envisages the introduction of ESRS as a set of common and mandatory reporting standards for all companies, so as to ensure a high degree of comparability of the reported information on an international level. Indeed, comparing the regulatory frameworks for non-financial information in 19 countries worldwide, it appears that only in six countries of those examined, there was a legal obligation to monitor the situation of equal opportunities and diversity protection in companies (Bird and Bird, 2022). Furthermore, only four out of 19 sampled countries have specific laws ensuring the protection of data collected when monitoring diversity. This represents a challenge that companies certainly face, as diversity information is particularly sensitive and its processing requires taking high privacy risks (Bellringer, 2022). The CSRD (2022) and the ESRS aim to enhance the compulsoriness and comparability of sustainability reporting. On 22 November 2022, after a lengthy consultation process, EFRAG provided the first draft of ESRS that is related to environmental, social and corporate governance issues. Diversity is addressed in detail in the four social standards which are labelled ESRS S. The first social standard (ESRS S1 'Own workforce'), which is the most extensive one and is also referred to in the other three, within the section 'Metrics and targets', contains the 'Disclosure Requirement S1-9' regarding diversity indicators with an emphasis on gender and age variables. Specifically, it requires disclosing the distribution of top management by gender and the age distribution among employees by distinguishing three categories (i.e. under 30, 30–50, over 50). Therefore, the CSRD (2022) is leading (through a phasing-in as of 1 January 2024) to a significant change in corporate reporting with reference also to diversity disclosure. It represents an external and regulatory pressure for companies to comply. As aforementioned, this pressure has increased over time for reasons both external (e.g. stakeholder demand) and internal (e.g. new policies) to the organisation. However, companies do not effectively adopt DEI policies if their corporate culture does not recognise their importance. Therefore, companies that do not have a history of formalising their commitment and readily recognising social logic may only promote DEI policies under strong external pressure and only from a strictly formal point of view. This may result in corporate reporting characterised by low volume and low relevance of the reported DEI information, complying with the minimum regulatory requirements.

4 Concluding Remarks

The analysis of the literature highlights that most of the papers selected in the relevant area 'Business, management and accounting' deal with the general discussion of DEI issues, while only a few academic articles focus on the communication and reporting of these items. Furthermore, the analysis of the selected journals emphasises that very few journals specialised in corporate reporting have so far published on the main topic of this chapter. This evidence reveals that disclosure inherent to DEI policies in the corporate context is still a topic in its infancy and developmental stage, awaiting adequate dissemination in the literature.

The introduction of more specific regulations (CSRD, 2022) and standards (ESRS) concerning non-financial disclosure should favour DEI reporting. Indeed, diversity can be measured, and its results can be represented through reporting (Gagnon et al., 2022). Organisations are called upon to implement and communicate DEI policies within their structure (Waples & Botsford Morgan, 2023). Failure to change course in this regard could result in significant disadvantages for organisations, such as the establishment of intercultural barriers between employees, a lack of adequate communication, and an increase in ethnocentrism, which could also lead to a decrease in company performance (Feitosa et al., 2022). These patterns of conduct are unproductive because they can cause organisational inefficiencies (Anderson, 2023). For this reason, in addition to implementing DEI measures and reporting on them, it is essential to analyse in advance what are the advantages and disadvantages that companies can (still theoretically) gain from their adoption and the most appropriate actions to be pursued in this regard. One measure frequently used by companies is targeted recruitment. This certainly increases the rate of diversity within the organisation, but at the same time, it can make new recruits feel as if they were brought into the company solely for the purpose of fulfilling specific strategic objectives related to diversity policies that the company had set itself to pursue. This perception can lead to the opposite effect, making people feel more excluded and less involved in the company itself (Hoang et al., 2022). Similarly, the literature shows that so-called 'diversity councils', training courses or employee resource groups (ERGs) often fail to bring about significant change in the organisation (Miller & Davis-Howard, 2023). Therefore, it is first of all necessary to identify practices aimed at integrating diversity in the company and to choose them according to the specific corporate situation. It is also useful to understand which of the three values (diversity, equity and inclusion) is the most appropriate to develop first in an organisation. Currently, it seems that the natural first step would be to increase diversity in the company. This would be followed by inclusion measures and policies that also pursue equity (Roberson & Scott, 2022; Russen & Dawson, 2023; Sakr et al., 2023). The inclusive environment is primarily created through fair treatment of employees, which is implemented despite their personal features. This may require a redefinition of the corporate structure in order to incorporate the concept of inclusion into the organisation's mission (Adamson et al., 2021). The benefits of this are manifold. The same pursuit of sustainable growth is inextricably tied to job satisfaction, productivity, safety and well-being, all of which are significantly impacted by the work environment (Torres et al., 2023). Through the perception of greater inclusion, people will feel freer to express their thoughts and come up with new ideas to experiment with. Instead of being reactive to what is experienced externally, the company can thus become proactive and lead the market towards change (Amin et al., 2023). This, in turn, generates a significant economic and financial impact: the mere announcement of inclusive actions by companies increases the value of their actions, to the detriment of those that do not take them. This is because such initiatives are viewed positively by shareholders and the market, which will therefore expect positive returns for the company in the future (Pandey et al., 2005). The economic benefit that the inclusive company obtains from these policies derives primarily from the effect they have on corporate reputation (Khan & Kalra, 2022). Thus, a positive link is established between the pursuit of corporate policies, adequate communication and reporting of the implemented actions and improvement of corporate reputation and economic-financial return. The recent measures (CSRD, 2022 and ESRS) highlight both the great attention paid to sustainability reporting (by capital markets, civil society organisations and governments around the world) and the willingness of the European Union to make sustainability reporting a regulated practice. Traditionally, initiatives relating to the corporate social domain have been associated with so-called soft regulation, which is not an alternative to legislative action, but an additional tool, which is reinforced by government action and stakeholder pressure (Torres et al., 2023). The exclusively voluntary approach to reporting proved to be ineffective because relevant information, useful to foster transparency and comparability of information, was often not included. Therefore, it was deemed appropriate to adopt an integrative approach in which even voluntary corporate initiatives are reinforced by mandatory regulation and public policy. The results of the analysis implemented in this chapter support the idea that the accounting system should remain flexible in order to respond to corporate changes introduced by DEI policies, as the effect of corporate culture is needed to implement effective change in diversity disclosure (Agarwal et al., 2024; Lepori & Montauti, 2020). The implemented analysis shows that corporate reporting on DEI issues is still in its early stages. There are still a few contributions specific to the topic under analysis, but all of them are recent, and this suggests the urgency and current relevance of the topic.

Appendix 1: Journals with the Largest Number of Articles Published on the Subject

Journal	No. of published papers
Equality Diversity and Inclusion	31
Advances in Developing Human Resources	7
Frontiers in Sports and Active Living	5
Gender, Work and Organization	5
Issues in Accounting Education	5
Journal of Business and Psychology	5
Public Integrity	5
Gender in Management	4
International Journal of Educational Management	4
Business Horizons	3
Cross Cultural and Strategic Management	3
Evaluation and Program Planning	3
Human Resource Management	3
Journal of Advertising Education	3
Journal of Management and Organization	3
Journal of Management Education	3
Journal of Park and Recreation Administration	3
Journal of Sport Management	3
Organization Development Journal	3
Recreational Sports Journal	3
Review of Public Personnel Administration	3
School Leadership & Management	3
American Journal of Evaluation	2
Applied Economic Perspectives and Policy	2
Australasian Marketing Journal	2
Breaking The Zero-Sum Game	2
Cities	2
Collection Management	2

Journal	No. of published papers
Educational Management Administration and Leadership	2
Employee Relations	2
Futures	2
Human Relations	2
Human Service Organizations Management, Leadership and Governance	2
Humanities and Social Sciences Communications	2
IEEE Transactions on Professional Communication	2
International Journal of Ethics and Systems	2
International Journal of Human Resource Management	2
International Journal of Intercultural Relations	2
Journal of Applied Behavioral Science	2
Journal of Applied Psychology	2
Journal of Business Ethics	2
Journal of Cultural Marketing Strategy	2
Journal of Healthcare Management	2
Journal of Higher Education Policy and Leadership Studies	2
Journal of Leadership Studies	2
Journal of Management	2
Journal of Management in Engineering	2
Journal of Public and Nonprofit Affairs	2
Journal of Public Policy and Marketing	2
Journal of the Academy of Marketing Science	2
Management Communication Quarterly	2
Management Decision	2
Managing Sport And Leisure	2
Museum Management and Curatorship	2
Personnel Review	2
Public Personnel Management	2
Research in Organizational Behavior	2
Sport Management Education Journal	2
Total	**182**

Appendix 2: Categorisation of the Sampled Papers According to Four Different Perspectives

Authors	Year	Cat. 1—General overview of DEI policies	Cat. 2—Integration of disabled people	Cat. 3—Corporate policies for women	Cat. 4.—DEI policy reporting
Adamson M.; Kelan E.; Lewis P.; Śliwa M.; Rumens N.	2021	X			
Amin, S; Yasin, I; Rutkowska-Ziarko, A	2022	X			
Anderson, JC	2023	X			
Annabi H.; Locke J.	2019		X		
Bellringer M.	2022				X
Bender, AF; Pigeyre, F	2016			X	
Bonaccio S.; Connelly C.E.; Gellatly I.R.; Jetha A.; Martin Ginis K.A.	2020		X		
Carrero J.; Krzeminska A.; Härtel C.E.J.	2019		X		
Chordiya R.; Hubbell L.	2023			X	
Daily C.M.; Dalton D.R.	2003			X	
Davis P.L.; Dickins D.; Higgs J.L.; Reid J.D.	2021	X			
Feitosa J.; Hagenbuch S.; Patel B.; Davis A.	2022	X			
Gagnon S.; Augustin T.; Cukier W.	2022				X
Hoang T.; Suh J.; Sabharwal M.	2022	X			
Ingram, P; Choi, Y	2022	X			
Jang S.; Ardichvili A.	2020				X
Jizi, MI; Nehme, R	2017			X	

Authors	Year	Cat. 1—General overview of DEI policies	Cat. 2—Integration of disabled people	Cat. 3—Corporate policies for women	Cat. 4.—DEI policy reporting
Khan N.; Korac-Kakabadse N.; Skouloudis A.; Dimopoulos A.	2019				X
Khan U.; Kalra A.	2022	X			
Knowlton K.; Carton A.M.; Grant A.M.	2022	X			
Le H.; Palmer Johnson C.; Fujimoto Y.	2021			X	
Miller F.A.; Davis-Howard V.	2022	X			
Pandey V.K.; Shanahan K.J.; Hansen S.W.	2005	X			
Roberson, Q; Scott, W	2022	X			
Rogers A.M.	2020	X			
Rudel E.M.; Derr B.; Ralston M.; Williams T.B.; Young A.	2021	X			
Russen M.; Dawson M.	2023	X			
Sakr N.; Son Hing L.S.; González-Morales M.G.	2023	X			
Schloemer-Jarvis A.; Bader B.; Böhm S.A.	2022		X		
Schultheiss D.E.	2021			X	
Seijts G.H.; Milani K.Y.	2022	X			
Simmons S.V.; Yawson R.M.	2022	X			
Sims C.M.	2018	X			
Stein M.A.; Bantekas I.	2021		X		
Stephens N.M.; Rivera L.A.; Townsend S.S.M.	2020	X			
Waples E.P.; Botsford Morgan W.	2023	X			

Authors	Year	Cat. 1—General overview of DEI policies	Cat. 2—Integration of disabled people	Cat. 3—Corporate policies for women	Cat. 4.—DEI policy reporting
Weak E.	2022	X			
Wiggins-Romesburg C.A.; Githens R.P.	2018	X			

References

Adamson, M., Kelan, E., Lewis, P., Śliwa, M., & Rumens, N. (2021). Introduction: Critically interrogating inclusion in organisations. *Organization, 28*(2), 211–227.

Agarwal, N., Krishnan, R., & Weiler, L. (2024). Institutional theory and hybrid accounting and control systems. *Journal of Management Accounting Research, 36*(1), 1–26.

Amin, S., Yasin, I., & Rutkowska-Ziarko, A. (2023). Diversity-inclusion nexus: Assessing the role of ethnic and religious diversity in financial inclusion; a global perspective. *Economic Research-Ekonomska Istraživanja, 36*(1), 1205–1225.

Amis, J., Barney, J., Mahoney, J. T., & Wang, H. (2020). From the editors—Why we need a theory of stakeholder governance—And why this is a hard problem. *Academy of Management Review, 45*(3), 499–503.

Anderson-Gough, F., Edgley, C., Robson, K., & Sharma, N. (2022). Organizational responses to multiple logics: Diversity, identity and the professional service firm. *Accounting, Organizations and Society, 103*, 101336.

Anderson, J. C. (2023). Implicit social cognition: The hidden element affecting equity, inclusion, and belonging on diverse collaborative teams. *Journal of Leadership Studies, 17*(1), 30–37.

Bellringer, M. (2022). Worthy of trust: Protecting minority privacy in diversity reporting. *Journal of Data Protection & Privacy, 5*(2), 173–182.

Bird and Bird. (2022). *"HR data essentials: Equality, diversity and inclusivity monitoring", A multi-country guide and chart* (pp. 1–92). Bird and Bird LLP. https://www.twobirds.com/-/media/new-website-content/pdfs/2022/bird-bird-2022-edi-chart.pdf

CSRD. (2022). *European Union (EU) Directive 2022/2464/EU*. Retrieved March 2024, from https://eur-lex.europa.eu/legal-content/EN/TXT/HTML/?uri=CELEX:32022L2464

Dixon-Fyle, S., Hunt, V., Dolan, K., & Prince, S. (2020). *Diversity wins: How inclusion matters*. McKinsey & Company. Retrieved February 20, 2024 from https://www.mckinsey.com/~/media/mckinsey/featured%20insights/diversity%20and%20inclusion/diversity%20wins%20how%20inclusion%20matters/diversity-wins-how-inclusion-matters-vf.pdf

European Commission. (2003, October 31). The costs and benefits of diversity. Luxembourg: European Commission - Directorate-General for Employment, Industrial Relations and Social Affairs. Retrieved February 20, 2024, from https://migrant-integration.ec.europa.eu/library-document/costs-and-benefits-diversity_en

Feitosa, J., Hagenbuch, S., Patel, B., & Davis, A. (2022). Performing in diverse settings: A diversity, equity, and inclusion approach to culture. *International Journal of Cross-Cultural Management, 22*(3), 433–457.

Gagnon, S., Augustin, T., & Cukier, W. (2022). Interplay for change in equality, diversity and inclusion studies. *Human Relations, 75*(7), 1327–1353.

Gardenswartz, L., & Rowe, A. (1994). Diversity management: Practical application in a health care organization. *Frontiers of Health Services Management, 11*(2), 36–40.

Gardenswartz, L., & Rowe, A. (2003). *Diverse teams at work: Capitalising on the power of diversity*. Society for Human Resource Editors.

GDEIB. (2021). *'Global Diversity, Equity & Inclusion Benchmarks. Standards for Organisations around the World', Center for Global Inclusion*. Retrieved March 2024, from https://centreforglobalinclusion.org/wp-content/uploads/2021/06/GDEIB-APRIL-2021-1.pdf

Gray, R., Owen, D., & Maunders, K. (1987). *Corporate social reporting: Accounting and accountability*. Prentice-Hall.

Hoang, T., Suh, J., & Sabharwal, M. (2022). Beyond a numbers game? Impact of diversity and inclusion on the perception of organizational justice. *Public Administration Review, 82*(3), 537–555.

Hunt, V., Layton, D., & Prince, S. (2015). *Diversity matters* (pp. 15–29). McKinsey & Company. Retrieved February 20, 2024, from: https://www.mckinsey.com/~/media/mckinsey/business%20functions/people%20and%20organizational%20performance/our%20insights/why%20diversity%20matters/diversity%20matters.pdf

Jang, S., & Ardichvili, A. (2020). The role of HRD in CSR and sustainability: A content analysis of corporate responsibility reports. *European Journal of Training and Development, 44*(6/7), 549–573.

Khan, N., Korac-Kakabadse, N., Skouloudis, A., & Dimopoulos, A. (2019). Diversity in the workplace: An overview of disability employment disclosures among UK firms. *Corporate Social Responsibility and Environmental Management, 26*(1), 170–185.

Khan, U., & Kalra, A. (2022). It's good to be different: How diversity impacts judgments of moral behavior. *Journal of Consumer Research, 49*(2), 177–201.

Lepori, B., & Montauti, M. (2020). Bringing the organization back in: Flexing structural responses to competing logics in budgeting. *Accounting, Organizations and Society, 80*, 101075. https://doi.org/10.1016/j.aos.2019.101075

Littell, J. H., Corcoran, J., & Pillai, V. (2008). *Systematic reviews and meta-analysis*. Oxford University Press.

Massaro, M., Dumay, J., & Guthrie, J. (2016). On the shoulders of giants: Undertaking a structured literature review in accounting. *Accounting, Auditing & Accountability Journal, 29*(5), 767–801.

Miller, F. A., & Davis-Howard, V. (2023). It is time for organizations to take a leap forward. *Organization Development Journal, 41*(3).

Mongeon, P., & Paul-Hus, A. (2016). The journal coverage of web of science and Scopus: A comparative analysis. *Scientometrics, 106*, 213–228.

NFRD. (2014). *European Union (EU) Directive 2014/95/EU*. Retrieved March 2024, from https://eur-lex.europa.eu/legal-content/EN/TXT/?uri=CELEX%3A32014L0095

Pandey, V. K., Shanahan, K. J., & Hansen, S. W. (2005). The relationship between shareholder wealth effects, diversity, and publicity as a marketing strategy. *Journal of the Academy of Marketing Science, 33*, 423–431.

Roberson, Q., & Scott, W. (2022). Contributive justice: An invisible barrier to workplace inclusion. *Journal of Management, 50*(3), 877–897.

Russen, M., & Dawson, M. (2023). Which should come first? Examining diversity, equity and inclusion. *International Journal of Contemporary Hospitality Management, 36*(1), 25–40.

Sakr, N., Son Hing, L. S., & González-Morales, M. G. (2023). Development and validation of the marginalized-group-focused diversity climate scale: Group differences and outcomes. *Journal of Business and Psychology, 38*(3), 689–722.

Sivarajah, U., Kamal, M. M., Irani, Z., & Weerakkody, V. (2017). Critical analysis of big data challenges and analytical methods. *Journal of Business Research, 70*, 263–286.

Torres, L., Ripa, D., Jain, A., Herrero, J., & Leka, S. (2023). The potential of responsible business to promote sustainable work–an analysis of CSR/ESG instruments. *Safety Science, 164*, 106151.

United Nations. (2015). *Transforming our world: The 2030 agenda for sustainable development. Outcome document of the summit for the adoption of the post-2015 development agenda.*

United Nations. 25–27 September 2015. Retrieved February 20, 2024, from https://sustainabledevelopment.un.org/post2015/transformingourworld/publication
United Nations. (2021). *The sustainable development goals report*. United Nations. Retrieved February 20, 2024, from https://unstats.un.org/sdgs/report/2021/
Waples, E. P., & Botsford Morgan, W. (2023). Leveraging mega-threats to reduce prejudice: A model for multi-level changes. *Management Decision, 61*(4), 1013–1037.WBCSD. (2022). *World Business Council for Sustainable Development and Korn Ferry, 'Diversity, Equity & Inclusion in the Workplace The journey to leading practice'*, GENEVA, 21 April 2022. Retrieved March 2024, from https://www.google.com/url?sa=t&rct=j&q=&esrc=s&source=web&cd=&cad=rja&uact=8&ved=2ahUKEwj4gm5jeWEAxU5Q_EDHdkcBvgQFnoECA4QAw&url=https%3A%2F%2Fwww.wbcsd.org%2FImperatives%2FEquity-Action%2FNews%2FWBCSD-and-Korn-Ferry-launchreport-exploring-key-dimensions-of-maturity-when-it-comes-to-Diversity-Equity-Inclusion-DEI&usg=AOvVaw1K_hRqY2-IFM5BWzgmn0oZ&opi=89978449

Diversity, Equity, and Inclusion in Environmental Social and Governance Disclosure: An Empirical Analysis of Governance Determinants

Arcangelo Marrone, Vincenzo Pontrelli, and Lara Oliva

1 Introduction

In recent times, a paradigm shift towards emphasizing economic and social sustainability, along with a heightened awareness of environmental responsibility, has been observed (Marrone et al., 2023). Influenced by the aftermath of the pandemic and socio-political movements such as "Me Too" and "Black Lives Matter," firms are increasingly confronted with social challenges that include addressing inequality, improving quality of life, and balancing work and family life (García-Sánchez et al., 2023; Manoharan et al., 2021). This shift has led to a growing call for organizations to take tangible steps to address these issues (Shohaieb et al., 2022), with nearly 49% of companies in the G250 now recognizing social factors as potential operational risks (KPMG, 2022).

Among social aspects, various studies highlight the growing importance of diversity, equity, and inclusion (DEI) issues. For instance, McKinsey's "Delivering through Diversity" report shows that companies with ethnic diversity enjoy a performance advantage ranging from 15% to 35%. Similarly, Accenture's "The Disability Inclusion Advantage" study reveals a significant 28% increase in revenue for enterprises prioritizing disability inclusion. Additionally, BlackRock's Investment Stewardship emphasizes the pivotal role of DEI in facilitating capital access, further underlining its significance within financial contexts.

A. Marrone (✉) · V. Pontrelli
Department of Management, Finance and Technology, LUM University, Casamassima, Italy
e-mail: marrone@lum.it; pontrelli@lum.it

L. Oliva
Department of Biosciences and Territory, University of Molise, Campobasso, Italy
e-mail: lara.oliva@unimol.it

M. Agostini et al. (eds.), *Diversity and Equity in Accounting*, SIDREA Series in Accounting and Business Administration,
https://doi.org/10.1007/978-3-031-78247-3_6

This concern is translated into a growing expectation among stakeholders for companies to transparently share information related to their sustainability commitment (Vuontisjärvi, 2006), supported by comprehensive disclosure policies (Chauvey et al., 2015; Raimo et al., 2021).

Furthermore, governments actions (e.g., European Union's Directive 2022/2464) are progressively mandating larger corporations to evaluate and disclose their societal and environmental impacts (Haji et al., 2022). The regulatory pressure is driving companies to enhance their approaches to engaging and sharing information with stakeholders (Ruiz et al., 2021), indicating a wider movement towards increased corporate transparency and accountability concerning social and environmental concerns. However, studies suggest that companies tend to offer scant disclosure regarding DEI practices (García-Sánchez et al., 2023; Shohaieb et al., 2022).

Given this context, the aim of this chapter is two-fold. Firstly, it seeks to assess the quality of DEI disclosure within the sustainability reports of companies belonging to the S&P 500 index. Secondly, employing agency theory as a theoretical framework, it investigates the influence of certain governance variables on this disclosure quality.

The following sections of this chapter are organized as follows: Sect. 2 presents a literature review, while Sect. 3 outlines the theoretical background and introduces research hypotheses. Section 4 details the methodology, and Sect. 5 presents and discusses the results. Section 6 draws conclusions.

2 Literature Review

To the best of our knowledge, only two contributions have investigated the disclosure of DEI themes and their determinants.

Shohaieb et al. (2022) found that governance variables like size, independence, and gender diversity positively influenced diversity management disclosure in UK FTSE all-share non-financial organizations' annual reports from 2013 to 2019.

García-Sánchez et al. (2023) explored how governance factors, including gender diversity and board expertise, influenced the quality of diversity and inclusion disclosure in 189 European multinational corporations from 2011 to 2020, revealing that diversity and expertise enhance communication effectiveness, while board independence does not; the study also underscores the impact of European regulation and the COVID-19 pandemic in bolstering transparency in diversity practices among these companies.

The scant research in this area creates a significant gap in understanding the impact of board characteristics on DEI disclosure; indeed, this review broadens its focus to include various forms of non-financial disclosure.

Regarding sustainability disclosures, Michelon and Parbonetti (2012), in their study of 57 companies from the Dow Jones index, found no relationship between board independence and disclosure quality. Conversely, Mahmood et al. (2018), analyzing 100 Pakistani companies, observed a positive relationship between board independence and size with sustainability disclosures. Ong and Djajadikerta (2020) found that gender diversity and independence positively influenced sustainability disclosures in Australian companies.

In terms of corporate social responsibility (CSR) disclosures, Barako and Brown (2008) showed that board independence and gender diversity positively affected disclosure levels in Kenyan banks. Khan (2010) highlighted the positive impact of independence on Bangladeshi banks CSR disclosures but found no significant effect of gender diversity. Pucheta-Martínez and Gallego-Álvarez (2019) noted a positive impact of board size and gender diversity but a negative effect of independence on CSR disclosures across 13,178 companies in 39 countries.

In terms of environmental, social, and governance (ESG) disclosures, McBrayer (2018) highlighted the pivotal role of governance factors in shaping the quality and consistency of such disclosures. Faisal (2018), in a study of 73 Indonesian listed companies, discovered that board size had a negative impact on ESG disclosure. Conversely, Giannarakis (2014) analyzed a larger sample of 366 Fortune 500 companies and found a significant positive relationship between board size and ESG disclosure, while gender diversity has no effect. Similarly, Khoiriawati and Nuswantara (2021) observed a positive relationship between board size, independence, gender diversity, and the level of ESG disclosure in Asian companies. Lavin and Montecinos-Pearce (2021) confirmed that both board independence and gender diversity positively influence ESG disclosure. Additionally, Cucari et al. (2018) noted a positive effect of board independence on ESG disclosure, while average board age had no significant effect on ESG disclosure in Italian companies. Husted and de Sousa-Filho (2019) highlighted the positive influence of board size and board independence on ESG disclosure, while board gender diversity had a negative impact. Conversely, Wasiuzzaman and Wan Mohammad (2020) found a positive impact of gender diversity on ESG disclosure in a sample of 78 Malaysian companies.

3 Theoretical Background and Hypothesis Development

This study, in line with prior research on the impact of board characteristics on disclosure quality (e.g., Frias-Aceituno et al., 2013; Vitolla et al., 2020a), is grounded in agency theory (Jensen & Meckling, 1976). This theory suggests that the division between management and ownership, due to the information asymmetry between shareholders and managers, generates agency costs within a firm (Barako et al., 2006). Managers, deeply involved in business operations, possess significant informational advantages, creating ethical dilemmas for shareholders who lack insight into managerial decisions (Barako et al., 2006). This information asymmetry allows managers to potentially act against shareholders' interests (Donnelly & Mulcahy, 2008), prioritizing short-term gains for personal benefit, while shareholders focus on the long-term value of the company, affecting the valuation of economic capital (Healy & Palepu, 2001). Disclosure serves as a tool to reduce information asymmetry, aligning the interests of shareholders and managers and consequently decreasing agency costs (Bozzolan et al., 2006; Healy & Palepu, 2001). Therefore, maintaining an appropriate level of oversight is crucial for disclosure to effectively fulfill its role in mitigating information asymmetry.

The principal control mechanism is the board of directors, responsible for supervising management's disclosure practices (Donnelly & Mulcahy, 2008); indeed, the board assumes a supervisory function, closely examining the actions of top management to safeguard shareholder interests (Donnelly & Mulcahy, 2008; Fama & Jensen, 1983; Jensen & Meckling, 1976).

Within this framework, the board effective oversight enhances disclosure quality, thereby reducing information asymmetry and related agency costs, necessitating specific board attributes.

Several studies show that board diversity enhances decision-making and performance (Post et al., 2011). Gender diversity, in particular, has sparked significant scholarly debate (Alfiero et al., 2017; Frias-Aceituno et al., 2013), with evidence suggesting women on boards contribute essential skills, perspectives, and values, fostering a positive work environment and improving information dissemination (e.g., Hichri, 2022; Hofstede et al., 2010). Women are also found to be more effective communicators, more transparent, and more ethical than their male counterparts, positively influencing CSR (Barako & Brown, 2008). Furthermore, gender diversity can reduce groupthink and cognitive biases, thereby enhancing the quality of decision-making and disclosure in organizations. Based on this, it can be hypothesized that

H1 The quality of DEI disclosure is positively influenced by board gender diversity.

Several studies emphasize the positive impact of non-executive directors on transparency, with Donnelly and Mulcahy (2008) and López et al. (2007) pointing out their role in enhancing transparency to safeguard their reputations. Omran et al. (2021) found that a higher proportion of independent directors correlates with increased disclosure, reducing agency costs and encouraging more comprehensive information sharing. This aligns with agency theory, which posits that independent board members can better oversee management and decrease information asymmetries (Vitolla et al., 2020b). Several scholars underscore the importance of non-executive directors in enhancing oversight, engaging with external environments, and meeting stakeholder expectations (e.g., Biswas et al., 2018; Cucari et al., 2018).

Additionally, independent board members offer an impartial perspective that enhances transparency, helping to prevent conflicts of interest and promote genuine DEI communication. This impartiality helps ensure that important issues are not understated, thereby improving the reliability of disclosures. Based on this, it can be hypothesized that

H2 The quality of DEI disclosure is positively influenced by board independence.

Many scholars argue that larger boards—varying in expertise, perspectives, gender, and education—improve management oversight, transparency in non-financial reporting, and operational efficiency (e.g., Hichri, 2022; Vitolla et al., 2020b). Furthermore, De Villiers and Hsiao (2018) suggested that a larger board enhances disclosure policies and transparency, with Fiori et al. (2016) adding that they are more likely to adopt non-financial reporting initiatives. Therefore, a larger board can incorporate more diverse skills, perspectives, and backgrounds, which may facilitate addressing a wider range of DEI issues and improving related disclosure practices. Based on this, it can be hypothesized that

H3 The quality of DEI disclosure is positively influenced by board size.

4 Methodology

4.1 Sample

As a starting sample, the S&P 500 index is chosen. This index is selected for its wide representation across various countries and industries, providing a reliable source for examining firms sustainability disclosure practices. However, data on the independent and control variables were available for only 247 out of the 498 companies in the index. Among these, sustainability reports for the year 2022 were found for only 157 companies. Therefore, the sample under investigation consists of 157 companies, with all data used pertaining to the year 2022.

4.2 Dependent Variable

The DEI disclosure quality index (DE&ID), constructed by the authors using content analysis methodology (Krippendorff, 2018), represents the independent variable. The selection of the items for the content analysis was guided by the GRI standards, which are recognized as the international benchmark for sustainability reporting excellence (Ferraro & Cristiano, 2022). An evaluative scale ranging from 0 to 3 was utilized for each item, where 0 indicates no disclosure, 1 represents a basic mention (descriptive, vague, or immaterial information), 2 signifies a qualitative disclosure, and 3 denotes a quantitative disclosure. As a result, the maxim score for the DE&ID index ranges from 0 to 51. A full list of the items searched is provided in Appendix. The "Requirements," "Recommendations," and "Guidance" sections provided by the GRIs were considered for content analysis and thus for words to be searched within the reports.

4.3 Independent and Control Variables

Three independent variables were integrated. Board gender diversity (BGD) is represented by the percentage of female board members (e.g., Alfiero et al., 2017; Frias-Aceituno et al., 2013; Liao et al., 2015). Board independence (BDI) is defined by the percentage of independent board members (e.g., Frias-Aceituno et al., 2013; Vitolla et al., 2020b). Board size (BDS) is the total number of board members (e.g., Frias-Aceituno et al., 2013; Vitolla et al., 2020a).

To bolster the model's validity, following precedents in board influence on sustainability disclosure quality research (e.g., Esposito et al., 2023; Frias-Aceituno et al., 2013), we included firm size (logarithm of total assets) and financial leverage (total assets to equity ratio) as control variables.

4.4 Model

The hypotheses were tested using a cross-sectional regression model represented by the following equation:

$$\text{DE \& ID} = \beta_0 + \beta_1\,\text{BGD} + \beta_2\,\text{BDI} + \beta_3\,\text{BDS} + \beta_4\,\text{FSIZE} + \beta_5\,\text{LEV} + \varepsilon$$

5 Results

5.1 Descriptive Statistics, VIFs, and Correlation Analysis

Table 1 presents the results of the descriptive analysis. The dependent variable DE&ID has an average score of 34.21, ranging from 5 to 51, indicating substantial variation in disclosed information among the sampled firms. In terms of independent variables, the sampled firms have an average board gender diversity (BGD) of 31.04%, ranging from 10% to 60%. The average value for board independence

Table 1 Descriptive statistics

Variables	Obs.	Mean	Std. dev.	Min.	Max
DE&ID	157	34.21	13.36	5	51
BGD	157	31.04	8.31	10	60
BDI	157	87.64	6.56	50	93.75
BDS	157	11.32	1.88	7	21
FSIZE	157	10.507	1.15	7.99	14.95
LEV	157	68.16	785.51	1.33	96.56

(BDI) is 87.64%, with a range from 50% to 93.75%. Furthermore, the average board size (BDS) for the sampled firms is 11.32 members, varying from 7 to 21 members.

Pearson's correlation analysis was conducted to assess the relationships among governance dimensions, control variables, and the DE&ID index, with the results detailed in Table 2. The highest correlation coefficient, between BDS and FSIZE, was 0.5350, which is below the multicollinearity thresholds of ±0.8 or ±0.9 suggested by Farrar and Glauber (1967). Furthermore, variance inflation factor (VIF) analysis indicated VIF values ranging from 1.02 to 1.47, with an average of 1.21, well below the critical threshold of 10 recommended by Myers (1990). These findings confirm that multicollinearity is not a significant concern in this study.

5.2 *Results and Discussion*

The three hypotheses were evaluated using a multiple linear regression model, with the results summarized in Table 3. This table presents the regression coefficients for all the variables with DE&ID as the dependent variable.

The adjusted R^2 score of 0.2793 indicates that the model can explain 28% of the variability observed in the dependent variable.

The results support hypothesis 1 (H1). The findings indicate a significant ($p = 0.023$) positive association between board gender diversity (BGD) and DEI disclosure (DE&ID). This result suggests that companies with higher female representation on their boards are more likely to disclose information on DEI issues. This evidence could be attributed to women's greater emphasis on social responsibility, ethical decision-making, and their active engagement in board activities (Liao et al., 2015). Additionally, female inclusion on corporate boards is associated with a positive organizational climate and increased inclusiveness (Hofstede et al., 2010). Gender diversity also reduces the risk of groupthink, as decision-making by homogeneous groups can lead to cognitive biases that negatively affect disclosure levels.

The results support hypothesis 2 (H2). The findings indicate a significant ($p = 0.024$) positive association between board independence (BDI) and DEI disclosure (DE&ID). This finding suggests that companies with a higher proportion of independent members on their board of directors are more inclined to disclose information related to DEI issues. The involvement of non-executive members is

Table 2 VIFs and Pearson's correlation coefficients

Variables	VIF	DE&ID	BGD	BDI	BDS	FSIZE	LEV
DE&ID		1					
BGD	1.04	0.1407*	1				
BDI	1.07	0.2119***	0.1543*	1			
BDS	1.45	0.4944***	0.0020	0.1517*	1		
FSIZE	1.47	0.2262***	0.1057	0.1794**	0.5350***	1	
LEV	1.02	0.0471	−0.0104	−0.0946	−0.0572	0.0297	1

Table 3 OLS regression model results

Variables	Coefficient	Standard error	p-value	Sign.
Cons	−29.304	13.770	0.035	**
BGD	0.261	0.113	0.023	**
BDI	0.327	0.143	0.024	**
BDS	3.867	0.593	0.000	***
FSIZE	−1.617	0.960	0.094	*
LEV	0.001	0.001	0.157	

Note: n = 157; Adj R^2 = 27.93
***Significant at the 1% level; **significant at the 5% level; *significant at the 10% level

crucial for overseeing firm operations, meeting stakeholder expectations, and safeguarding the rights of minority shareholders (Birindelli et al., 2018; Chintrakarn et al., 2021; Elmagrhi et al., 2019). Moreover, independent board members introduce an external and objective perspective, fostering transparency and reducing the likelihood of concealing or downplaying problems. Additionally, independent members bring extensive expertise in sustainability and governance, essential for creating effective DEI strategies, accurately interpreting relevant data, and ensuring their disclosure.

The results support hypothesis 3 (H3). The findings indicate a significant (p = 0.000) positive relationship between board size (BDS) and DEI disclosure (DE&ID). This indicates that companies with larger boards are more likely to disclose information on DEI issues. Larger boards bring a wider range of skills and experiences, potentially enhancing problem-solving and decision-making capabilities (Vitolla et al., 2020a, 2020b). This diversity of competencies is particularly beneficial in the complex area of DEI disclosure, enabling effective oversight of information gathering and dissemination related to all aspects of management, thus improving disclosure quality. Additionally, a larger board can provide stricter oversight of company activities, ensure adherence to DEI policies, and exert pressure for compliance with rigorous ESG reporting standards.

6 Conclusions

This study aims to examine, on the one hand, the quality of DEI disclosure within sustainability reports and, on the other hand, the impact of three governance dimensions such as gender diversity, size, and independence on this quality.

To evaluate three hypotheses grounded in agency theory, this study utilizes a cross-sectional OLS regression model on a sample of 157 global firms operating in different sectors. Results indicate that all three board characteristics examined positively influence the quality of DEI disclosures.

This research holds considerable implications both theoretically and practically. From an academic standpoint, it significantly enriches the body of literature on ESG disclosure by broadening the understanding of DEI disclosures and their determinants—a realm that has not been extensively explored. Additionally, it extends the application of agency theory to a new area of disclosure. Practically, by delving into the quality of DEI disclosures and identifying their determinants, this study could stimulate increased transparency in this area, thus facilitating the incorporation of these elements into corporate policies and strategic planning. Furthermore, it offers critical insights for policymakers aimed at improving corporate disclosure norms. For firms, the findings of this study suggest strategic directions for board-level interventions and the alignment of communication practices with the evolving regulatory landscape, particularly in light of new directives from the European Union.

Although this study yields significant theoretical and practical insights, it is imperative to acknowledge its limitations. The methodology used is cross-sectional, a choice thoroughly explained and justified in the model section, which might limit the ability to identify subtle temporal variations in the analysis outcomes. Secondly, certain board characteristics scrutinized in this study may be constrained. For instance, while diversity primarily refers to gender diversity, factors like educational background, nationality, and ethnicity could broaden the scope of the examination. Furthermore, despite the authors' adherence to rigorous analysis protocols, the inherent subjectivity of content analysis remains a factor to consider. Lastly, this study focuses solely on the content quality of reports and does not address other critical aspects such as relevance, comparability, verifiability, clarity, and neutrality, which are equally important.

The aforementioned limitations do not diminish the usefulness of the results; instead, they provide valuable insights for future research directions.

Future studies could longitudinally investigate this phenomenon over multiple years, facilitating a more comprehensive understanding of the interplay among board characteristics, and DEI disclosure quality. Furthermore, future research could explore previously uncharted governance dimensions, including diverse attributes and activities. Additionally, future research could explore additional parameters of disclosure quality, including the relevance, comparability, verifiability, clarity, and neutrality of information. Lastly, investigations could delve into the impact of both governance and non-governance factors—such as company size, industry, and ownership structure—on disclosure levels.

Appendix: Content Analysis Items

GRI Code	Topic	Score
401-1	New employee hires and employee turnover	0–3
401-2	Benefits provided to full-time employees that are not provided to temporary or part-time employees	0–3
401-3	Parental leave	0–3

GRI Code	Topic	Score
404-1	Average hours of training per year per employee	0–3
404-2	Programs for upgrading employee skills and transition assistance programs	0–3
404-3	Percentage of employees receiving regular performance and career development reviews	0–3
405-1	Diversity of governance bodies and employee	0–3
405-2	Ratio of basic salary and remuneration of women to men	0–3
406-1	Incidents of discrimination and corrective actions taken	0–3
408-1	Operations and suppliers at significant risk for incidents of child labor	0–3
409-1	Operations and suppliers at significant risk for incidents of forced or compulsory labor	0–3
410-1	Security personnel trained in human rights policies or procedures	0–3
411-1	Incidents of violations involving the rights of Indigenous peoples	0–3
413-1	Operations with local community engagement, impact assessments, and development programs	0–3
413-2	Operations with significant actual and potential negative impacts on local communities	0–3
414-1	New suppliers that were screened using social criteria	0–3
414-2	Negative social impacts in the supply chain and actions taken	0–3
Total score		0–51

References

Alfiero, S., Cane, M., Doronzo, R., & Esposito, A. (2017). Board configuration and IR adoption. Empirical evidence from European companies. *Corporate Ownership & Control, 15*(1), 444–458. https://doi.org/10.22495/cocv15i1c2p13

Barako, D. G., & Brown, A. M. (2008). Corporate social reporting and board representation: Evidence from the Kenyan banking sector. *Journal of Management & Governance, 12*, 309–324. https://doi.org/10.1007/s10997-008-9053-x

Barako, D. G., Hancock, P., & Izan, H. Y. (2006). Factors influencing voluntary corporate disclosure by Kenyan companies. *Corporate Governance: An International Review, 14*(2), 107–125. https://doi.org/10.1111/j.1467-8683.2006.00491.x

Birindelli, G., Dell'Atti, S., Iannuzzi, A. P., & Savioli, M. (2018). Composition and activity of the board of directors: Impact on ESG performance in the banking system. *Sustainability, 10*(12), 4699. https://doi.org/10.3390/su10124699

Biswas, P. K., Mansi, M., & Pandey, R. (2018). Board composition, sustainability committee and corporate social and environmental performance in Australia. *Pacific Accounting Review, 30*(4), 517–540. https://doi.org/10.1108/PAR-12-2017-0107

Bozzolan, S., O'Regan, P., & Ricceri, F. (2006). Intellectual capital disclosure (ICD) a comparison of Italy and the UK. *Journal of Human Resource Costing & Accounting, 10*(2), 92–113. https://doi.org/10.1108/14013380610703111

Chauvey, J. N., Giordano-Spring, S., Cho, C. H., & Patten, D. M. (2015). The normativity and legitimacy of CSR disclosure: Evidence from France. *Journal of Business Ethics, 130*, 789–803. https://doi.org/10.1007/s10551-014-2114-y

Chintrakarn, P., Jiraporn, P., & Treepongkaruna, S. (2021). How do independent directors view corporate social responsibility (CSR) during a stressful time? Evidence from the financial crisis. *International Review of Economics & Finance, 71*, 143–160. https://doi.org/10.1016/j.iref.2020.08.007

Cucari, N., Esposito De Falco, S., & Orlando, B. (2018). Diversity of board of directors and environmental social governance: Evidence from Italian listed companies. *Corporate Social Responsibility and Environmental Management, 25*(3), 250–266. https://doi.org/10.1002/csr.1452

De Villiers, C., & Hsiao, P. C. K. (2018). A review of accounting research in Australasia. *Accounting & Finance, 58*(4), 993–1026. https://doi.org/10.1111/acfi.12424

Donnelly, R., & Mulcahy, M. (2008). Board structure, ownership, and voluntary disclosure in Ireland. *Corporate Governance: An International Review, 16*(5), 416–429. https://doi.org/10.1111/j.1467-8683.2008.00692.x

Elmagrhi, M. H., Ntim, C. G., Elamer, A. A., & Zhang, Q. (2019). A study of environmental policies and regulations, governance structures, and environmental performance: The role of female directors. *Business Strategy and the Environment, 28*(1), 206–220. https://doi.org/10.1002/bse.2250

Esposito, B., Raimo, N., Malandrino, O., & Vitolla, F. (2023). Circular economy disclosure and integrated reporting: The role of corporate governance mechanisms. *Business Strategy and the Environment*. https://doi.org/10.1002/bse.3427

Faisal, F. (2018). Board Characteristics, Environmental Social Governance Disclosure and Corporate Performance: Evidence From Indonesia Public Listed Companies. *In International Conference on Governance and Accountability*.

Fama, E. F., & Jensen, M. C. (1983). Agency problems and residual claims. *The Journal of Law and Economics, 26*(2), 327–349. https://www.jstor.org/stable/725105

Farrar, D. E., & Glauber, R. R. (1967). Multicollinearity in regression analysis: The problem revisited. *The Review of Economic and Statistics, 49*(1), 92–107. https://doi.org/10.2307/1937887

Ferraro, O., & Cristiano, E. (2022). Investigating the quality of gender equality non-financial information disclosed in the cooperative credit sector: A case study. *Journal of Risk and Financial Management, 15*(12), 595. https://doi.org/10.3390/jrfm15120595

Fiori, G., Di Donato, F., & Izzo, M. F. (2016). Exploring the effects of corporate governance on voluntary disclosure: An explanatory study on the adoption of integrated report. *Studies in Managerial and Financial Accounting, 31*, 83–108. https://doi.org/10.1108/S1479-351220160000031003

Frias-Aceituno, J. V., Rodriguez-Ariza, L., & Garcia-Sanchez, I. M. (2013). The role of the board in the dissemination of integrated corporate social reporting. *Corporate Social Responsibility and Environmental Management, 20*(4), 219–233. https://doi.org/10.1002/csr.1294

García-Sánchez, I. M., Aibar-Guzmán, B., & Aibar-Guzmán, C. (2023). Transparencia en materia de diversidad e inclusión: el papel de independientes, mujeres y especialistas en el consejo de administración. *Revista de Contabilidad y Tributación. CEF, 488*, 199–230. https://doi.org/10.51302/rcyt.2023.18823

Giannarakis, G. (2014). The determinants influencing the extent of CSR disclosure. *International Journal of Law and Management, 56*(5), 393–416. https://doi.org/10.1108/IJLMA-05-2013-0021

Haji, A. A., Coram, P., & Troshani, I. (2022). Consequences of CSR reporting regulations worldwide: A review and research agenda. *Accounting, Auditing & Accountability Journal, 36*(1), 177–208. https://doi.org/10.1108/AAAJ-05-2020-4571

Healy, P. M., & Palepu, K. G. (2001). Information asymmetry, corporate disclosure, and the capital markets: A review of the empirical disclosure literature. *Journal of Accounting and Economics, 31*(1–3), 405–440. https://doi.org/10.1016/S0165-4101(01)00018-0

Hichri, A. (2022). Corporate governance and integrated reporting: Evidence of French companies. *Journal of Financial Reporting and Accounting, 20*(3–4), 472–492. https://doi.org/10.1108/JFRA-09-2020-0261

Hofstede, G., Hofstede, G. J., & Minkov, M. (2010). *Cultures and organizations: Software of the mind: Intercultural cooperation and its importance for survival*. McGraw-Hill.

Husted, B. W., & de Sousa-Filho, J. M. (2019). Board structure and environmental, social, and governance disclosure in Latin America. *Journal of Business Research, 102*, 220–227. https://doi.org/10.1016/j.jbusres.2018.01.017

Jensen, M. C., & Meckling, W. H. (1976). Theory of the firm: Managerial behavior, agency costs and ownership structure. *Journal of Financial Economics, 3*(4), 305–360. https://doi.org/10.1016/0304-405X(76)90026-X

Khan, H. U. Z. (2010). The effect of corporate governance elements on corporate social responsibility (CSR) reporting: Empirical evidence from private commercial banks of Bangladesh. *International Journal of Law and Management, 52*(2), 82–109. https://doi.org/10.1108/17542431011029406

Khoiriawati, N., & Nuswantara, D. A. (2021). Board characteristics and disclosure of environmental, social, and governance (Esg) matters: Evidence from Asean countries. *Review of Business, Accounting, & Finance, 1*(4), 374–391.

KPMG. (2022). *Survey of sustainability reporting*. KPMG.

Krippendorff, K. (2018). *Content analysis: An introduction to its methodology*. Sage Publications.

Lavin, J. F., & Montecinos-Pearce, A. A. (2021). ESG disclosure in an emerging market: An empirical analysis of the influence of board characteristics and ownership structure. *Sustainability, 13*(19), 10498. https://doi.org/10.3390/su131910498

Liao, L., Luo, L., & Tang, Q. (2015). Gender diversity, board independence, environmental committee and greenhouse gas disclosure. *The British Accounting Review, 47*(4), 409–424. https://doi.org/10.1016/j.bar.2014.01.002

López, M. V., Garcia, A., & Rodriguez, L. (2007). Sustainable development and corporate performance: A study based on the Dow Jones sustainability index. *Journal of Business Ethics, 75*, 285–300. https://doi.org/10.1007/s10551-006-9253-8

Mahmood, Z., Kouser, R., Ali, W., Ahmad, Z., & Salman, T. (2018). Does corporate governance affect sustainability disclosure? A mixed methods study. *Sustainability, 10*(1), 207. https://doi.org/10.3390/su10010207

Manoharan, A., Madera, J. M., & y Singal, M. (2021). Walking the talk in diversity management: Exploring links between strategic statements, management practices, and external recognition. *International Journal of Hospitality Management, 94*, 102864. https://doi.org/10.1016/j.ijhm.2021.102864

Marrone, A., Pontrelli, V., & Oliva, L. (2023). Boards of directors and high-tech sectors affect ESG disclosure quality: An empirical analysis of global firms. *International Journal of Business and Management, 18*(6).

McBrayer, G. A. (2018). Does persistence explain ESG disclosure decisions? *Corporate Social Responsibility and Environmental Management, 25*(6), 1074–1086. https://doi.org/10.1002/csr.1521

Michelon, G., & Parbonetti, A. (2012). The effect of corporate governance on sustainability disclosure. *Journal of Management & Governance, 16*, 477–509. https://doi.org/10.1007/s10997-010-9160-3

Myers, R. H. (1990). *Classical and modern regression with applications* (Vol. 2, p. 488). Duxbury Press.

Omran, M., Ramdhony, D., Mooneeapen, O., & Nursimloo, V. (2021). Integrated reporting and board characteristics: Evidence from top Australian listed companies. *Journal of Applied Accounting Research, 22*(4), 732–758. https://doi.org/10.1108/JAAR-04-2020-0077

Ong, T., & Djajadikerta, H. G. (2020). Corporate governance and sustainability reporting in the Australian resources industry: An empirical analysis. *Social Responsibility Journal, 16*(1), 1–14. https://doi.org/10.1108/SRJ-06-2018-0135

Post, C., Rahman, N., & Rubow, E. (2011). Green governance: Boards of directors' composition and environmental corporate social responsibility. *Business & Society, 50*(1), 189–223. https://doi.org/10.1177/0007650310394642

Pucheta-Martínez, M. C., & Gallego-Álvarez, I. (2019). An international approach of the relationship between board attributes and the disclosure of corporate social responsibility issues. *Corporate Social Responsibility and Environmental Management, 26*(3), 612–627. https://doi.org/10.1002/csr.1707

Raimo, N., Caragnano, A., Zito, M., Vitolla, F., & Mariani, M. (2021). Extending the benefits of ESG disclosure: The effect on the cost of debt financing. *Corporate Social Responsibility and Environmental Management, 28*(4), 1412–1421. https://doi.org/10.1002/csr.2134

Ruiz, S., Romero, S., & Fernandez-Feijoo, B. (2021). Stakeholder engagement is evolving: Do investors play a main role? *Business Strategy and the Environment, 30*(2), 1105–1120. https://doi.org/10.1002/bse.2674

Shohaieb, D., Elmarzouky, M., & Albitar, K. (2022). Corporate governance and diversity management: Evidence from a disclosure perspective. *International Journal of Accounting & Information Management, 30*(4), 502–525. https://doi.org/10.1108/IJAIM-03-2022-0058

Vitolla, F., Raimo, N., & Rubino, M. (2020a). Board characteristics and integrated reporting quality: An agency theory perspective. *Corporate Social Responsibility and Environmental Management, 27*(2), 1152–1163. https://doi.org/10.1002/csr.1879

Vitolla, F., Raimo, N., Marrone, A., & Rubino, M. (2020b). The role of board of directors in intellectual capital disclosure after the advent of integrated reporting. *Corporate Social Responsibility and Environmental Management, 27*(5), 2188–2200. https://doi.org/10.1002/csr.1957

Vuontisjärvi, T. (2006). Corporate social reporting in the European context and human resource disclosures: An analysis of Finnish companies. *Journal of Business Ethics, 69*, 331–354. https://doi.org/10.1007/s10551-006-9094-5

Wasiuzzaman, S., & Wan Mohammad, W. M. (2020). Board gender diversity and transparency of environmental, social and governance disclosure: Evidence from Malaysia. *Managerial and Decision Economics, 41*(1), 145–156. https://doi.org/10.1002/mde.3099

Are the European Sustainability Reporting Standards Effective to Fight Modern Slavery Risk?

Paola Demartini and Silvia Soriano

1 Introduction

Modern slavery, also known as contemporary slavery, encompasses various forms of exploitation where individuals are deprived of their freedom and exploited for personal or commercial gain (Bales, 2005). It is a grave violation of human rights and a pressing global issue and refers to the exploitation of individuals through forced labour, human trafficking, debt bondage, and other forms of coercion. Modern slavery is fueled by factors such as poverty, inequality, and weak governance, making it essential for businesses to play a significant role in combating this heinous practice (Bales, 2012, 2017).

Eradicating the phenomenon of modern slavery is a challenge for sustainable development that can only be fought through the joint effort of supranational organisations, NGOs, governments, the business world, and civil society in general (Burritt & Christ, 2023).

Countries such as the UK, in 2015, and Australia, in 2018, have implemented legislation requiring businesses to disclose their efforts to eradicate modern slavery from their operations and supply chains. In those countries, reporting and disclosure regarding modern slavery have become crucial for corporate responsibility, generating growing interest and debate among policymakers, professionals, and scholars (Christ et al., 2019; Mai et al., 2023).

Human rights reporting will be further integrated into the GRI standards, following the launch in 2022 of a project to update labour topic standards (including GRI 408: Child Labor; GRI 409: Forced or Compulsory Labor). The European

P. Demartini · S. Soriano (✉)
Department of Business Studies, Roma Tre University, Rome, Italy
e-mail: paola.demartini@uniroma3.it; ssoriano@uniroma3.it

M. Agostini et al. (eds.), *Diversity and Equity in Accounting*, SIDREA Series in Accounting and Business Administration,
https://doi.org/10.1007/978-3-031-78247-3_7

Sustainability Reporting Standards (ESRS), adopted in July 2023, provide a framework that includes reporting on the identification and management of modern slavery risk, although, as in the GRI standards, the issue is not directly addressed in a devoted standard.

Since, to our knowledge, no accounting researchers have investigated the EU regulatory framework on modern slavery reporting, we are interested in understanding how the GRI standards and ESRS may support European companies in their disclosure and play a role in raising awareness of this phenomenon. To this end, we pose the following research question:

RQ 1—How do the GRI standards and the ESRS raise awareness by addressing modern slavery?

Furthermore, regarding ESRS that are being implemented by companies, we will examine whether those standards alone may be a tool for effective change to eradicate modern slavery and protect human rights, so we formulate the following research question:

RQ 2—Are the ESRS enough to guide companies in the fight against modern slavery?

For this reason, our critical analyses of the above-mentioned standards will be implemented by discussion on co-enforcement mechanisms to make the ESRS more effective.

This chapter is structured as follows: Sect. 2 focuses on the background and literature on modern slavery reporting. Section 3 describes the methodology we followed, and Sect. 4 presents a critical analysis of GRI standards and European Social Sustainability Reporting Standards regulating companies' disclosure obligations. Finally, Sect. 5 presents our conclusions.

2 Background and Literature Review

2.1 Modern Slavery: An Umbrella Term

Modern slavery is an umbrella term scoping several human rights issues including forced labour, bonded labour, worst forms of child labour, human trafficking, and slavery-like practices. The term modern slavery is not defined in law, but it generally refers to situations of exploitation a person cannot refuse or leave because of threats, violence, coercion, deception, or abuse of power (Walk Free Foundation, 2023; International Labour Organisation, 2019).

Despite the different interpretations of the scope of the term, as well as different cultural sensitivity to this term across the globe, the concept has gained international attention due to the introduction of the 2015 UK Modern Slavery Act and 2018 Australian Modern Slavery Act. The GRI-ILO report 'Advancing modern slavery reporting to meet stakeholder expectations' (2019)[1] recognises the relevance of the theme worldwide, both in more developed and developing countries, focusing the attention on the characteristics that are most relevant for businesses, as outlined in Fig. 1.

The relation between the impact of modern slavery and business activities is especially clear in the case of forced labour. This is not a problem that any one nation can address and solve on their own, and as such, the eradication of modern slavery has become the focus of multilateral organizations like the United Nations (UN), as part of the 2030 Agenda for Sustainable Development. The primary SDG relating to human rights is SDG 8, which focuses on 'promot[ing] inclusive and sustainable economic growth, employment and decent work for all.'; actually, Target 8.7 directly calls for the end of human trafficking and modern slavery by stating: '*Take immediate and effective measures to eradicate forced labour, end modern slavery and human trafficking and secure the prohibition and elimination of the worst forms of child labour, including recruitment and use of child soldiers*' (UN, 2015).[2]

In this context, the antecedent of our research is that the responsibility of companies should translate, from an economic point of view, into the return of a fair economic value to the workforce involved in the production process and the generation of a positive social impact for the community (Gold et al., 2015).

2.2 *How Reporting and Disclosure on Modern Slavery Can Be a Driver of Social Change?*

Reporting and disclosure regarding modern slavery have become critical aspects of corporate responsibility and accountability in recent years (Christ et al., 2019; Mai et al., 2023). Some countries, such as the UK and Australia, adopted Modern Slavery Acts requiring businesses to draw an annual statement detailing the actions they have taken to prevent modern slavery within their operations and supply chains.

Not surprisingly, the UK has moved first in this direction. The belief that companies, as social actors, and accounting, as a socio-technical system, can be agents of change is rooted in Anglo-Saxon accounting studies (Burchell et al., 1980). Accounting is not a neutral technical phenomenon, but an intensely social process that impacts society in many ways. As a result of such perspective, accounting has gained its current organisational and social significance (Hopwood & Miller, 1994). More recently, the commitment of some scholars to challenging environmental

[1] https://www.globalreporting.org/media/r1ydr40k/rli-gri_advancing-modern-slavery-reporting--to-meet-stakeholder-expectations.pdf

[2] https://sdgs.un.org/goals/goal8#targets_and_indicators

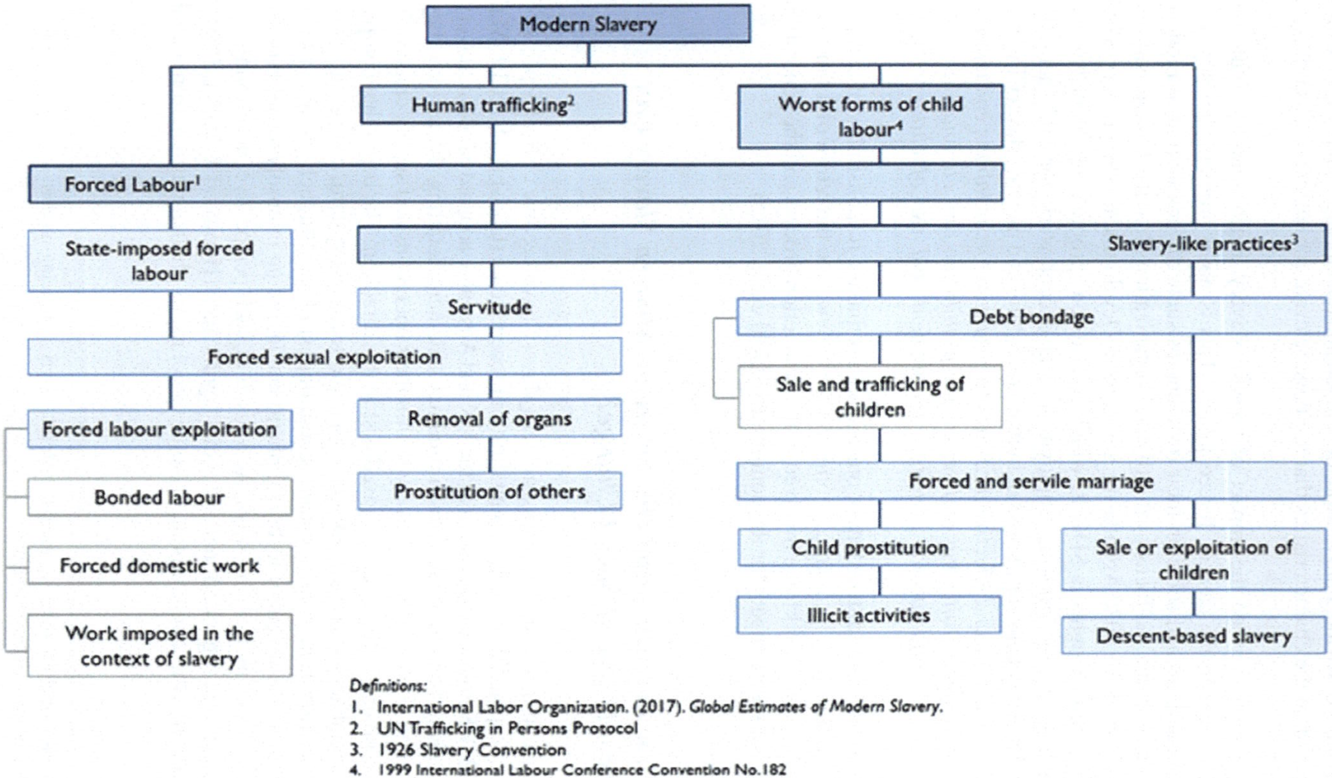

Fig. 1 The modern slavery phenomenon (GRI-ILO, 2019). (Source: 2019 GRI-ILO report 'Advancing Modern Slavery Reporting to Meet Stakeholder Expectations')

degradation and social injustice has given rise to the field of social and environmental accounting (SEA) research and practice (Gray, 2002).

Effective reporting and disclosure may play a crucial role in raising awareness, fostering transparency, and holding businesses accountable for their actions in combating modern slavery (Schaper & Pollach, 2021; Ahmad et al., 2023). However, accounting literature pertaining to modern slavery also highlights several gaps in effectively guiding companies to design their reporting and control system as well as to improve stakeholder engagement and accountability, as shown in Table 1. By addressing these gaps, researchers can contribute to the development of more effective accounting practices and regulatory frameworks for combating modern slavery and promoting ethical business practices.

In light of the above gaps and considering the lack of specific regulatory frameworks and reporting requirements on modern slavery for EU companies, our interest is to focus on how GRI standards and ESRS may support companies in their

Table 1 Shortcomings highlighted in the accounting literature

Shortcomings highlighted in the accounting literature	
Design and implementation of a reporting and control system	*Measurement and disclosure standards*: While there has been progress in developing frameworks and guidelines for reporting on modern slavery, there is a lack of standardized measurement and disclosure practices across industries and jurisdictions. This inconsistency hampers comparability and transparency in assessing companies' efforts to address modern slavery (Hess, 2019). *Supply chain transparency and traceability*: More research is needed on innovative accounting techniques and technologies, such as blockchain and supply chain mapping tools, to enhance supply chain transparency and traceability (Cole et al., 2019) and to mitigate modern slavery risk (Flynn & Walker, 2021). *Auditing and assurance practices*: There is a need for more standardized audit methodologies and assurance frameworks to provide stakeholders with greater confidence in the accuracy and reliability of modern slavery disclosure (Benstead et al., 2021). *Costs and benefits of compliance*: There is no empirical research on the costs and benefits of compliance with anti-slavery regulations and standards and limited research on companies' compliance behaviour (Flynn, 2020). Understanding the cost-effectiveness of anti-slavery initiatives can help companies make more informed decisions and allocate resources more efficiently.
Stakeholder engagement/ collaboration and accountability	*Stakeholder engagement and accountability*: There is a need for research on the effectiveness of stakeholder engagement mechanisms, in driving corporate accountability and promoting responsible business conduct (Christ & Burritt, 2023). *Co-enforcement*: it involves participation by workers, worker organisations, influential firms, and government bodies in mutually enforcing labour standards (Guthrie et al., 2022; Dodd et al., 2023). There is a need for further research on the mechanisms that help to eradicate modern slavery thanks to strategic co-enforcement initiatives (Boersma & Bedford, 2023).

disclosure and may play a role in raising awareness of this phenomenon, so we formulate the following research questions:

RQ 1—How do the GRI standards and the ESRS raise awareness by addressing modern slavery?

RQ 2—Are the ESRS enough to guide companies in the fight against modern slavery?

3 Methodology

From a methodological perspective, we performed a critical analysis of the relevant sections of SDGs, GRI, and ESRS, which, as for our background, set out the fundamental guidelines for addressing the phenomenon of modern slavery to respond to our research questions.

- First, considering the definition of modern slavery, we emphasised the close interconnection between the GRI standards and the achievement of Target 8.7 of the SDGs which aims to eliminate forced labour, modern slavery, human trafficking, and child labour.
- Then, we analysed the GRI standards and the ESRS, on the basis of their interoperability. The latter concept is highlighted in the [draft] GRI-ESRS Interoperability Index, which '*is a mapping tool, prepared from an EU standpoint, that helps entities understand the commonalities between the two sustainability reporting standards*' (GRI & EFRAG, 2023).[3] In addition, we proceeded with a comprehensive analysis of the European social standards, underling the data points (DPs) and sub-narrative elements of a disclosure requirement, relevant to reporting on the risk of modern slavery.

Table 2 Sources analyzed

Source	Section analyzed
UN Sustainable Development Goals (SDGs)	Goal 8-decent work and economic growth: Target 8.7
GRI STANDARDS	GRI 408-Child Labor and GRI 409-Forced or Compulsory Labor
European Sustainability Reporting Standards (ESRS)	ESRS S1-Own workforce; ESRS S2-Workers in the value chain; ESRS S3-Affected communities; ESRS S4-Consumers and end-users
Corporate Sustainability Due Diligence Directive (CSDDD)	Whole proposal directive

[3] chrome-extension://efaidnbmnnnibpcajpcglclefindmkaj/https://www.globalreporting.org/media/z2vmxbks/gri-standards-and-esrs-draft-interoperability-index_20231130-final.pdf

- Finally, we analysed the Corporate Sustainability Due Diligence Directive (CSDDD) as a tool that could be used alongside the implementation of a co-enforcement model to amplify the revolutionary impact of European standards.

In the following Table 2, sources and the specific sections analysed are summarised.

4 Discussion

4.1 How Do the GRI Standards and the ESRS Raise Awareness by Addressing Modern Slavery?

4.1.1 The Role of the GRI Standards

The GRI standards do not address modern slavery in a specific standard. However, they do provide a framework for companies to disclose their efforts to address human rights issues, including modern slavery risk in their operations and supply chains.

Moreover, the GRI has taken steps to promote awareness and action to fight modern slavery through various initiatives and collaborations. This organization collaborates with other ones focused on combating modern slavery, including the United Nations Global Compact (UNGC) and the Alliance 8.7, a global partnership committed to achieving Target 8.7 of the UN Sustainable Development Goals (SDGs). As the report 'Linking the SDGs and the GRI standards' states, the GRI standards '*play a key role in shaping the very process of having sustainability reporting reflected in the SDGs*' (GRI, 2022).[4] More specifically, there is a strong

SDG	Target	Available Disclosures	Disclosure	Sources
8 DECENT WORK AND ECONOMIC GROWTH	8.7 Take immediate and effective measures to eradicate forced labour, end modern slavery and human trafficking and secure the prohibition and elimination of the worst forms of child labour, including recruitment and use of child soldiers, and by 2025 end child labour in all its forms	a. Operations and suppliers considered to have significant risk for incidents of: i. child labor; ii. young workers exposed to hazardous work. b. Operations and suppliers considered to have significant risk for incidents of child labor either in terms of: i. type of operation (such as manufacturing plant) and supplier; ii. countries or geographic areas with operations and suppliers considered at risk. c. Measures taken by the organization in the reporting period intended to contribute to the effective abolition of child labor.	408-1	GRI 408: Child Labor 2016
		Operations and suppliers considered to have significant risk for incidents of forced or compulsory labor either in terms of: i. Type of operation (such as manufacturing plant) and supplier; ii. Countries or geographic areas with operations and suppliers considered at risk.	409-1	GRI 409: Forced or Compulsory Labor 2016
		Measures taken by the organization in the reporting period intended to contribute to the elimination of all forms of forced or compulsory labor.	409-1-b	GRI 409: Forced or Compulsory Labor 2016

Fig. 2 Representation of the linkage between Target 8.7 and the GRI 408 and GRI 409. (Source: GRI (last update 2022), the report 'Linking the SDGs and the GRI Standards')

[4] GRI (last update 2022) available at https://www.globalreporting.org/search/?query=Linking+the+SDGs+and+the+GRI+Standards

interconnection between the 'GRI 408-Child labor' and the 'GRI 409—Forced or Compulsory Labor' and the achievement of Target 8.7 as highlighted in Fig. 2.

As a consequence, the decision of a company to be compliant with the abovementioned two GRI standards (408 and 409) consents to individuate and mitigate risks inextricably linked to modern slavery ones.

Therefore, by including specific human rights indicators (see 'Available Disclosure' in Fig. 2), the GRI standards encourage companies to assess and disclose their human rights performance, highlighting their efforts to address child labour and forced and compulsory labour, all of which are included in the definition of modern slavery.

The relevance of the information required by GRI standards 408 and 409 in addressing human rights risks is also demonstrated, in our view, by EFRAG's decision to ensure interoperability with these standards by introducing similar requirements in the ESRS.

In addition, the GRI encourages companies to take proactive measures to address modern slavery risk in their sustainability reporting, highlighting the importance of transparency and accountability in combating this scourge. An example of this type of GRI awareness-raising effort is the 2019 GRI-ILO report 'Advancing Modern Slavery Reporting to Meet Stakeholder Expectations',[5] which provides a toolkit useful for reporting on due diligence and supportive measures related to modern slavery across the value chain. In summary, the report calls for collaborative action between companies, governments, NGOs, and other stakeholders to improve reporting practices, strengthen regulatory frameworks, and promote ethical business conduct, and the GRI can play a role in facilitating these efforts.

However, while the GRI standards provide a valuable, even if voluntary, framework for companies to disclose their efforts to address human rights issues, their effectiveness in combating modern slavery ultimately depends on how companies interpret and implement these standards in practice.

4.1.2 The Role of the ESRS

The European Sustainability Reporting Standards have emerged as a crucial tool in promoting corporate responsibility and sustainable development. Their architecture is characterized by two standards cross-cutting, which are applicable crosswise, and ten topical standards divided according to the three ESG themes (ESRS, (EU) 2023/2772).[6]

Regarding our research concern, the ESRS provide a framework that includes reporting on the identification and management of modern slavery risk, although, as in the GRI standards, there is currently no specific standard or data point focused solely on modern slavery.

---

[5] https://www.globalreporting.org/media/r1ydr40k/rli-gri_advancing-modern-slavery-reporting--to-meet-stakeholder-expectations.pdf

[6] For the future, it is expected the elaboration and the adoption of sector specific standards

The ESRS encourage companies to conduct due diligence to identify, assess, and manage social and human rights risks, which includes modern slavery as a human rights violation, and emphasise the importance of engaging with suppliers to promote responsible practices throughout the supply chain.

More specifically, to express the role of the ESRS in raising awareness of modern slavery, it is important to focus on social topical standards.

- In the ESRS S1-Own workforce and in the ESRS S2-Workers in the value chain, the sub-topic *Other work-related rights* clearly considers also the sub-subtopic *Child labour and Forced labour*.
- In the ESRS S3-Affected communities, the sub-topic *Communities' civil and political rights* is specified by considering also the sub-subtopic *Impacts on human rights defenders*.
- In the S4-Consumers and end-users, the sub-topic *Personal safety of consumers and/or end-users* is expressed by also considering the sub-subtopics *Health and safety*, *Security of a person*, and *Protection of children*.[7]

The requirement for disclosure on these different topics and sub-topics occurs through the data points. In the ESRS S1-Own workforce and in the ESRS S2-Workers in the value chain, there are different data points connected with the issue of human rights, but if we consider, as an example, exclusively, the ones with a direct reference to child labour, we have to underline the request of:

- '*information about type of operations at significant risk of incidents of child labour*' (S1-SBM 3);
- '*information about countries or geographic areas with operations considered at significant risk of incidents of child labour*' (S1-SBM 3);
- '*disclosure of geographies or commodities for which there is significant risk of child labour, or of forced or compulsory labour, among workers in undertaking's value chain*' (S2-SBM 3);
- '*policies explicitly address trafficking in human beings, forced labour or compulsory labour and child labour*' (S1-1 and S2-1).

More broadly, the link between European social standards and the themes, encompassed by the term 'modern slavery', is evident, also considering the topics of the data points of the ESRS S2, the ESRS S3, and the ESRS S4, which are listed below[8]:

- description of relevant human rights policy commitments;
- disclosure of general approach for human rights and measures to provide and (or) enable remedy for human rights impacts;

[7] For more details about topics, sub-topics, and sub-sub-topics of the ESRS, see the table 'Sustainability matters covered in topical ESRS' in ESRS 1-General requirements.

[8] For the details about all the data points of the ESRS, see the 'List of ESRS Data Points - Implementation Guidance 3' available at https://www.efrag.org/en/projects/esrs-implementation-guidance-documents

- disclosure of the extent and indication of nature of cases of non-respect of the UN Guiding Principles on Business and Human Rights, ILO Declaration on Fundamental Principles, and Rights at Work or OECD Guidelines for Multinational Enterprises;
- disclosure of severe human rights issues and incidents;
- initiatives or processes whose primary aim is to deliver positive impacts for the specific category considered in the standard, which is designed also to support the achievement of one or more of SDGs.

In summary, European social standards include data points that, if reported appropriately by companies, can ensure an objective and clear description of the risks and incidents of modern slavery. This includes respecting internationally recognised human rights standards and principles, such as those set out in the ILO Declaration on Fundamental Principles and Rights at Work.

In conclusion, while ESRS could play an important role in tackling modern slavery, their effectiveness depends on several factors, including the rigour of companies' due diligence processes and the robustness of regulatory enforcement mechanisms. We believe that both the GRI standards and the ESRS, with their high degree of interoperability, have the potential to contribute to the fight against modern slavery by providing frameworks and guidelines for sustainability reporting.

Table 3 Strengths and shortcomings of ESRS

	European Sustainability Reporting Standards
Strengths	*Regulatory and mandatory compliance*. Compliance with the ESRS ensures that companies, within the scope of the Corporate Sustainability Reporting Directive (CSRD)[a], fulfil their reporting obligations also regarding modern slavery. Non-compliance may result in reputational damage, legal risks, and regulatory sanctions. *Consistency and comparability*. Standardized reporting requirements and metrics under the ESRS can enhance consistency and comparability in reporting among European companies, facilitating stakeholders to benchmark companies' performance and identify leaders and laggards in addressing modern slavery risks. Standardized reporting also encourages companies to adopt best practices and improve their performance over time. *Integration of human rights due diligence*. The ESRS encourage companies to conduct and disclose human rights due diligence processes to identify, prevent, and mitigate adverse human rights impacts, including modern slavery. *Stakeholder engagement*. The ESRS promote stakeholder engagement as an integral part of the reporting process. Companies are encouraged to engage with a wide range of stakeholders, including workers, affected communities, NGOs, and trade unions, to identify and address human rights risks effectively. Stakeholder engagement fosters transparency, builds trust, and helps companies understand the diverse perspectives and concerns related to modern slavery.

Table 3 Continued

	European Sustainability Reporting Standards
Shortcomings	*Implementation challenges*. There may be gaps in coverage or effectiveness, both because modern slavery is not directly addressed in the standards and because for companies it is possible to omit all disclosure requirements in a topical standard if it is assessed that is not material, so they have to perform a correct double materiality assessment. *Need for implementation guidance*. Companies may require additional guidance and support to implement reporting requirements effectively, particularly if they lack experience or expertise in addressing modern slavery within their operations and supply chains.[b] *Enforcement challenges*. Even with regulatory support, enforcement mechanisms may be necessary to ensure compliance with reporting requirements and drive accountability for addressing modern slavery risks. Without robust enforcement, companies may not prioritize or adequately disclose information on modern slavery.

[a]Directive, 2022/2464 on corporate sustainability reporting, which among other innovations introduced the adoption of the European Sustainability Reporting Standards (ESRS)

[b]Currently, EFRAG has prepared implementation guidance on materiality assessment, value chain and detailed ESRS data points. They are available at https://www.efrag.org/en/projects/esrs-implementation-guidance-documents (EFRAG, 2024).

4.2 *Are the ESRS Enough to Guide Companies in the Fight Against Modern Slavery?*

4.2.1 Strengths and Shortcomings of ESRS

This section examines the effectiveness of the ESRS in guiding companies to combat modern slavery. As illustrated in Table 3, the ESRS' primary strengths regard mandatory requirements also on modern slavery risk. Furthermore, the ESRS' standardised reporting encourages companies to adopt best practices, such as disclosing their human rights due diligence processes and engaging stakeholders as an integral part of the reporting process.

Conversely, as evidenced by the ESRS shortcomings, there is a need for more specific guidance on how companies should engage with stakeholders to ensure their meaningful participation in eradicating modern slavery. Furthermore, robust enforcement mechanisms must be established. As a consequence, it is necessary to develop tools that will enable the transformative potential of European standards and that will encourage companies to take proactive measures to manage the risk of modern slavery, rather than merely complying with a disclosure requirement. Instruments that can lead companies in this direction are the Corporate Sustainability Due Diligence Directive (CSDDD) and, more generally, the implementation of a co-enforcement model.

4.2.2 The Corporate Sustainability Due Diligence Directive and Other Co-enforcement Mechanisms

The CSDDD[9] is the European legislation that sets out the obligations of companies for actual and potential adverse human rights and environmental impacts arising from their operations, those of their subsidiaries, and carried out by their business partners in companies' chains of activities, as well as liability for violations of these obligations (Art. 1, 'Subject matter', CSDDD, 2024).

As for human rights, the directive regulates the due diligence obligation and at the same time covers corporate directors' duties to implement it through specific processes and measures. To comply with the directive, companies should map their supply chain to identify and address potential risks and impacts (Kortelainen, 2022), while today the ESRS only cover the last stage of the due diligence obligation, i.e. the reporting stage.

However, it is important to note that excessive regulatory obligations may sort out unexpected results linked to merely formal implementation of the directive. Therefore, it is crucial to guarantee its effectiveness to generate real changes in the companies' behaviour.

Additionally, the implementation of a co-enforcement model, activated through mechanisms of collaborative governance, can be another effective approach to address the root causes of modern slavery and bring about systemic change, by leveraging the expertise, resources, and collaboration of multiple stakeholders, including government agencies, non-governmental organizations (NGOs), industry associations, and other relevant actors. It emphasises formal, consensus-oriented, and deliberative decision-making processes (Fine, 2017) and requires trust building and the development of commitment and shared understanding (Ansell & Gash, 2008). However, the effectiveness of co-enforcement depends on the willingness and capacity of all parties to collaborate effectively, which may vary depending on the context and stakeholders involved.

5 Conclusion and Future Research

In this chapter, our contribution unfolds through a critical analysis of the texts regulating companies' disclosure obligations on modern slavery, with particular reference to the recently introduced European social sustainability reporting standards that are being implemented by companies and the CSDDD, which can help the ESRS to provide a clearer framework for addressing modern slavery across industries and jurisdictions by imposing a due diligence process.

[9] The CSDDD is expected to be applied to all EU companies and parent companies with more than 1000 employees on average and a net worldwide turnover of more than EUR 450 million. The Directive 2024/1760 on corporate sustainability due diligence (CSDDD) is available at https://eur-lex.europa.eu/legal-content/EN/TXT/?uri=OJ:L_202401760.

In line with previous literature (Amengual & Fine, 2017; Hampton, 2019; Boersma & Bedford, 2023), we agree that by combining legislative requirements with a collaborative enforcement approach, policymakers can create a more holistic and robust response to modern slavery, addressing both the regulatory and practical challenges associated with this complex issue. It is important, indeed, to recognise that in some countries, there are 'grey areas' where working in conditions that may border on human rights violations is the only income opportunity for certain populations. This generates a need for true social responsibility, a process that requires the involvement of governments, NGOs, members of civil society, and all companies themselves.

In conclusion, we envisage two main research streams for future research. From a regulatory and institutional perspective, there is a need to explore how the CSDDD can be an effective tool to help the ESRS address the complex challenges associated with modern slavery. At the same time, future research should adopt a standpoint that involves the companies themselves and should analyse, from a cost-benefit perspective, how the implementation of new standards and regulations can generate processes of real sustainable change.

References

Ahmad, N., Haque, S., & Islam, M. A. (2023). Modern slavery disclosure regulations in the global supply chain: A world-systems perspective. *Critical Perspectives on Accounting, 99*, 102677.

Amengual, M., & Fine, J. (2017). Co-enforcing labor standards: The unique contributions of state and worker organizations in Argentina and the United States. *Regulation & Governance, 11*(2), 129–142.

Ansell, C., & Gash, A. (2008). Collaborative governance in theory and practice. *Journal of Public Administration Research and Theory, 18*(4), 543–571.

Bales, K. (2005). *Understanding global slavery: A reader*. University of California Press.

Bales, K. (2012). *Disposable people: New slavery in the global economy, updated with a new preface*. University of California Press.

Bales, K. (2017). Slavery in its contemporary manifestations. In *Critical readings on global slavery* (pp. 1660–1686). Brill.

Benstead, A. V., Hendry, L. C., & Stevenson, M. (2021). Detecting and remediating modern slavery in supply chains: A targeted audit approach. *Production Planning & Control, 32*(13), 1136–1157.

Boersma, M., & Bedford, D. S. (2023). The role of market devices in addressing labour exploitation: An analysis of the Australian cleaning industry. *The British Accounting Review, 55*(3), 101129.

Burchell, S., Clubb, C., Hopwood, A., Hughes, J., & Nahapiet, J. (1980). The roles of accounting in organizations and society. *Accounting, Organizations and Society, 5*(1), 5–27.

Burritt, R. L., & Christ, K. L. (2023). Modern slavery and the global reporting initiative–a bridge too far? *Business Strategy & Development, 6*(3), 296–309.

Christ, K. L., & Burritt, R. L. (2023). Exploring effectiveness of entity actions to eliminate modern slavery risk–early Australian evidence. *The British Accounting Review, 55*(1), 101065.

Christ, K. L., Rao, K. K., & Burritt, R. L. (2019). Accounting for modern slavery: An analysis of Australian listed company disclosures. *Accounting, Auditing & Accountability Journal, 32*(3), 836–865.

Cole, R., Stevenson, M., & Aitken, J. (2019). Blockchain technology: Implications for operations and supply chain management. *Supply Chain Management: An International Journal, 24*(4), 469–483.

CSDDD. (2024). https://eur-lex.europa.eu/legal-content/EN/TXT/?uri=OJ:L_202401760

Directive 2022/2464 on corporate sustainability reporting (CSRD).

Directive 2024/1760. on corporate sustainability due diligence (CSDDD, 2024) available at https://eur-lex.europa.eu/legalcontent/EN/TXT/?uri=OJ:L_202401760

Dodd, T., Guthrie, J., & Dumay, J. (2023). Management controls and modern slavery risks in the building and construction industry: Lessons from an Australian social housing provider. *The British Accounting Review, 55*(3), 101098.

EFRAG. (2024). https://www.efrag.org/en/projects/esrs-implementation-guidance-documents.

Fine, J. (2017). Enforcing labor standards in partnership with civil society: Can co-enforcement succeed where the state alone has failed? *Politics and Society, 45*(3), 359–388.

Flynn, A. (2020). Determinants of corporate compliance with modern slavery reporting. *Supply Chain Management: An International Journal, 25*(1), 1–16.

Flynn, A., & Walker, H. (2021). Corporate responses to modern slavery risks: An institutional theory perspective. *European Business Review, 33*(2), 295–315.

Gold, S., Trautrims, A., & Trodd, Z. (2015). Modern slavery challenges to supply chain management. *Supply Chain Management: An International Journal, 20*(5), 485–494.

Gray, R. (2002). The social accounting project and accounting organizations and society privileging engagement, imaginings, new accountings and pragmatism over critique? *Accounting, Organizations and Society, 27*(7), 687–708.

Guthrie, J., Dumay, J., Michelson, G., & Dodd, T. (2022). Australian modern-day slavery: A social systems perspective. *Journal of Behavioural Economics and Social Systems, 4*(2), 7746.

Hampton, D. B. (2019). Modern slavery in global supply chains: Can national action plans on business and human rights close the governance gap? *Business and Human Rights Journal, 4*(2), 239–263.

Hess, D. (2019). The transparency trap: Non-financial disclosure and the responsibility of business to respect human rights. *American Business Law Journal, 56*(1), 5–53.

Hopwood, A. G., & Miller, P. (Eds.). (1994). *Accounting as social and institutional practice* (Vol. 24). Cambridge University Press.

GRI-ILO. (2019). Ending child labour, forced labour and human trafficking in global supply chains. Available at https://www.globalreporting.org/media/r1ydr40k/rli-gri_advancing-modern-slavery-reporting-tomeet-stakeholder-expectations.pdf, downloaded 01.01.24.

GRI & EFRAG. (2023). chromeextension://efaidnbmnnnibpcajpcglclefindmkaj/https://www.globalreporting.org/media/z2vmxbks/gri-standards-andesrs-draft-interoperability-index_20231130-final.pdf.

GRI. (2022). https://www.globalreporting.org/search/?query=Linking+the+SDGs+and+the+GRI+Standards

Kortelainen, S. (2022). *Impacts of the corporate sustainability due diligence directive (CSDDD)–a supply chain and competition perspective*. UTUPub.

Mai, N., Vourvachis, P., & Grubnic, S. (2023). The impact of the UK's modern slavery act (2015) on the disclosure of FTSE 100 companies. *The British Accounting Review, 55*(3), 101115.

UN. (2015). https://sdgs.un.org/goals/goal8#targets_and_indicators

Schaper, S., & Pollach, I. (2021). Modern slavery statements: From regulation to substantive supply chain reporting. *Journal of Cleaner Production, 313*, 127872.

Walk Free Foundation. (2023). *The global slavery index 2023*. Walk Free Foundation.

Social Equity Reporting and Practices in Local Governments: Insights from an Exploratory Case Study

Eleonora Cardillo, Antonio Leotta, Carmela Rizza, and Daniela Ruggeri

1 Introduction

In recent decades, social equity has risen to prominence as a dominant paradigm for scholars and governments, driven by institutional pressures that advocate for translating this broad principle into management practices (Zeemering, 2018; Svara & Brunet, 2020). Coherently, the 2030 Agenda, with its Sustainable Development Goals (SDGs), has provided great impetus to sustainable development, urging public administrations to prioritize economic growth, inclusion and social cohesion, and eco-sustainability.

Following these guidelines, local governments are promoting several initiatives aimed at transforming social equity challenges into opportunities through profound socio-economic transformations.

The relevance of the social equity challenge has encouraged local governments to implement innovative forms of reporting, in order to illustrate to citizens, civil society, and various stakeholders the performance achieved in these areas (Hinna, 2004; Tanese, 2004; Caperchione et al., 2017; Grossi et al. 2017, Grossi et al., 2023).

In the Italian context, local governments can select the tools through which they disclose social equity policies and actions. Recent studies (Grossi & Argento, 2022) have shown that public governance development not only alters the way public services are delivered, but also changes the roles of social actors and public administrations' practices. Despite this, scant attention has been paid to understanding how various actors influence goals within public administrations and their role in shaping the development of social equity practices (Grossi et al., 2020). Accordingly, this chapter delves into social equity reporting in the context of local governments,

E. Cardillo · A. Leotta · C. Rizza · D. Ruggeri (✉)
Department of Economics and Business, University of Catania, Catania, Italy
e-mail: cardillo@unict.it; antonio.leotta@unict.it; carmela.rizza@unict.it; d.ruggeri@unict.it

M. Agostini et al. (eds.), *Diversity and Equity in Accounting*, SIDREA Series in Accounting and Business Administration,
https://doi.org/10.1007/978-3-031-78247-3_8

exploring the following questions: How are communication tools used to disclose social equity policies? How are these policies translated into social practices able to affect social equity?

To achieve this objective, a case study was conducted in a municipality in Southern Italy to depict how social equity policies are disclosed and accomplished, underlying their impact on social equity. The results offer such implications for further research on this issue, pinpointing potential guidelines for more extensive studies aimed at exploring and explaining similarities and differences in disclosure processes related to social equity among various local governments. Additionally, the findings offer insights to policymakers on how to enhance the regulation of local government disclosure processes, thereby improving transparency. The chapter is structured as follows: Sect. 2 presents the literature review, Sect. 3 is devoted to the methodology and the municipality profile, Sect. 4 shows the findings of the case study, and Sect. 5 offers final remarks.

2 Literature Review

Studies have recognized the central role of local authorities in innovating and implementing new managerial systems and forms of sharing based on social equity, as they are in direct contact with citizens, serving as a crucial institutional lever to support social programs aimed at balanced social well-being (Frederickson, 2005; Salvador & Sancho, 2021; De Matteis & Borgonovi, 2021).

Local governments play a crucial role in providing cultural, environmental, and planning services to promote health and well-being, in order to educate the community to respect ecological rules and adopt ethical behaviour (Cohen & Karatzimas, 2015). In doing so, the institutional mandate guides political actors in defining a framework for incorporating social interventions aimed at achieving positive outcomes for the community (Zeemering, 2018).

In particular, some studies have analyzed the administrative and organizational structures responsible for social initiatives (Jepson, 2004), identifying the mechanisms used to encourage stakeholder participation in the decision-making process (Hawkins & Wang, 2012), the managerial tools adopted to promote social policies, and the interconnection between municipal functions and services that produce social effects on the territory (Feiock & Soun, 2009).

Scholars have also questioned the internal and external motivations behind producing and publishing social reports (Marcuccio & Steccolini, 2009; Bracci & Tallaki, 2013), investigating their impact on internal decision-making processes and stakeholder engagement (Farneti & Guthrie, 2009; Goswami & Lodhia, 2014), underscoring the significance of reporting in the implementation of social policies and its impact in the allocation of financial funds.

Recognizing this relevance, recent studies have focused on local governments' approach to promoting social equity as a critical aspect of social policies (Vakkuri et al., 2021; Grossi & Argento, 2022). Scholars particularly acknowledge social equity as fairness and justice in the provision of governmental policies and services (Riccucci, 2009; Guy & McCandless, 2012; Gooden, 2015), revealing that social equity is critical in shaping our thinking about and evaluating government (Frederickson, 2015; Cepiku & Mastrodascio, 2021). The renewed interest in equity as a component of sustainability requires that local government planning processes clearly reflect this emphasis, reporting on the availability of resources and opportunities for disadvantaged citizens and seeking to distribute public resources in favour of those who are less well off.

On this matter, prior contributions have highlighted that while various planning subfields emphasize different aspects of equity, an effective approach to social equity should ensure that equity concerns are relevant in planning decisions and debates. In public participation, the expectation is for an inclusive planning process where residents, stakeholders, and experts converge to participate in shared plan and decision-making, with the aim of transferring at least some power to non-experts (Innes & Booher, 2000, 2004).

Scholars concur in defining an equitable comprehensive plan as the outcome of an inclusive public participation process wherein inequities are identified and corrective actions are planned. The plan would recommend economic development strategies that benefited the community as a whole, including its most vulnerable members (Loh & Kim, 2021).

On this issue, further research is required on how local governments make decisions regarding the data they choose to store, analyze, and use for social equity purposes (Ruijer et al., 2023; Stokan et al., 2023). In particular, Gooden and Rissler (2017) highlighted that the approach of local government to social equity may best be described as the strategic attempt to meet the needs of the community, both through direct services and long-term relational connections built on trust. They emphasized that even if specific policy focus areas may vary, the significance of institutional structures and the human dimension of public service reveals differences in the real local government commitment. In this context, a challenge is to develop and implement appropriate assessment tools and promote accountability via performance measures specifically designed to support jurisdictional work in advancing equity. Ultimately, social equity efforts at the local level require engagement with community stakeholders not just connected to a specific initiative, but as an ongoing, organic conversation (Gooden & Rissler, 2017; Rivera & Knox, 2023).

Studies and institutions have long stressed the relevance of social equity topic and highlighted the benefits of reporting as a means of internal and external communication of the social equity policies and the interdependencies between policies and practices, calling for more research on this issue (Gooden, 2017; Niemann et al., 2017; Cardillo & Longo, 2020; Manes-Rossi et al., 2020; Grossi et al., 2023).

Coherently, this paper aims to investigate social equity reporting in the context of local governments, exploiting how communication tools are used to disclose social equity policies and how these are translated into social practices able to effectively affect social equity.

3 Methodology and Local Authority Profile

According to the research aim, we conducted an exploratory case study in a Municipality of Southern Italy to depict the disclosure process related to social equity, aiming to identify opportunities and criticalities in managing this process (Yin, 2003). The analysis carried out within the institution highlighted how the administration addresses issues pertaining to social equity objectives and measurement. This approach is valuable in assessing the level of awareness achieved by the local government in managing crucial aspects of social equity, as well as pinpointing strengths and areas for improvement that can effectively impact social equity outcomes (Otley & Berry, 1994).

The case study was chosen because it was involved in various projects linked to social inclusion, integration, and co-responsible citizenship which make the Municipality a significant case with respect to social equity issues. Notably, the Municipality developed the Urban Agenda for Sustainable Urban Development (SUS) promoting strategies and initiatives for increasing territorial quality, economic development, and social cohesion.

The Municipality under observation boasts a population of 299,730 residents as of 2022 and demonstrates a strong commitment to social equity policies, as shown by some indexes such as the number of households, the number of foreign residents, and the old-age dependency ratio which has shown improvement in recent years.

To address the research question previously stated, data were gathered through document analysis and interviews. This approach aimed to collect all relevant information necessary for describing how the disclosure process related to social equity policies is carried out and how social actions and practices introduced are able to effectively impact social equity. The research period spanned from 2021 to 2023, with the data collection process taking place from September 2023 to February 2024. Aiming to investigate the disclosure process, a crucial step was the introduction of the Integrated Plan of Activities and Organization (PIAO). This document, introduced by art. 6 DL 80/2021, serves as an integrated managerial planning and governance tool which, with the aim of overcoming the excessive documentary fragmentation of the public administration, collects the plan for personnel needs and agile working, the three-year anti-corruption plan, and the performance plan and the objectives plan of local authorities as further provided for by art. 2 of Presidential Decree 81/2022. Specifically, within the Public Value section of the PIAO, required by law, the local authority highlights the initiatives and policies in terms of objectives whose measurement will explain the public value achieved.

The analysis considered two PIAOs (2022–2024, 2023–2025) as well as the related planning documents including the DUP linked to the mayor's mandate lines and related actions and projects to be implemented during the administrative mandate, the three-year budget forecast, the technical annexes to the PIAO, the management control reports, and the evaluators' report.

The purpose of the analysis was, on the one hand, to evaluate how the Municipality disclosed social equity policies, looking for the related actions and initiatives, and,

Table 1 Plan of interviews

Interviewees	Number of interviews
General secretary	2
Management control manager 1	3
Management control manager 2	4
Performance plan manager	2
Social policies manager	4
Member of social policy staff	3

on the other hand, to examine results and criticalities reported in the documents in order to understand changes occurring in the development of the two plans.

In addition, we conducted eighteen interviews (the duration was approximately 40 minutes) with the organizational actors who were involved in social policies as reported in Table 1.

Certain extracts from the interviews were directly included in the text, while others were reported indirectly in a narrative form. Reflective questions were extensively used during the interviews. Asking for social policies and typology of social actions and interventions encouraged the interviewees to provide detailed information on the phenomena under investigation, paying attention to how objectives and initiatives were defined and monitored (Dumay et al., 2016). We triangulated the data collected from the documentary analysis with interviews to enhance the comprehensiveness of our analysis (Eisenhardt & Graebner, 2007).

4 The Disclosure Process of Social Equity Policies and Practices

The introduction of the PIAO occurred within the Municipality with specific objectives, which serve as a critical foundation for comprehending the approach followed in the development of strategic and operational objectives. The local body states that the main purposes of PIAO are to enhance coordination and streamline planning activities while also ensuring enhanced quality and transparency in administrative activities and services provided to citizens and businesses. As reported by the management control manager, '*When we began working on the PIAO 2022-2024, we were aware that it was not a merely collection of plans and programming acts, but rather a tool that encapsulates strategies implemented across various fields and their alignment toward achieving public value*'. The management control managers and General Secretary emphasized the significance of disclosing the public value in terms of economic, social, welfare and environmental well-being. On this point, the social policies manager argued, '*We are accustomed to recognizing the various norms that dictate the utilization of financial funds. However, in the planning process, we also give significant weight to our experience and knowledge of the needs of vulnerable citizens. As a result, we try to allocate financial funds to prompt specific actions aimed at improving social conditions*'. Interviews in general revealed a strong commitment of municipality managers to the social equity policies disclosed in the two PIAOs under consideration. Furthermore, the policies disclosed in the two PIAOs signify the outcome of an inclusive process that involves citizens and social associations. On one hand, this is evident in certain social objectives that are shaped based on citizens' requests and suggestions collected through the social web forum. In particular, the Municipality paid attention to social actions, making them visible on the website and trying to stay close to citizens through a new social practice called 'the citizen's room', an online forum that leads the Municipality to activate communication actions in order to promote participatory democracy, through the active involvement of the citizens in the decision-making processes of the Municipality. The citizen's room represents the online environment through which citizens can interact with the Municipality and submit reports, suggestions, and proposals. On the other hand, a dedicated social objective was devoted to establishing a network of social associations aimed at proposing new actions. On this point, the social policies manager said, '*We usually arrange meetings with social associations to gather their feedback on the actions we have taken, and consequently to act accordingly*'.

Specifically, the analysis of the two PIAOs was focused on mission no. 12 called 'Social, family and inclusion policies' aimed at improving the citizens' life quality by the involvement of social forces, social private entities, volunteering, third-sector organizations, and institutional agencies responsible for education, growth, and safety towards the local community. The strategic objectives disclosed in both PIAO reflect the administrative mandate aims about social policy and are declined as follows:

- To enhance home-based and community services
- To promote inclusion, solidarity, and reciprocity policies, contrasting marginalization and social exclusion
- To ensure assistance services for the elderly and differently abled individuals, enhancing their participation and social life, improving their role in the community
- To strengthen policies against gender-based violence
- To implement educational services for children
- To enhance actions supporting parenthood
- To start training projects for the social workers operating in the field

In both plans, the strategic objectives were supported by a context analysis in order to justify how the objectives, actions, and initiatives were aligned with the community's needs. In particular, for each social area (inclusion, differently abled individuals, elderly individuals, minors), actions and activities were detailed, including the provisional number of citizens involved. This approach facilitated tracking the Municipality's progress in social policies over time and encouraged citizens' participation in each initiative. Regarding this, the social policies manager stated, '*Considering the minors' policies, the number of trusted families increased due to new actions carried on to improve the relationships between minors and trusted families. For example, we recently launched two initiatives: one focused training potential trusted families and another aimed at supporting trusted families in addressing misunderstandings with minors. The engagement of trusted families and minors has also led to the identification of another initiative devoted to providing cultural activities aligned with minors' needs*'.

The disclosure of social actions occurs through the Municipality's website, where a dedicated page is allocated to social policies to inform and engage citizens about the procedures and forms required for participation in each initiative. On this web page, the Municipality uploads municipal resolutions on social policies, and citizens are able to directly interact through a social forum. This platform enables citizens to communicate any issues they may encounter and provides an avenue for offering suggestions to enhance municipality policies and actions.

In response to some citizens' requests, new services were introduced in the social plans reported in the PIAO 2023–2025. An example is the 'integrated home care service', a new social initiative aimed at providing primarily health-related support to individuals, ensuring them the opportunity to remain in their own living environment. This represents a translation of social sustainability policies into new social practices that require a reallocation of financial funds.

The Municipality's strong inclusion approach was confirmed by the increased number of social projects introduced in the latter PIAO (see Table 2).

Discussing the neutral space project, the social policies manager explained, '*In response to difficulties noticed by social educators during house meetings involving minors, we established a dedicated space to address the conflictual separation between minors and their families. Initially, we designated two rooms for this*

Table 2 Social projects introduced in the PIAO 2023–2025

Action	Duration	Service characteristics	Provisional number of citizens involved
Development of personal autonomy for individuals with physical, autistic, and psychic disabilities	36 months	Evaluating individual functional abilities and needs, the project is aimed to activate individualized projects to stimulate individuals towards socialization and work autonomy	90 families
Housing First	36 months	The project is aimed at the inclusion of people in specific accommodations and to support them in promoting their autonomy and strengthening their personal resources	50 individuals
Access point for homeless people	12 months	This project is aimed to provide services to homeless people in different access points established around the city	50 individuals
Neutral space project	24 months	The neutral space aims to facilitate parent-child meetings in situations of distress and to manage encounters between children and parents	30 families

service, but observing users' habits of having lunch during the meetings, we allocated an additional room for the kitchen to re-create a family atmosphere'. On this point, the management control manager argued, 'During *performance monitoring, the identification of corrective actions often prompted us to revise the allocation of financial funds for the next period*'.

The strategic objectives outlined in the PIAOs are monitored by the management control office and the evaluation committee, which analyze how the Municipality achieved each objective and report the results for each performance indicator. The attainment of social objectives serves as a measurable way to assess how the actions undertaken effectively affected social equity. That was the case of the Housing First objective measured by three performance indicators: the first one was the updating of the ranking list measured by the number of official documents related to the ranking list process, the second one measured the number of houses provided to people registered in the final and approved ranking list, and the third indicator referred to the digitalized Housing First folders in order to make them available in 'the citizen's room'.

The results pertaining to social objectives are monitored on a semester basis, providing the opportunity to identify and implement corrective actions as needed. This was the case of the social objective related to 'differently abled individuals' measured as follows: number of parking passes for disabled individuals provided in the year, number of passes renewed, number of passes to control, and number of passes checked. In this case, during the semester monitoring, it was decided to send a formal communication to individuals who did not satisfy pass requirements. The verification activity stimulated also stronger communication with citizens about 'the Handicap desk', an online desk that gathers all necessary information for citizens to benefit from available healthcare and social interventions in the city area.

In summary, case evidence revealed that the PIAO could be an effective tool for managing and disclosing social equity policies. In particular, the evidence allowed us to define two main phases that characterized the disclosure process related to social equity policies, as shown in Fig. 1. Throughout this process, inclusiveness ensured by the engagement of social parties was recognized as fundamental, with their participation in the objectives definition process and in the updating of objectives based on the results monitoring process (Gooden & Rissler, 2017; Rivera & Knox, 2023). As emerged during the interviews, the experience and commitment of all internal actors involved in the planning process were also deemed essential. Similarly, the systematic monitoring of the performance results provided the Municipality with the opportunity to promptly evaluate the impact of actions undertaken, identifying potential criticalities to solve with corrective actions (Frederickson, 2015; Cepiku & Mastrodascio, 2021). Case findings suggested also further investigating into the role of specific governance mechanisms that could effectively influence the implementation of social equity practices.

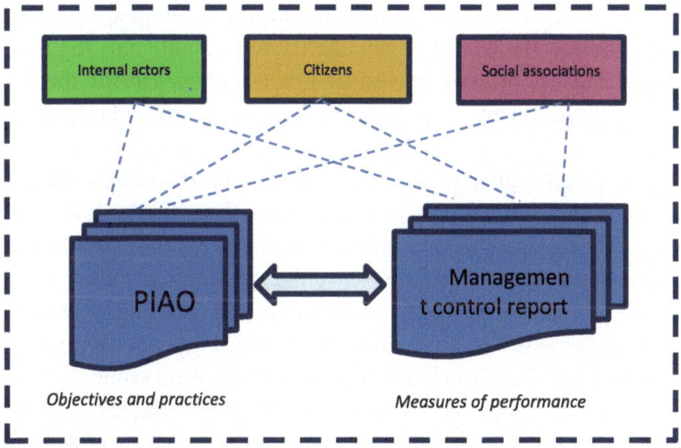

Fig. 1 The disclosure process related to social equity in the Municipality

5 Concluding Remarks

Acknowledging social sustainability as a relevant challenge for local governments, Italian local governments have embraced innovative social accountability reporting to disclose policies and actions focused on this topic.

Contributions on these issues have underlined the heterogeneity of disclosure processes, prompting further research to explore how different actors influence goals within public administrations and their role in developing social sustainability practices. Taking inspiration from this gap, we tried to shed light on social sustainability reporting, exploiting how communication tools are used to disclose social policies and how these policies are translated into social practices able to effectively affect social equity.

To deepen understanding of the disclosure process of the local government, an exploratory case study was conducted in a southern municipality. This study focused on the actors involved and the tools used to communicate with the citizens' communities regarding how social sustainability policy is accomplished and how it affects social equity. Findings showed that in the Municipality, the disclosure process related to social equity was characterized by two phases: the first one related to the identification of objectives and their inclusion in the planning tool, such as the PIAO, and the second one linked to how the Municipality measures and evaluates the effectiveness of actions through various performance indicators.

Case evidence revealed that within the Municipality, the recognition of objectives involved internal actors such as the secretary, the management control managers, the performance plan managers, and the social policies manager and its staff, as well as external actors such as the social associations' network and the citizens. This underlines an inclusive approach by the Municipality, which annually identifies new objectives and actions able to affect social equity.

Social equity policies and actions were monitored through specific performance indicators disclosed in the Management control report and analyzed by the evaluation committee. This monitoring served as a means of measuring the effectiveness of social actions undertaken and represented a stimulus for identifying corrective actions.

In this case, social equity objectives were disclosed through the performance plan contained in the PIAO, aligning with those outlined in the DUP. These objectives primarily aim to establish or strengthen services for the most vulnerable categories of citizens and promote initiatives to enhance access to public services. Some critical profiles pertain to limited programming and analysis of gender policies, which should be addressed through the preparation of a gender report and the reinforcement of the single committee responsible for ensuring equal opportunities.

This study contributes to the social equity literature underlining that effective social equity actions require an organic and ongoing conversation with the community to engage and stimulate continuous improvement (Frederickson, 2015; Cepiku & Mastrodascio, 2021). Similarly, an orientation towards social equity should involve the establishment of specific governance mechanisms such as the social association network or the committee for ensuring equal opportunities and their effective impact on social equity actions and practices.

Further contributions are related to the transparency of the documents used to disclose social equity policies and actions. Specifically, while the inclusion approach adopted by the Municipality was not clearly evident from document analysis, it was discerned through interviews. This reveals an opacity in the disclosure process as it only partially represents the Municipality's commitment towards social equity policies and actions (Ruijer et al., 2023; Stokan et al., 2023).

Findings also suggest practical implications for policymakers, providing guidelines to improve transparency and commitment among social actors. Additionally, the case study sheds light on social practices developed by the Municipality, inspiring a managerial approach to defining social equity policies and strategies aimed at influencing social equity.

The main limitation lies in the analysis of a single case study. Further research could explore the main aspects of the disclosure process related to social equity through a survey aimed at gathering and elucidating similarities and differences among different local governments in their disclosure processes related to social equity.

References

Bracci, E., & Tallaki, M. (2013). Socio-environmental reporting trends in the Italian local government: Thrive or wither? *Socio-environmental reporting trends in the Italian local government: Thrive or Wither?* 27–46.

Caperchione, E., Demirag, I., & Grossi, G. (2017). Public sector reforms and public private partnerships: Overview and research agenda. *Accounting Forum, 41*(1), 1–7.

Cardillo, E., & Longo, M. C. (2020). Managerial reporting tools for social sustainability: Insights from a local government experience. *Sustainability, 12*(9), 3675.

Cepiku, D., & Mastrodascio, M. (2021). Equity in public services: A systematic literature review. *Public Administration Review, 81*(6), 1019–1032.

Cohen, S., & Karatzimas, S. (2015). Tracing the future of reporting in the public sector: Introducing integrated popular reporting. *International Journal of Public Sector Management, 28*(6), 449–460.

De Matteis, F., & Borgonovi, E. (2021). A sustainability management model for local government: An explorative study. *Administrative Sciences, 11*, 126.

Dumay, J., Bernardi, C., Guthrie, J., & Demartini, P. (2016). Integrated reporting: A structured literature review. *Accounting Forum, 40*(3), 166–185.

Eisenhardt, K. M., & Graebner, M. E. (2007). Theory building from cases: Opportunities and challenges. *Academy of Management Journal, 50*(1), 25–32.

Farneti, F., & Guthrie, J. (2009). Sustainability reporting by Australian public sector Organisations: Why they report. *Accounting Forum, 33*, 89–98.

Feiock, R. C., & Soun, J. H. (2009). The role of nonprofits in local service delivery. *Public Administration Review, 70*(July/August), 668–680.

Frederickson, H. G. (2005). The state of social equity in American public administration. *National Civic Review, 94*(4), 31–38.

Frederickson, H. G. (2015). *Social equity and public administration: Origins, developments, and applications*. Routledge.

Gooden, S. T. (2015). From equality to social equity. *Public Administration Evolving*, 210–231.

Gooden, S. T. (2017). Social equity and evidence: Insights from local government. *Public Administration Review, 77*(6), 822–828.

Gooden, S. T., & Rissler, G. E. (2017). Local government: Social equity "first responders". *State and Local Government Review, 49*(1), 37–47.

Goswami, K., & Lodhia, S. (2014). Sustainability disclosure patterns of south Australian local councils: A case study. *Public Money & Management, 34*(4), 273–280.

Grossi, G., & Argento, D. (2022). The fate of accounting for public governance development. *Accounting, Auditing and Accountability Journal, 35*(9), 272–303.

Grossi, G., Kallio, K. M., Sargiacomo, M., & Skoog, M. (2020). Accounting, performance management systems and accountability changes in knowledge-intensive public organisations. *Accounting, Auditing and Accountability Journal, 33*(1), 256–280.

Grossi, G., Steccolini, I., Adhikari, P., Brown, J., Christensen, M., Cordery, C., & Vinnari, E. (2023). The future of public sector accounting research. A polyphonic debate. *Qualitative Research in Accounting & Management, 20*(1), 1–37.

Guy, M. E., & McCandless, S. A. (2012). Social equity: Its legacy, its promise. *Public Administration Review, 72*(s1), S5–S13.

Hawkins, C. V., & Wang, X. (2012). Sustainable development governance: Citizen participation and support networks in local sustainability initiatives. *Public Works and Management Policy, 17*, 7–29.

Hinna, L. (2004). *Il bilancio sociale nelle amministrazioni pubbliche. Processi, strumenti, strutture e valenze*. FrancoAngeli.

Innes, J. E., & Booher, D. E. (2000). *Public participation in planning: New strategies for the 21st century*. University of California.

Jepson, E. J. (2004). The adoption of sustainable development policies and techniques in U.S. cities: How wide, how deep, and what role for planners? *Journal of Planning Education and Research, 23*(2), 229–241.

Loh, C. G., & Kim, R. (2021). Are we planning for equity? Equity goals and recommendations in local comprehensive plans. *Journal of the American Planning Association, 87*(2), 181–196.

Manes-Rossi, F., Nicolò, G., & Argento, D. (2020). Non-financial reporting formats in public sector organizations: A structured literature review. *Journal of Public Budgeting. Accounting & Financial Management, 32*(4), 639–669.

Marcuccio, M., & Steccolini, I. (2009). Patterns of voluntary extended performance reporting in Italian local authorities. *International Journal of Public Sector Management, 22*(2), 146–167.

Niemann, L., Hoppe, T., & Coenen, F. (2017). On the benefits of using process indicators in local sustainability monitoring: Lessons from a Dutch municipal ranking (1999–2014). *Environmental Policy and Governance, 27*(1), 28–44.

Otley, D. T., & Berry, A. J. (1994). Case study research in management accounting and control. *Management Accounting Research, 5*(1), 45–65.

Riccucci, N. M. (2009). The pursuit of social equity in the federal government: A road less traveled? *Public Administration Review, 69*(3), 373–382.

Rivera, J. D., & Knox, C. C. (2023). Bureaucratic discretion, social equity, and the administrative legitimacy dilemma: Complications of new public service. *Public Administration Review, 83*(1), 65–77.

Ruijer, E., Porumbescu, G., Porter, R., & Piotrowski, S. (2023). Social equity in the data era: A systematic literature review of data-driven public service research. *Public Administration Review, 83*(2), 316–332.

Salvador, M., & Sancho, D. (2021). The role of local government in the drive for sustainable development public policies. An analytical framework based on institutional capacities. *Sustainability, 13*(11), 5978.

Stokan, E., Hatch, M. E., & Overton, M. (2023). Fifty years as the fourth pillar of public administration: A polycentric extension of the social equity framework. *Public Administration, 101*(4), 1427–1442.

Svara, J. H., & Brunet, J. R. (2020). The importance of social equity to prevent a hollow public administration. *The American Review of Public Administration, 50*(4–5), 352–357.

Tanese A., (a cura di), (2004). Rendere conto ai cittadini. Il Bilancio Sociale nelle amministrazioni pubbliche, Edizioni Scientifiche Italiane Roma.

Vakkuri, J., Johanson, J. E., Feng, N. C., & Giordano, F. (2021). Governance and accountability in hybrid organizations–past, present and future. *Journal of Public Budgeting, Accounting & Financial Management, 33*(3), 245–260.

Yin, R. K. (2003). Designing case studies. *Qualitative Research Methods, 5*(14), 359–386.

Zeemering, E. S. (2018). Comparing governance and local engagement in the St. Marys River area of concern. *American Review of Canadian Studies, 48*(1), 20–40.

Assessing Italian B-Corps Commitment to Diversity and Inclusion and Its Linkage with Financial Performance

Selena Aureli, Monica Bartolini, and Giorgia Moschini

1 Introduction

According to the literature, diversity and inclusion (D&I) initiatives are driven by two main factors (Edmans et al., 2023a, b). Firstly, there would be a financial incentive, as fostering D&I can enhance a company's long-term financial outlook (Boustanifar & Kang, 2022). This is because employees' value is not solely determined by their skills; it also encompasses their cognitive diversity—their distinct backgrounds, experiences, and problem-solving approaches. Furthermore, achieving optimal financial performance also relies on cultivating a work environment of fairness and inclusivity that enables organizations to leverage employees' abilities and viewpoints effectively (Herring, 2009; Nederveen Pieterse et al., 2013). Secondly, there is a social imperative behind D&I initiatives, grounded in the idea that companies bear a responsibility to contribute to broader societal objectives (Van Dijk et al., 2012). While some research argues that only top-down policies and regulations stemming from moral frameworks may drive companies to integrate D&I, other studies also explore internal ethical motivations (Warren & Warren, 2023).

In this regard, certified B-Corporations (B-Corps) are companies that stand out for their commitment to social responsibility (Mion & Loza Adaui, 2020). They are certified by the B Lab, which evaluates rigorous standards of transparency and social and environmental performance (Castellini et al., 2019; Liute & De Giacomo, 2022). Certification is obtained after undergoing a process called B Impact Assessment (BIA) that evaluates five dimensions. Two of them, workers and community, dedicate particular attention to people. D&I is a related sub-dimension that gets a specific score.

S. Aureli (✉) · M. Bartolini · G. Moschini
Department of Management, Bologna University, Bologna, Italy
e-mail: selena.aureli@unibo.it; monica.bartolini4@unibo.it; giorgia.moschini2@unibo.it

M. Agostini et al. (eds.), *Diversity and Equity in Accounting*, SIDREA Series in Accounting and Business Administration,
https://doi.org/10.1007/978-3-031-78247-3_9

Given that D&I is a fundamental driver of company innovation, competitiveness, and long-term success (Cox & Blake, 1991; Herring, 2009; Nederveen Pieterse et al., 2013), which can be reflected in financial outcomes, this study aims to answer the following question: are higher scores on D&I positively related to financial performance in B-Corps?

To shed light on this aspect, this study focuses on a sample of Italian B-Corps whose commitment to D&I is measured by a score provided by the B-Corp database. Results show that the D&I score is only weakly correlated with ROA and other measures of financial performance achieved during the 2 years after the certification. This suggests that a strong commitment to enhancing employees' well-being does not automatically translate into financial benefits in the short term. Future research should check for possible favourable long-term impacts on company performance.

2 Literature Review

2.1 *B-Corporations*

B-Corps represent a paradigm shift in the corporate world, proving that profitability and responsibility toward society and the environment can coexist. Unlike traditional corporations solely focused on maximizing shareholder value, B-Corps prioritize a triple-bottom-line approach, considering people, the planet, and profit (Elkington & Rowlands, 1999; Stubbs, 2017). They are considered hybrid organizations, like benefit corporations, because they manage to pursue social value while generating economic value (Rawhouser et al., 2015; Gamble et al., 2020; Ferlito & Faraci, 2022a). Furthermore, previous studies show how being a benefit corporation increases the likelihood of small and medium sized enterprises of adopting a self-resilient approach, when coping with crises (Bartolini et al., 2023).

However, while benefit corporations have opted for a permanent change in the corporate structure (their bylaws include the commitment to make a positive material impact on the environment and society) (Mion et al., 2021), B-Corps are usually for-profit companies that integrate social and environmental challenges in their strategies and policies and undergo an assessment process to get the B-Corp certification. Although different, B-Corps share with benefit corporations the same commitment to transparency (they both publish reports evaluating social and environmental performance) and accountability (their directors are required to assess the impact of their decisions on workers, the community, and the environment, besides shareholders).

Despite its temporality, the B-Corp certification is of great value because it categorizes the company as committed to transparency and accountability. Such categorization helps gain legitimacy in the eyes of key stakeholders (Chauhan & O'Neill, 2020), illustrates key differences with competitors, facilitates stakeholder relationships, and helps attract employees, investors, and customers (Bagdadli & Gianecchini, 2023). At the same time, the B-Corp certification is held as reliable because it is provided by a third party (Moroz & Gamble, 2021), and its associated evaluation process stimulates organizations to assess and revise their practices in the light of sustainability (Sharma et al., 2018). However, also opposite findings have been reported, as in the case of companies analyzed by Villela et al. (2021) that appeared to be less concerned with the processual learning aspects of being a certified B-Corp and more concerned with getting a certification as a badge of reputation.

The certification can be obtained by any type of company (i.e. large, small, social, or profit entities) that undergoes the certification process (BIA). The BIA is performed by a private entity named B Lab that evaluates five broad dimensions: environment, workers, customers, community, and governance (Castellini et al., 2019; Gazzola et al., 2019; Liute & De Giacomo, 2022). If the company achieves a minimum score based on the dimensions analyzed and pays a fee, it obtains a 3-year certification.

All dimensions contribute to business value creation and delivery (Ferlito & Faraci, 2022b); however, in our paper, we focus on the specific sub-dimension of D&I because of its capacity to drive innovation, competitiveness, and long-term success (Herring, 2009; Nederveen Pieterse et al., 2013).

2.2 *Diversity and Inclusion and Its Assessment*

Diversity represents a major challenge (and an opportunity) for businesses. Promoting a diverse work environment, where people of different genders, ethnicities, ages, religious beliefs, work experiences, and sexual and affective orientations coexist (Herring, 2009), means being able to integrate different perspectives into an organization. Yet integration needs inclusion, which means 'ensuring that people of all backgrounds are respected and made to feel welcome, and that employees are encouraged to speak up, express their views, and be themselves without pressure to conform' (Edmans et al., 2023a, p. 9). Hiring minorities to tick a box, without ensuring they can thrive and be themselves in the workplace, will not deliver the benefits of diversity (Cole & Salimath, 2013). An inclusive environment should ensure equitable access to resources and opportunities for all, where individuals can feel safe, respected, engaged, motivated, and valued for their contributions towards organizational and societal goals. Programs focusing on gender pay gap reductions as well as talent acquisition and development programs supporting equal opportunities (Blau & Kahn, 2007; Bear et al., 2010; Badal & Harter, 2014) are examples of approaches currently adopted by organizations, while new organizational roles have been created, such as the D&I manager.

Companies are prompted to implement D&I policies by different supranational authorities and governments. For example, the United Nations 2030 Agenda has a specific SDG (no. 4) that seeks to ensure an '*inclusive and equitable quality education and promoting lifelong learning opportunities for all*'. The European Union also motivates companies to consider and adopt D&I policies. Both the EU Non-Financial Reporting Directive (NFD) and the latest Corporate Sustainability Reporting Directive (CSRD), effective from January 2024, require increased transparency regarding D&I policies. More specifically, the requirement DR S1-9 mandates the use of diversity indicators to ensure more comprehensive and impactful disclosure.

To address the increasing need for disclosure on D&I, companies can apply GRI, SASB, and ESR standards, IIRC guidelines, and other reporting frameworks provided by national and international organizations and standard setters. In addition, companies may obtain different certifications to signal their concerns and commitment to D&I and related policies (the B-Corp certification, the Great Place to Work (GPTW) certification, etc.). These certifications provide ratings and rankings.

Reporting standards and certification assessment procedures have several differences, but some of them are now converging due to a continued call for harmonization (Tschopp & Nastanski, 2014; Afolabi et al., 2022; Adams & Abhayawansa, 2022; Zaid & Issa, 2023). Nevertheless, the accounting discipline is still struggling to design a proper scorecard of performance indicators able to capture all dimensions that must be reported (Chomsky, 2023). The mere measurement of diversity in demographic terms (e.g. the number of women on the board) is not enough as it does not necessarily reflect dedicated company policies or strategies. Therefore, real and deep inclusion cannot be achieved by just hiring a higher percentage of a diverse workforce; rather, inclusion occurs when a company creates an environment based on mutual respect, where freedom of expression and absence of discrimination dominate.

According to Edmans et al. (2023a), analyzing proprietary data on D&I measures used to compile the list of the 100 Best Companies to Work For in America (the list prepared by Great Place to Work®), two-thirds of the final score stems from employee responses to questions on employee satisfaction, while the remaining one-third arises from checks on company's demographic makeup, pay and benefit programs, and culture. This has implications for diversity metrics, to which investors, employees, media, regulators, and ESG rating agencies pay increasing attention. In practice, such metrics only capture a small portion of the overall picture, whereas there are other important factors to consider. Additional dimensions should be embedded in a scorecard assessing D&I. Therefore, it is crucial to take a more comprehensive approach to diversity and inclusion assessment, and this is the reason why managers and accountants need to be trained.

2.3 *The Impact of D&I Management on Performance*

Academic research is devoting much attention to the connection between D&I, as part of a company's social responsibility strategy, and corporate financial performance (Williams & O'Reilly, 1998; Rowley & Berman, 2000). According to the literature, teams' diversity boosts innovation, knowledge, growth, and profitability

(Cox & Blake, 1991; Ely & Thomas, 2020; Herring, 2009; Nederveen Pieterse et al., 2013). Furthermore, diversity enhances the functioning and the decision-making quality of both organizational and top-management teams (Harrison & Klein, 2007). It allows them to adopt multiple perspectives and recognize different environmental signals; consequently, they acquire a greater ability to capture different stakeholders' needs. Compared to a uniform board, diverse boards lead to better social and environmental performance (Orazalin & Baydauletov, 2020) as well as financial performance (Maxfield et al., 2018; Birindelli et al., 2018).

Already in the early 1990s, Cox and Blake brought to light early evidence of how cultural diversity drives competitive advantages. First, a diverse work team provides *cost advantages* because of lower turnover and absenteeism rates. Greater corporate diversity fosters a more stimulating environment, where employees develop a greater sense of belonging and attachment. Second, an inclusive company that is attentive to different social minorities *attracts more and diverse talents*; together with diversity policies that encourage companies to look beyond traditional recruitment sources, more *effective human talent acquisition* is achieved. Third, *marketing benefits* derived from the reputation of being attentive to diversity, favouring relationships with consumers and the community. Fourth, in a diverse and inclusive environment, *creativity* is also encouraged. Heterogeneous teams create a 'market of ideas' (Kanter, 1984), thinking 'out of the box' and adopting multiple points of view. Different cultural and/or professional backgrounds stimulate non-obvious ideas that increase innovation (Page, 2007). Fifth, *problem-solving* is favoured, because the more different backgrounds you have in a group, the greater number of solutions to the same problem are identified (Hoffman & Maier, 1961; Page, 2007). Finally, greater *system flexibility*, due to different approaches and cognitive systems, characterizes inclusive organizations, which appear to be less standardized and more fluid and responsive to environmental changes.

Empirical evidence demonstrates that the best companies ranked for their D&I performance usually enjoy superior long-term shareholder returns. Already in 2011, Edmans observed an increase in earnings over 28 years (from 1984 to 2011). More recently, Boustanifar and Kang (2022) demonstrated that this outperformance continues up to 2020, while Edmans et al. (2023b) have extended these results outside the US. Economic gains are also reported in the study of Ely and Thomas (2020). On the other hand, some controversial results exist. For example, Maznevski and Di Stefano (2000) stated that diverse teams may perform worse than homogeneous ones.

Research investigating the effect of B-Corp certification on company growth or financial performance (Paelman et al., 2020; Parker et al., 2019; Romi et al., 2018) shows that being certified is not always a guarantee of higher financial performance. For example, the study by Parker et al. (2019) identifies a short-term growth slowdown arising from certification, which is more pronounced for the smallest and youngest firms, while the study of Paelman et al. (2020) reported that B-Corp certification positively impacts the turnover growth rates 1 year before versus one year post certification. No significant effects on employee growth rates or total asset growth rates are found, instead. A limitation of these studies is that they search for an association between B-Corps' total scores and overall financial performance. As demonstrated by the study of Romi et al. (2018), focusing on single CSR dimensions may reveal more interesting findings. Their study investigates the financial impact of obtaining and reporting on excellence in two specific dimensions: employees and consumers. In detail, it shows that B-Corps with excellent scores in the worker dimension record higher employee productivity, while one-year and three-year sales growth is significantly higher when excellence refers to the customer's dimension.

Moving from these academic studies, we explored the relationship between a company's commitment to D&I and its financial outcomes, answering the following question: are higher scores on D&I positively related to financial performance in B-Corps?

3 Method and Sample Description

This research analyzes the relationship between D&I scores and financial KPIs of Italian B-Corps. D&I scores are sourced from the BIA dataset provided by B Lab, which collects information on more than 1300 B-Corps at the EU level and about 239 Italian B-Corps. KPIs refer to ROA, ROE, ROS, sales, and EBITDA, which are sourced from the Aida-Bureau Van Dijke database.

Our research focuses on Italian B-Corps because Italy is the second country in the EU in terms of the total number of B-Corps (following France). This community has proven to be one of the most active in Europe, playing a significant role in the adoption of the legal form of benefit corporations within the Italian legislation.

Italian B-Corps comprehensively employ over 16,000 individuals and collectively generate a turnover exceeding 10 billion euros. Table 1 provides a

Table 1 Characteristics of all 239 Italian B-Corps by size at the end of 2023 (total sample)

	Size[a]			
Characteristics	Small	Medium	Large	Total
No. of corporations	184	42	13	239
% of corporations	77,0	17,6	5,4	100.0
% Sector: agriculture/growers	1.3	1.3	0.0	2.5
% Sector: manufacturing	18.0	8.8	2.5	29.3
% Sector: service with minor environmental footprint	42.7	3.8	1.3	47.8
% Sector: service with significant environmental footprint	5.0	2.1	0.8	7.9
% Sector: wholesale/retail	10.0	1.7	0.8	12.6
Geographical area: north (No.)	138	32	13	183
Geographical area: centre (No.)	37	6	0	43
Geographical area: south (No.)	9	4	0	13
Geographical area: north (%)	57.7	13.4	5.4	76.6
Geographical area: centre (%)	15.5	2.5	0.0	18.0
Geographical area: south (%)	3.8	1.7	0.0	5.4

[a] Size is proxied by the no. of employees

breakdown of the Italian B-Corps based on size, sector, and geographical area. Small corporations constitute the majority (77%), and service companies dominate across all size categories. The majority (76.6%) is located in the north of Italy. This type of company has experienced a rapid increase over the years, especially since 2020 (Fig. 1).

B-Corps undergo an assessment procedure that evaluates five Impact Areas (IAs) or dimensions. Figure 2 reports average scores on the five IAs and the specific D&I score, which is included in the Community IA.

The Community and Workers Impact Areas appear to be the most relevant and systematically score average higher values over the period, thus having a more

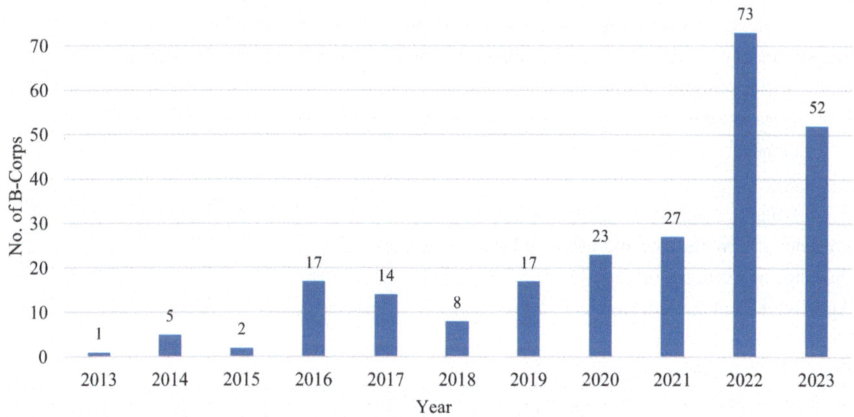

Fig. 1 No. of assessed Italian B-Corps per year

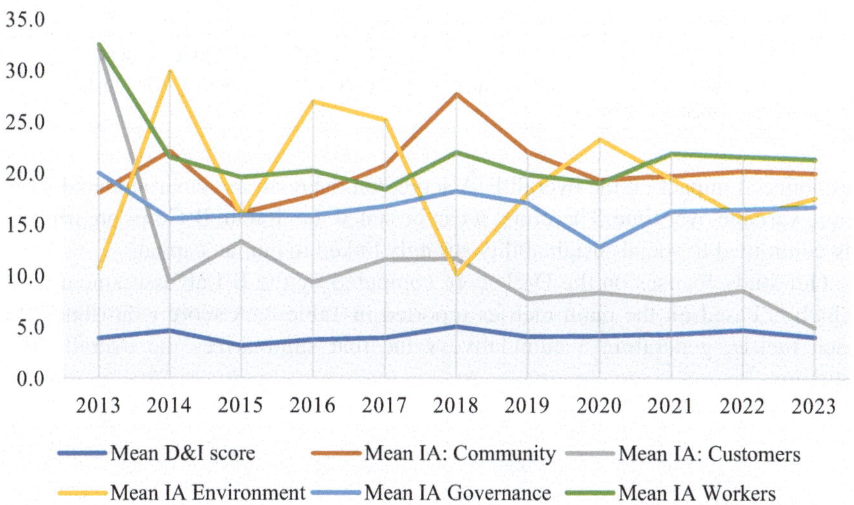

Fig. 2 Average scores of each Impact Area and D&I score over time for Italian B-Corps

Table 2 D&I metrics included in the D&I score

D&I metrics included in the D&I scores
Diverse ownership and leadership—role of underrepresented groups
Creating and managing inclusive work environments—practices:
– Statement in all job postings with a commitment to D&I
– Anonymous or 'blind' review of applications or resumes without attaching names or identifiable characteristics
– Analyses of job description language and requirements to ensure they are inclusive and equitable
– Training for all employees on topics related to D&I
– Setting of specific and measurable D&I goals
– Pay equity analysis by gender, race/ethnicity, or other demographic factors
– Implementation of equal compensation improvement plans or policies
Measurement of diversity, through anonymous surveys or other legal methods about:
– Socioeconomic status
– Race or ethnicity
– Gender
– Age
– Other
Presence of low-income and/or low-education workers
Presence of women workers
Age diversity in the workforce
High- to low-pay ratio
Presence of female managers
Presence of managers from underrepresented populations
Supplier diversity—policies, programs, and characteristics:
– Track of diversity of ownership among suppliers
– Policy to give preferences to suppliers with ownership from underrepresented populations
– Formal targets to make purchases from suppliers with diverse ownership
– Formal program to purchase and provide support to suppliers with diverse ownership
– % of purchases from companies that are majority owned by women or individuals from underrepresented populations

pronounced impact on the overall BIA score. On the contrary, environmental AI is more variable over time. Therefore, it can be stated that Italian B-Corps are primarily committed to social sustainability strongly linked to human capital.

Our study focuses on the D&I score computed by the B Lab assessment tool, which is based on the main metrics reported in Table 2. A score is attributed to each metric, generating a cumulative value that summarizes the overall D&I situation.

4 Findings

In order to explore our research question, we considered the relationship between D&I and financial performance not necessarily in a causal sense. In other words, it also holds that better financial performance may favour more commitment to D&I. Therefore, we searched for a positive correlation between the two variables because, if confirmed, it would attenuate concerns that D&I mainly generates expenses to the detriment of financial performance.

The correlation analysis is limited to B-Corps that underwent the certification assessment in 2020 and 2021. This choice allows us to collect B-Corps' financial KPIs over a three-year period (from 2020 to 2022); the final sample counts no. 138 B-Corps with the following sizes: 80% small-sized, 18% medium-sized, and the remaining 2% large-sized. More than 50% of the final sample consists of businesses founded after 2010; of these, 18.7% were established after 2018. Hence, it can be concluded that our companies are mainly start-ups whose mission is strongly rooted in sustainable principles.

Financial data include growth rates for ROE (return on equity), ROA (return on assets), ROS (return on sales), sales, and EBITDA.

Table 3 describes the univariate correlations between the D&I scores and the growth rate of the selected financial KPIs.

Our results show that the D&I score from the B Lab assessment is only weakly correlated with company growth. The highest correlation (at 0.18) is observed for the ROE growth rate, reinforcing our previous considerations about the potential of D&I in driving shareholders' value and sustaining overall profitability. Results also show a positive, even if weak, correlation with the EBITDA growth rate (0.11), while the correlation with the ROS growth rate is negative (−0.02).

Past studies posit that B-Corps expand their business by devoting a great portion of their resources to socially responsible and environmentally friendly investments

Table 3 Correlation between D&I score, overall score, and financial performance

	Score D&I	Overall score	ROE growth %	ROA growth %	ROS growth %	Sales growth %	EBITDA growth %
Score D&I	1						
Overall score	0.15684	1					
ROE growth %	0.17991	0.02196	1				
ROA growth %	−0.05025	0.08848	0.19815	1			
ROS growth %	−0.02109	0.07191	0.24594	0.99026	1		
Sales growth %	−0.22169	0.06986	−0.25307	−0.08228	−0.08626	1	
EBITDA growth %	0.10676	−0.06275	0.16576	0.06724	0.05554	−0.50191	1

(Chen & Kelly, 2015). Therefore, it could be argued that the negative correlation between D&I and some financial performance ratios is due to the additional efforts companies put into such investments. Furthermore, B-Corps are likely to include B-Corp certification assessment expenses in their marketing efforts, which further increases expenses in the short period.

The most surprising result is the negative correlation with sales growth (−0.22), contrary to what is found in the literature that investigates the impact of the B-Corp certification on sales. We should mention, though, the study by Parker et al. (2019) that had already identified a short-term growth slowdown arising from certification, even more pronounced in the case of the smallest and youngest firms, like the B-Corps of our sample. Very small-sized companies are inevitably more subject to profitability fluctuations when compared to more established businesses. Additionally, we should not forget that the period considered for the analysis is influenced by the consequences of the COVID-19 pandemic at a global economic level. Lastly, the increasing inflation experienced in the EU (particularly in the Italian context) and the slowdown in certain sectors may be other factors explaining the results obtained.

5 Conclusions

Our research investigates the relationship between D&I policies and financial performance in B-Corps. Results show that the D&I score obtained during the certification process is weakly positively associated with ROE and EBITDA growth achieved in the following 2 years. Emerging investments and expenses for training and additional services to support workers' inclusion and well-being could partially explain this outcome. However, the lack of a strong generalized positive relationship between the variables investigated also prompts future research that should investigate long-term impacts (e.g. over a 5-year period) and use other metrics to assess D&I.

The assessment framework and metrics adopted by B Lab to describe a company's D&I commitment may actually fail to fully capture the scope of D&I policies within an organization. In line with the critics of Edmans et al. (2023a, 2023b) on the Great Place to Work ranking, our results call for more investigations on possible limitations of the D&I score used as it focuses on age, gender, and economic status, while other aspects are not accounted for. A comprehensive assessment of D&I should incorporate additional dimensions such as belief system, culture, language and accent, disability, mental health, education, work experience, thinking, and personality type. The B Lab score for D&I does not include all of them. For example, inclusion policies that address chronically underemployed populations and remove barriers to employment are currently included in the Impact Area dedicated to workers, while they could be aggregated to the D&I section. The exclusion of such important elements from the D&I score may lead to a potential distortion of the correlation results between D&I and financial performance. Incorporating the company's dedication to these aspects would increase transparency and clarity and probably result in a more holistic D&I score.

From a theoretical point of view, in line with the results of Parker et al. (2019), our study confirms that higher D&I investments are not so clearly related to financial success. Yet a weak positive relation to ROE advises shareholders that D&I does not negatively curb profitability and B-Corps are businesses from which managers may learn how social responsibility and profit can go hand in hand. At the same time, our results contribute to the ongoing discussion on how to assess a very heterogeneous and intangible dimension like D&I, reiterating the need for further studies to develop appropriate tools for its measurement.

This study is not free of limitations. Most of all, the correlation between D&I policies and financial performance has been investigated only in the short period; hence, it would be beneficial to also consider the long-term effects. The literature suggests that the impact of profitability may be more pronounced on long-term profitability measures. A long-term perspective would also address a second issue, about start-ups and young firms. More precisely, since their profitability is greatly influenced by their initial investments, the potential benefits of D&I investments could be partially offset by negative profitability impacts commonly experienced during the early stages of the business life cycle.

References

Adams, C. A., & Abhayawansa, S. (2022). Connecting the COVID-19 pandemic, environmental, social and governance (ESG) investing and calls for 'harmonisation' of sustainability reporting. *Critical Perspectives on Accounting, 82*, 102309.

Afolabi, H., Ram, R., & Rimmel, G. (2022). Harmonization of sustainability reporting regulation: Analysis of a contested arena. *Sustainability, 14*(9), 5517.

Badal, S., & Harter, J. K. (2014). Gender diversity, business-unit engagement, and performance. *Journal of Leadership & Organizational Studies, 21*(4), 354–365.

Bagdadli, S., & Gianecchini, M. (2023). Italy: Human resource Management in Italian Family-Owned SMEs: Sustaining the competitive advantage through B Corp transformation. In *The global human resource management casebook* (pp. 169–176). Routledge.

Bartolini, M., Aurelim S., & Tinti, S. (2023). Resilience to Covid-19 pandemic crisis as Benefit Corporation - The case of an Italian SME. *Piccola Impresa/Small Business, Special Issue SMEs and humane entrepreneurship overcoming the COVID-19 pandemic 1*, 109–134.

Bear, S., Rahman, N., & Post, C. (2010). The impact of board diversity and gender composition on corporate social responsibility and firm reputation. *Journal of Business Ethics, 97*, 207–221.

Blau, F. D., & Kahn, L. M. (2007). The gender pay gap. *The Economists' Voice, 4*(4).

Birindelli, G., Dell'Atti, S., Iannuzzi, A., & Savioli, M. (2018). Composition and activity of the board of directors: Impact on ESG performance in the banking system. *Sustainability, 10*, 1–10.

Boustanifar, H., & Kang, Y. D. (2022). Employee satisfaction and long-run stock returns, 1984–2020. *Financial Analysts Journal, 78*(3), 129–151.

Castellini, M., Marzano, M., & Riso, V. (2019). How B-corporations' mobilize IC (unawares) to create value. Evidence from the Italian ecosystem. Corporate governance e scenari di settore delle imprese, (p. 82).

Chauhan, Y., & O'Neill, H. M. (2020). Strategic advantages through social responsiveness: The case of certified B-corps. Available at SSRN 3627399.

Chen, X., & Kelly, T. F. (2015). B-corps—a growing form of social enterprise: Tracing their progress and assessing their performance. *Journal of Leadership & Organizational Studies, 22*(1), 102–114.

Chomsky, R. (2023). Measuring sustainability in business, sustainability review, posted in August 20, 2023. Retrieved from: https://sustainablereview.com/measuring-sustainability-in-business/.

Cole, B. M., & Salimath, M. S. (2013). Diversity identity management: An organizational perspective. *Journal of Business Ethics, 116*, 151–161.

Cox, T. H., & Blake, S. (1991). Managing cultural diversity: Implications for organizational competitiveness. *Academy of Management Perspectives, 5*(3), 45–56.

Edmans, A., Flammer, C., & Glossner, S. (2023a). Diversity, equity, and inclusion (No. w31215). National Bureau of Economic Research.

Edmans, A., Pu, D., Zhang, C., & Li, L. (2023b). Employee satisfaction, labor market flexibility, and stock returns around the world. *Management Science*.

Elkington, J., & Rowlands, I. H. (1999). Cannibals with forks: The triple bottom line of 21st century business. *Alternatives Journal, 25*(4), 42.

Ely, R. J., & Thomas, D. A. (2020). Getting serious about diversity. *Harvard Business Review, 98*(6), 114–122.

Ferlito, R., & Faraci, R. (2022a). Sustainable hybrid business model of benefit corporation: The case of an Italian film production company. *Sustainability, 14*(10), 5836.

Ferlito, R., & Faraci, R. (2022b). Business model innovation for sustainability: A new framework. *Innovation & Management Review, 19*(3), 222–236.

Gamble, E. N., Parker, S. C., & Moroz, P. W. (2020). Measuring the integration of social and environmental missions in hybrid organizations. *Journal of Business Ethics, 167*, 271–284.

Gazzola, P., Grechi, D., Ossola, P., & Pavione, E. (2019). Certified benefit corporations as a new way to make sustainable business: The Italian example. *Corporate Social Responsibility and Environmental Management, 26*(6), 1435–1445.

Harrison, D. A., & Klein, K. J. (2007). What's the difference? Diversity constructs as separation, variety, or disparity in organizations. *Academy of Management Review, 32*(4), 1199–1228.

Herring, C. (2009). Does diversity pay?: Race, gender, and the business case for diversity. *American Sociological Review, 74*(2), 208–224.

Hoffman, L. R., & Maier, N. R. (1961). Quality and acceptance of problem solutions by members of homogeneous and heterogeneous groups. *The Journal of Abnormal and Social Psychology, 62*(2), 401.

Kanter, R. M. (1984). *Change masters*. Simon and Schuster.

Liute, A., & De Giacomo, M. R. (2022). The environmental performance of UK-based B Corp companies: An analysis based on the triple bottom line approach. *Business Strategy and the Environment, 31*(3), 810–827.

Maxfield, S., Wang, L., & Magaldi de Sousa, M. (2018). The effectiveness of bank governance reforms in the wake of the financial crisis: A stakeholder approach. *Journal of Business Ethics, 150*, 485–503.

Maznevski, J. J. D. M. L., & Di Stefano, J. J. (2000). Creating value with diverse teams in global management. *Organizational Dynamics, 29*(1), 45–63.

Mion, G., & Loza Adaui, C. R. (2020). Understanding the purpose of benefit corporations: An empirical study on the Italian case. *International Journal of Corporate Social Responsibility, 5*(1), 4.

Mion, G., Loza Adaui, C. R., & Bonfanti, A. (2021). Characterizing the mission statements of benefit corporations: Empirical evidence from Italy. *Business Strategy and the Environment, 30*(4), 2160–2172.

Moroz, P. W., & Gamble, E. N. (2021). Business model innovation as a window into adaptive tensions: Five paths on the B Corp journey. *Journal of Business Research, 125*, 672–683.

Nederveen Pieterse, A., Van Knippenberg, D., & Van Dierendonck, D. (2013). Cultural diversity and team performance: The role of team member goal orientation. *Academy of Management Journal, 56*(3), 782–804.

Orazalin, N., & Baydauletov, M. (2020). Corporate social responsibility strategy and corporate environmental and social performance: The moderating role of board gender diversity. *Corporate Social Responsibility and Environmental Management, 27*(4), 1664–1676.

Paelman, V., Van Cauwenberge, P., & Vander Bauwhede, H. (2020). Effect of B Corp certification on short-term growth: European evidence. *Sustainability, 12*(20), 1–18.

Page, S. E. (2007). Making the difference: Applying a logic of diversity. *Academy of Management Perspectives, 21*(4), 6–20.

Parker, S. C., Gamble, E. N., Moroz, P. W., & Branzei, O. (2019). The impact of B lab certification on firm growth. *Academy of Management Discoveries, 5*(1), 57–77.

Rawhouser, H., Cummings, M., & Crane, A. (2015). Benefit corporation legislation and the emergence of a social hybrid category. *California Management Review, 57*, 13–35.

Romi, A., Cook, K. A., & Dixon-Fowler, H. R. (2018). The influence of social responsibility on employee productivity and sales growth: Evidence from certified B corps. *Sustainability Accounting, Management and Policy Journal, 9*, 392–421.

Rowley, T., & Berman, S. (2000). A brand new brand of corporate social performance. *Business & Society, 39*(4), 397–418.

Sharma, G., Beveridge, A. J., & Haigh, N. (2018). A configural framework of practice change for B corporations. *Journal of Business Venturing, 33*(2), 207–224.

Stubbs, W. (2017). Sustainable entrepreneurship and B corps. *Business Strategy and the Environment, 26*(3), 331–344.

Tschopp, D., & Nastanski, M. (2014). The harmonization and convergence of corporate social responsibility reporting standards. *Journal of Business Ethics, 125*, 147–162.

Van Dijk, H., van Engen, M., & Paauwe, J. (2012). Reframing the business case for diversity: A values and virtues perspective. *Journal of Business Ethics, 111*(1), 73–84.

Villela, M., Bulgacov, S., & Morgan, G. (2021). B Corp certification and its impact on organizations over time. *Journal of Business Ethics, 170*, 343–357.

Warren, M. A., & Warren, M. T. (2023). The EThIC model of virtue-based allyship development: A new approach to equity and inclusion in organizations. *Journal of Business Ethics, 182*(3), 783–803.

Williams, K. Y., & O'Reilly, C. A., III. (1998). *Demography and Research in Organizational Behavior, 20*, 77–140.

Zaid, M. A., & Issa, A. (2023). A roadmap for triggering the convergence of global ESG disclosure standards: Lessons from the IFRS foundation and stakeholder engagement. *Corporate Governance: The International Journal of Business in Society, 23*(7), 1648–1669.

Part III
Organisational Challenges on Diversity and Equity

Diversity in Accounting: Implications for Environmental Sustainability

Zeila Occhipinti, Salvatore Tallarico, and Roberto Verona

1 Introduction

Promoting and nurturing diversity are key challenges in addressing the complex societal issues that are critical to achieving social justice and equity. In formulating the Sustainable Development Goals (SDGs) to be achieved by 2030, the United Nations explicitly included (at least) two SDGs aimed specifically at societal diversity: gender equality (SDG 5) and reduced inequalities (SDG 10). In line with the perspectives of numerous human rights organisations, such as the United Nations Human Rights Council and the European Institute for Gender Equality, diversity is understood to encompass a wide range of human qualities and characteristics that define the identity of an individual, group, or organisation (Ghio et al., 2024).

For a significant period, accounting tended to align with societal norms that favoured a profession predominantly dominated by Western, white, heterosexual males (Anderson-Gough et al., 2005; Haynes, 2017). This orientation reflects the prevalence of a neoliberal capitalist ethos in accounting practice and has fostered a culture of power dynamics (Lehman et al., 2016). However, social and cultural changes are occurring rapidly, which is why a reassessment of the current accounting model is required (Alawattage et al., 2021).

Current research in this field highlights the increasing attention that accounting firms are devoting to diversity (Ghio et al., 2024; Anderson-Gough et al., 2022). As noted by Ghio et al. (2024, p. 17), there is 'a noticeable trend towards hiring a more diverse workforce', largely driven by stakeholders such as investors and clients, who are pushing for greater diversity on boards and greater transparency around diversity-related information. However, the extent to which these changes affect the

Z. Occhipinti (✉) · S. Tallarico · R. Verona
University of Pisa, Pisa, Italy
e-mail: zeila.occhipinti@unipi.it; salvatore.tallarico@ec.unipi.it; roberto.verona@unipi.it

M. Agostini et al. (eds.), *Diversity and Equity in Accounting*, SIDREA Series in Accounting and Business Administration,
https://doi.org/10.1007/978-3-031-78247-3_10

commercial, performative, and hierarchical organisational culture typical of accounting contexts remains uncertain and subject to debate (Baudot et al., 2022). Evidence suggests that power imbalances related to diversity (or lack thereof) are widespread in the accounting profession and are perpetuated by accounting techniques. While the apparent increase in the representation of diverse social identities in accounting and reporting may seem positive at first, it often overlooks issues of social justice and equity and fails to address power inequalities. Efforts to promote diversity in accounting often fail to redistribute power resources and inadvertently reinforce existing inequalities. Moreover, current diversity practices in accounting often exacerbate the marginalisation of certain social identities, particularly of those groups that contribute less to organisational performance, thereby perpetuating organisational structures that reproduce power imbalances (Bigoni & Mohammed, 2023).

In line with the growing interest in social and environmental accounting, we also observe an increasing interest in understanding the impact of diversity on companies' environmentally sustainable activities (e.g. Rahi, 2024; Issa & Zaid, 2021; Liao et al., 2015). Environmentally sustainable development has become a global challenge for humanity. Economic development has had a devastating impact on our planet, with the potential to cause irreversible damage to the ecosystem and the future population. A growing number of studies have attempted to examine the potential of accounting as a useful tool for achieving economic development in a way that is not harmful to the environment (Bigoni et al., 2023; Bigoni & Occhipinti, 2023; Sobkowiak et al., 2020; Thomson et al., 2014). Nevertheless, it is important to understand how this strand of studies relates to accounting research on diversity. In light of the above, we aim to answer the following research question:

RQ: How is accounting research on diversity intertwined with corporate environmental sustainability?

In order to answer the research question, we conducted a systematic literature review on studies that bring together accounting research on diversity and environmental sustainability issues. Both descriptive and content analyses were conducted (Cerchione & Esposito, 2016). The descriptive analysis provides an overview of the trends in this stream of literature. The content analysis, on the other hand, seeks to systematise the contributions on diversity, accounting, and environmental sustainability by providing implications for future research. For the descriptive analysis, we conducted a bibliometric analysis using the Bibliometrix R package. For the content analysis, we used a main path analysis using VOSViewer® and Pajek® software, together with the interpretation and systematisation of the results.

This chapter is structured as follows: after the introduction, the methodology adopted is explained. The results of the application obtained from the implementation of the methodology are presented. Finally, the chapter concludes with a discussion of the results and the contributions of the work.

2 Methodology

In line with established systematic literature review practices (Bankins et al., 2023), we have defined our methodological protocol in order to ensure transparency and replicability of our approach (Greenhalgh, 1997). The main steps are illustrated in Fig. 1. The latter illustrates the PRISMA (Preferred Reporting Items for Systematic Reviews and Meta-Analyses) framework. This framework outlines the entire process, including article identification, screening, eligibility assessment, and final inclusion. These steps will be explained in the following paragraphs.

2.1 Article Selection Process

The article selection process involved two stages. First, a comprehensive search was conducted to identify relevant keywords and formulate an appropriate search query. We then used Scopus-Elsevier, a well-established database dating back to 2004, to retrieve the documents. The second stage involved the actual selection of articles based on predetermined inclusion and exclusion criteria.

2.1.1 Search Query

The search query used in this study was adapted from Ghio et al.'s (2024) recent literature review on diversity in accounting. Given our focus on exploring the extent to which accounting research on diversity addresses aspects of environmental corporate sustainability—i.e. a subset of the broader topic investigated by Ghio et al. (2024)—we employed the same query to select the initial sample of articles.

Ghio et al. (2024) focused their search query on specific journals, including notable interdisciplinary accounting journals with a score of B or above in the Australian Business Deans Council (ABDC) journal list.

The timeframe for the search of articles to be selected, as considered by Ghio et al. (2024), spans from 1956 (the oldest Scopus-Elsevier publications) to the present day (April 2024).

Using the search query specified by Ghio et al. (2024) in Scopus-Elsevier, we retrieved 1076 articles.

2.1.2 Article Selection Criteria

In order to ensure the relevance of the articles selected for our research topic (Kraus et al., 2022), we applied specific inclusion and exclusion criteria to the articles identified through the Ghio et al. (2024) search query.

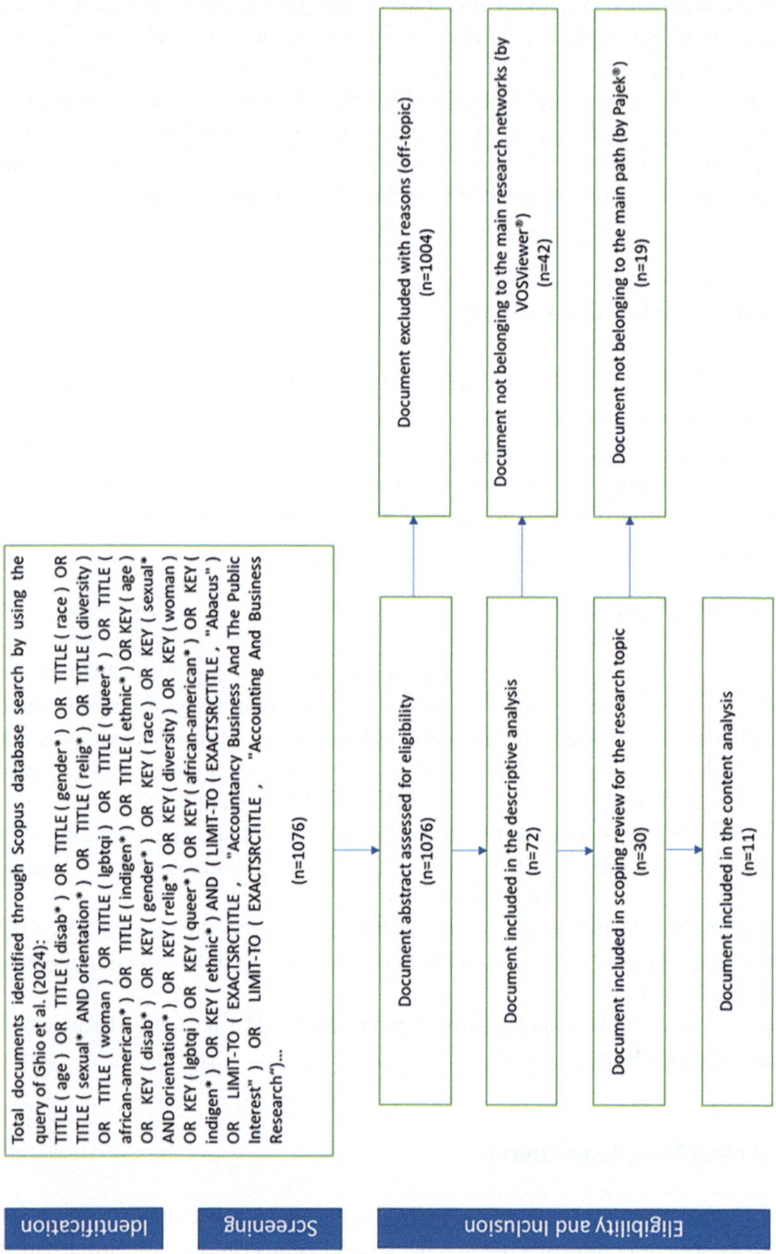

Fig. 1 PRISMA framework

The initial stage of the process involved screening the abstracts to identify those that discussed diversity, accounting, and environmental sustainability. The principal researcher reviewed all abstracts, with input from other researchers when needed.

The second step involved a comprehensive examination of the main body of selected articles to identify sections that specifically addressed the impact of diversity on companies' environmentally sustainable activities.

Following these criteria, 72 papers were identified as suitable for the subsequent descriptive analysis phase. These papers will be used to synthesise and categorise research findings in order to provide an overview of the literature.

2.2 Descriptive Analysis

Bibliometric analysis is employed to provide a snapshot of the trend of the literature, which brings together accounting research on diversity and environmental sustainability issues.

To implement this analysis, the Bibliometrix R package was used to analyse the 72 articles. We have depicted the selected articles from four distinct viewpoints: papers over time, papers by countries, papers by journal, and papers by keywords.

2.3 Content Analysis

The content analysis was conducted using the VOSViewer® software, which constructed the primary network of articles interconnected by citations from the initial pool of 72 articles. The resulting network comprised 30 articles linked through citations.

To focus solely on foundational articles relevant to our research topic, we employed main path analysis using Pajek® software. Pajek® identifies and organises highly cited articles from a larger network presenting them in chronological order. The main path analysis enables us to monitor the evolution of theories or literature traditions related to a specific topic over time, identifying the most influential articles along a chronological path. From the initial 30 documents in the VOSViewer® main network, Pajek® produced a path comprising 11 articles (see Fig. 2), spanning from 2015 to 2024 (the current year of writing this chapter).

By analysing the content of these 11 articles, we were able to trace the development of discourse concerning the studies which bring together the accounting research on diversity and environmental sustainability issues.

Figure 2 presents the network of main articles related to the topic under study in the form of a pathway. The study by Liao et al. (2015), identified as the main node (i.e. most cited) of the network according to the analysis conducted with VosViewer®, serves as the starting point in Pajek® for the stream of articles that branches out into

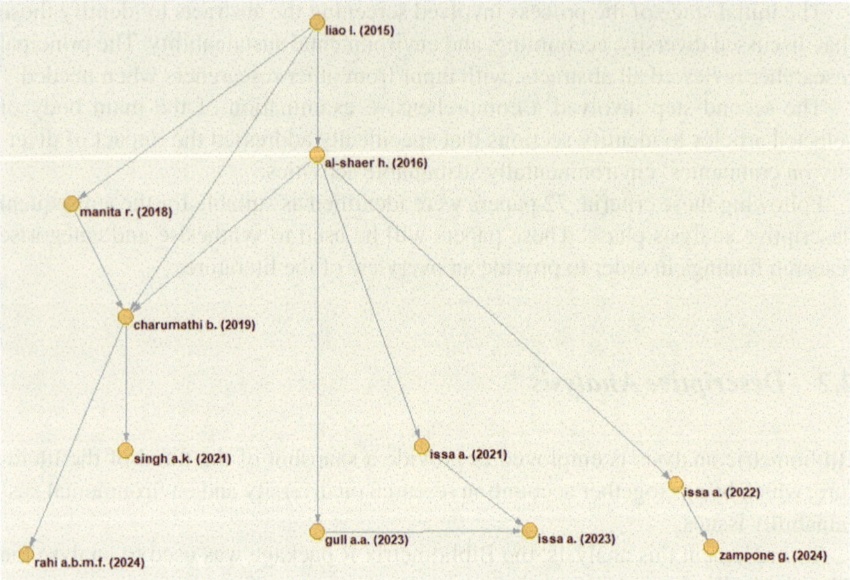

Fig. 2 Article main path by Pajek®

various subtopics, ultimately leading to Rahi (2024), Issa and Hanaysha (2023), and Zampone et al. (2024), which will be examined in the content analysis of this study.

Overall, the evidence from VosViewer® and Pajek® demonstrates that the topic under study is currently a subject of discussion and development within the scientific community.

3 Results

3.1 Descriptive Analysis

This paragraph presents the main findings of the descriptive analysis conducted through the Bibliometrix R package to examine the 72 articles according to the following four perspectives.

Table 1 in the appendix provides an overview of the selected articles for analysis.

3.1.1 Papers Over Time

Figure 3 illustrates the temporal distribution of the 72 selected articles.

The landscape of these articles begins in 2008, with a notable concentration towards more recent years, particularly experiencing a substantial surge in publications from 2020 onward. This observation suggests that the debate about diversity within accounting sectors concerning environmental sustainability aspects has emerged as a prominent and rapidly evolving topic within the academic literature.

3.1.2 Papers by Countries

Figure 4 illustrates the distribution of the 72 selected articles by country.

The map generated by the Bibliometrix R package considers the nationalities of authors contributing to the collection, with colour intensity proportional to the number of publications.

Australia is the country with the highest number of papers. Following closely are the United States of America, Canada, England, Italy, New Zealand, and China, with notable contributions. Furthermore, several other European Union countries, including France, Spain, and Germany, as well as non-EU countries such as India, also make significant contributions to the literature.

This distribution suggests that the discourse on diversity within accounting fields to bolster environmental sustainability is particularly pronounced in the most developed countries globally.

3.1.3 Papers by Journal

Figure 5 displays the distribution of articles according to the most significant sources.

It is notable that journals with substantial contributions, each surpassing seven publications, include *Sustainability Accounting, Management and Policy Journal* (eight contributions), *Meditari Accountancy Research* (six contributions), *Critical Perspectives on Accounting* (five contributions), *International Journal of Accounting and Information* (five contributions), and *Journal of Applied Accounting Research* (five contributions).

These journals have emerged as key platforms for scholarly discourse and dissemination of research findings pertaining to diversity within accounting fields and its implications for environmental sustainability.

3.1.4 Papers by Keywords

The Bibliometrix R package was used to create a TreeMap visualisation of the keywords present in the selected articles.

Figure 6 illustrates the treemap of keywords among the papers analysed in this research. The most frequently used keywords included ‘corporate social

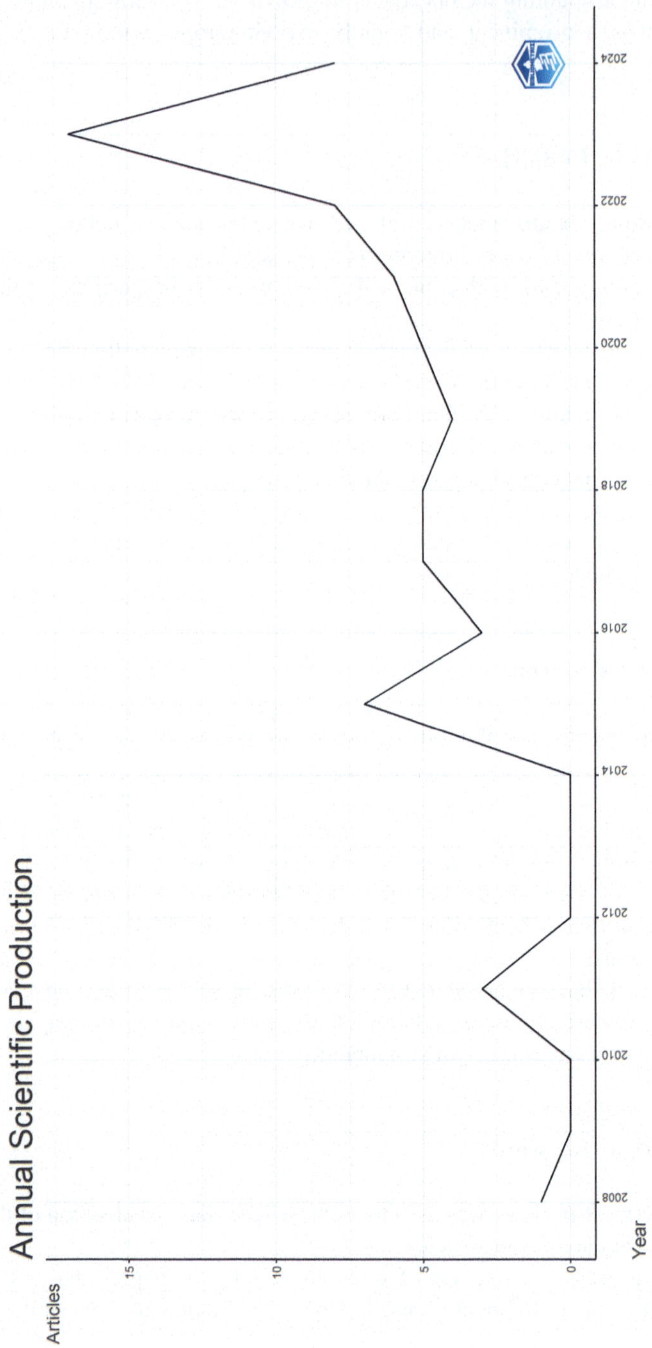

Fig. 3 Papers over time

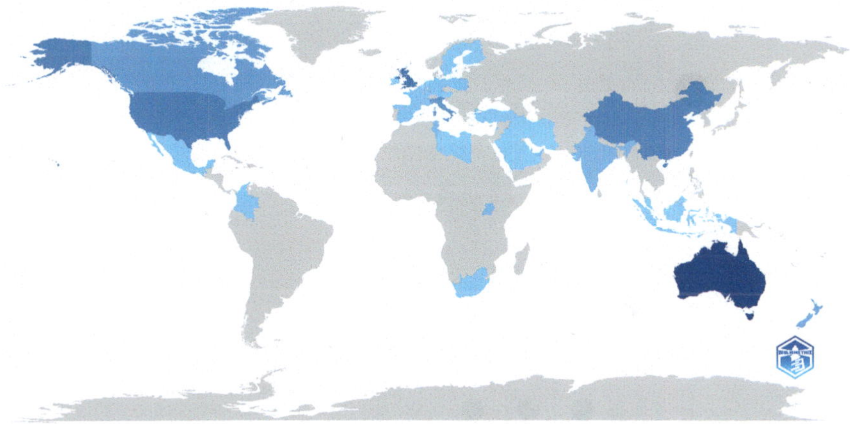

Fig. 4 Papers by countries

responsibility', 'corporate governance', 'gender diversity', 'sustainability', and 'board gender diversity'. These keywords serve as the foundational elements framing the background topic of this study.

Furthermore, it is notable that emerging keywords include 'ESG', 'disclosure', 'environmental', and 'climate change'. These emerging keywords provide insights into the evolving discourse surrounding diversity within accountability fields. In particular, they shed light on the trajectory towards environmental sustainability, as indicated by the presence of keywords such as 'environmental' and 'climate change'. Moreover, the inclusion of keywords such as 'disclosure', 'accountability', and 'sustainability' indicates an increasing focus on the relationship between diversity initiatives and their impact on firms' environmental sustainability-related performance.

Overall, the distribution of keywords offers valuable insights into the evolving landscape of research related to diversity in accounting, particularly in the context of advancing environmental sustainability goals and improving corporate performance in this regard.

3.2 Content Analysis

In this section, we conducted a content analysis of the articles that, according to the main path obtained from the implementation of Pajek®, constitute the traditional foundation of research on diversity, accounting, and environmental sustainability. These studies investigate the relationship between board diversity and environmental sustainability in terms of both disclosure and performance. In particular, all the articles belonging to the main path (Fig. 2) focus on the role of gender diversity

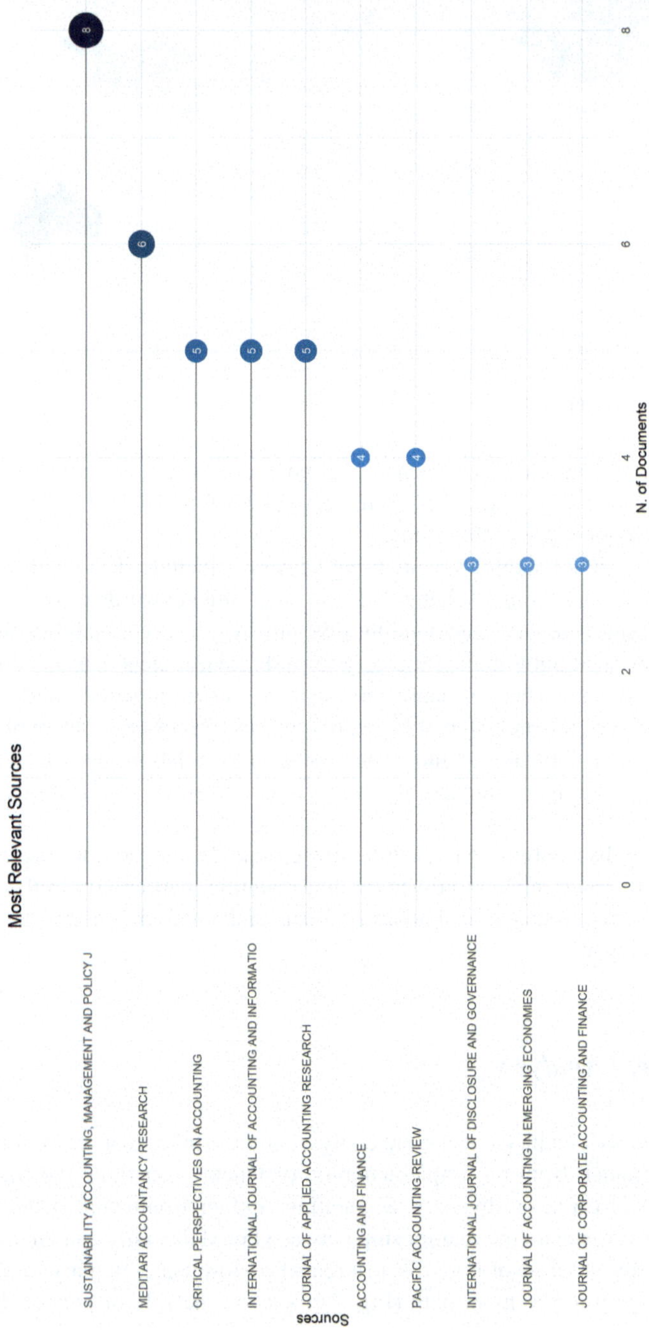

Fig. 5 Papers by journal

Fig. 6 Papers by keywords

within corporate boards and investigate the implications in terms of corporate environmental sustainability.

3.2.1 The Role of Women Within Corporate Boards

The inclusion of women on corporate boards appears to bring a diverse set of values, skills, and experiences that differ from those of men. Past research shows that women tend to be more attuned to environmental risks. Consequently, achieving a balanced gender representation in the boardroom is considered essential for the effective implementation of environmental strategies (Rahi, 2024; Singh et al., 2021; Issa & Zaid, 2021).

Critical mass theory has been used by researchers to estimate the critical number of women on corporate boards needed to improve corporate environmental policy (Issa & Hanaysha, 2023). The percentage of women on the board is used as a measure of board gender diversity (number of women directors/total directors on the board as of the last date of the financial year) (Charumathi & Rahman, 2019). The Blau and Shannon indexes (Singh et al., 2021; Al-Shaer & Zaman, 2016) can also be used.

The ability of women on corporate boards to influence the environmental strategies implemented by companies depends on several contextual factors, including the country's cultural tradition, industry, regulatory environment, and corporate governance mechanisms (Issa & Hanaysha, 2023; Issa et al., 2022; Singh et al., 2021).

Previous studies have highlighted the challenges faced by women in male-dominated countries in participating in environmental sustainability decision-making. In contrast, female-friendly countries that mandate gender equality in corporate governance structures create a favourable working environment for women, enabling them to freely express their ideas to help the company achieve better environmental performance (Rahi, 2024; Al-Shaer & Zaman, 2016).

Scholars have highlighted that women's attitudes towards environmental strategies are influenced by their professional experience and education. The professional skills of women on corporate boards in developing countries are comparatively less advanced than those of their counterparts in Western countries, and thus, their presence on corporate boards may not have a positive impact on environmental sustainability. For instance, Issa et al. (2022) investigated the phenomenon within companies in the Arabian Gulf Council region and found a negative effect of women's presence on corporate boards on environmental disclosure, while Singh et al. (2021) focused on the Indian context and found no significant impact on environmental performance.

Other scholars have highlighted that the ability of women to influence the environmental sustainability of the firm depends not only on their educational and professional skills, but also on their relationships with other board members (Rahi, 2024; Issa & Hanaysha, 2023; Manita et al., 2018). When the composition of the board includes around 30% of women, the latter can work together and apply their skills in a synergistic manner, which has a positive impact on corporate sustainability performance (Rahi, 2024). Conversely, when only one woman is appointed or elected to a board, a 'minority invisibility/neutralisation phenomenon' occurs. This results in her being relegated to the sidelines of power, her role and status being symbolically and socially diminished, her voice being silenced, and her ability to influence and drive change being reduced. Consequently, her impact on corporate environmental sustainability is ineffective and possibly negative (Manita et al., 2018, p. 218).

3.2.2 Environmental Corporate Performance and Voluntary Disclosure

As mentioned above, all the contributions belonging to the Pajek® main path assess the role of board gender diversity in enhancing corporate environmental sustainability. These studies can be classified into two main groups: (1) studies focusing on the relationship between board gender diversity and corporate environmental performance, from Liao et al. (2015) to Issa and Hanaysha (2023) and Rahi (2024), in the main path (Fig. 2), and (2) studies focusing on the relationship between board gender diversity and environmental disclosure, from Liao et al. (2015) to Zampone et al. (2024), in the main path (Fig. 2).

Both groups include exclusively quantitative research studies.

The first group (1) assessed environmental performance using the environmental, social, and governance (ESG) score (Rahi, A., 2024; Issa & Hanaysha, 2023; Manita et al., 2018) or the corporate social responsibility (CSR) score (Singh et al., 2021), or other environmental scores created by the authors themselves (Issa & Zaid, 2021; Charumathi & Rahman, 2019) as proxies.

The environmental dimension of the ESG score comprises information on energy consumption, recycled water, carbon emissions, waste management, spills, and pollution issues. The CSR score is calculated as the expenditure on CSR initiatives undertaken by the firm. The author's environmental scores are based on environmental information such as resource use, emissions, and environmental product innovation.

The majority of studies have indicated that gender diversity in corporate boards can be a trigger for improving corporate environmental performance (Rahi, 2024; Issa & Zaid, 2021; Charumathi, B., & Rahman, 2019). However, the studies by Issa and Hanaysha (2023) and Singh et al. (2021) found no significant relationship between gender board diversity and corporate environmental sustainability. This can be explained by some contextual factors, such as corporate governance mechanisms and the country's cultural tradition, which may mitigate the positive relationship between gender board diversity and corporate environmental sustainability.

The second group of studies (2) examines the relationship between gender board diversity and environmental disclosure, focusing on the attitudes of firms with women on their boards towards voluntary disclosure of environmental information, such as the reporting of greenhouse gas (GHG) emissions (Liao et al., 2015), CSR disclosure (Issa et al., 2022), and Sustainable Development Goal (SDG) disclosure (SDGs 13—climate action—and 8—decent work and economic growth) (Zampone et al., 2024).

In accordance with the findings of the first group of studies (1), the majority of the subsequent group of studies (2) found a significant positive correlation between gender board diversity and environmental disclosure (Zampone, 2024; Liao et al., 2015). The inclusion of diverse gender representation on corporate boards is widely acknowledged as an effective corporate governance indicator in promoting greater transparency and accountability (Zampone et al., 2024). Moreover, this relationship can be weakened by contextual factors, in particular, those related to the country's cultural tradition (Issa et al., 2022).

Further enriching our understanding, the study conducted by Zampone et al. (2024) identifies the mediating role of sustainability committees in bridging board diversity with SDG disclosure, especially regarding SDG 13 and SDG 8. This highlights the importance of corporate governance mechanisms within organisations in translating diversity initiatives into tangible sustainability outcomes.

4 Discussion and Conclusion

This chapter systematises studies that bring together accounting research on diversity and environmental sustainability issues.

Our findings show that, since 2008, the literature on diversity accounting has focused on issues of environmental sustainability, with a notable concentration since 2015. This is because the topic of sustainable development became more important after the UN member states adopted the SDGs in 2015 as part of the 2030 Agenda for Sustainable Development (Bebbington & Unerman, 2018). The accounting literature on diversity and environmental sustainability is mostly written by authors from developed countries. This is similar to the distribution of the broader diversity and accounting literature (Ghio et al., 2024). The journals that have emerged as key platforms for academic debate and dissemination of the accounting literature on diversity and its implications for environmental sustainability are different from those that have published more about diversity and accounting (Ghio et al., 2024). This suggests that environmental sustainability is a niche topic that is distinct from the broader literature on accounting and diversity.

Our findings demonstrate the positive impact of board gender diversity on corporate environmental disclosure and performance. They also highlight the importance of contextual factors such as cultural traditions, industry dynamics, regulatory frameworks, and corporate governance mechanisms in understanding the relationship between board gender diversity and environmental sustainability outcomes (Issa & Hanaysha, 2023; Naz et al., 2023). In particular, our findings indicate that women's ability to influence corporate environmental sustainability depends on their educational and professional qualifications, as well as their interactions with other board members (Rahi, 2024; Issa & Hanaysha, 2023; Manita et al., 2018).

The findings from such research could help identify the elements that shape women's behaviour on boards and shed light on the factors driving women's leadership in corporate environmental decision-making. We emphasise the need to open the 'black box' and gain insight into the factors that influence women's decisions on boards. This can be achieved through field studies, interviews, and psychometric tests. Furthermore, cross-country comparative studies between developed and developing countries would assist in deepening the role of women's education in influencing the decisions made by women on boards about environmental policies.

Future studies could also explore how new regulatory issues can promote effective female board leadership.

Our findings suggest that companies with female board members tend to demonstrate increased voluntary disclosure of sustainability information and improved environmental performance (Rahi, 2024; Issa & Zaid, 2021; Zampone et al., 2024). The presence of women on the board is associated with an increased focus on information transparency. It would be beneficial to explore whether the increased transparency associated with female board representation could mitigate phenomena like greenwashing. Women are more inclined towards genuine environmental policies within companies, which could lead to a more transparent approach to environmental disclosure.

Further research is needed to determine the interest of female board members in implementing environmentally friendly policies. The studies reviewed investigate the impact of female board members on environmental performance. Researchers often rely on proxies to measure environmental performance. These proxies, however, may not always fully represent the true 'environmental impact'. Future research should improve these proxies by creating indices that more accurately reflect the various facets of environmental impact.

Additionally, future studies could adopt a critical approach to women's pro-environment actions and identify the accounting tools most used by women to inform their decision-making. It would be beneficial to examine more closely the adoption of environmental accounting practices by companies with women on their boards. Indeed, the integration of a culture inspired by diversity in accounting, both in the profession and in the technique, can enhance the ability of accounting to shape a more environmentally sustainable world. The concept of diversity is inextricably linked to accounting, which is fundamentally shaped by social constructs (Hopwood, 1987a, 1987b). Accounting is a technical, social, and moral practice (Carnegie et al., 2021) with the potential to shape the world (Hines, 1988). By preparing, using, and applying accounting principles, people can incorporate their perspectives and life experiences into accounting practices. Consequently, integrating a culture that values diversity into the field of accounting could enhance its ability to contribute towards creating a more sustainable global environment.

A step forward in the accounting literature on diversity intertwined with environmental issues would be to extend the research to primary/surface-level dimensions of diversity that relate to types of core social identity other than gender, i.e. age, ethnicity (cultural), race, disability, sexual orientation, and religion (Ghio et al., 2024). Quantitative and qualitative methods can shed light on the impact of board members' social identity on corporate environmental disclosure and performance. Using a critical approach, future studies could investigate the perception of environmental risk by people with different social identities and shed light on their different attitudes towards the use of environmental accounting practices. For a broader understanding of the phenomenon, the perception of environmental risk by people with different social identities should be estimated taking into account the profession of the people within the company, such as a board member or a chief financial officer.

Finally, our findings provide an impetus for future studies to systematise the accounting literature on diversity on the basis of the social dimension of corporate ESG activities, thus considering the multiple profiles of sustainable development that emerge from the SDGs.

This chapter contributes to the accounting literature on diversity (Ghio et al., 2024) by mapping the discussion of diversity in accounting with the very warm topic of environmental sustainability and offering implications for future research. It also contributes to the literature that views accounting as a technical, social, and moral practice with the power to shape the world (Carnegie et al., 2021). This is achieved by demonstrating how diversity can enhance the ability of accounting to foster a better world, inspired by environmental sustainability (Carnegie et al., 2021). Our research can also inform central government and private organisations of the importance of promoting diversity within the accounting profession while mitigating any form of marginalisation.

Appendix

Data Collection Information

Table 1 Main information about the collection

Description	Results
MAIN INFORMATION ABOUT DATA	
Timespan	2008:2024
Sources (Journals, Books, etc)	30
Documents	72
Annual Growth Rate %	13,88
Document Average Age	4,14
Average citations per doc	43,97
References	5477
DOCUMENT CONTENTS	
Author's Keywords	264
AUTHORS	
Authors	183
Authors of single-authored docs	10
AUTHORS COLLABORATION	
Single-authored docs	10
Co-Authors per Doc	2,71
International co-authorships %	26,39
DOCUMENT TYPES	
article	71
review	1

References

Alawattage, C., Arjaliès, D.-L., Barrett, M., Bernard, J., de Castro Casa Nova, S. P., Cho, C. H., Cooper, C., Denedo, M., D'Astros, C. D., Evans, R., Ejiogu, A., Frieden, L., Ghio, A., McGuigan, N., Luo, Y., Pimentel, E., Powell, L., Navarro Pérez, P. A., Quattrone, P., … Sorola, M. (2021). Opening accounting: A manifesto. *Accounting Forum*, 45(3), 227–246. https://doi.org/10.1080/01559982.2021.1952685.

Al-Shaer, H., & Zaman, M. (2016). Board gender diversity and sustainability reporting quality. *Journal of Contemporary Accounting & Economics, 12*(3), 210–222. https://doi.org/10.1016/j.jcae.2016.09.001

Anderson-Gough, F., Edgley, C., Robson, K., & Sharma, N. (2022). Organizational responses to multiple logics: Diversity, identity and the professional service firm. *Accounting, Organizations and Society, 103*, 101336. https://doi.org/10.1016/j.aos.2022.101336

Anderson-Gough, F., Grey, C., & Robson, K. (2005). "Helping them to forget …": The organizational embedding of gender relations in public audit firms. *Accounting, Organizations and Society, 30*(5), 469–490. https://doi.org/10.1016/j.aos.2004.05.003

Bankins, S., Ocampo, A. C., Marrone, M., Restubog, S. L., & Woo, S. E. (2023). A multilevel review of artificial intelligence in organizations: Implications for organizational behavior research and practice. *Journal of Organizational Behavior*. https://doi.org/10.1002/job.2735

Baudot, L., Kelly, K., & McCullough, A. (2022). Contemporary conflicts in perspectives on work hours across hierarchical levels in public accounting. *The Accounting Review, 97*(6), 67–89. https://doi.org/10.2308/TAR-2020-0106

Bebbington, J., & Unerman, J. (2018). Achieving the United Nations Sustainable Development Goals: An enabling role for accounting research. *Accounting, Auditing & Accountability Journal, 31*(1), 2–24. https://doi.org/10.1108/AAAJ-05-2017-2929

Bigoni, M., & Mohammed, S. (2023). Critique is unsustainable: A polemic. *Critical Perspectives on Accounting, 97*, 102555.

Bigoni, M., & Occhipinti, Z. (2023). Early forms of accounting for sustainable development: The Grand Duchy of Tuscany in the XVI and XVII centuries. CONTABILITÀ E CULTURA AZIENDALE, (2023/2).

Bigoni, M., Lazzini, S., Occhipinti, Z., & Verona, R. (2023). Environmental accounting and state power in the Grand Duchy of Tuscany (1537–1621). *Accounting, Auditing & Accountability Journal, 36*(6), 1503–1528. https://doi.org/10.1108/AAAJ-12-2021-5572

Carnegie, G., Parker, L., & Tsahuridu, E. (2021). It's 2020: What is accounting today? *Australian Accounting Review, 31*(1), 65–73.

Cerchione, R., & Esposito, E. (2016). A systematic review of supply chain knowledge management research: State of the art and research opportunities. *International Journal of Production Economics, 182*, 276–292. https://doi.org/10.1016/j.ijpe.2016.09.006

Charumathi, B., & Rahman, H. (2019). Do women on boards influence climate change disclosures to CDP?—Evidence from large Indian companies. *Australasian Accounting, Business and Finance Journal, 13*(2), 5–31. https://doi.org/10.14453/aabfj.v13i2.2

Ghio, A., Occhipinti, Z., & Verona, R. (2024). The consideration of diversity in the accounting literature: A systematic literature review. European Accounting Review, 33(5), 1667–1691. https://doi.org/10.1080/09638180.2024.2330089

Greenhalgh, T. (1997). How to read a paper: Papers that summarize other papers (systematic reviews and meta-analyses). *BMJ, 315*(7109), 672–675. https://doi.org/10.1136/bmj.315.7109.672

Haynes, K. (2017). Accounting as gendering and gendered: A review of 25 years of critical accounting research on gender. *Critical Perspectives on Accounting, 43*, 110–124. https://doi.org/10.1016/j.cpa.2016.06.004

Hines, R. D. (1988). Financial accounting: In communicating reality, we construct reality. *Accounting, Organizations and Society, 13*(3), 251–261. https://doi.org/10.1016/0361-3682(88)90003-7

Hopwood, A. G. (1987a). Accounting and gender: An introduction. *Accounting, Organizations and Society, 12*(1), 65–69. https://doi.org/10.1016/0361-3682(87)90016-X

Hopwood, A. G. (1987b). The archeology of accounting systems. *Accounting, Organizations and Society, 12*(3), 207–234. https://doi.org/10.1016/0361-3682(87)90038-9

Issa, A., & Hanaysha, J. R. (2023). Breaking the glass ceiling for a sustainable future: The power of women on corporate boards in reducing ESG controversies. *International Journal of Accounting & Information Management, 31*(4), 623–646. https://doi.org/10.1108/IJAIM-03-2023-0053

Issa, A., & Zaid, M. A. A. (2021). Boardroom gender diversity and corporate environmental performance: A multi-theoretical perspective in the MENA region. *International Journal of Accounting & Information Management, 29*(4), 603–630. https://doi.org/10.1108/IJAIM-05-2021-0101

Issa, A., Zaid, M. A. A., Hanaysha, J. R., & Gull, A. A. (2022). An examination of board diversity and corporate social responsibility disclosure: Evidence from banking sector in the Arabian Gulf countries. *International Journal of Accounting & Information Management, 30*(1), 22–46. https://doi.org/10.1108/IJAIM-07-2021-013

Kraus, S., Breier, M., Lim, W. M., et al. (2022). Literature reviews as independent studies: Guidelines for academic practice. *Review of Managerial Science, 16*, 2577–2595. https://doi.org/10.1007/s11846-022-00588-8

Lehman, C., Annisette, M., & Agyemang, G. (2016). Immigration and neoliberalism: Three cases and counter accounts. *Accounting, Auditing & Accountability Journal, 29*(1), 43–79. https://doi.org/10.1108/AAAJ-09-2013-1470

Liao, L., Luo, L., & Tang, Q. (2015). Gender diversity, board independence, Environmental Committee and Greenhouse Gas Disclosure. *The British Accounting Review, 47*(4), 409–424. https://doi.org/10.1016/j.bar.2014.01.002

Manita, R., Bruna, M. G., Dang, R., & Houanti, L. (2018). Board gender diversity and ESG disclosure: Evidence from the USA. *Journal of Applied Accounting Research, 19*(2), 206–224. https://doi.org/10.1108/JAAR-01-2017-0024

Naz, F., et al. (2023). Board gender diversity and the financial performance of Pakistani non-financial firms: A fuzzy-set QCA approach. *Journal of Corporate Accounting & Finance, 34*(2), 258–272. https://doi.org/10.1002/jcaf.22607

Rahi, A. (2024). Unpacking women's power on corporate boards: Gender reward in board composition. *International Journal of Disclosure and Governance*. https://doi.org/10.1057/s41310-024-00228-5

Singh, A. K., Kota, H. B., Sardana, V., & Singhania, S. (2021). Does gender diversity on board promote corporate social responsibility? An empirical analysis of sustainable development goals. *Australasian Accounting, Business and Finance Journal, 15*(5), 22–40. https://doi.org/10.14453/aabfj.v15i5.3

Sobkowiak, M., Cuckston, T., & Thomson, I. (2020). Framing sustainable development challenges: Accounting for SDG-15 in the UK. *Accounting, Auditing and Accountability Journal, 33*(7), 1671–1703. https://doi.org/10.1108/AAAJ-01-2019-3810

Thomson, I., Grubnic, S., & Georgakopoulos, G. (2014). Exploring accounting sustainability hybridisation in the UK public sector. *Accounting, Organizations and Society, 39*(6), 453–476. https://doi.org/10.1016/j.aos.2014.02.003

Zampone, G., Nicolò, G., Sannino, G., & De Iorio, S. (2024). Gender diversity and SDG disclosure: The mediating role of the sustainability committee. *Journal of Applied Accounting Research, 25*(1), 171–193. https://doi.org/10.1108/JAAR-06-2022-0151

Queer Dimensions and Other Diversities: Valorization and Positive Language Within Organizations

Katia Giuseppponi

1 Introduction

Individual, organizational, and social benefits achievable through diversity inclusion are emphasized by many authors (Ely & Thomas, 2001; Page, 2007; Mor Barak, 2011; Shore et al., 2011, among others). However, the slow progress of organizations in this direction remains evident, and a need for cultural evolution to bridge the gap between the rhetoric and concreteness of inclusion clearly emerges (Shore et al., 2011; Nkomo, 2013; Barak et al., 2016). Recurrent "exclusionary dynamics" are observed (Bernstein et al., 2020:395); these are often automatisms not easy to deactivate, arising from assumptions that form a ground for practices geared de facto toward excluding who is different (Bernstein et al., 2020; Nkomo, 2013; Schein, 1990; Argyris & Schön, 1974). Calls for research widely emerge in literature (Shore et al., 2011; Mor Barak et al., 2016; Shore et al., 2018; Adamson et al., 2021), and the importance of broadening research horizons strongly emerges with specific reference to the diversity of sexual orientation and gender identity (Ng & Rumens, 2017; Burchiellaro, 2021, among others).

Within this framework, the perspective of language use offers important insights for understanding approaches to inclusion. Perales et al. (2022) discussed the positive impact of inclusive language on people's sense of organizational belonging and well-being. In Zimman, language represents a crucial context of delegitimization or affirmation of identities depending on its marginalizing or constructive direction (2017:101–102). From the educational perspective, Nemi Neto saw the consistency of language as a necessary foundation for inclusive orientations (2018:601); Knisely

K. Giuseppponi (✉)
Department of Education, Cultural Heritage and Tourism, University of Macerata, Macerata, Italy
e-mail: katia.giuseppponi@unimc.it

M. Agostini et al. (eds.), *Diversity and Equity in Accounting*, SIDREA Series in Accounting and Business Administration,
https://doi.org/10.1007/978-3-031-78247-3_11

and Paiz emphasized the importance of fostering a critical approach that allows for the conscious deconstruction of pre-constituted schemas (2021:39); Carlson argued that an evolved and democratic educational system should go beyond categories of diversity to truly support the development of identities (1998:114). However, normativity is seen as pervasive, and language is considered always at risk of stereotyping. With respect to issues of diversity in sexual orientation and gender identity, some interesting studies highlight such risks with attention to media, work environments, and social contexts (Hall et al., 2019; Calder, 2020; Leap, 2015; Motschenbacher & Stegu, 2013; DeSouza et al., 2017).

Nevertheless, this field of research is in its early stages and offers countless areas yet to be explored in both private (profit and nonprofit) and public organizations. Particularly significant among these areas is the one concerning the language used and the reality outlined by those who have successfully proposed themselves as administrators of a municipality, thus as representatives of the community. Actually, no studies emerge on the mandate programs of incumbent mayors in the perspective of analysis considered here. The content of such programs is of huge interest because it can be observed as a megaphone of widespread thinking and feeling (read through the administrator's lens) and studied to understand the terrain of inclusion. With an exploratory approach, this work is therefore conceived to help bridge the gap observed and, welcoming the multiple calls for research, participate in the advancement of knowledge on language use from an inclusive and valorizing perspective of diversity of sexual orientation and gender identity.

The mandate programs of mayors of a sample of Italian municipalities, representing more than 20% of Italian residents, are analyzed to extract and discuss references to LGBTQ+ and fluid dimensions. The main results reveal that while gender dimensions in a binary perspective are referred to in the vast majority of the cases observed, the use of terms expressive of sexual orientation diversity is much less common. For instance, references to LGBT* spheres are present in only 24% of cases and to non-binary dimensions in only 6%. Furthermore, queer and fluid dimensions are lacking. A use of words mainly highlighting an anti-discriminatory orientation also emerges. These results cannot be interpreted in terms of the absence of sensitivity but have to be contextualized as expressing a lack of explicit and valorizing orientation toward the dimensions here considered. To include the reference to different perspectives in understanding the outcomes of the qualitative content analysis of the mandate programs and formulating possible responses, a group of experts in the field of diversity enhancement is involved through interviews.

Based on the observed emblematic context, this work highlights gaps in the expression of diversity and analyzes obstacles that limit openness—often merely declined in an anti-discriminatory sphere—and inhibit the richness of full inclusion. Furthermore, the study proposes a framework of actions to encourage valorizing approaches in attitudes and language within public and private organizations. The prospect is to extend openness to the valorization of plurality, with favorable implications in terms of higher inclusiveness in management and accounting research, effectiveness and attitude to involvement in organizational governance, and individual and social well-being.

2 Variety, Queerness, and Visibility: The Role of Language

Widely unexplored is the potential for well-being and value—regarding individuals, organizations, and societies—related to the awareness of human chaos and the ability to move through it without artificial categories. The queer approach is understood here in a broad sense, as an approach that valorizes human chaos and freedom of being and that prescinds from categories derived from social constructs and often from confusions between performing and being in defining people's identities, as pointed out by Butler (1990). Queer dimensions—in different contexts of life—are often read as "anti" and "non" dimensions, that is, dimensions of rupture. However, queer dimensions have a deeply "pro" root (particularly pro a person's self-determination and freedom to be) and possess a constructively disorienting perspective, as highlighted by Ahmed (2006). In a broad sense, the queer perspective derives from the choice to observe reality with a non-normative approach (Motschenbacher & Stegu, 2013:520; Rumens et al., 2019:594; Ghio et al., 2021:235).

Variety—as a source of value—cannot be lacking in language if it is to represent reality and help shape it positively, toward higher and more widespread levels of awareness. This is true in all contexts of society and with reference to all human profiles, outward and inward, of thought, faith, attitude, experience, sexual orientation, and gender identity. This is also true in the disciplines of management and accounting and in every business organizational context. However, broad limitations have been observed in these disciplines regarding attention to LGBTQI+ perspectives (Rumens, 2016; Burrell, 1987; Bendl et al., 2008). Reflecting the variety of existences through the use of language means helping to make variety visible and habitual so that everyone feels not only welcomed but also fully at home; in other words, so that no one feels "out of time" or "out of place" (Ahmed, 2006:13). In this sense, the queer perspective finds natural terrain in the analysis of language and discourse, as queer linguistics (Motschenbacher, 2011; Leap & Motschenbacher, 2012).

3 Exploring the Approach to Queer Dimensions in Language: An Investigation into the Mandate Programs of Incumbent Mayors

To appreciate the habituality of the approach to diversity and variety within language, this work observes the context of public organizations—given the huge scope of their impact—with a specific focus on the mandate programs of incumbent mayors in a sample of Italian municipalities. These programs were studied to extract specific references to LGBTQ+ and fluidity dimensions. It should be emphasized that the content of mandate programs was analyzed as a mirror, a megaphone of widespread thinking and feeling, and was in no way subjected to political analysis or evaluations concerning individual politicians' directions. The content was studied solely as an indicator of widespread perceptions that found indirect expression through the political representative (indirect economic subject).

The logical basis for this choice lies in the reference to pragmalinguistics, which studies language in relation to the environment, considering language as a system of real action constructed by the actor for its recipients. From this perspective, if it is true that context is essential for understanding language, it is also true that the linguistic factors used provide important cognitive elements for understanding the target context (Morris, 1938; Levinson, 1983). In public contexts, to which we refer here, we can study the use of a language inspired by the search for legitimization, support, and consensus, matching the interests of audiences of citizens (Cap, 2008). The reference to queer dimensions within the mandate programs was therefore considered an indirect indicator of the habituality and widespread attitudes of the citizen communities regarding these dimensions, that is, an (imperfect) reflection of common feeling.

4 Methodological Framework and Investigation Process

A qualitative approach was adopted in the analysis, as it is consistent with the fields of exploratory research concerning contexts that do not have defined boundaries (Yin, 1994; Nickols, 2000). This approach concerned both the contents of the mandate programs of mayors of a sample of Italian municipalities, as available online in May 2023, and the contents expressed by the experts interviewed on the topic between May and July 2023. The qualitative content analysis was carried out through the collection of resources, the organization of the same with the identification and use of relevant coding frames, and the extraction of meanings based on the study of relationships and concordances (Schreier, 2012; Khan & VanWynsberghe, 2008).

The sample of municipalities includes 33 cities: all Italian cities with more than 150,000 residents (25) and all regional capitals independent of their size (Table 1). To appreciate the significance of this sample, consider that overall the reference population is 11,975,040 residents, 20.35% of the 58 million and 851 thousand residents in Italy according to provisional ISTAT data as of January 1, 2023 (ISTAT, 2023b; Tuttitalia.it, 2023). All geographic areas of the country are represented: there are 16 northern cities with a total of 5,260,094 residents, 43.93% of the sample residents; five central cities with 3,564,879 residents, 29.77%; and 12 southern cities with 3,150,067 residents, 26.31% (ISTAT, 2023a). Consider that the results are never associated with specific mayors or cities and that the order in which the municipalities of reference are listed in Table 3, Figs. 1, 2, and Graph 1 is neither alphabetical nor by size.

The experts involved are people who, within their activities, have been able to develop reflections and share experiences on the topics of inclusion,

Table 1 The Italian municipalities in the sample

Municipality	Population residents
1. Roma	2,748,109
2. Milano	1,354,196
3. Napoli	913,462
4. Torino	841,600
5. Palermo	630,167
6. Genova	558,745
7. Bologna	387,971
8. Firenze	360,930
9. Bari	316,015
10. Catania	298,762
11. Verona	255,588
12. Venezia	250,369
13. Messina	218,786
14. Padova	206,496
15. Trieste	198,417
16. Parma	196,764
17. Brescia	196,446
18. Prato	195,736
19. Taranto	188,098
20. Modena	184,153
21. Reggio Calabria	170,951
22. Reggio Emilia	169,545
23. Perugia	161,748
24. Ravenna	155,751
25. Livorno	152,914
26. Cagliari	148,117
27. Trento	118,046
28. Ancona	98,356
29. Catanzaro	84,670
30. L'Aquila	69,558
31. Potenza	64,406
32. Campobasso	47,075
33. Aosta	33,093

Source: ISTAT (2023b); Tuttitalia.it (2023). Access: May 1, 2023

intersectionality, and sexual orientation (Table 2). A purposeful sampling was carried out based on a direct evaluation of the evidence of competence expressed in the context under consideration (Fazey et al., 2006; Krueger et al., 2012). All interviews (each lasting 20–25 min) were conducted by telephone directly by the author. The opinions of the experts were acquired with respect to the main evidence emerging from the analysis of the mandate programs and the widespread perceptions that these reflected. The contents of the interviews were analyzed to better interpret the theme, especially in its evolutionary perspectives. To ensure anonymity, experts are only referred to by their initials.

Frequency and concordance analysis and interpretation of linguistic contexts covered both the corpus of mandate programs (33 files for 533,779 tokens) and the corpus of interviews (11 files for 1464 tokens). In particular, the search for references to specific content was conducted by analyzing the corpora through the AntConc software, developed by Laurence Anthony (2022). Before proceeding with the analysis, a check was made on the software's access to all mandate documents in the relevant corpus. For four PDF documents related to mandate programs, a conversion to Word was necessary. All findings were checked by the author through direct textual analysis, verifying their relevance to what was studied, with respect to sexual orientation and gender identity. For example, with respect to Fluid*, findings related to traffic fluency or management were excluded. Frequencies and concordances were then analyzed to understand the ways and contexts of terms used and thus extract meanings.

5 Discussion of the Findings of the Investigation on the Mandate Programs

The study was developed with attention to the use, recurrence, and contextualization of certain relevant terms in the representation of sexual orientation and gender identity. The selection made here includes central terms in this perspective but can only be considered a contribution to an area of research that certainly requires the convergence of further efforts, also through reflections on the use of other elements of language and additional terminological nuances. KWIC (key-word-in-context) concordance analyses were developed for the words considered here, yielding the results highlighted below. Reference is to the original terms, researched in Italian-language mandate programs, for which a translation is provided here.

From the analysis on the *LGBT** root (a nodal term for the issues addressed here), 25 pieces of evidence emerge that relate to the mandate programs of the incumbent mayors of eight municipalities out of the 33 analyzed, about one in four (Table 3). Concordance analysis shows that the *LGBT** dimensions and related extensions are linked to indications of *comunità* [community] (eight cases), *persone* [people] (six), *associazioni* [associations] (one), *mondo* [world] (one), *istanze* [instances] (one), *organizzazioni* [organizations] (one), *tematiche* [themes] (two), *temi* [themes] (one), *cultura* [culture] (one), *questioni* [matters] (one), and not applicable (two). Analytical reference to concordances reveals the important connection with ideas of protection in favor of spaces, rights, spheres, and sensitivities and against discrimination and homotransphobia. In general, a broadly focused perspective on the important issue of protection emerges; however, an approach to enhancement (in debates, plural decision-making, stakeholder engagement, and so on) does not emerge. There is no shortage of interesting perspectives, for example, in terms of attention to *LGBT** culture, but a prevention orientation remains largely prevalent.

Absent are references to *Queer* and *Fluid**. More specifically, the reference to *Queer* does not appear at all, while the reference to *Fluid** is present but never relevant to the themes discussed here, as revealed by the author's direct analysis of context. Very limited are the references to *Intersezion** [Intersection*], *Stereotip** [Stereotyp*], and *Non-binari** [Non-binary]. In particular, *Intersezion** recurs pertinently with the dimensions considered here in only two instances (concerning two mandate programs), among the total five observed instances. *Stereotip** has three relevant recurrences (across two programs) among the total 18. For *Non-binari**, there are two pieces of evidence, both relevant (concerning two programs).

To also be considered limited, but less rare than seen above, are references to *Fobi** [Phobi*] and *Sessual** [Sexual*]. Specifically, ten relevant pieces of evidence are linked to the *Fobi** root (among the total 11). These evidences concern seven mandate programs, one in five indicatively. With respect to *Sessual**, 23 pieces of evidence (among the total 32) are relevant to the topic discussed here. These evidences concern 11 programs, thus one in three programs, although in some cases the reference is only hinted at. The terms here discussed, together with the nodal term *LGBT**, are certainly less distant than the terms treated in the previous points that reflect dimensions which are not usual (*Intersezion**, *Stereotip**, *Non-binari**) or altogether left out (*Queer*, *Fluid**). However, it should still be considered that, overall, a minority of the mandate programs show the reference to *Fobi**, *Sessual**, or *LGBT** (13 programs out of 33).

More intense, but still confined to a minority of mandate programs, is the reference to discrimination in a manner relevant to the topics discussed here. Relevant occurrences of *Discrimina** are 67 (among the total 93) and concern 14 programs (42.42%). The terms of discrimination turn out to be associated with the words *genere*, *violenza*, *sessuale*, *razzismo*, *stereotipi*, and *orientamento* [gender, violence, sexual, racism, stereotypes, orientation] and with reflections on the need to fight and counter, in a struggle for prevention and rights. More widespread among the programs is the theme of *Diversità/Diversity* (92 pieces of evidence across 23 programs) which, however, appears to be predominantly projected on environmental perspectives and biodiversity, according to what emerges from the textual investigation and the context analysis (in connection with themes of conservation, protection, valorization). Some interesting examples of positive language and approaches with reference to human and social diversity as a resource, as a source of wealth for the community, also emerge.

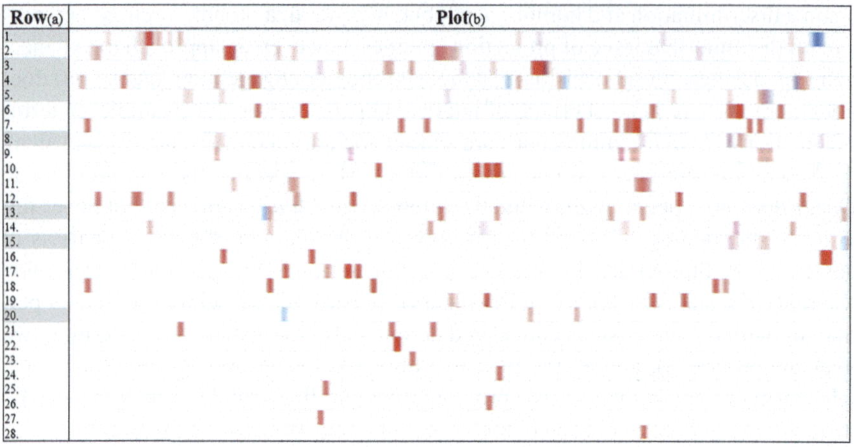

Fig. 1 Concordance plot: *Generi/i*, *Gender*, and *LGBT**. (*Software*: Anthony, L. (2022), *AntConc (Version 4.2.0)*. (**a**) The eight *LGBT**-referenced programs are distinguished in gray. (**b**) *Genere/i* and *Gender* in red scale, *LGBT** in blue)

Highly significant is the comparison between the reference to *LGBT** and the reference to *Genere/i* or *Gender* (in a binary approach). Consider that the term *Genere/i* is relevant in 230 cases (among the total 241) across 28 programs; the term *Gender* has a frequency of 12 across five of these programs. Overall, the reference to *Genere/i* or *Gender* recurs in 242 valid cases across 28 programs (84.85%) with an average of 8.64 occurrences, confirming the known familiarity with respect to the topic in the public debate. Comparison with the frequency and distribution of the *LGBT** root reveals two very distant perspectives. The concordance plot (Fig. 1) clearly shows the different distribution. The habituality of gender discourse is clear versus the very limited and certainly unaccustomed LGBT* reference.

In Fig. 2 and Graph 1, the picture of a language that largely flows toward dimensions of gender understood in a normative sense while minimally incorporating themes related to non-normative dimensions of sexual orientation and gender identity is evident. As noted in the introduction, these findings do not have to be read as an expression of absence of attention, but as evidence of a widespread gap in valorizing approaches to diversity. These findings highlight the impact of normativity on language—therefore on the representation of reality—adding a new perspective, relevant to managers and organizations, which reinforces what is evidenced in studies based on different resources and developed with different focuses (particularly: Hall et al., 2019; Calder, 2020; Leap, 2015; Motschenbacher & Stegu, 2013; DeSouza et al., 2017).

Municipalities	Queer	Fluid*	Intersezion*	Stereotip*	Non-binari*	Fobi*	LGBT*	Sessual*	Discrimin*	Genere+ Generi+ Gender(a)
a				2		2	3	2	15	21
b			1		1	1	2	3	8	12
c			1			2	15		8	28
d				1		1	1	3	4	28
e							1	4	5	7
f							1		2	9
g							1	2	2	6
h							1	1	3	2
i						1		1	3	8
j					1	2		2	4	6
k						1		2	5	8
l								1	3	2
m									1	5
n										5
o								2	4	12
p										4
q										8
r										35
s										9
t										13
u										5
v										3
w										1
x										1
y										1
z										1
aa										1
bb										1
cc										
dd										
ee										
ff										
gg										
total evidences	0	0	2	3	2	10	25	23	67	242
total programs	0	0	2	2	2	7	8	11	14	28
% programs with evidence	0.00%	0.00%	6.06%	6.06%	6.06%	21.21%	24.24%	33.33%	42.42%	84.85%
average of evidences			1.00	1.50	1.00	1.43	3.13	2.09	4.79	8.64
max			1	2	1	2	15	4	15	35
min			1	1	1	1	1	1	1	1
mode			1	#N/D	1	1	1	2	4	1
median			1	1,5	1	1	1	2	4	6
standard deviation			0.00	0.71	0.00	0.53	4.85	0.94	3.58	9.00

Fig. 2 Keyword reference: overview. (*Software*: Anthony, L. (2022), *AntConc (Version 4.2.0)*. (**a**) [Queer; Fluid; Intersection*; Stereotyp*; Non-binary; Phobi*; LGBT*; Sexual*; Discrimin*; Gender])

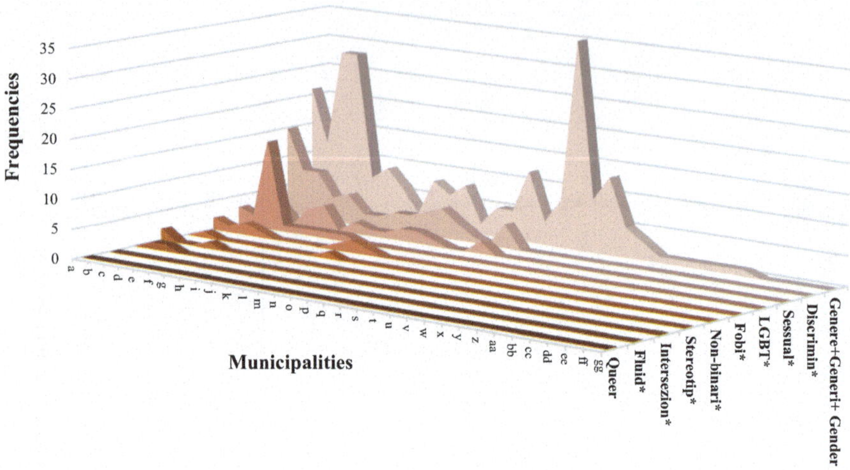

Graph 1 Keyword reference: overview

Table 2 Experts interviewed

Experts	Cited here as
– A psychologist and psychotherapist, expert in developmental and educational psychology	PN
– A pedagogist, psychologist, and psychotherapist, expert in pedagogical epistemology	MC
– A PhD student, member of the National Conference of Equality Bodies of Italian Universities	NI
– An executive director and strategic advisor	EF
– A co-founder of a cultural organization and art director	FB
– A scholar of empowerment and gender equality policies	SG
– A professor of private law and of private law and differences, expert in gender policies	IC
– A senior HR consultant and company coach	MCa
– A finance and planning advisor	SA
– An entrepreneur and consultant on sustainability and innovation	SD
– An account and business development director, member of the D&I Global Council	PA

Table 3 LGBT*: key-word-in-context

Row	FileTokens	Freq	NormFreq	Dispersion
1	32057	3	93,583	0.491
2	15116	2	132,310	0.333
3	47993	15	312,546	0.000
4	8286	1	120,685	0.000
5	40381	1	24,764	0.000
6	25074	1	39,882	0.000
7	35276	1	28,348	0.000
8	14432	1	69,290	0.000

Software: Anthony, L. (2022), *AntConc (Version 4.2.0)*

6 Discussion of Evidence and Meanings That Emerged from the Interviews

From the qualitative content analysis on the expert interviews, focuses of attention emerged concerning three main areas: language *(Linguagg*)*, diversity and differences *(Divers*/Differ*)*, and evolutionary design from the perspective of inclusion as a convergent system of culture, knowledge, training, education, valorization, sharing, awareness, and equality (*Cultur**, *Conosc**, *Forma**, *Educ**, *Valor**, *Condiv**, *Consapevol**, *Ugua**). Italian word roots used within the research are indicated in brackets.

The theme of inclusive language *(Linguagg**), in general, was brought to the attention of the experts in the introduction to the interview, with a brief presentation of the findings from the analysis of the mandate programs. From the KWIC analysis and the author's direct analysis, it emerges how this theme was explored in depth by the experts, emphasizing its relevance as a central tool and a determining context for giving visibility, spreading knowledge and culture, enabling understanding, fostering sharing, and overcoming fears. In particular, experts highlight that language has a fundamental impact on people's well-being and the balance of organizations and therefore needs to be carefully attended to. Nevertheless, it often encompasses stereotypes which are fed seamlessly. Bad habits that need to be overcome are discussed, including in the area of language. It is noted that language which ensures space for all is especially necessary in the current stage of development of perceptions of differences in sexual orientation and gender. "Care must be taken to give evidence, to give visibility. Distinguishing belongs to a stage of understanding" (NI). "The sharing of studies and language is needed, to spread knowledge and awareness" (PN). However, the reference to normativity is strong, generating "the fear of not being 'normal', and language reflects this fear" (MC). "We need to work for freedoms and make the languages that express the recognition of freedoms habitual" (SD). The translations of the contents expressed by the experts and here reported are by the author.

Through the discussion on language, the experts delved into the analysis of the reality to be represented by language: specifically, into the analysis of diversity and differences *(Divers*/Differ*)*, with their value and right to be, versus the formality of inclusive forms that often remain only on the surface. "It's about dimensions of diversity that touch deep chords, that are unseen, that lead others to almost want to defend themselves for fear of what is unknown. Spreading knowledge is crucial" (FB). The importance of encouraging everyone to explain and share the dimensions of diversity they experience so that other people can understand is highlighted. "We all carry diversities. We must work both to understand and value those of others and to make others understand and appreciate our own" (SA) by overcoming "the fear of being labeled that talking about our peculiarities brings" (MCa). However, in order to enable richer and broader perspectives, it is necessary to bridge wide gaps in the attitude of valorizing diversity. "There is an emphasis on equality but not one that takes diversity into account. [...] we still do not understand how added value can arise from difference, we fail to overcome patterns and then equality becomes only appearance" (SG).

The need for change is strongly expressed by the experts, toward an evolutionary plan represented as a convergent system of culture, knowledge, training, education, valorization, sharing, awareness, and equality *(Cultur*, Conosc*, Forma*, Educ*, Valor*, Condiv*, Consapevol*, Ugua*)*. "It is necessary to distinguish in order to understand, in order to evolve and no longer need to distinguish" (NI). Nonetheless, overall, experts observe confusion regarding different sexual orientations and gender identities, also on the part of organizations: "on the one hand we avoid talking about it, on the other we abuse the topic to obtain consensus. We need to talk about it naturally, without excesses" (EF). Furthermore, it is noted that there is a lack of studies that enhance the strengths of these differences "we talk about them by default, we don't have enough positive references to understand" (PN). "Distinguishing and talking about differences is important to stop talking about them" (IC). "There is a need to go into organizations and schools to raise awareness, adopting different modalities based on the target audience. Alliances need to be developed" (PA). The importance of being spontaneously inclusive toward others, on the one hand, and of always being able to count on the openness of others to our peculiarities, on the other, is widely reiterated. However, achieving this openness "needs internal communication and training" (MCa). The evolutionary plan that emerges is based on education to respect and recognize freedoms in all dimensions of being, acting, thinking, and believing, including sexual orientation and gender identity. Even today, this must not be taken for granted. "The social construct is very strong in directing what is appropriate and what is not, and the value of dialogue is often tainted by this aspect" (SD).

Dimensions of training, education, and sharing are discussed by experts as foundations for advancing culture and spreading awareness of the variety of human profiles. Approaches emerge that are consistent with evolutionary visions expressed in literature (Nkomo, 2013; Barak et al., 2016; Shore et al., 2018, among others). Care for inclusive language is seen as an integral part of this path, since language is considered a key systemic tool to highlight and eradicate the assumptions underlying exclusionary behaviors (behaviors evidenced by Bernstein et al., 2020; Nkomo,

Experts interviewed	Linguagg*	Divers* + Differ*	Cultur*	Conosc*	Forma*	Valor*	Condiv*	Consapevol*	Ugua*	Educ* (a)
1	1			1			1			1
2	1		2					1		
3	4	1			2				1	
4	1	1		1			2			
5	1	1	1	2						
6	2	4				4			4	
7	1	2	1		1					
8	1	1			1			1		
9	1	3	1			2	1	1		
10	1			2	1	1				2
11	2	1	2		1		1	1		1
Total evidences	16	14	7	6	6	7	5	4	5	4

Fig. 3 Thematic focuses expressed by the experts: overview. (*Software*: Anthony, L. (2022), *AntConc (Version 4.2.0)*. (**a**) [Languag*; Divers* + Differ*; Cultur*; Know*; Train*; Valoriz*; Shar*; Aware*; Equal*; Educat*])

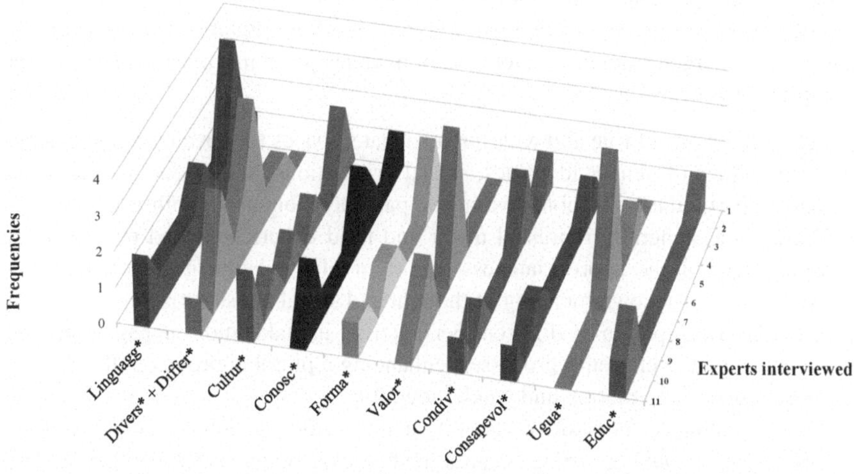

Graph 2 Thematic focuses expressed by the experts: overview

2013; Argyris & Schön, 1974; Schein, 1990, among others). The interpretative key offered by the experts—undoubtedly that of a call to action—highlights a ferment to be made extensive by understanding and removing barriers to inclusion in organizations and societies. In Fig. 3 and Graph 2, the experts' focuses are represented in an overall picture.

7 Conclusion on the Recognition of Hindering Factors and the Definition of a Possible Agenda

Important and deep-rooted hindering factors emerge, factors that prevent openness or limit it to an anti-discriminatory sphere, thus inhibiting the systemic value of full inclusion. These are specifically:

- Knowledge gap regarding queer and fluid dimensions;
- Uncertainties and fears about the perception of these dimensions by the majority of stakeholders (uncertainties and fears that lead to limiting the individual's exposure);
- Entrenched fear of diversity.

Actions are needed, within public and private organizations, to encourage valorizing approaches in attitudes and language. The prospect is to extend openness to the appreciation of the richness of plurality, also through the diffusion of a positive language that sweeps away negative expressions unfortunately still present in organizations and that need to be countered without compromise, since language also directs reality. Giving visibility to diversity is a fundamental element, but certainly not to be confused with full inclusion which always presupposes a profoundly valorizing approach, as effectively underlined by Roberson (2006).

With respect to the *knowledge gap* of queer and fluid dimensions, based on the results that emerged from the exploration of mandate programs and the involvement of experts, it is necessary to:

- Create moments of true and widespread debate, spaces for developing awareness on the issues of gender identities, sexual orientations, and freedoms (moments that are particularly valuable in strategic pathways for sustainability);
- Narrate and generally represent queer and fluid experiences and perspectives, taking care of the appropriateness and rigor of the language, because every expression has its own meaning of thought and social construct;
- Seek the participation of different perspectives in stakeholder engagement and organizational well-being processes, enhancing a plural approach in the discussion on sexual orientation and gender identity;
- Foster an alliance for positive visibility and evolution of culture and awareness; this alliance should be strong because the brake on change is strong; it should be kept in mind that homosexuality is still considered a crime in some places in the world and that until 1973 it was included as a diagnosis in the Diagnostic and Statistical Manual of Mental Disorders of the American Psychiatric Association (Drescher, 2015).

With reference to *uncertainties and fears regarding the perception* of queer and fluid dimensions by the majority of stakeholders, it is important to:

- Take first steps, inspiring also by the example of rigorous empathy-based language, language that never labels or contains false humor but always derives from a careful evaluation of the effects on the recipients, to avoid, as highlighted by the Linguistic Society of America, stereotypes and manners that cause marginalization and exclusion (LSA, 2016);
- Dismantle the rhetoric of "I would, but…" by taking on the responsibility for participating in the common discourse, individually and as members of organizations, and demonstrating that it is possible (Thein, 2013:172–174).

Regarding the deep-rooted *fear of diversity*, it is strategic:

- To speak, to represent, insisting until diversity becomes familiar, because non-normativity is scary as long as it is perceived as an element extraneous to the usual scenario;
- To facilitate the spread of the attitude to change and the ability to grasp the positive aspects of the new against a status quo that penalizes everyone;
- To facilitate the paths of people who face radical changes in life, at all levels, supporting, speaking out, and creating plural value based on their experiences and testimonies.

As highlighted by Boje et al. (2004), organizations and organizational processes can be observed as phenomena *in* and *of* language, not as independent and detached from it. Indeed, in speaking, individuals express their representation of the organization, and through speaking, they influence others' perceptions of the organization. As we have noted and discussed here, when a part of reality does not find space in language, dimensions of invisibility and extraneousness are fueled with complex impacts. Exclusion operated through language is reflected in visions, interpretations, and actions. Much has been said, for instance, about the impact of dimensions of invisibility in school textbooks (among others, Goldstein, 2015). It is imperative to enrich language codes and broaden the boundaries of the communities that recognize themselves in them, that is, *speech communities*, in the meaning of Barrett (1997), with the awareness that even simple changes in words have large-scale impacts (Tavits & Pérez, 2019:16786). The evolutionary path outlined here necessarily also requires the dissemination of positive language, valorizing diversity, for visibility that does not overlap with normativity. This work represents only a contribution. There is an urgent need for continuous engagement, plural research, and expanded debate on these issues, too often seen as minor precisely because they are alternatives to the norm.

References

Adamson, M., Kelan, E., Lewis, P., Śliwa, M., & Rumens, N. (2021). Introduction: Critically interrogating inclusion in organisations. *Organization, 28*(2), 211–227.

Ahmed, S. (2006). *Queer phenomenology: Orientations, objects*. Duke University Press.

Anthony, L. (2022). *AntConc (Version 4.2.0) [Computer Software]*. Waseda University. Available from https://www.laurenceanthony.net/software.html

Argyris, M., & Schön, D. (1974). *Theory in practice. Increasing professional effectiveness*. Jossey-Bass.

Barak, M. E. M., Findler, L., & Wind, L. H. (2016). Diversity, inclusion, and commitment in organizations: International empirical explorations. *Journal of Behavioral and Applied Management, 2*(2).

Barrett, R. (1997). The "homo-genius" speech community. In Livia & Hall (Eds.), *Queerly phrased: Language, gender, and sexuality* (pp. 181–201). Oxford University Press.

Bendl, R., Fleischmann, A., & Walenta, C. (2008). Diversity management discourse meets queer theory. *Gender in Management: An International Journal, 23*(6), 382–394.

Bernstein, R. S., Bulger, M., Salipante, P., & Weisinger, J. Y. (2020). From diversity to inclusion to equity: A theory of generative interactions. *Journal of Business Ethics, 167*, 395–410.

Boje, D. M., Oswick, C., & Ford, J. D. (2004). Language and organization: The doing of discourse. *Academy of Management Review, 29*(4), 571–577.

Burchiellaro, O. (2021). Queering control and inclusion in the contemporary organization: On 'LGBT-friendly control' and the reproduction of (queer) value. *Organization Studies, 42*(5), 761–785.

Burrell, G. (1987). No accounting for sexuality. *Accounting Organisations and Society, 12*(1), 89–101.

Butler, J. (1990). *Gender trouble: Feminism and the subversion of identity*. Routledge.

Calder, J. (2020). Language, gender and sexuality in 2019: Interrogating normativities in the field. *Gender & Language, 14*(4).

Cap, P. (2008). Towards the proximization model of the analysis of legitimization in political discourse. *Journal of Pragmatics, 40*(1), 17–41.

Carlson, D. (1998). Who am I? Gay identity and democratic politics of the self. In Pinar (Ed.), *Queer theory in education* (pp. 107–120). Lawrence Erlbaum Associates.

DeSouza, E. R., Wesselmann, E. D., & Ispas, D. (2017). Workplace discrimination against sexual minorities: Subtle and not-so-subtle. *Canadian Journal of Administrative Sciences, 34*(2), 121–132.

Drescher, J. (2015). Out of DSM: Depathologizing homosexuality. *Behavioral Sciences, 5*(4), 565–575.

Ely, R. J., & Thomas, D. A. (2001). Cultural diversity at work: The effects of diversity perspectives on work group processes and outcomes. *Administrative Science Quarterly, 46*(2), 229–273.

Fazey, I., Fazey, J. A., Salisbury, J. G., Lindenmayer, D. B., & Dovers, S. (2006). The nature and role of experiential knowledge for environmental conservation. *Environmental Conservation, 33*(1), 1–10.

Ghio, A., McGuigan, N., & Powell, L. (2021). Queer accounting. In A. Alawattage, B. Barrett, C. de Castro Casa Nova, et al. (Eds.), *Opening accounting: A manifesto* (Vol. 45, pp. 227–246). Accounting Forum.

Goldstein, B. (2015). LGBT invisibility in language learning materials. *Language Issues, 26*(2), 35–40.

Hall, K., Levon, E., & Milani, T. M. (2019). Navigating normativities: Gender and sexuality in text and talk. *Language in Society, 48*(4), 481–489.

ISTAT – Istituto Nazionale di Statistica. (2023a). Demographic indicators, 7th April 2023, https://www.istat.it/it/files/2023/04/indicatori-anno-2022.pdf.

ISTAT – Istituto Nazionale di Statistica. (2023b). *Population and households*, https://www.istat.it/en/population-and-households?data-and-indicators.

Khan, S., & VanWynsberghe, R. (2008). Cultivating the under-mined: Cross-case analysis as knowledge mobilization. *Forum: Qualitative Social Research, 9*(1), 34.

Knisely, K. A., & Paiz, J. M. (2021). Bringing trans, non-binary, and queer understandings to bear in language education. *Critical Multilingualism Studies, 9*(1), 23–45.

Krueger, T., Page, T., Hubacek, K., Smith, L., & Hiscock, K. (2012). The role of expert opinion in environmental modelling. *Environmental Modelling & Software, 36*, 4–18.

Leap, W. L. (2015). Queer linguistics as critical discourse analysis. In H. Tannen & Schiffrin (Eds.), *The handbook of discourse analysis* (pp. 661–680). Wiley Blackwell.

Leap, W. L., & Motschenbacher, H. (2012). Launching a new phase in language and sexuality studies. *Journal of Language and Sexuality, 1*(1), 1–14.

Levinson, S. C. (1983). *Pragmatics*. Cambridge University Press.

LSA – Linguistic Society of America. (2016). *Guidelines for inclusive language*. https://www.linguisticsociety.org/resource/guidelines-inclusive-language.

Mor Barak, M. E. (2011). *Managing diversity: Toward a globally inclusive workplace* (2nd ed.). Sage.

Mor Barak, M. E., Lizano, E. L., Kim, A., Duan, L., Rhee, M. K., Hsiao, H. Y., & Brimhall, K. C. (2016). The promise of diversity management for climate of inclusion: A state-of-the-art review and meta-analysis. *Human Service Organizations: Management, Leadership & Governance, 40*(4), 305–333.

Morris, C. W. (1938). *Foundations of the theory of signs. International encyclopedia of unified science* (pp. 1–59). Chicago University Press.
Motschenbacher, H. (2011). Taking queer linguistics further: Sociolinguistics and critical heteronormativity research. *International Journal of the Sociology of Language*, 149–179.
Motschenbacher, H., & Stegu, M. (2013). Queer linguistic approaches to discourse. *Discourse & Society, 24*(5), 519–535.
Nemi Neto, J. (2018). Queer pedagogy: Approaches to inclusive teaching. *Policy Futures in Education, 16*(5), 589–604.
Ng, E. S., & Rumens, N. (2017). Diversity and inclusion for LGBT workers: Current issues and new horizons for research. *Canadian Journal of Administrative Sciences, 34*(2), 109–120.
Nickols, F. (2000). The tacit and explicit nature of knowledge: The knowledge in knowledge management. In Woods & Cortada (Eds.), *The knowledge management yearbook 2000–2001* (pp. 12–21). Butterworth-Heinemann.
Nkomo, S. M. (2013). Inclusion: Old wine in new bottles? In Ferdman & Deane (Eds.), *Diversity at work: The practice of inclusion* (pp. 580–592). Jossey-Bass.
Page, S. E. (2007). Making the difference: Applying a logic of diversity. *Academy of Management Perspectives, 21*(4), 6–20.
Perales, F., Ablaza, C., & Elkin, N. (2022). Exposure to inclusive language and well-being at work among transgender employees in Australia, 2020. *American Journal of Public Health, 112*(3), 482–490.
Roberson, Q. M. (2006). Disentangling the meanings of diversity and inclusion in organizations. *Group & Organization Management, 31*(2), 212–236.
Rumens, N. (2016). Sexualities and accounting: A queer theory perspective. *Critical Perspectives on Accounting, 35*, 111–120.
Rumens, N., De Souza, E. M., & Brewis, J. (2019). Queering queer theory in management and organization studies: Notes toward queering heterosexuality. *Organization Studies, 40*(4), 593–612.
Schein, E. H. (1990). Organizational culture. *American Psychologist, 45*(2), 109–119.
Schreier, M. (2012). *Qualitative content analysis in practice*. Sage.
Shore, L. M., Cleveland, J. N., & Sanchez, D. (2018). Inclusive workplaces: A review and model. *Human Resource Management Review, 28*(2), 176–189.
Shore, L. M., Randel, A. E., Chung, B. G., Dean, M. A., Holcombe Ehrhart, K., & Singh, G. (2011). Inclusion and diversity in work groups: A review and model for future research. *Journal of Management, 37*(4), 1262–1289.
Tavits, M., & Pérez, E. O. (2019). Language influences mass opinion toward gender and LGBT equality. *Proceedings of the National Academy of Sciences, 116*(34), 16781–16786.
Thein, A. H. (2013). Language arts teachers' resistance to teaching LGBT literature and issues. *Language Arts, 90*(3), 169–180.
Tuttitalia.it. (2023). *Comuni italiani per popolazione*. https://www.tuttitalia.it/comuni/popolazione/.
Yin, R. K. (1994). *Case study research: Design and methods* (2nd ed.). Sage.
Zimman, L. (2017). Transgender language reform: Some challenges and strategies for promoting trans-affirming, gender-inclusive language. *Journal of Language and Discrimination, 1*(1), 84–105.

Female Leadership

Barbara Sveva Magnanelli and Elisa Raoli

1 Introduction and Reason of the Study

In the intricate tapestry of human progress, leadership emerges as a crucial thread woven by minds of diverse backgrounds, perspectives, and experiences. As we navigate the complexities of the twenty-first century, we realize that the narrative of leadership is incomplete without exploring the unique contributions and challenges faced by women in leadership roles. This chapter embarks on a journey to unravel the multifaceted dimensions of female leadership, delving into the remarkable traits, daunting challenges, and inspiring stories that shape the leadership landscape for women.

Female leadership encompasses a distinctive blend of skills and perspectives, enriching the fabric of effective leadership. Advocating for the integration of female leadership, rather than its segregation, emphasizes the untapped potential women bring. Focusing on female leadership is pivotal for promoting gender equality and enhancing organizational and societal well-being by understanding and addressing the challenges encountered by female leaders.

This chapter uncovers narratives of resilience, innovation, and empowerment. To comprehend the present, it is imperative to acknowledge the past. From ancient matriarchal societies to the struggles of the suffragette movement, history has

B. S. Magnanelli (✉)
Department of Business Administration, John Cabot University, Rome, Italy
e-mail: bmagnanelli@johncabot.edu

E. Raoli
Department of Scienze dell'Economia e della Gestione Aziendale (SEGESTA), Catholic University of the Sacred Heart, Milan, Italy
e-mail: elisa.raoli@unicatt.it

M. Agostini et al. (eds.), *Diversity and Equity in Accounting*, SIDREA Series in Accounting and Business Administration,
https://doi.org/10.1007/978-3-031-78247-3_12

witnessed the gradual evolution of women's roles in leadership. Understanding this historical context provides a lens to appreciate the progress made and identify persistent barriers yet to be dismantled.

Female leadership brings a diversity of thought, experience, and perspective to decision-making processes. Embracing female leadership fosters an environment where different viewpoints can prosper, leading to more comprehensive problem-solving and strategic planning. The relevance of gender diversity has been emphasized by research, evidencing its positive impact on business performance, particularly in terms of innovation. Studies by Herring (2009) and Catalyst (2011) further underscore the correlation between gender diversity and organizational outcomes. Scholars like Eagly and Carli (2007) and Kochan et al. (2003) highlighted the positive relationship between gender diversity in leadership and improved organizational performance, including higher financial returns and better employee satisfaction.

Female leaders often excel in interpersonal skills, empathy, and communication, contributing to higher levels of employee engagement. Employees are more likely to feel valued, understood, and supported in a work environment where female leadership is acknowledged and encouraged. In many industries, women constitute a significant portion of the consumer base. Having women in leadership positions enables organizations to better understand and respond to the needs of their diverse customer base, leading to improved market responsiveness and customer satisfaction.

Global efforts toward gender diversity in leadership include countries and organizations implementing legal and ethical frameworks for equal opportunities. The European Institute for Gender Equality and the Global Gender Gap Report, published annually by the World Economic Forum, assess the effectiveness of initiatives and provide insights into gender disparities and societal progress. The Organization for Economic Co-operation and Development (OECD) offers a toolkit for women's economic empowerment, including leadership strategies, while the European Commission outlines key actions for gender equality in various sectors, emphasizing policy initiatives and legal frameworks for achieving gender parity.

Research on female leadership is integral to advancing broader goals of social and economic equality, exploring the challenges and opportunities women face in leadership roles, and advocating for societal change and strategies to advance women's leadership across sectors.

In conclusion, studying female leadership transcends addressing gender disparities; it is about leveraging the unique strengths and perspectives that women bring to leadership roles, ultimately enriching organizations and societies alike. This chapter will present examples of well-known female leaders, highlighting the resilience, innovation, and empowerment of women who have achieved top leadership positions.

2 Key Traits of Successful Female Leaders

2.1 Emotional Intelligence

Emotional intelligence (EI) is crucial for business success, enhancing organizational effectiveness and leadership. High EI improves communication, collaboration, and decision-making. Leaders with strong EI navigate interpersonal dynamics, build trust, and inspire teams (Cherniss & Goleman, 2001). EI also boosts customer relations through empathetic service (Carmeli et al., 2009). Organizations emphasizing EI see higher employee engagement, satisfaction, and retention, leading to better performance and competitive advantage.

Female leadership is closely linked with high EI, as women often excel in understanding and managing emotions. Female leaders typically demonstrate strong empathy, social awareness, and relationship management. They connect well on an emotional level, fostering trust, collaboration, and team cohesion. Female leaders create inclusive, supportive environments where employees feel valued and motivated (Barbuto & Burbach, 2006). Organizations led by emotionally intelligent female leaders often enjoy higher employee engagement, satisfaction, and retention. By leveraging EI, female leaders effectively navigate interpersonal dynamics, inspire teams, and drive success.

2.2 Collaboration and Team Building

Effective collaboration drives innovation, problem-solving, and organizational performance, encouraging diverse perspectives, idea exchange, and creativity (Edmondson & Lei, 2014). Collaboration fosters ownership, accountability, and engagement among team members. Trust and mutual respect in team building create resilient and adaptable teams that navigate challenges and drive growth. In dynamic environments, collaboration and team building are vital for organizational agility, innovation, and resilience.

Female leadership is closely linked with effective collaboration and team building. Women excel at creating inclusive environments where diverse perspectives are valued, and team members feel empowered to contribute (Eagly & Carli, 2007). They prioritize open communication, encouraging dialogue, and idea-sharing. Female leaders build trust and strong interpersonal relationships within teams, fostering camaraderie and mutual support (Wolff & Pescosolido, 2010). Teams led by women often exhibit higher cohesion, collaboration, and innovation, leading to improved performance (Barbuto & Burbach, 2006). By leveraging relational skills and emotional intelligence, female leaders create inclusive cultures where individuals feel valued and motivated to work toward common goals (Kramer, 2010). As organizations recognize the importance of collaboration in driving success, the leadership qualities of women are increasingly valued.

2.3 Resilience and Adaptability

Resilience involves bouncing back from adversity and learning from challenges. It requires robust systems and cultures to withstand shocks. Adaptability, the ability to adjust to changing circumstances, is crucial for sustained success (Teece et al., 1997). Prioritizing resilience and adaptability enables organizations to weather crises and seize opportunities (Meyer & Gaba, 2005). A culture of resilience fosters innovation and continuous improvement, making businesses more agile and competitive (Williams & Gruber, 2017). In the modern economy, resilience and adaptability are essential for organizational growth and sustainability.

Female leadership exemplifies resilience and adaptability, vital for navigating today's business challenges. Women leaders often demonstrate high resilience, using emotional intelligence and interpersonal skills to cope with adversity and recover from setbacks (Eagly & Carli, 2007). They remain composed under pressure, maintain a positive outlook, and lead teams through turbulent times. Additionally, women foster cultures of resilience, promoting open communication, collaboration, and a growth mindset (Barbuto & Burbach, 2006). Adaptability is also a hallmark of female leadership, with women leaders pivoting and innovating in response to changing circumstances and market dynamics (Wolff & Pescosolido, 2010). They embrace change, seize opportunities, and leverage diverse perspectives to drive success.

2.4 Effective Communication

Research underscores the critical role of effective communication in fostering internal collaboration, customer engagement, and stakeholder relations. Clear communication aligns employees with organizational goals, fostering a sense of purpose. It facilitates efficient teamwork and transparent management of organizational change (Cameron & Green, 2015). Externally, effective communication builds trust and credibility, enhancing brand reputation. Strong communication practices help organizations adapt to market dynamics and seize opportunities, making it a vital skill for innovation, collaboration, and overall performance.

Effective communication is integral to female leadership, as women often excel in both verbal and nonverbal communication, enhancing their leadership success. Women are adept at actively listening to team members, understanding their perspectives, and responding with empathy (Eagly & Carli, 2007). Female leaders articulate clear and concise messages, ensuring organizational goals are effectively communicated to all stakeholders (Kramer, 2010). By prioritizing transparent and inclusive communication, female leaders create environments where diverse viewpoints are valued, fostering collaboration, trust, and mutual respect (Barbuto & Burbach, 2006). Research also indicates that women naturally excel at building and nurturing relationships through effective communication, enhancing their ability to influence and inspire others (Wolff & Pescosolido, 2010).

3 Challenges Faced by Female Leaders

3.1 Gender Stereotypes and Bias

Gender stereotypes are shared societal beliefs that dictate expectations about the behavior and characteristics of women and men. As explained and shown in the work of Gipson et al. (2017), these stereotypes can be descriptive, defining how women and men are perceived, as well as prescriptive, specifying how they should behave. Descriptive stereotypes often depict women as communal and warm (Fiske et al., 2007), while prescriptive stereotypes prescribe that women should display communal traits (Eagly & Karau, 2002). In contrast, men are often associated with agentic traits such as confidence and assertiveness (Huddy & Terkildsen, 1993). These agentic characteristics are commonly seen as essential qualities for leadership (Koenig et al., 2011). Schein's (1973) think-manager-think-male paradigm suggested that successful leaders are perceived as possessing characteristics, attitudes, and temperaments aligned with the global masculine stereotype. Koenig et al.'s meta-analysis (2011) found that prototypical leader traits had a stronger correlation with masculine traits than feminine traits across various studies. Overall, the literature suggests that managerial roles are often associated with masculine traits and behaviors and asserts that the stereotypical attributes associated with women are incongruent with the attributes typically required for senior leadership positions. However, research has revealed that women who exhibit agentic behaviors may face denigration and backlash for deviating from the prescriptive stereotype of being communal (Phelan et al., 2008). Therefore, women leaders must navigate the challenge of displaying agentic characteristics expected in leadership roles without violating gender stereotypes.

3.2 Glass Ceiling and Career Advancement

While women are increasingly entering diverse occupational activities and organizations, certain spaces, particularly leadership positions, remain challenging and somewhat closed for them. In 2021, data from The Catalyst, a nonprofit organization focused on creating safe and inclusive workplaces for women, revealed that women held top managerial positions (CEO) around 5% in the USA, 7% in Japan, and only about 1.8% in Europe.

There is a remarkable amount of literature focusing on women's careers examining the obstacles hindering career advancement. Following Lyness and Judiesch (2008), career advancement can be defined as promotions to higher levels in a management hierarchy.

Hutchings et al. (2012) found that North American and Middle Eastern women identified work–life balance and societal expectations as common career influencers. They also highlighted discrimination based on "culture" and the "lack of protective legislation and government support" as additional obstacles. Studies on China and UAE (Metcalfe, 2008; Tatli et al., 2017) revealed how societal status and family connections significantly influenced women's career choices, limiting their development. Addressing women's underrepresentation in managerial roles, Mainiero and Sullivan (2005) argued for a holistic approach to defining career success.

The reasons behind women's underrepresentation in corporate leadership positions and, by extension, societal leadership roles are diverse and have been extensively researched over decades (Eagly & Karau, 2002; Oakley, 2000). This body of research has generated various theories, ranging from global patriarchal systems favoring male power to gender role ideologies, beliefs, and socialization in specific cultures that perceive leadership and responsibility as masculine activities, thereby excluding women from leadership roles. The congruity theory suggests that the perceived incongruity between the female gender role and leadership roles leads to prejudice, resulting in less favorable views of women as potential leaders and a less favorable evaluation of their behavior in leadership roles compared to men (Eagly & Karau, 2002). Consequently, these perceptions contribute to less favorable attitudes toward female leaders compared to their male counterparts.

3.3 *Female Leadership and Motherhood*

Examining women in leadership must include the impact of motherhood, which significantly influences career progression. While research often focuses on the effects of female leadership on firms, the role of motherhood in leadership is less explored. Pregnancy-related leaves and the challenges of returning to work have lasting career implications.

Family-related issues, particularly pregnancy and childbirth, pose challenges for women aspiring to leadership roles (Mäkelä, 2005). Working mothers often struggle with balancing career and childcare responsibilities, which aligns with traditional gender stereotypes (Park et al., 2008). Women prioritizing work over family may face judgments of inadequacy as parents and partners (Morgenroth & Heilman, 2017).

The "Think Manager-Think Parent" paradigm by Morgenroth et al. (2021) extends Schien's "Think Manager-Think Male" (TMTM) association, integrating the motherhood penalty and fatherhood advantage. Schein's study categorized attributes traditionally linked to men (agency) and women (communality), showing how these stereotypes affect leadership perceptions. Morgenroth et al. argued that parenthood alters these stereotypes, with motherhood reducing women's desirability for leadership due to leadership roles being viewed as masculine and agentic. Conversely, fathers are seen as providers, aligning with workplace norms, and thus receive benefits like higher pay, known as the fatherhood bonus (Banchefsky & Park, 2016; Ely & Meyerson, 2000; Glauber, 2008).

3.4 *Behavioral Differences Between Male and Female in Leadership*

The differences between the male and the female gender are undoubtedly leading individuals to behave and act differently, as suggested by upper echelon theory (Hambrick & Mason, 1984). Literature about female leadership highlights the differences between males and females when it comes to decisions; women tend to be more risk-averse, less overconfident, and more detailed and accurate while researching before deciding (Charness & Gneezy, 2012). These different behavioral approaches will have implications on firm outcomes, especially in contingent situations, leading to eventual bias when it comes to their decision-making process. These behavioral differences, in fact, contribute to the complexities and nuances that leaders face in their roles.

The upper echelon theory framework (Hambrick & Mason, 1984) emphasizes how the cognitive features of individuals in leadership positions are fundamental determinants for firm results. According to studies developed on the behavioral differences in the most recent years, men tend to be more competitive, less risk-averse, more overconfident, and less ethical than women (Charness & Gneezy, 2012; Niederle & Vesterlund, 2007). Bliss and Potter (2002) posited that besides being more risk-averse, they also worry more about how the company spends money, and in addition, they usually extract fewer personal benefits from the company compared to their male counterparts. Ravasi and Schultz (2006) stated that women, within organizational contexts, tend to be more collaborative and less hierarchical than men. Reguera-Alvarado et al. (2017) underlined that females are more long-term oriented than males when it comes to strategy and strategic decisions.

Moreover, previous literature on the attributes of female leaders indicates that they have better communication and listening capabilities than males, are more reluctant to increase debt leverage, and are more people-oriented (Dallas, 2002; Faccio et al., 2016; Rosa et al., 1996) These characteristics impact firm performance because they imply a different attitude when making decisions.

4 Stories of Inspiring Female Leaders: Highlighting Successful Female Leaders in Various Industries

This section aims to present three different examples of women who, despite biases and difficulties stemming from gender, as highlighted by the literature, broke the glass ceiling. The analysis of the three presented stories of female leaders demonstrates common behavioral traits among the three women, including resilience, innovation, and empowerment. Choosing Barra, Kelly, and Nooyi highlights the diverse and impactful leadership styles of women in traditionally male-dominated industries—automotive, banking, and consumer goods. Detailing the achievements and leadership styles of these three women will describe diverse, rich examples of how female leaders can excel, innovate, and inspire within their respective fields. These stories underscore the multifaceted nature of leadership and the profound impact of female executives in shaping the future of their industries.

4.1 Indra Nooyi: Former CEO of PepsiCo

Indra Nooyi, an Indian-American business executive, served as chairperson and CEO of PepsiCo from 2006 to 2018, making her one of the most powerful women in business (Tandon, 2018). Fortune ranked her #1 in the Most Powerful Women in Business list in 2009 and 2010 and #2 in 2015 and 2017 (Forbes, 2017). She also serves on Amazon's board.

A key accomplishment of Nooyi's tenure was steering PepsiCo toward healthier product offerings to meet changing consumer preferences. Her "Performance with a Purpose" strategy categorized products into "fun for you" (e.g., potato chips, regular soda), "better for you" (e.g., diet snacks and sodas), and "good for you" (e.g., oatmeal). This initiative included significant investment in healthier options, such as removing aspartame from Diet Pepsi in 2015 (Reingold, 2015).

Nooyi emphasized sustainability, redesigning packaging to reduce waste, conserving water, transitioning to renewable energy, and implementing recycling practices. By 2020, all PepsiCo-operated U.S. facilities used 100% renewable electricity. She also focused on employee retention, fostering a supportive workplace culture. Notably, she personally corresponded with the parents of her leadership team and visited their homes to build personal connections (Freeland, 2020; Novak, 2018).

4.1.1 Indra Nooyi's Leadership Style

She is known for her transformative leadership and strategic vision. Her ability to balance financial success with social responsibility has made her a role model for aspiring female leaders, showcasing that it is possible to lead with both empathy and business acumen. **Her leadership style can be defined as visionary and inclusive leadership.** Visionary leaders have a clear sense of purpose and a long-term vision for the organization, while inclusive leaders prioritize diversity, creating an environment where different perspectives are valued. Indra Nooyi's leadership at PepsiCo involved a focus on long-term strategic goals, such as shifting toward healthier products and sustainable practices. She actively promoted diversity in the workplace, emphasizing the importance of inclusivity in decision-making and fostering a culture of innovation. Nooyi's leadership style has been summarized in the **"5 Cs" that leaders must have for driving business success:** competency, courage and confidence, communication, consistency, and compass.

4.2 *Mary Barra: CEO of General Motors*

Mary Barra made history by becoming the first female CEO of a major global automaker when she took the reins at General Motors (GM) in 2014. Barra was listed as 1st on *Forbes*' Most Powerful Women list in 2017 (Forbes, 2017). She is also the chair of the Business Roundtable, a collection of America's most influential corporate CEOs. Barra also sits on the board of directors for the Walt Disney Company.

Barra's leadership became particularly noteworthy during a challenging period for GM, marked by a major ignition switch recall crisis. Barra demonstrated resilience and accountability during this crisis, taking swift action to address the issues, cooperating with regulators, and implementing changes to ensure product safety (Quartz at Work, 2018). Under her leadership, GM rebounded, achieving strong financial performance and innovation in electric and autonomous vehicles.

Barra's emphasis on innovation, diversity, and sustainability has shaped her leadership at GM. She aims to lead the company and the industry toward achieving zero emissions and is determined to eradicate both the financial and physical toll of vehicle accidents. Moreover, she has actively advocated for the advancement of women in the automotive industry and has championed the development of electric vehicles, positioning GM for the future. Mary Barra's case is inspiring for several reasons. She not only shattered the glass ceiling in a traditionally male-dominated industry but also showcased effective crisis management and forward-thinking leadership. Her commitment to innovation and inclusivity serves as a model for aspiring female leaders in the corporate world.

4.2.1 Mary Barra's Leadership Style

Barra's leadership style can be defined as adaptive leadership. Adaptive leaders are those skilled at navigating change and uncertainty and adjusting strategies to meet evolving challenges. Barra showcased adaptive leadership during the ignition switch recall crisis at General Motors, showing resilience. Resilience in the face of challenges and a commitment to accountability are essential traits of effective leaders. Barra's handling of the ignition switch recall crisis at General Motors underscores the importance of taking responsibility, making tough decisions, and leading with transparency during difficult times (Yale School of management, 2018).

Barra's leadership style also involves a focus on innovation, showcasing adaptability in response to industry shifts. Her leadership style relies also on the concept of servant leadership, which is grounded on protecting and preserving the well-being of community members, helping them also to grow and succeed. Thus, the servant leader philosophy is a fundamental component of Barra's decision-making attitude.

Moreover, Barra's leadership style reflects her commitment to open communication, empowering employees, and maintaining unwavering integrity. This approach revolves around emphasizing teamwork, treating everyone with respect, and cultivating a community where the voices of all individuals are acknowledged and valued.

4.3 *Gail Kelly: Former CEO of Westpac*

Born in South Africa, Gail Kelly is an Australian businesswoman. In 2002, she achieved the milestone of becoming the first female CEO of Westpac, a major Australian bank from 2008 to 2015. By 2005, she held the distinction of being the highest-paid woman in an Australian corporation, and the *Australian Banking & Finance* magazine gave her an award for "Best Financial Services Executive" in 2003 and 2004 (The Age, 2005). In 2010, *Forbes* recognized her as the 8th most powerful woman in the world.

Kelly's leadership style has been defined as a beacon of transformation and inclusivity. In fact, Kelly employs a transformational leadership style that has made a lasting impact on the banking sector. Her leadership at Westpac not only led to substantial financial growth but also instigated a cultural transformation, prioritizing values such as trust, inclusivity, and sustainability. During a period marked by various challenges in the banking industry, including economic downturns and technological disruptions, Kelly's leadership played a pivotal role in ensuring Westpac's resilience. Her innovative strategies and focus on customer centricity positioned the bank as a frontrunner in the industry, promoting also a cultural transformation.

Kelly also emphasized the importance of workplace diversity and inclusion, advocating for women in leadership roles and implementing policies to support work-life balance.

Gail Kelly gained recognition for her outstanding communication abilities, employing a range of platforms, including town hall meetings and internal communications, to articulate her vision for Westpac. By providing a vivid depiction of the bank's future, she ensured that all employees, spanning from top-level executives to frontline staff, comprehended and shared alignment with this vision. Her communication approach extended beyond conveying the "what" to also encompass the "why." By elucidating the reasoning behind her vision and strategies, she secured buy-in and commitment from her team.

4.3.1 Gail Kelly's Leadership Style

Kelly's leadership style can be defined as transformational leadership, given that transformational leaders are known for inspiring and motivating their teams to achieve extraordinary results. Kelly demonstrated transformational leadership through her emphasis on cultural change at Westpac, focusing on customer satisfaction and instilling a customer-centric mindset within the organization. She promoted a collaborative and inclusive work environment, valuing diversity and recognizing the importance of engaging employees in the company's mission. Kelly boosts change and cultivates an atmosphere conducive to innovation. Characterized by her capacity to instigate substantial transformations in individuals and the organization as a whole, her transformational leadership involves inspiring teams by crafting a future vision, motivating them to realize it, and offering unwavering support and encouragement. Leaders who adopt this approach often serve as role models, instilling pride, respect, and trust within their teams.

4.4 Conclusions

In conclusion, the exemplary leadership journeys of Indra Nooyi, Mary Barra, and Gail Kelly illuminate common traits and principles that have propelled these women to the pinnacle of success in their respective fields. Each of these leaders embodies resilience, innovation, and empowerment, showcasing their ability to overcome obstacles and break through barriers.

Indra Nooyi's visionary and inclusive leadership style enabled PepsiCo's transformation toward healthier product offerings and sustainable practices, demonstrating a balance between financial success and social responsibility. Mary Barra's adaptive leadership approach was evident during the ignition switch recall crisis at General Motors, emphasizing resilience, accountability, and innovation. Gail Kelly's transformational leadership at Westpac fostered cultural change, prioritizing values of trust, inclusivity, and sustainability while championing workplace diversity and communication.

Despite operating in traditionally male-dominated industries, these women have not only shattered the glass ceiling but have also redefined leadership paradigms, inspiring others with their unwavering commitment to excellence, integrity, and inclusivity. Their leadership legacies serve as guiding beacons for aspiring female leaders worldwide, demonstrating that resilience, innovation, and empowerment are indeed the cornerstones of effective and impactful leadership.

References

Banchefsky, S., & Park, B. (2016). The "new father": Dynamic stereotypes of fathers. *Psychology of Men & Masculinity, 17*, 103.

Barbuto, J. E., & Burbach, M. E. (2006). The emotional intelligence of transformational leaders: A field study of elected officials. *The Journal of Social Psychology, 146*(1), 51–64.

Bliss, R. T., & Potter, M. E. (2002). Mutual fund managers: Does gender matter? *The Journal of Business and Economic Studies, 8*(1), 1.

Cameron, E., & Green, M. (2015). *Making sense of change management: A complete guide to the models, Tools and techniques of organizational change*. Kogan Page Publishers.

Carmeli, A., Yitzhak-Halevy, M., & Weisberg, J. (2009). The relationship between emotional intelligence and psychological well-being. *Journal of Managerial Psychology, 24*(1), 66–78.

Catalyst. (2011). The bottom line: Corporate performance and women's representation on boards. *Catalysts*.

Catalyst. (2021). *Quick take: Women in the workforce—global.*
Charness, G., & Gneezy, U. (2012). Strong evidence for gender differences in risk taking. *Journal of Economic Behavior & Organization, 83*(1), 50–58.
Cherniss, C., & Goleman, D. (2001). *The emotionally intelligent workplace: How to select for, measure, and improve emotional intelligence in individuals, groups, and organizations.* John.
Dallas, L. L.: 2002, The new managerialism and diversity on corporate boards of directors', *Public Law and Legal Theory Working Paper* 38, University of San Diego School of Law.
Eagly, A. H., & Carli, L. L. (2007). *Through the labyrinth: The truth about how women become leaders.* Harvard Business Press.
Eagly, A. H., & Karau, S. J. (2002). Role congruity theory of prejudice toward female leaders. *Psychological Review, 109*, 573–598.
Edmondson, A. C., & Lei, Z. (2014). Psychological safety: The history, renaissance, and future of an interpersonal construct. *Annual Review of Organizational Psychology and Organizational Behavior, 1*(1), 23–43.
Ely, R. J., & Meyerson, D. E. (2000). Theories of gender in organizations: A new approach to organizational analysis and change. *Research in Organizational Behavior, 22*, 103–151.
Faccio, M., Marchica, M. T., & Mura, R. (2016). CEO gender, corporate risk-taking, and the efficiency of capital allocation. *Journal of Corporate Finance, 39*, 193–209.
Fiske, S. T., Cuddy, A. J. C., & Glick, P. (2007). Universal dimensions of social cognition: Warmth and competence. *Trends in Cognitive Sciences, 11*(2), 77–83.
Freeland, G. Indra Nooyi's passions: People, performance & purpose at PepsiCo and beyond. *Forbes*. Retrieved August 12, 2020.
Gipson, A. N., Pfaff, D. L., Mendelsohn, D. B., Catenacci, L. T., & Burke, W. W. (2017). Women and leadership: Selection, development, leadership style, and performance. *The Journal of Applied Behavioral Science, 53*(1), 32–65.
Glauber, R. (2008). Race and gender in families and at work: The fatherhood wage premium. *Gender & Society, 22*, 8–30.
Hambrick, D. C., & Mason, P. A. (1984). Upper echelons: The organization as a reflection of its top managers. *Academy of Management Review, 9*, 195–206.
Herring, C. (2009). Does diversity pay? Race, gender, and the business case for diversity. *American Sociological Review, 74*(2), 208–224.
Huddy, L., & Terkildsen, N. (1993). Gender stereotypes and the perception of male and female candidates. *American Journal of Political Science, 37*(1), 119–147.
Hutchings, K., Lirio, P., & Metcalfe, B. D. (2012). Gender, globalisation and development: A re-evaluation of the nature of women's global work. *The International Journal of Human Resource Management, 23*(9), 1763–1787.
Kochan, T., Bezrukova, K., Ely, R., Jackson, S., Joshi, A., Jehn, K., & Thomas, D. (2003). The effects of diversity on business performance: Report of the diversity research network. *Human Resource Management, 42*(1), 3–21.
Koenig, A. M., Eagly, A. H., Mitchell, A. A., & Ristikari, T. (2011). Are leader stereotypes masculine? A meta-analysis of three research paradigms. *Psychological Bulletin, 137*(4), 616.
Kramer, M. W. (2010). *Communication and organizational culture: A key to understanding work experiences.* SAGE Publications.
Lyness, K. S., & Judiesch, M. K. (2008). Can a manager have a life and a career? International and multisource perspectives on work-life balance and career advancement potential. *Journal of Applied Psychology, 93*(4), 789.
Mainiero, L. A., & Sullivan, S. E. (2005). Kaleidoscope careers: An alternate explanation for the "opt-out" revolution. *Academy of Management Perspectives, 19*(1), 106–123.
Mäkelä, L. (2005). Pregnancy and leader-follower dyadic relationships: A research agenda. *Equal Opportunities International, 24*(3/4), 50–72.
Metcalfe, B. D. (2008). Women, management and globalization in the Middle East. *Journal of Business Ethics, 83*, 85–100.

Meyer, A. D., & Gaba, V. (2005). Innovation through time-management practices. *Academy of Management Journal, 48*(3), 489–505.

Morgenroth, T., Ryan, M. K., & Sønderlund, A. L. (2021). Think manager–think parent? Investigating the fatherhood advantage and the motherhood penalty using the think manager–think male paradigm. *Journal of Applied Social Psychology, 51*, 237–247.

Morgenroth, T., & Heilman, M. E. (2017). Should I stay or should I go? Implications of maternity leave choice for perceptions of working mothers. *Journal of Experimental Social Psychology, 72*, 53–56.

Niederle, M., & Vesterlund, L. (2007). Do women shy away from competition? Do men compete too much? *The Quarterly Journal of Economics, 122*(3), 1067–1101.

Novak, D. (September 12, 2018). Follow Indra Nooyi's example: Be a leader people want to follow. www.cnbc.com. Retrieved August 12, 2020.

Oakley, J. G. (2000). Gender-based barriers to senior management positions: Understanding the scarcity of female CEOs. *Journal of Business Ethics, 27*, 321–334.

Park, B., Smith, J. A., & Correll, J. (2008). "Having it all" or "doing it all"? Perceived trait attributes and behavioral obligations as a function of workload, parenthood, and gender. *European Journal of Social Psychology, 38*, 1156–1164.

Phelan, J. E., Moss-Racusin, C. A., & Rudman, L. A. (2008). Competent yet out in the cold: Shifting criteria for hiring reflect backlash toward agentic women. *Psychology of Women Quarterly, 32*(4), 406–413.

Ravasi, D., & Schultz, M. (2006). Responding to organizational identity threats: Exploring the role of organizational culture. *Academy of Management Journal, 49*(3), 433–458.

Reguera-Alvarado, N., De Fuentes, P., & Laffarga, J. (2017). Does board gender diversity influence financial performance? Evidence from Spain. *Journal of Business Ethics, 141*, 337–350.

Reingold, J. (2015). PepsiCo's CEO Indra Nooyi was right. Now what?. Fortune.

Rosa, P., Carter, S., & Hamilton, D. (1996). Gender as a determinant of small business performance: Insights from a British study. *Small Business Economics, 8*, 463–478.

Schein, V. E. (1973). The relationship between sex role stereotypes and requisite management characteristics. *Journal of Applied Psychology, 57*, 95–100.

Tatli, A., Ozturk, M. B., & Woo, H. S. (2017). Individualization and marketization of responsibility for gender equality: The case of female managers in China. *Human Resource Management, 56*(3), 407–430.

Teece, D. J., Pisano, G., & Shuen, A. (1997). Dynamic capabilities and strategic management. *Strategic Management Journal, 18*(7), 509–533.

Williams, T. A., & Gruber, D. A. (2017). A practice perspective on dynamic capabilities: Connecting strategic choice, learning, and competition. *Academy of Management Annals, 11*(1), 589–659.

Wolff, S. B., & Pescosolido, A. T. (2010). The leadership is sinking: A temporal investigation of narcissistic leadership. *Journal of Applied Social Psychology, 40*(12), 3094–3128.

How Do Cultural and Personnel Controls Influence Inclusive Workplace Climate for People with Disability? Insights from the Italian Context

Domenico Raucci and Manuela Paolini

1 Introduction

Over the past 50 years, several international organizations advocating for the rights of people with disabilities (PwD), the UN 2030 Agenda on Sustainable Development Goals, the European Employment Equality Directive, the European Disability Strategy 2021–2030, civil society, and stakeholders have emphasized the values of equity and inclusion within CSR principles, particularly the inclusion of PwD in the workplace. In Italy, the legislative evolution, beginning with L. 68/1999 and culminating in L. 227/2021, has fostered the development of disability management practices to ensure a 'reasonable accommodation' of PwD and, consequently, their workplace involvement and valorization (Agovino & Rapposelli, 2020). This regulation on the inclusive workplace climate (IWC) for PwD is more binding for public organizations, due to the links between the public value of their actions and the social responsibility principles they embody (Burns & Jollands, 2020; Hammon et al., 2023).

Nevertheless, for PwD to really feel included in the workplace and for this inclusion not to be 'merely' a compliance obligation, it is of the utmost importance that public organizations' efforts are directed at enhancing the sense of belonging of PwD (Coll & Mignonac, 2023; Metallo et al., 2009; Palumbo et al., 2023), putting back these social dimensions of CSR principles in the traditional public sector values (Aguilera et al., 2007). To achieve these CSR objectives, public organizations should pay attention to all employees, as organizational agents, and how they relate to PwD in stakeholder management and engagement approaches (Migliaccio, 2019). In particular, public organizations should foster and disseminate among their

D. Raucci (✉) · M. Paolini
Department of Economics, University of Studies G. d'Annunzio Chieti-Pescara, Chieti, Italy
e-mail: domenico.raucci@unich.it; manuela.paolini@unich.it

M. Agostini et al. (eds.), *Diversity and Equity in Accounting*, SIDREA Series in Accounting and Business Administration,
https://doi.org/10.1007/978-3-031-78247-3_13

employees the sense of social responsibility associated with the IWC for PwD, through the induction of individual processes of internalization of its value as a CSR principle (Bracci et al., 2019; Nelissen et al., 2017).

In this context, research on the integration of CSR principles within management control systems (Johnstone, 2019) suggests extending the traditional uses of these systems to unleash their potential to support the implementation of such principles. Indeed, organizations can adopt different management control approaches (Tessier & Otley, 2012) to align individual behaviours with organizational goals consistent with CSR values. Merchant and Van der Stede (Merchant & Van der Stede, 2007) theorized four types of control: results, actions, cultural, and personnel. The latter two types of controls aim, respectively, to foster an organizational climate by building shared norms and values and to manage personnel to induce desired employee behaviours.

The purposes of these controls and the informal nature of their use can be usefully interpreted through the lenses of self-determination theory (Ryan & Deci, 2000). According to this, when a person relates to the organization and his/her need for relatedness is fulfilled, a series of positive effects are produced in the process of organizational identification (OI) and individual internalization of the organizational aims and values. If effectively managed, personnel and cultural controls could be used by public organizations to induce perceptions of an IWC for PwD as an expression of the organization's broader sense of social responsibility. The focus on these CSR values can engender employees' sense of 'relatedness', by addressing their beliefs that the organization incorporates values and expectations of social responsibility consistent with those of their personal identity. Consequently, higher levels of OI, developed in these affective-relational dimensions of CSR (D'Aprile & Talò, 2014), can shape employees' sense of responsibility, as conveyed by public organizations. This, in turn, can result in the induction of positive feelings and attitudes towards IWC for PwD.

In public organizations, recent research on the drivers of social responsibility has explored the individual-level determinants of CSR and how to induce employees' motivation and prosocial behaviours consistent with CSR values and goals (Aguinis & Glavas, 2012; Hammon et al., 2023). However, studies on the managerial use of management control systems, from the perspectives of public subordinate employees (Van der Kolk et al., 2019), have not yet investigated how personnel and cultural controls interface with IWC for PwD.

Rooted in the research on the implementation of CSR through management control systems and framed in the self-determination theory, our work aimed to contribute to this literature by assuming that cultural and personnel controls, as experienced by non-managerial public employees, can increase their levels of OI, which, in turn, can induce positive perceptions and attitudes in terms of IWC for PwD.

To test the research design, a survey was conducted among employees of southern Italian municipalities.

The paper is structured as follows: paragraph 2 presents the background and the hypotheses, paragraph 3 describes the sample and the methodology, paragraph 4 presents the results, paragraph 5 provides the discussions, and paragraph 6 drives conclusions.

2 Background and Hypothesis Development

The implementation of an IWC for PwD would serve as a foundation for the development of more effective, shared, and integrated disability management practices within public organizations (Angeloni, 2013; Palumbo et al., 2023). In the latter, the more stringent regulatory requirements, alone, may not guarantee the substantial achievement of IWC for PwD. Beyond mere compliance, such organizations should incorporate this sense of social responsibility by internally sharing and fostering this value with all employees. As indicated by CSR studies in the public context (Abdelmotaleb & Saha, 2019; Aguilera et al., 2007), the promotion of social responsibility principles should reinvigorate the traditional public sector values, which include, among others, accountability, solidarity, justice, fairness, and social inclusion. These values are operationalized in the dynamics of stakeholder engagement (Migliaccio, 2019), with positive effects both within and outside of organizations.

In fact, PwD, as employees and internal stakeholders, are the first and main beneficiaries of the IWC, which allows them to experience a sense of belongingness to their organizations while still feeling free to express their differences and uniqueness (Metallo et al., 2009; Mor Barak et al., 2021). Furthermore, as highlighted by studies on the outcomes of inclusive workplace contexts (Mor Barak et al., 2021; Oware & Mallikarjunappa, 2021; Palumbo et al., 2023), perceptions of IWC can result in improvements in work well-being, attitudes, and behaviours of all employees, with positive influences on the individual and organizational performance. These effects facilitate the promotion, from within, of principles like that of social integration and equal opportunity, which are the basis of public values and aims that public organizations embody (Aguinis & Glavas, 2012; Burns & Jollands, 2020; Hammon et al., 2023). Employees' positive perceptions of IWC for PwD, by enhancing their propensity to align themselves with such organizational CSR values, would also be conveyed beyond organizational boundaries, inducing in them prosocial motivations and behaviours in public service delivery relationships with PwD as external users (Abdelmotaleb & Saha, 2019; Migliaccio, 2019). In the role of organizational agents, employees would convey similar perceptions of an inclusive and supportive climate also towards these external stakeholders, going beyond the mere formal removal of architectural barriers required by law.

To achieve these objectives, public organizations must nurture feelings of social responsibility amongst all employees by establishing, from within, an IWC for PwD that is grounded in more profound individual processes of internalization of its value of CSR (Aguilera et al., 2007; Burns & Jollands, 2020).

Studies on management control systems in public organizations have highlighted their role in aligning employees' motivation, behaviours, and performance with the expected organizational ones (Amici & Cepiku, 2020; Van der Kolk et al., 2019).

Generalist studies have explored various approaches to the design and use of management control systems with the aim of internally integrating CSR principles and supporting the pursuit of related goals in a balanced manner with economic ones (Johnstone, 2019; Laguir et al., 2019).

Management control systems are essentially used to direct employee behaviours and to achieve goal congruence (Amici & Cepiku, 2020; Tessier & Otley, 2012). Merchant and Van der Stede (Merchant & Van der Stede, 2007) conceptualized four types of control based on its object. They distinguish according to whether the control relies on formal mechanisms (control over actions or results) or informal mechanisms (control over personnel or culture). Action controls monitor the actions that need to be executed to reach organizational goals, while results control focuses on examining the achieved results compared to the expected ones. Personnel controls encompass all employee management mechanisms, from the initial selection to ongoing training and career development, to increase the likelihood that employees' behaviour aligns with the organization's goals. Cultural controls are used to communicate and disseminate the organization's core values and norms to employees through various means.

The latter two types of informal controls operate according to the social control dynamics while focusing the employees' attention on organizational goals.

Several studies have emphasized the importance of their use in an integrated manner with other control mechanisms, as they are at least as effective in affecting organizational outcomes as formal controls (Laguir et al., 2019). They can create a work environment that fosters the internalization and sharing of organizational values with employees, including CSR principles. For public organizations, having complex objectives and responsibilities linked to public value (Abdelmotaleb & Saha, 2019; Amici & Cepiku, 2020), the motivational and attitudinal potential of cultural and personnel controls can be crucial (Van der Kolk et al., 2019).

The interface between management control systems and micro-CSR outcomes is an emerging issue within public organizations. Here, recent studies have explored the motivations and behaviours driven by individuals' CSR perceptions (Aguinis & Glavas, 2012; Hammon et al., 2023), while there is a lack of research on how management control systems, specifically cultural and personnel controls, support the pursuit of CSR goals. Relatively little is known about how employees without managerial roles react to these types of control. Management control system literature has primarily focused on the managerial intention of control, as managers are the primary users of these systems (Cepiku et al., 2017; Raucci & Paolini, 2022). Nevertheless, if managerial uses of management control systems convey to subordinates behavioural norms and values that are consistent with the organization's CSR principles, the perceptions of managerial use of control experienced by employees are equally crucial (Tessier & Otley, 2012). Indeed, the perceptions of the latter facilitate the operationalization of the organization's sense of social responsibility towards IWC for PwD in everyday work. Few studies have explored the potential for managerial uses of informal controls, as perceived by public subordinates' employees, to enhance their motivation and performance (Van der Kolk et al., 2019).

Mostly, there is a dearth of studies that examine the functions of these types of informal controls in promoting an IWC for PwD (Tucker & Nash, 2023).

The role of personnel and cultural controls as drivers of micro-CSR at the executive-employee level can be explored through the interpretive lens of self-determination theory. This theory (Ryan & Deci, 2000) posits that individuals aim to fulfil three basic needs: competence, autonomy, and relationships. Competence expresses the perception of having opportunities for development and self-fulfilment. Autonomy refers to the freedom to make independent choices. Relatedness is the sense of belonging and significance to a reference community. Employees' need for relatedness is satisfied when they relate to the organization personified by its internal actors. A sense of relatedness facilitates the individuals' identification with the organizational goals and values (Gagné & Deci, 2005). By helping to satisfy employees' needs for relatedness, cultural and personnel controls enable a process of adaptation between employees' values, goals, and beliefs and those of the organization. This process deepens their emotional attachment and affective bond to the organization, increasing the internalization of organizational CSR goals and values (Aguilera et al., 2007; D'Aprile & Talò, 2014). OI dynamics (Abdelmotaleb & Saha, 2019; Coll & Mignonac, 2023; Smidts et al., 2001) feed employees' perceptions that there are expectations and norms consistent with their personal identity and that they should take an active part in the pursuit of the organization's values of social responsibility. Therefore, it is likely that through these influences on the psychological schemes, personal and cultural controls contribute to increasing employees' propensity to align themselves with prosocial and inclusive values conveyed by their public organizations. This, in turn, may lead them to feel and promote an IWC for PwD (Fig. 1).

Based on this rationale, we hypothesize that

Hp 1: Cultural control positively influences organizational identification of public subordinate employees.

Hp 2: Personnel control positively influences organizational identification of public subordinate employees.

Hp 3: Organizational identification positively influences inclusive workplace climate for PwD among public subordinate employees.

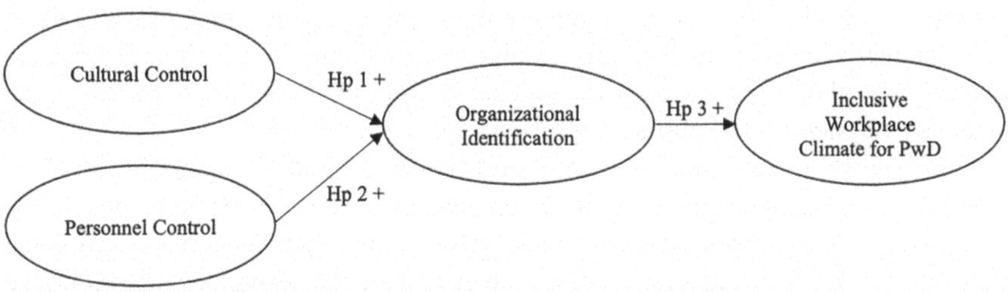

Fig. 1 Research design

3 Method

3.1 Sample

The units of analysis are all non-managerial employees of municipalities located in the eight regions of southern Italy, namely, Abruzzo, Molise, Campania, Puglia, Basilicata, Calabria, Sicilia, and Sardegna. The southern Italian municipalities were selected because the problem of workplace inclusion of PwD is widely felt in this area of Italy. Indeed, in the southern regions of Italy, the high levels of indebtedness, the scarcity of resources available to municipalities, the socio-cultural factors, and the less developed economic conditions compared to other areas of Italy have resulted in greater employment challenges for all individuals, with and without disabilities. For PwD, this condition results in greater discrimination in job opportunities and higher levels of unemployment, further increasing the risk of social exclusion (Agovino & Rapposelli, 2017; ISTAT, 2023).

The study focused on the 170 Southern municipalities with a population between 20,000 and 59,999 according to the ISTAT classification. The selected population range characterizes several municipalities in southern Italy. Furthermore, these medium-small dimensions reflect the size of the range of employees in the municipality, making it more likely that all of them know each other within the organization. This increases the likelihood that informal aspects of management control systems will be unleashed. Of these municipalities, we selected those with more than 50,000 inhabitants (equal to 22), and within these, we further identified those with more than 200 employees. These selection criteria allow to focus on those municipalities that are obliged to implement disability management practices and appoint a figure responsible for them, in accordance with the provisions of the 2009 'White Paper on Accessibility and Urban Mobility', L.D. 75/2017 and L. 227/2021. These municipalities should therefore be more attentive to encouraging an IWC for PwD. The selection process yielded a total of nine municipalities that met the selected criteria. These municipalities were contacted by telephone to request their participation in the study. Of these, five (56% of the sample) agreed to participate.

A survey was conducted to investigate the relationship between cultural and personnel controls, OI and IWC for PwD. The survey was sent to the email address (Yammarino et al., 1991) of the municipality, requesting that it be addressed to all non-managerial employees. The privacy and confidentiality of the respondents were assured. A total of 149 responses were received; thus, the final sample for statistical analysis consisted of 149 public employees (Table 1).

The majority of respondents (46%) are between 51 and 60 years old, 30% are over 60 years old, and only 15% of the respondents are up to 40 years old. Fifty-three percent of the respondents are male. Almost all respondents have completed high school (42%) or university (42%). Over half of the respondents (51%) have more than 20 years of public service; 13% have less than 5 years of public service, while only 8% have between 5 and 10 years of public service.

Table 1 Sample composition

Sample composition
Age
Up to 30 years: 2%
Between 31 and 40 years: 13%
Between 41 and 50 years: 22%
Between 51 and 60 years: 46%
More than 60 years: 17%
Gender
Male: 53%
Female: 47%
Education
Middle school: 5%
High school: 42%
Bachelor's or master's degree: 40%
Higher than master's degree: 13%
Years of public employment
Less than 5 years: 13%
Between 5 and 10 years: 8%
Between 11 and 20 years: 28%
More than 20 years: 51%

3.2 Survey

The questionnaire contains items aimed at measuring the characteristics of respondents, their perceptions of cultural and personnel controls, the degree of OI, and the IWC for PwD.

Cultural and personnel controls were each measured by five items based on Merchant and Van der Stede (Merchant & Van der Stede, 2007), as adopted by Van der Kolk et al. (Van der Kolk et al., 2019). These are 5-point Likert-type scales that explore employees' feelings regarding the informal controls implemented by their organizations, which are, respectively, culturally based ('Employees provide each other with solicited and unsolicited feedback'; 'Norms and values are seldom communicated to employees'; 'Employees know what is expected from them from the prevailing culture'; 'Employees check each other's activities regularly'; 'Employees know what is expected from them from the exemplary behavior of superiors') and personnel-based (e.g. 'Job and task descriptions are being used to provide employees with clarity about their tasks'; 'Many opportunities for training and education are being offered'; 'Employees receive possibilities to become more self-managed'; 'New hires receive elaborate training and learning time'; 'New employees are being selected by a strong selection process'). Cronbach's alpha of 0.944 and 0.968, respectively, which is above the threshold of 0.70, confirmed the reliability of the scale.

OI consists of five items from Smidts et al.'s (Smidts et al., 2001) scale. These items measure the degree of employees' attachment and affective bond to the municipality on a 7-point Likert-type scale ('I feel strong ties with my organization'; 'I experience a strong sense of belonging to my organization'; 'I am sufficiently acknowledged in my organization'; 'I feel proud to work for my organization'; 'I am glad to be a member of my organization'). Cronbach's alpha is 0.863.

IWC was captured by the Nelissen et al.'s (Nelissen et al., 2017) scale. It includes five items measuring on a 5-point Likert-type scale the extent to which executive employees perceive their municipalities to include PwD in their work activities ('In my organization people with disabilities are accepted'; 'In my organization people with disabilities are helped'; 'In my organization people with disabilities are treated as other colleagues', 'In my organization we are attentive to the needs of people with disabilities'; 'In my organization we are attentive to the opportunities of people with disabilities'). Cronbach's alpha is 0.795.

The measurement scales have been slightly adapted to relate them to the context of municipalities and also following the input of a pilot test of the questionnaire with a small group of public employees. Therefore, the validity of these scales was tested by an exploratory factor analysis; factor loadings above 0.50 for all the items allowed to verify the convergent validity of all the scales; the absence of significant cross-loadings confirmed their discriminant validity.

4 Statistical Analyses

4.1 Descriptive and Correlation Analyses

Descriptive and correlation analyses were performed. Table 2 presents the descriptive statistics of the variables.

The mean values of cultural control (3.64), personnel control (3.20), and IWC for PwD (3.04) are well above the neutrality threshold, based on the five-point extension of the scales. In line with the seven-point extension of the scale measuring OI, the average score of this construct (4.06) is also positioned above the neutrality threshold.

The results of the correlation analysis provide some preliminary evidence on the relationship between the variables, showing that cultural control is positively correlated with personnel control ($r = 0.762$, $p \leq 0.001$) and OI ($r = 0.348$, $p \leq 0.001$),

Table 2 Descriptive statistics and correlations

Variable	Mean	SD	1	2	3	4
1. Cultural control	3.64	1.08	1			
2. Personnel control	3.20	1.19	0.762***	1		
3. Organizational identification	4.06	1.24	0.348***	0.337***	1	
4. Inclusive workplace climate for PwD	3.04	0.83	0.145	0.096	0.366***	1

*p-value ≤0.05; **p-value ≤0.01; ***p-value ≤0.001

Table 3 Regression analysis

	Independent variable			Control variable			
Dependent variable	Cultural control	Personnel control	Organiz. Identif.	Gender	Education	R^2	Hp
Organizational identification	0.416*** (0.09)			0.048 (0.19)	0.16 (0.19)	0.13	Hp 1
		0.358*** (0.08)		0.029 (0.19)	0.16 (0.19)	0.12	Hp 2
Inclusive workplace climate for PwD			0.244*** (0.05)	0.306* (0.13)	−0.06 (0.13)	0.17	Hp 3

Standard error in brackets
**p*-value ≤0.05; ***p*-value ≤0.01; ****p*-value ≤0.001

which, in turn, is positively correlated with personnel control ($r = 0.337$, $p \leq 0.001$) and IWC for PwD ($r = 0.366$, $p \leq 0.001$).

4.2 Regression Analysis

The research hypotheses were tested using linear regression analysis, with gender and education included as control variables. Table 3 presents the results obtained.

The evidence demonstrated that both cultural and personnel controls had the expected significant effect on OI ($\beta = 0.416$, $p \leq 0.001$ and $\beta = 0.358$, $p \leq 0.001$, respectively), confirming research hypotheses 1 and 2. Our evidence also documented a positive significant relationship between OI and an IWC for PwD ($\beta = 0.244$, $p \leq 0.001$), consistently with Hp 3. Additionally, the control variable gender is also significant in this path ($\beta = 0.306$, $p \leq 0.05$). Therefore, all the hypothesized relationships were verified.

5 Discussion

The study aimed to explore the role and the effectiveness of informal controls, namely, cultural and personnel controls, as perceived by non-managerial employees, in promoting a better IWC for PwD within public organizations. To address this issue, an empirical analysis was conducted on a sample of municipalities in southern Italian, where the workplace inclusion of PwD is a particularly pressing concern. This is due to the specific socio-cultural factors and more critical economic development conditions, which result in a greater risk of workplace discrimination and fewer employment opportunities especially for PwD.

The results revealed that both cultural and personnel controls contribute to the alignment of public employees' values and goals with those of their organization, thus reinforcing OI. Therefore, these findings confirmed research hypotheses 1 and

2. They enriched the extant evidence on the motivational role of the informal dynamics of management control systems functioning from the perspective of public employees without managerial responsibilities.

Furthermore, such findings are consistent with the previous research on the efficacy of cultural and personnel controls in satisfying employees' need for relatedness (Van der Kolk et al., 2019). This facilitates the sharing of organizational values, including those of social responsibility, which in public organizations have complex roots intertwined with public value (Abdelmotaleb & Saha, 2019; Bracci et al., 2019). In this context, the findings indicated that OI strengthens employees' emotional ties and affective bond with the organization and the goals, as public servants, thereby reinforcing their relations with the public service. This, in turn, feeds a greater IWC for PwD. Consequently, the results also validated Hp 3, providing further insights into the relational drivers of IWC for PwD as micro-CSR outcomes in public organizations (Aguinis & Glavas, 2012; D'Aprile & Talò, 2014). They represent an enabling driver of CSR perceptions of these organizational actors, as they operate on the links between the sense of social responsibility, which is internally transmitted by their public organization, and the values, prosocial behaviours, and public service motivation as public servants (Abdelmotaleb & Saha, 2019; Nelissen et al., 2017). These insights are valuable, because they provide a better understanding of the effectiveness of personnel and cultural controls, concurrent with that of formal management controls, in positively influencing employees' organizational outcomes, even if personnel and cultural controls are less visible and typically not a deliberately designed means of focusing employees' attention on organizational goals (Laguir et al., 2019).

All in all, these findings validated the dynamics described by self-determination theory (Gagné & Deci, 2005). Furthermore, they support the need for integration of the relational dimensions induced by informal controls within the mechanistic structure of management control systems used to increase the probability of alignment of individual behaviours with public organizations' objectives and values, including those linked to the social dimension of CSR. This would allow for a substantial increase in the workplace inclusion of PwD, as opposed to the mere CSR behaviours of 'inclusion washing', which are often induced by the traditional bureaucratic orientation to the fulfilment of requirements, particularly in public organizations. Such inclusion is substantial if it is built on the interiorization of a felt and shared value in public organizations, where the individual's 'disability' is to be perceived, accepted, and at the centre of the managerial approaches for the enhancement of PwD's contribution to the organizational performance (Mor Barak et al., 2021; Oware & Mallikarjunappa, 2021).

6 Conclusions

This work contributes to the research applied to public organizations on the integration of management control systems with micro-foundations of social responsibility (Bracci et al., 2019; Johnstone, 2019) and to emerging studies on the drivers of CSR in the public context (Aguilera et al., 2007; Aguinis & Glavas, 2012; Hammon et al., 2023).

Along these lines, the study complements existing findings relying on managerial perceptions about management control systems with additional insights based on the largely overlooked employees' perceptions of control (Tessier & Otley, 2012). In these terms of contribution, our study values the role cultural and personnel controls play in inducing public employees to foster feelings of relatedness (Van der Kolk et al., 2019), thereby creating an environment that supports an IWC for PwD (Coll & Mignonac, 2023; Metallo et al., 2009). In these dimensions of CSR outcomes, the paper adds some relevant insights on the micro-foundations of the IWC for PwD in the context of public organizations, contributing to the literature on disability management practices (Angeloni, 2013; Palumbo et al., 2023).

Research suggests that public management and policymakers should search for stronger integration and coordination of personnel and cultural controls with human resource management practices, which are more directly involved in disability management issues. The promotion of principles of social inclusion and equal opportunities, from within, would allow for the common building of fair and sustainable development models, thereby ensuring the pursuit of broader public values and aims that public organizations embody (Aguinis & Glavas, 2012; Burns & Jollands, 2020).

Despite our results, it must be noted that findings are survey-driven and based on a restricted number of observations. This limits the potential for generalizations, as the responses are influenced by the organizational context and the subjective interpretation of the respondents. Enlarging the research sample would allow to test the validity of the observed dynamics within other municipalities and other types of public organizations. Furthermore, in the future development of the research, it would be beneficial to explore the role of some intervening factors, such as work engagement, intrinsic motivation, or well-being. Additionally, the link between the IWC of PwD with the performance outcomes from public employees' perspective can be scrutinized in future studies. Finally, since this study considers the perceptions of all non-managerial employees as a whole, it might be interesting to distinguish these two perspectives to verify convergences and differences in the analyzed paths.

References

Abdelmotaleb, M., & Saha, S. K. (2019). Corporate social responsibility, public service motivation and organizational citizenship behavior in the public sector. *International Journal of Public Administration, 42*(11), 929–939.

Agovino, M., & Rapposelli, A. (2017). Regional performance trends in providing employment for persons with disabilities: Evidence from Italy. *Social Indicators Research, 130*, 593–615.

Agovino, M., & Rapposelli, A. (2020). Laws for the right to work of disabled people: The Italian experience. *The Palgrave Handbook of Disability at Work*, 79–95.

Aguilera, R. V., Rupp, D. E., Williams, C. A., & Ganapathi, J. (2007). Putting the S back in corporate social responsibility: A multilevel theory of social change in organizations. *Academy of Management Review, 32*(3), 836–863.

Aguinis, H., & Glavas, A. (2012). What we know and don't know about corporate social responsibility: A review and research agenda. *Journal of Management, 38*, 932–968.

Amici, M., & Cepiku, D. (2020). Performance management: A theoretical framework. In *Performance management in international organizations* (pp. 97–114). Palgrave Pivot.

Angeloni, S. (2013). Integrated disability management: An interdisciplinary and holistic approach. *SAGE Open, 3*(4), 1–15.

Bracci, E., Papi, L., Bigoni, M., Deidda Gagliardo, E., & Bruns, H. J. (2019). Public value and public sector accounting research: A structured literature review. *Journal of Public Budgeting, Accounting & Financial Management, 31*(1), 103–136.

Burns, J., & Jollands, S. (2020). Acting in the public interest: Accounting for the vulnerable. *Accounting and Business Research, 50*(5), 507–534.

Cepiku, D., Hinna, A., Scarozza, D., & Savignon, A. B. (2017). Performance information use in public administration: An exploratory study of determinants and effects. *Journal of Management & Governance, 21*, 963–991.

Coll, C., & Mignonac, K. (2023). Perceived organizational support and task performance of employees with disabilities: A need satisfaction and social identity perspectives. *The International Journal of Human Resource Management, 34*(10), 2039–2073.

D'Aprile, G., & Talò, C. (2014). Measuring corporate social responsibility as a psychosocial construct: A new multidimensional scale. *Employee Responsibilities & Rights Journal, 26*(3), 153–175.

Gagné, M., & Deci, E. L. (2005). Self-determination theory and work motivation. *Journal of Organizational Behavior, 26*(4), 331–362.

Hammon, S. D., Gillis, W. E., & Icenogle, M. L. (2023). From social responsibility to employee engagement: Evidence from the public sector. *Journal of Management and Governance, 27*(4), 1223–1247.

ISTAT. (2023). *Disabilità in Cifre.* Retrieved from https://disabilitaincifre.istat.it/.

Johnstone, L. (2019). Theorising and conceptualising the sustainability control system for effective sustainability management. *Journal of Management Control, 30*(1), 25–64.

Laguir, L., Laguir, I., & Tchemeni, E. (2019). Implementing CSR activities through management control systems: A formal and informal control perspective. *Accounting, Auditing & Accountability Journal, 32*(2), 531–555.

Merchant, K. A., & Van der Stede, W. A. (2007). *Management control systems: Performance measurement, evaluation and incentives*. Prentice Hall.

Metallo, G., Ricci, P., & Migliaccio, G. (Eds.). (2009). *La risorsa umana "diversamente abile" nell'economia dell'azienda*. Giappichelli.

Migliaccio, G. (2019). Disabled people in the stakeholder theory: A literature analysis. *Journal of the Knowledge Economy, 10*(4), 1657–1678.

Mor Barak, M. E., Luria, G., & Brimhall, K. C. (2021). What leaders say versus what they do: Inclusive leadership, policy-practice decoupling, and the anomaly of climate for inclusion. *Group & Organization Management, 47*, 840–871.

Nelissen, P. T. J. H., Hülsheger, U. R., Van Ruitenbeek, G. M. C., & Zijlstra, F. R. H. (2017). Lending a helping hand at work: A multilevel investigation of prosocial motivation, inclusive climate and inclusive behavior. *Journal of Occupational Rehabilitation, 27*, 467–476.

Oware, K. M., & Mallikarjunappa, T. (2021). Disability employment and financial performance: The effect of technological innovation of listed firms in India. *Social Responsibility Journal, 17*(3), 384–398.

Palumbo, R., Hinna, A., & Manesh, M. F. (2023). Aiming at inclusive workplaces: A bibliometric and interpretive review at the crossroads of disability management and human resource management. *Journal of Management & Organization*, 1–24.

Raucci, D., & Paolini, M. (2022). Informazioni budgetarie e prospettive di behavioral management accounting nelle aziende sanitarie pubbliche italiane. *Management Control, 2*, 117–139.

Ryan, R. M., & Deci, E. L. (2000). Self-determination theory and the facilitation of intrinsic motivation, social development, and well-being. *American Psychologist, 55*(1), 68–78.

Smidts, A., Pruyn, A. T. H., & Van Riel, C. B. (2001). The impact of employee communication and perceived external prestige on organizational identification. *Academy of Management Journal, 44*(5), 1051–1062.

Tessier, S., & Otley, D. (2012). A conceptual development of Simons' levers of control framework. *Management Accounting Research, 23*(3), 171–185.

Tucker, B. P., & Nash, E. (2023). Good for business: Towards a management control research agenda relating to the employment of workers with intellectual disability. *Journal of Accounting Literature*.

Van der Kolk, B., Van Veen-Dirks, P. M., & ter Bogt, H. J. (2019). The impact of management control on employee motivation and performance in the public sector. *European Accounting Review, 28*(5), 901–928.

Yammarino, F. J., Skinner, S. J., & Childers, T. L. (1991). Understanding mail survey response behavior a meta-analysis. *Public Opinion Quarterly, 55*(4), 613–639.

Exploring Gender Disparities in the Era of AI

Tommaso Fornasari and Mariasole Bannò

1 Introduction

Automation technologies like artificial intelligence, big data analytics, and industrial robots have played a significant role in the recent drastic changes in the world of work. These technologies have led to changes in the occupational hierarchy, work location and schedule, and career trajectories. Automation technologies have rapidly improved, allowing for a variety of work tasks to be performed more efficiently. This has led to the possibility of replacing workers, regardless of gender, in an increasing number of jobs (Blanas et al., 2019; Wajcman, 2017).

Artificial intelligence (AI) has made significant progress over the last two decades, allowing for the accomplishment of non-routine tasks that were once believed to be possible only for humans. AI has the capacity to supplant workers in a range of professions, encompassing both low-skill and high-skill positions, potentially leading to widespread job displacement in the upcoming years. There has been much debate about the impact of technology on work, particularly regarding AI in accounting. Gusai (2019) has examined the role of AI in accounting and emphasized how AI is replacing the traditional roles of accountants while highlighting the superior efficiency of AI systems in accounting tasks. Hasan (2021) provided insights into how the job roles of accountants are rapidly evolving due to AI, forecasting a significant shift towards consulting and advisory roles over the next decade.

T. Fornasari (✉)
Department of Economics and Management, University of Brescia, Brescia, Italy
e-mail: tommaso.fornasari@unibs.it

M. Bannò
Department of Mechanical Engineering, University of Brescia, Brescia, Italy
e-mail: mariasole.banno@unibs.it

M. Agostini et al. (eds.), *Diversity and Equity in Accounting*, SIDREA Series in Accounting and Business Administration,
https://doi.org/10.1007/978-3-031-78247-3_14

However, there is a lack of studies that specifically analyze how AI affects work from a gender standpoint (Filippi et al., 2023). Our research aims to address this gap by conducting an initial qualitative analysis of the risks of substitution for women compared to men in the accounting field by gathering insights from various stakeholders with different perspectives. We aim to uncover workforce inequalities and understand how AI could affect individuals differently based on their gender by analyzing the outcomes through a gender lens.

This research employs qualitative methods with the specific aim of deeply investigating gender disparities. Since this process is closely dependent on the context and the variables influencing it are complex, interconnected, and difficult to measure, the decision was made to gather as much information as possible, including dimensions that might not be considered through quantitative techniques. The resulting description is, therefore, richer, and ambiguities, exceptions, and best practices can be more easily identified. Specifically, we adopt direct interviews as the primary research tool.

2 The Impact of AI on Women's Work

2.1 The Impact of AI: Positive and Negative Aspects

AI implementation can result in both favourable and unfavourable outcomes that may raise non-economic issues. AI could lead to a reduction in company employment and employee contentment and well-being, even though it has the potential to boost firm efficiency. AI affects employment through two contrasting effects: substitution, where AI replaces workers or enhances labour productivity, and compensation, which offsets the initial decrease in employment by indirect means. Acemoglu and Restrepo (2019) suggested that the ultimate outcome may result in an overall reduction in employment. Some studies suggest that investments in AI have a slightly beneficial influence on firm employment, while other studies indicate that AI is linked to job loss and has a detrimental impact on recruiting at both the business and plant levels.

The effects of AI could vary based on numerous aspects. Some studies suggest that AI has no effect on jobs at the occupational level (Caselli et al., 2021), while others indicate that it generates employment for middle-skilled workers in manufacturing companies in central China but leads to job losses for low-skilled workers in different areas (Xie et al., 2021). AI has employment consequences related to altering work organizations rather than replacing workers (Boavida & Candeias, 2021). AI does not have any discernible impact on hiring at the industry level, maybe due to its consequences not being realized yet, despite its capacity to replace labour in certain activities. AI raises the need for skills in medium-tech sectors, but not in low-tech sectors (Xie et al., 2021). Research examining the influence of AI on productivity indicates that it has a modest beneficial effect on enterprises' productivity, estimated at approximately 5% on average (Bessen and Righi, 2019).

AI promotes job growth in high-income occupations but has little impact on low- and middle-income occupations (Felten et al., 2019). AI boosts non-routine tasks in both low-skill and high-skill jobs but reduces routine tasks in middle-skill jobs. When AI is integrated with other technologies, even high-skill jobs can experience a decrease in demand (Tschang & Almirall, 2021). AI adoption results in the displacement of low-skilled production workers and the recruitment of high-skilled tech workers, with the magnitude of this effect growing over time (Xie et al., 2021). Jobs with minimal exposure to AI require skills in complicated problem-solving, interpersonal communication, and non-repetitive manual tasks (Webb, 2019).

Although there is hope that more job opportunities will emerge in the market, some occupations may experience a slight decline in employment as a result of AI (Vermeulen et al., 2018). The occupations most vulnerable to AI are office and administrative support and production, while those least vulnerable are healthcare, management, architecture and engineering, academia, and art. Overall, there is a trend of decline in low- and medium-skill professions and an increase in high-skill occupations, although there are exceptions, with some low- and medium-skill occupations experiencing growth as well (Vermeulen et al., 2018).

Finally, AI may impact intangible factors influencing employees' well-being, like expectations, job opportunities, career fulfilment, mental health, and stress (Schwabe & Castellacci, 2020). When a company contemplates implementing AI, employees may start to worry about potential job losses and financial challenges (Schwabe & Castellacci, 2020). Job satisfaction declines as a result of employees feeling undervalued and ignored by their employers. Prolonged work insecurity might heighten the likelihood of experiencing psychological stress, anxiety, and burnout.

When analysing women and men, the research on the impact of AI on employment is lacking, and the results are frequently inconclusive and inconsistent (Bannò et al., 2023; Filippi et al., 2023). Women may experience a greater impact because they are underrepresented in both employment and education in the rapidly expanding STEM fields (Avolio et al., 2020). García-Holgado et al. (2019) have confirmed that the low representation of women in STEM fields is a disadvantage that could lead to a significant number of women being pushed out of the job market. Another reason for the adverse effects of AI on women is the utilization of automation technologies to carry out basic repetitive tasks, typically handled by women.[1] Only a limited number of studies have indicated that AI will have a lesser effect on women (Filippi et al., 2023).

[1] According to previous research, the nature of women's occupations and the particular tasks they perform have an impact on their risk of substitution. Previous research indicates that women and men are exposed to varying levels of replacement risk from automation as they engage in distinct occupations and work tasks, even within the same field (Mason, 2021).

2.2 The Impact of AI on Accounting

The integration of AI into the accounting field is reshaping job roles, skill requirements, and career trajectories, presenting challenges and opportunities.

AI is primarily affecting routine and repetitive tasks within accounting—roles that have historically seen higher women's participation at the entry level. The use of AI in this field could potentially displace jobs but also opens doors for a transition to more strategic and analytical roles that are less prone to automation (Alderman, 2021). Moreover, the adoption of AI in accounting could influence work-life balance positively (Gupta et al., 2022). AI can replace long hours and manual labour, offering a more flexible work environment (Wisskirchen et al., 2017).

However, this technological shift also necessitates attention to training and access (Kulkov, 2021). There is a risk that women could lag in skill acquisition if they face barriers to educational resources or bias in workplace training opportunities. While AI introduces some risks, it also holds significant potential for empowering women in the accounting profession, provided there is a conscious effort towards equitable training, opportunity distribution, and ethical AI usage (Dwivedi et al., 2021).

These theoretical premises allow us to elaborate on the research question:

What is the different impact of AI on men and women in the accounting field?

3 Method

3.1 Data Collection

Due to the intricate and interconnected nature of the variables influencing AI and work in the accounting field, a decision was made to collect extensive information through interviews, including dimensions that may not be captured using quantitative methods. Consequently, the description becomes more detailed, allowing for clearer identification of ambiguities, exceptions, and best practices. In particular, we use direct interviews as the main method of research.

The strategy used for choosing the respondents for the interviews is the information-oriented selection, which aims to maximize the utility of information from small samples (Flyvbjerg, 2006). In this type of selection, respondents are chosen based on expectations about their information content. Among the possible forms of sampling, we selected Italian respondents with the maximum variation with the aim of obtaining information about how various circumstances are significant in explaining case processes and outcomes. The interview features a varied panel consisting of a chartered accountant, an entrepreneur with an engineering background, a manager from an AI company, and a researcher, all aged between 40 and 50 years. Every participant contributes distinct viewpoints and specialized knowledge to the conversation, ensuring a thorough examination of the influence of AI on different job functions, particularly accounting.

Respondent 1: Fifty-year-old Chartered Accountant and Councillor of the Institute of Chartered Accountants:

(a) He/she provides a historical view of the development of accounting and the significant impact of AI over time.
(b) He/she analyzes the difficulties and advantages that AI brings to experienced accounting professionals, such as changes in work procedures and skill demands.

Respondent 2: Forty-year-old Entrepreneur with engineering background:

(a) He/she shares firsthand experiences about incorporating AI into their business operations and its impact on financial management and planning.
(b) Examines the strategic financial decision-making and operational optimization improved by implementing AI.

Respondent 3: Fifty-year-old Manager from an artificial intelligence company:

(a) He/she provides a detailed examination of AI's precise uses in the accounting field, including advancements in technology and upcoming trends.
(b) He/she explores the profound influence of AI on accounting services and how businesses in the industry are adjusting their business models in response.

Respondent 4: Forty-year-old Researcher:

(a) He/she provides an academic analysis of AI and accounting, covering current research, trends, and potential future implications.
(b) He/she explores ethical and legal considerations associated with AI utilization in accounting and advocates for measures to ensure responsible implementation.

The paper seeks to provide a thorough understanding of how AI is changing the accounting field by comparing different perspectives and insights from various respondents.

3.2 *Interview Structure*

The interview consists of four primary questions and several sub-questions.

- How has AI impacted labor force[2] participation among men and women, particularly in relation to both skilled and unskilled job roles?

[2] When we refer to the labor market, we are talking about the overall job market, not just the one specific to your company.

  - Is there a disparity in access to AI-related job opportunities based on gender? If yes, for what reason?
  - Are there gender differences in the effects of AI on high-skilled work in terms of horizontal segregation? If so, how?
  - What about vertical segregation in career paths?

- What is the specific influence of AI on the workforce, particularly in terms of gender differences within your company or working environment?
  - What is your company's specific experience with automation, and how has it impacted your workforce overall? Are there gender-specific differences?
  - Can you provide specific instances of how AI has enhanced or altered daily operations in your organization or context? Are there gender-specific differences?
  - How have automation and AI impacted the skills needed for your company's workforce? Are there gender-specific differences?

- How has AI impacted highly skilled jobs, and what are the resulting gender disparities?
  - Are there disparities in the allocation of high-skilled positions between men and women in the era of AI?
  - How do disparities in educational and professional access based on gender affect participation in high-skilled jobs affected by AI?

- How can strategies be used to lessen the adverse impacts of automation and AI on the workforce, taking into account gender disparities?
  - Are there targeted policies in place to safeguard and assist female employees in industries significantly impacted by automation and AI?
  - What strategies or policies could be enacted at the corporate or governmental level to reduce the adverse impacts of automation and AI on the workforce? And according to gender?

3.3 Data Analysis

Initially, we concentrated on each individual case during the analysis. The interviews, ranging from 45 to 90 min in duration, were transcribed after being digitally recorded. To prevent errors caused by halo effects and interpretation biases, only a specific group of authors, which included those who did not participate in the interviews, utilized the transcribed notes to analyze the effects of AI on female work. We utilized the transcribed notes to create an initial framework. We proceeded with an iterative process by marking quotes and concepts and then reviewing our notes to identify patterns or themes among interviewees from the same firm (Thomas, 2006).

A cross-case analysis was conducted in the second step to identify consistent patterns and themes, including both commonalities and contradictions (Miles and Huberman, 1994).

The findings were discussed and compared with existing literature to ensure reliability and validity according to current case study research standards (De Massis and Kotlar, 2014).

4 Results

The section presents themes that have been identified through original quotations (Kallmuenzer et al., 2018). The quotation's source (interviewee's role) is provided in brackets.

- How has AI impacted labor force participation among men and women, particularly in relation to both skilled and unskilled job roles?

Respondent 1 (Chartered Accountant): *AI has impacted labor market participation differently for men and women. AI contributes to bridging the age gap more than the gender gap by enhancing service provision to clients and reducing disparities. A broad spectrum of skills is crucial in AI management, encompassing both technical and humanistic abilities. Women frequently perform exceptionally well in control roles because of their accuracy and capacity to collaborate effectively with AI technologies.*

Respondent 2 (Entrepreneur with engineering background): *AI's effect on labor market participation is similar for both genders across various job levels. There are more women in lower-skilled positions, and men dominate higher-skilled positions.*

Respondent 3 (Manager from an AI company): *Recently, there has been a significant rise in the number of women with STEM backgrounds, especially among those under 35. This trend has resulted in decreased differences in labor market involvement.*

Respondent 4 (Researcher): *AI has contributed to an increase in female participation in the labor market by reducing execution times for tasks. Access to AI-related opportunities varies because of the limited number of female graduates in STEM fields. It emphasizes the need to tackle gender disparities in STEM education to guarantee equal access to AI-related job opportunities for both genders.*

- What is the specific influence of AI on the workforce, particularly in terms of gender differences within your company or working environment?

Respondent 1 (Chartered Accountant): *AI has not been integrated into our accounting firm, but larger firms such as the Big 4 may be considering its implementation. Currently, there is no discernible difference in the impact of AI on men and women in our workplace.*

Respondent 2 (Entrepreneur with engineering background): *Our companies have a higher proportion of male employees due to the larger number of qualified men in STEM fields, which are frequently required for the positions we provide. The gender imbalance in our workforce mirrors larger patterns seen in STEM fields.*

Respondent 3 (Manager from an AI company): *At our fledgling AI company, we have not observed notable disparities between the effects of AI on the workforce based on gender. Technical positions typically draw a larger number of male applicants, possibly because there are more male CVs submitted for those roles.*

Respondent 4 (Researcher): *As a researcher, the impact of AI on the workforce isn't directly relevant to my field. Research settings usually prioritize competency and credentials over gender differences when evaluating the implementation of AI technologies.*

- How has AI impacted highly skilled jobs, and what are the resulting gender disparities?

Respondent 1 (Chartered Accountant): *Basic tasks are likely to be automated, which could lead to a reduction in gender disparities as it streamlines processes and removes gender biases inherent in manual tasks.*

Respondent 2 (Entrepreneur with engineering background): *AI within our company elevates skilled jobs by enabling humans to concentrate on more advanced tasks. In our situation, men mostly hold these skilled positions. Although AI can enhance workflow and efficiency, it is essential to focus on rectifying gender disparities in hiring and promotion procedures.*

Respondent 3 (Manager from an AI company): *AI can greatly enhance human abilities in professions that demand high levels of creativity. For example, a collaboration between one individual and AI can achieve the output of three people. Combining human and AI capabilities can result in increased efficiency and productivity, without regard to gender.*

Respondent 4 (Researcher): *In university settings, there isn't a gender disparity in the distribution of highly skilled jobs, but rather in roles within those positions. Encouraging women to pursue STEM courses can help bridge the gender gap and promote diversity and inclusivity in AI-related fields.*

- How can strategies be used to lessen the adverse impacts of automation and AI on the workforce, taking into account gender disparities?

Respondent 1 (Chartered Accountant): *In accounting, we expect significant benefits from automation and AI, without anticipating any negative impacts. Integrating AI can improve processes and open up opportunities for more significant contributions, maximizing women's potential in the workforce.*

Respondent 2 (Entrepreneur with engineering background): *So far, automation and AI have not had any adverse effects on our industry. It is crucial to stay alert and take proactive steps to evaluate possible future obstacles and put in place measures to reduce any negative impacts, thus guaranteeing gender equality in light of technological progress.*

Respondent 3 (Manager from an AI company): *AI has the potential to enhance output levels significantly, with the same results achievable with only a fraction of the current effort. This principle is in line with the concept of Pareto efficiency, where individuals stay one step ahead of machines. Women excel in strategic thinking and execution in tasks with high value addition, making them ideal for collaborating with AI technologies.*

Respondent 4 (Researcher): *We expect automation and AI to bring multiple benefits without causing any negative effects. Enhanced time management with the help of AI can help women showcase their full potential in the workplace by managing professional and personal duties more efficiently. Improved work-life balance can help promote increased gender equality in the workplace.*

The interviews revealed that the influence of AI on labour market participation differs between men and women in various situations.

While some respondents noted a shift in job dynamics with AI facilitating the provision of additional services and potentially reducing gender disparities, others highlighted persisting gender imbalances, particularly in highly skilled positions.

A recurring theme is the significance of STEM education in tackling these disparities. Respondents observed a favourable trend of increased women's participation in STEM fields, leading to a more equitable distribution of labour market involvement, particularly among young people. There is a necessity to motivate women to pursue STEM education in order to achieve equal representation in specialized positions and enhance diversity in AI-related fields.

Finally, strategies aimed at reducing the adverse impacts of automation and AI on the workforce need to take into account gender disparities. Proactive measures are essential to address potential challenges and ensure gender equality in utilizing AI's advantages and opportunities for women.

5 Discussion and Conclusion

Advancements in automation technologies, especially artificial intelligence (AI), are increasing the likelihood of job displacement in various occupations. Previous studies have examined the influence of AI advancements on the labour force without considering the gender-specific effects. In fact, limited attention has been paid to how the impact of automation and specifically AI differs between women and men (Rodriguez-Bustelo et al., 2020), and the few existing studies on the issue have yielded conflicting results (Egana-delSol et al., 2021; Nedelkoska & Quintini, 2018). Our study demonstrates how incorporating AI can improve productivity and effectiveness, complementing the strategic thinking and execution skills of women. Enhanced time management through AI can help women achieve a better equilibrium between work and personal life, leading to increased gender equality in the workplace.

These results have both managerial and policy implications.

Organizations can implement managerial strategies to tackle gender disparities in automation and AI, in addition to policy implications. It is essential to cultivate an inclusive and diverse culture within the organization. Managers should focus on establishing an inclusive environment that values and respects all employees, regardless of gender. This entails encouraging transparent communication, actively pursuing varied viewpoints, and confronting any prejudices or discriminatory conduct that may be present. Investing in training and development programs that focus on enhancing skills needed for the evolving work landscape influenced by automation and AI can empower employees, especially women, to successfully adjust and excel in their positions. This may involve programs that emphasize digital literacy, problem-solving, and creativity—skills that are becoming more crucial in AI-driven work environments.

Educational policies play a pivotal role: investing in STEM education programs tailored to encourage and support women's participation can cultivate a diverse talent pool equipped to thrive in the evolving job market (Castellano & Rocca, 2018). The programs should include scholarships, mentorship opportunities, and activities aimed at challenging gender stereotypes starting at a young age.

Legislative measures are equally important. Implementing stringent gender equality regulations can help create a fairer environment in workplaces. This could involve requirements for clear salary frameworks, quotas to guarantee gender diversity in leadership roles, and measures supporting work-life balance, like parental leave programs available to all genders. Encouraging continuous learning and skill enhancement is crucial. Offering financial assistance or tax breaks to encourage individuals to engage in ongoing training and requalification can help women adjust to evolving job demands due to automation and AI, promoting career adaptability and advancement (Spencer, 2018).

An integrated strategy incorporating educational, legislative, and supportive actions is crucial to minimize the adverse impacts of automation and AI on the labour market and advance gender equality. Societies can establish inclusive and equitable environments by enacting these policies, ensuring that both men and women have equal opportunities for success in the digital era. Achieving gender equality is not easy and is a long-term investment (Beer, 2009): it requires time and effort by the entire society, national governments, and international organizations. Full participation of both women and men is essential for any economy to achieve its maximum potential (Georgieva et al., 2019).

References

Acemoglu, D., & Restrepo, P. (2019). Artificial intelligence, automation, and work. In A. Agrawal, J. Gans, & A. Goldfarb (Eds.), *The economics of artificial intelligence: An agenda* (pp. 197–236). The University of Chicago Press.

Alderman, J. (2021). Women in the smart machine age: Addressing emerging risks of an increased gender gap in the accounting profession. *Journal of Accounting Education, 55*, 100715.

Avolio, B., Chávez, J., & Vílchez-Román, C. (2020). Factors that contribute to the underrepresentation of women in science careers worldwide: A literature review. *Social Psychology of Education, 23*(3), 773–794.

Bannò, M., Filippi, E., & Trento, S. (2023). Automation technologies and their impact on employment: A review, synthesis and future research agenda. *Technological Forecasting and Social Change, 191.*

Beer, D. (2009). Power through the algorithm? Participatory web cultures and the technological unconscious. *New Media & Society, 11*(6), 985–1002.

Bessen, J., & Righi, C. (2019). Shocking technology: What happens when firms make large IT investments? (Research Paper No. 19–6; Law & Economics Series Paper). Boston University School of Law.

Blanas, S., Gancia, G., & (Tim) Lee, S. Y.. (2019). Who is afraid of machines? *Economic Policy, 34*(100), 627–690.

Boavida, N., & Candeias, M. (2021). Recent automation trends in Portugal: Implications on industrial productivity and employment in automotive sector. *Societies, 11*(3).

Caselli, M., Fracasso, A., Scicchitano, S., Traverso, S., & Tundis, E. (2021). *Stop worrying and love the robot: An activity-based approach to assess the impact of robotization on employment dynamics* (Working Paper No. 67). Istituto Nazionale per l'Analisi delle Politiche Pubbliche (INAPP).

Castellano, R., & Rocca, A. (2018). Gender disparities in European labour markets: A comparison of conditions for men and women in paid employment. *International Labour Review, 157*(4), 589–608.

De Massis, A., & Kotlar, J. (2014). The case study method in family business research: Guidelines for qualitative scholarship. *Journal of Family Business Strategy, 5*(1), 15–29.

Dwivedi, Y. K., Hughes, L., Ismagilova, E., Aarts, G., Coombs, C., Crick, T., et al. (2021). Artificial intelligence (AI): Multidisciplinary perspectives on emerging challenges, opportunities, and agenda for research, practice and policy. *International Journal of Information Management, 57*, 101994.

Egana-delSol, P., Bustelo, M., Ripani, L., Soler, N., & Viollaz, M. (2021). Automation in Latin America: Are women at higher risk of losing their jobs? *Technological Forecasting and Social Change.*

Felten, E. W., Raj, M., & Seamans, R. (2019). *The occupational impact of artificial intelligence: Labor, skills, and polarization.* NYU Stern School of Business.

Filippi, E., Bannò, M., & Trento, S. (2023). Automation technologies and the risk of substitution of women: Can gender equality in the institutional context reduce the risk? *Technological Forecasting and Social Change, 191*, 122528.

Flyvbjerg, B. (2006). Five misunderstandings about case-study research. *Qualitative Inquiry, 12*(2), 219–245.

García-Holgado, A., Díaz, A. C., & García-Peñalvo, F. J. (2019, October). Engaging women into STEM in Latin America: W-STEM project. In *Proceedings of the seventh international conference on technological ecosystems for enhancing multiculturality* (pp. 232–239).

Georgieva, A., Abry, P., Chudáček, V., Djurić, P. M., Frasch, M. G., Kok, R., et al. (2019). Computer-based intrapartum fetal monitoring and beyond: A review of the 2nd workshop on signal processing and monitoring in labor (October 2017, Oxford, UK). *Acta Obstetricia et Gynecologica Scandinavica, 98*(9), 1207–1217.

Gupta, C., Rao, K. R., & Datta, P. (2022). Support vector machine-based prediction of work-life balance among women in information technology organizations. *IEEE Engineering Management Review, 50*(2), 147–155.

Gusai, O. P. (2019). Robot human interaction: Role of artificial intelligence in accounting and auditing. *Indian Journal of Accounting, 51*(1), 59–62.

Hasan, A. R. (2021). Artificial intelligence (AI) in accounting & auditing: A literature review. *Open Journal of Business and Management, 10*(1), 440–465.

Kallmuenzer, A., Nikolakis, W., Peters, M., & Zanon, J. (2018). Trade-offs between dimensions of sustainability: Exploratory evidence from family firms in rural tourism regions. *Journal of Sustainable Tourism, 26*(7), 1204–1221.

Kulkov, I. (2021). The role of artificial intelligence in business transformation: A case of pharmaceutical companies. *Technology in Society, 66*, 101629.

Mason, P. L. (2021). Computerization and occupational change: Assessing the impact of automation on racial and gender employment densities. *Review of Black Political Economy*.

Miles, M. B., & Huberman, A. M. (1994). *Qualitative data analysis: An expanded sourcebook*. Sage.

Nedelkoska, L., & Quintini, G. (2018). *Automation, skills use and training* (OECD social, employment and migration working papers no. 202). OECD Publishing. https://www.oecd-ilibrary.org/employment/automation-skills-use-and-training_2e2f4eea-en.

Rodriguez-Bustelo, C., Batista-Foguet, J. M., & Serlavós, R. (2020). Debating the future of work: The perception and reaction of the Spanish workforce to digitization and automation technologies. *Frontiers in Psychology, 11*, 1965.

Schwabe, H., & Castellacci, F. (2020). Automation workers' skills and job satisfaction. *PLOS ONE, 15*(11), e024292. https://doi.org/10.1371/journal.pone.0242929.

Spencer, D. A. (2018). Fear and hope in an age of mass automation: Debating the future of work. *New Technology, Work and Employment, 33*(1), 1–12.

Thomas, D. R. (2006). A general inductive approach for analyzing qualitative evaluation data. *American Journal of Evaluation, 27*(2), 237–246.

Tschang, F. T., & Almirall, E. (2021). Artificial intelligence as augmenting automation: Implications for employment. *Academy of Management Perspectives, 35*(4), 642–659.

Vermeulen, B., Kesselhut, J., Pyka, A., & Saviotti, P. (2018). The impact of automation on employment: Just the usual structural change? *Sustainability, 10*(5), 1661.

Wajcman, J. (2017). Automation: Is it really different this time? *The British Journal of Sociology, 68*(1), 119–127.

Webb, M. (2019). The impact of artificial intelligence on the labor market. *SSRN Electronic Journal*.

Wisskirchen, G., Biacabe, B. T., Bormann, U., Muntz, A., Niehaus, G., Soler, G. J., & von Brauchitsch, B. (2017). Artificial intelligence and robotics and their impact on the workplace. *IBA Global Employment Institute, 11*(5), 49–67.

Xie, M., Ding, L., Xia, Y., Guo, J., Pan, J., & Wang, H. (2021). Does artificial intelligence affect the pattern of skill demand? Evidence from Chinese manufacturing firms. *Economic Modelling, 96*, 295–309.

Do Women Behave More Ethically Than Men? Evidence from the Impact of Female CEO on the Level of Earnings Management

Davide Rizzotti and Claudia Frisenna

1 Introduction

Over the last few years, the issue of female representation on corporate boards has become a central topic in corporate governance debate (e.g., Krishnan & Parsons, 2008; Terjesen et al., 2009; Srinidhi et al., 2011; Gull et al., 2018; Mnif Sellami & Cherif, 2020; Chen et al., 2022; Ongsakul et al., 2022).

Prior studies show that, under certain conditions, the female presence in the board of directors could be a driver of governance effectiveness, as gender diversity brings variegate perspectives to the board, which, in turn, enhances both problem-solving and decision-making processes (Terjesen et al., 2015).

Nevertheless, and notwithstanding the progress made, the presence of women in the boardroom still falls short of the desired levels (Reguera-Alvarado et al., 2017). In order to enhance the female presence in the board of directors, codes of good governance in 17 countries recommend gender diversity (Terjesen et al., 2015; Sultana et al., 2020; Bhattacharya et al., 2022). Moreover, some countries, such as Norway and Italy, have introduced compulsory quotas to guarantee, at least temporarily, the appointment of female directors on the boards of listed and state-owned firms (Bennouri et al., 2020).

While, on one hand, gender regulation has led to an increase in the number of female directors, on the other hand, the expected impact in terms of performance is still debated. Actually, while many studies provide evidence of a positive association between gender diversity and firm performance (Arora, 2022; Brahma et al., 2021; Gull et al., 2023; La Rocca et al., 2024), some studies provide inconsistent evidence (e.g., Arnaboldi et al., 2020a, b; Bianco et al., 2015; Rubino et al., 2016).

D. Rizzotti · C. Frisenna (✉)
Department of Economics and Business, University of Catania, Catania, Italy
e-mail: rizzotti@unict.it; claudia.frisenna@unict.it

M. Agostini et al. (eds.), *Diversity and Equity in Accounting*, SIDREA Series in Accounting and Business Administration,
https://doi.org/10.1007/978-3-031-78247-3_15

Thus, despite increasing interest from policymakers and scholars, the contribution that women can provide to corporate governance effectiveness is still an empirical question (Nielsen & Huse, 2010; Hoobler et al., 2018).

This paper aims to shed some light on the role of female presence on the corporate governance, investigating the impact of CEO gender on the level of earnings management. Focusing on the presence of a female CEO, rather than on the proportion of female directors, we aim to provide direct evidence on gender-based differences on CEO's motivations to act opportunistically.

Specifically, building on gender socialization theory (Gilligan, 1982), which predicts a stricter ethical judgment for women than men, we hypothesize a negative relationship between the presence of women CEOs and the level of earnings management.

In order to answer our research question, we conduct an econometric analysis based on a sample of 132 Italian listed firms in 2010–2019. Findings show that CEO gender affects the level of earnings management. In particular, we find that female CEOs are associated with a lower level of earnings management.

We focus on the Italian context because Italy is one of the European countries with greater gender inequalities (World Economic Forum, 2016). According to prior sociological studies, this could be due to two specific cultural features, that is, the level of education and the level of religious participation (e.g. Bozzano, 2017). Both factors can significantly affect the social perception about female role models (Beaman et al., 2009). In particular, a low level of education could feed backward conceptions about the role of women in the society and in the business environment. Similarly, a high level of religious participation can affect the conformation of gender roles, often based on traditional, hardly changeable stereotypes (Guiso et al., 2003).

That said, the Italian context appears to be a suitable research setting, since, among the European countries, Italy has a lower level of education (OECD Indicators, 2016) and a higher level of religious participation (Arruñada, 2010).

This paper contributes to the literature in three ways. First, unlike previous studies, which examined the impact of gender on firm performance, this study investigates the impact of gender on the level of earnings management. We focus on earnings management because literature shows that CEOs have strong incentives to manage earnings in order to gain private benefits (Healy, 1985). This allows us to explore whether, other things being equal, there are gender-driven differences in the way in which managers respond to incentives to manage accounting numbers.

Second, this study enriches the debate on the effects of women participation to the board of directors. Actually, while most of prior studies focus on the positive impact of gender diversity resulting from the provision of different set of skills to the boardroom (e.g., Lückerath-Rovers, 2013; Terjesen et al., 2016), our findings show that positive consequences may be also due to the provision of female-specific traits and characteristics, such as a stricter ethical judgment and a lower attitude toward opportunistic behaviors.

Third, this study provides a contribution for regulators. Actually, our findings stress the need to overcome those cultural gender prejudices that hinder the substantial affirmation of gender equality. While gender regulation is necessary in order to enlarge the pool of female qualified candidates (Bennouri et al., 2020), the mere imposition of compulsory gender quotas is not sufficient to guarantee the full recognition of women in the business world (Rizzotti & Frisenna, 2017). Regulators should promote social and cultural policies to encourage the removal of cultural barriers and prejudices.

2 Theoretical Background and Hypotheses Development

In a world characterized by the presence of asymmetric information between insiders and outsiders, the transparency and reliability of accounting information are fundamental requirements to ensure the protection of stakeholders' interests and the financial markets' stability (Bushman & Smith, 2001; Leuz et al., 2003). Therefore, violating the obligation to provide reliable accounting information is primarily an ethical issue (Bruns & Merchant, 1990; Levitt, 1998).

However, managers have incentives to use accounting discretion opportunistically, in order to gain private benefits, mostly related to compensation contracts and managerial bonus (Balsam, 1998; Efendi et al., 2007; Holthausen et al., 1995).

Managed accounting numbers are likely to mislead investors and other stakeholders, and, as the well-known accounting scandals have shown, the opportunistic adoption of accounting discretion may lead to dangerous consequences for financial markets' stability.

The gender socialization theory assumes that women and men have different approaches toward ethical judgment (Betz et al., 1989; Gilligan, 1982). The development of a different ethical profile is due to the socialization process, that is, the process through which infants acquire those shared expectations socially ascribed on the basis of their sex (Eagly & Karau, 2002). Societal gender roles lead women to develop traits and values such as altruism, concern of others, and diligence. Conversely, societal gender roles lead men to emphasize traits related to competitive success, mastery, and ambition (Gilligan, 1982; Betz et al., 1989).

These different values acquired in the childhood shape women and men behavior as adults at the workplace, determining different orientations toward ethical dilemmas and different responses to incentives to behave unethically (Ameen et al., 1996). While women will tend to respect rules and are less likely to adopt opportunistic actions, men will be more likely to act opportunistically and to break rules for self-achievement (Betz et al., 1989).

Therefore, the gender socialization perspective theorizes that the ethical judgment of women is stricter than the ethical judgment of men (Pan & Sparks, 2012).

Empirical evidence mostly supports this prediction (Chen et al., 2016). For instance, Ekin and Tezölmez (1999) find gender differences in managers' unethical business behavior. Dawson (1995) finds that women sales managers have stricter ethical judgment than their male counterparts. Similar findings are reported by Hoffman (1998), which examines ethical perception of financial managers.

Moreover, Ben-Amar et al. (2017) find that voluntary climate change disclosure increases with women percentage on boards.

Evidence on the existence of gender differences in ethical behavior is provided by prior studies investigating the relationship between gender and earnings quality, or financial misconducts, in general. In particular, Krishnan and Parsons (2008) find that gender diversity in senior management is positively associated to earnings quality. Similarly, Srinidhi et al. (2011) find that the presence of female directors is associated with higher earnings quality. Finally, Wahid (2019) finds that gender diversity is negatively associated with corporate misconducts and frauds.

Consistent with the assumption that women have a stricter ethical judgment than men (Pan & Sparks, 2012), we expect a negative relationship between the presence of a female CEO and the level of earnings management.

Therefore, we formulate our hypothesis as follows:

H1
The presence of a female CEO is negatively associated with earnings management.

3 Research Design

3.1 Research Setting and Sample

The empirical analysis is based on a sample of nonfinancial firms listed in the FTSE Italia All-Share. Our sample consists of 1014 firm-year observations extracted from an unbalanced panel of 132 Italian listed firms covering the period 2010–2019. The first year of the analysis is 2010 as it was the first year available in *Amadeus* (*Bureau Van Dijk*), at the time in which we start the data collection (January 2021). We stopped data collection at 2019 in order to exclude external disruptions of the pandemic that may impact working capital accruals. Table 1 summarizes the sampling process.

We collect accounting information from Amadeus dataset, while corporate governance data are hand-collected from each firm's governance report.

3.2 Model and Variables

In order to test our hypothesis, we run the following regression model:

$$\begin{aligned}&EM_{i.t} = ß_0 + ß_1 WCEO_{i.t} + ß_2 WCHAIR_{i.t} + ß_3 WBOARD_{i.t} + \\ &ß_4 BINDEPENDENCE_{i.t} + ß_5 BIG4_{i.t} + ß_6 DUALITY_{i.t} + ß_7 TURNOVER_{i.t} \\ &+ ß_8 SIZE_{i.t} + ß_9 LEV_{i.t} + ß_{10} SGROWTH_{i.t} + ß_{11} ROA_{i.t} + YearFE + IndustryFE\end{aligned}$$

EM is the absolute value of abnormal working capital accruals, measured following DeFond and Park (2001). Specifically, EMi,t = WCi,t − (WCt−1*St/St−1),

Table 1 Sample selection process

	# Firms
Firms listed in *FTSE Italia All-Shares*, as at January 2021	230
less Financial sector firms	*50*
less Football clubs	*3*
less Foreign headquartered firms	*8*
less Suspended firms	*4*
Initial Sample of firms	*165*
less New IPO firms (i.e., IPO in 2018, 2019, 2020)	*17*
less Firm not providing corporate governance report	*16*
Final sample of firms	132

where WCi,t is the actual level of working capital observed in year t for firm i, scaled by total assets. The second term of the first equation (WCt–1*St/St–1) is the predicted value of working capital, which is the prior year's working capital adjusted for the change in sales.

We choose this proxy of earnings management as it is particularly suitable for the Italian context, where the stock market is relatively young and small (Cameran et al., 2018; Wysocki, 2004). This measure of abnormal accruals is particularly suitable for our sample because the Italian stock market is relatively young and small. Moreover, other earnings management measures, such as the Jones' models, require a large number of industry-year observations and are less applicable in our context, as also suggested by previous Italian studies (e.g., Cameran et al., 2018; Marra et al., 2011).

The independent variable of interest is *WCEO*, a dummy variable equal to 1 if the CEO is a woman and 0 otherwise. The set of control variables includes *WCHAIR*, a dummy variable equal to 1 if the chair is a woman and 0 otherwise, and *WBOARD* which is the proportion of female directors. We include these two variables in order to control for the potential effects of gender diversity in the board of directors, as suggested by prior studies (Peni & Vähämaa, 2010; Gull et al., 2018). *BINDEPENDENCE* is the proportion of independent directors; we control for board independence because prior studies suggest that an independent board is associated with higher accruals quality (García-Meca & Sánchez-Ballesta, 2009). However, some studies, based on the Italian context, find weak association between the proportion of independent directors and earnings management (Prencipe & Bar-Yosef, 2011). *BIG4* is a dummy variable equal to 1 if the audit firm is a Big 4 and 0 otherwise. We control for audit quality because prior studies show that it is negatively associated with the level of earnings management (Francis et al., 1999). *DUALITY* is a dummy variable equal to 1 if the CEO is also the chair of the board and 0 otherwise. We control for CEO duality because the excess of CEO power could positively impact on the level of earnings management (Finkelstein & D'aveni, 1994). *TURNOVER* is a dummy variable equal to 1 in the case of CEO turnover and 0 otherwise. We control for CEO turnover because prior studies show that it is negatively related to earnings manipulation (Pourciau, 1993). *SIZE* is a measure of firm size, measured with the natural logarithm of total assets. We control for firm size because prior studies find a negative association between firm dimension and the level of earnings management (Watts & Zimmerman, 1990). *LEV* is the firm's leverage degree, measured with the ratio of total debt over total assets. We control for firm leverage because Sweeney (1994) find that it is positively related to the level of earnings manipulation. Finally, we control for sales growth (*SGROWTH*) and performance (*ROA*) because prior studies suggest a positive relationship with earnings management (Lee et al., 2006).

4 Results

4.1 Descriptive Statistics

Table 2 reports summary statistics of our key metrics.

The full sample consists of 1014 firm-year observation, of which 54 with a female CEO (5.3% of the total sample) and 72 with a female chair (7.1% of the total sample). On average, 25% of boards is composed by female directors.

4.2 Empirical Results

We conduct the correlation analysis among our main variables (untabulated), which gives preliminary evidence supporting our assumption. Consistent with our hypothesis, we find a negative correlation between the level of earnings management and

Table 2 Descriptive statistics

Variable	Mean	Std. dev.	Min	Max
EM	−0.007	0.054	−0.268	0.161
WCEO	0.053	0.224	0.000	1.000
WCHAIR	0.071	0.257	0.000	1.000
WBOARD	0.251	0.135	0.000	0.571
BINDEPENDENCE	0.431	0.164	0.000	0.857
BIG4	0.915	0.279	0.000	1.000
DUALITY	0.355	0.479	0.000	1.000
TURNOVER	0.101	0.301	0.000	1.000
SIZE	13.295	1.759	9.821	18.951
LEV	0.163	0.133	0.000	0.598
SGROWTH	0.042	0.201	−0.640	1.003
ROA	0.039	0.074	−0.230	0.263
Obs.# 1014				

Table 3 Empirical results

EM	Pred. sign	Coefficient	Std. err.	*p*-value
Intercept		0.004	0.016	0.801
WCEO	–	–0.018**	0.008	0.016
WCHAIR	–	–0.004	0.007	0.551
WBOARD	–	–0.008	0.019	0.659
BINDEPENDENCE	–	0.007	0.011	0.556
BIG4	–	–0.010	0.006	0.122
DUALITY	+	–0.004	0.004	0.247
TURNOVER	–	–0.004	0.006	0.438
SIZE	–	0.000	0.001	0.830
LEV	+	0.015	0.014	0.304
SGROWTH	–	–0.084***	0.009	0.000
ROA	–/+	0.125***	0.024	0.000
INDUSTRY FE	Yes			
FIRM FE	Yes			
N.Obs. 1014				
Adj. R^2 11.4%				

the presence of a female CEO. We also find a negative correlation between the presence of a female CEO and CEO duality, sales growth, and ROA. The correlation analysis shows the existence of significant correlations between some predictors. In order to establish whether there are multicollinearity concerns, VIF scores are examined. For all the models, the VIF scores of the variables are all lower than 5.0.

Table 3 reports the empirical results concerning the test of our hypothesis. As expected, we find that the presence of a female CEO has a significantly negative impact on the level of earnings management (*WCEO*, $\beta = -0.018$; *p*-value = 0.016). Findings also show that that neither the presence of a female chair nor the proportion of women within the board of directors influences the level of earnings management (*WCHAIR*, $\beta = -0.004$; *p*-value = 0.551; *WBOARD*, $\beta = -0.008$; *p*-value = 0.659). Consistently with prior studies, we find that the level of earnings management is negatively related to firm's sales growth (*SGROWTH*, $\beta = -0.084$; *p*-value = 0.000). Finally, the level of earnings management is positively related to firm's performance (*ROA*, $\beta = 0.125$; *p*-value = 0.000).

5 Conclusion

Over the last few years, the issue of gender inequalities has increasingly attracted the interests of regulators and scholars. While regulators enacted gender equality policies in order to facilitate female presence in the business world, research lacks clarity about the effect of women participation on corporate governance effectiveness (Nielsen & Huse, 2010).

In order to examine whether there are gender-based differences toward an ethical behavior, this study investigates the impact of female CEOs on the level of earnings management. Building on gender socialization theory (Gilligan, 1982), which predicts a stricter women's ethical judgment, we hypothesize and find a negative relationship between the presence of female CEOs and the level of earnings management.

Our findings support the view that the female presence in the corporate governance structure may improve corporate accountability, because of the provision of female-specific traits and characteristics, such as a stricter ethical judgment and a lower attitude toward opportunistic behaviors. Our results also show that the number of women directors does not affect the level of earnings management. This could be explained by the existence of cultural barriers and prejudices, such as tokenism and cultural stereotypes. That is, women may be appointed to fulfill mandatory gender quotas rather than for their effective contributions into decision-making processes (Rixom et al., 2023). These biases might lead to women' opinions being undervalued in board discussions, thereby diminishing their potential impact on ethical decision-making, especially considering the lack of critical mass in the board composition (e.g., Eagly & Karau, 2002; Bianco et al., 2015).

Future research exploring the moderating roles of cultural and contextual factors in corporate dynamics could enrich our understanding of gender's role in corporate governance.

Collectively, our findings suggest that regulators should continue to encourage the inclusion of women in the business environment. However, policies such as compulsory gender quotas should be supported by social and cultural policies aimed at removing gender prejudices. In this sense, our findings raise interesting opportunities for future research. For instance, future studies can investigate whether cultural and institutional context affects the actual impact of women on corporate governance effectiveness.

References

Ameen, E. C., Guffey, D. M., & McMillan, J. J. (1996). Gender differences in determining the ethical sensitivity of future accounting professionals. *Journal of Business Ethics, 15*(5), 591–597.

Arnaboldi, F., Casu, B., Kalotychou, E., & Sarkisyan, A. (2020a). Board diversity reforms: Do they matter for EU bank performance? *European Financial Management, 26*(2), 416–454.

Arnaboldi, F., Casu, B., Kalotychou, E., & Sarkisyan, A. (2020b). The performance effects of board heterogeneity: What works for EU banks? *The European Journal of Finance, 26*(10), 897–924.

Arora, A. (2022). Gender diversity in boardroom and its impact on firm performance. *Journal of Management and Governance, 26*(3), 735–755.

Arruñada, B. (2010). Protestants and Catholics: Similar work ethic, different social ethic. *The Economic Journal, 120*(547), 890–918.

Balsam, S. (1998). Discretionary accounting choices and CEO compensation. *Contemporary Accounting Research, 15*(3), 229–252.

Beaman, L., Chattopadhyay, R., Duflo, E., Pande, R., & Topalova, P. (2009). Powerful women: Does exposure reduce bias? *The Quarterly Journal of Economics, 124*(4), 1497–1540.

Ben-Amar, W., Chang, M., & McIlkenny, P. (2017). Board gender diversity and corporate response to sustainability initiatives: Evidence from the carbon disclosure project. *Journal of Business Ethics, 142*(2), 369–383.

Bennouri, M., De Amicis, C., & Falconieri, S. (2020). Welcome on board: A note on gender quotas regulation in Europe. *Economics Letters, 190*, 109055.

Betz, M., O'Connell, L., & Shepard, J. M. (1989). Gender differences in proclivity for unethical behavior. *Journal of Business Ethics, 8*(5), 321–324.

Bhattacharya, B., Khadka, I., & Mani, D. (2022). Shaking up (and keeping intact) the old boys' network: The impact of the mandatory gender quota on the Board of Directors in India. *Journal of Business Ethics, 177*(4), 763–778.

Bianco, M., Ciavarella, A., & Signoretti, R. (2015). Women on corporate boards in Italy: The role of family connections. *Corporate Governance: An International Review, 23*(2), 129–144.

Bozzano, M. (2017). On the historical roots of women's empowerment across Italian Provinces: Religion or family culture? *European Journal of Political Economy, 49*, 24–46.

Brahma, S., Nwafor, C., & Boateng, A. (2021). Board gender diversity and firm performance: The UK evidence. *International Journal of Finance & Economics, 26*(4), 5704–5719.

Bruns, W. J., Jr., & Merchant, K. A. (1990). The dangerous morality of managing earnings. *Strategic Finance, 72*(2), 22.

Bushman, R. M., & Smith, A. J. (2001). Financial accounting information and corporate governance. *Journal of Accounting and Economics, 32*(1), 237–333.

Cameran, M., Ditillo, A., & Pettinicchio, A. (2018). Audit team attributes matter: How diversity affects audit quality. *European Accounting Review, 27*(4), 595–621.

Chen, X., Torsin, W., & Tsang, A. (2022). International differences in the CEO gender pay gap. *Corporate Governance: An International Review, 30*(5), 516–541.

Chen, C. W., Velasquez Tuliao, K., Cullen, J. B., & Chang, Y. Y. (2016). Does gender influence managers' ethics? A cross-cultural analysis. *Business Ethics: A European Review, 25*(4), 345–362.

Dawson, L. M. (1995). Women and men, morality and ethics. *Business Horizons, 38*(4), 61–68.

DeFond, M. L., & Park, C. W. (2001). The reversal of abnormal accruals and the market valuation of earnings surprises. *The Accounting Review, 76*, 375–404.

Eagly, A. H., & Karau, S. J. (2002). Role congruity theory of prejudice toward female leaders. *Psychological Review, 109*(3), 573.

Efendi, J., Srivastava, A., & Swanson, E. P. (2007). Why do corporate managers misstate financial statements? The role of option compensation and other factors. *Journal of Financial Economics, 85*(3), 667–708.

Ekin, M. S., & Tezölmez, S. H. (1999). Business ethics in Turkey: An empirical investigation with special emphasis on gender. *Journal of Business Ethics, 18*(1), 17–34.

Finkelstein, S., & D'aveni, R. A. (1994). CEO duality as a double-edged sword: How boards of directors balance entrenchment avoidance and unity of command. *Academy of Management Journal, 37*(5), 1079–1108.

Francis, J. R., Maydew, E. L., & Sparks, H. C. (1999). The role of Big 6 auditors in the credible reporting of accruals. *Auditing: A Journal of Practice & Theory, 18*(2), 17–34.

García-Meca, E., & Sánchez-Ballesta, J. P. (2009). Corporate governance and earnings management: A meta-analysis. *Corporate Governance: An International Review, 17*(5), 594–610.

Gilligan, C. (1982). *In a different voice*. Harvard University Press.

Guiso, L., Sapienza, P., & Zingales, L. (2003). People's opium? Religion and economic attitudes. *Journal of Monetary Economics, 50*(1), 225–282.

Gull, A. A., Atif, M., & Hussain, N. (2023). Board gender composition and waste management: Cross-country evidence. *The British Accounting Review, 55*(1), 101097.

Gull, A. A., Nekhili, M., Nagati, H., & Chtioui, T. (2018). Beyond gender diversity: How specific attributes of female directors affect earnings management. *The British Accounting Review, 50*(3), 255–274.

Healy, P. M. (1985). The effect of bonus schemes on accounting decisions. *Journal of Accounting and Economics, 7*(1–3), 85–107.

Hoffman, J. J. (1998). Are women really more ethical than men? Maybe it depends on the situation. *Journal of Managerial Issues*, 60–73.

Holthausen, R. W., Larcker, D. F., & Sloan, R. G. (1995). Annual bonus schemes and the manipulation of earnings. *Journal of Accounting and Economics, 19*(1), 29–74.

Hoobler, J. M., Masterson, C. R., Nkomo, S. M., & Michel, E. J. (2018). The business case for women leaders: Meta-analysis, research critique, and path forward. *Journal of Management, 44*(6), 2473–2499.

Krishnan, G. V., & Parsons, L. M. (2008). Getting to the bottom line: An exploration of gender and earnings quality. *Journal of Business Ethics, 78*(1), 65–76.

La Rocca, M., Fasano, F., La Rocca, T., & Neha, N. (2024). Women in CEO duality and firm performance in Europe. *Journal of Management and Governance, 28*(1), 177–214.

Lee, C. W. J., Li, L. Y., & Yue, H. (2006). Performance, growth and earnings management. *Review of Accounting Studies, 11*, 305–334.

Leuz, C., Nanda, D., & Wysocki, P. D. (2003). Earnings management and investor protection: An international comparison. *Journal of Financial Economics, 69*(3), 505–527.

Levitt, A., Jr. (1998). The numbers game. *The CPA Journal, 68*(12), 14.

Lückerath-Rovers, M. (2013). Women on boards and firm performance. *Journal of Management & Governance, 17*(2), 491–509.

Marra, A., Mazzola, P., & Prencipe, A. (2011). Board monitoring and earnings management pre- and post-IFRS. *The International Journal of Accounting, 46*, 205–230.

Mnif Sellami, Y., & Cherif, I. (2020). Female audit committee directorship and audit fees. *Managerial Auditing Journal, 35*(3), 398–428.

Nielsen, S., & Huse, M. (2010). The contribution of women on boards of directors: Going beyond the surface. *Corporate Governance: An International Review, 18*(2), 136–148.

OECD Publishing. (2016). *Education at a glance 2016: OECD indicators.*

Ongsakul, V., Jaroenjitrkam, A., Treepongkaruna, S., & Jiraporn, P. (2022). Does board gender diversity reduce "CEO luck"? *Accounting & Finance, 62*(1), 243–260.

Pan, Y., & Sparks, J. R. (2012). Predictors, consequence, and measurement of ethical judgments: Review and meta-analysis. *Journal of Business Research, 65*(1), 84–91.

Peni, E., & Vähämaa, S. (2010). Female executives and earnings management. *Managerial Finance, 36*(7), 629–645.

Pourciau, S. (1993). Earnings management and nonroutine executive changes. *Journal of Accounting and Economics, 16*(1), 317–336.

Prencipe, A., & Bar-Yosef, S. (2011). Corporate governance and earnings management in family-controlled companies. *Journal of Accounting, Auditing & Finance, 26*(2), 199–227.

Reguera-Alvarado, N., De Fuentes, P., & Laffarga, J. (2017). Does board gender diversity influence financial performance? Evidence from Spain. *Journal of Business Ethics, 141*, 337–350.

Rixom, J. M., Jackson, M., & Rixom, B. A. (2023). Mandating diversity on the board of directors: Do investors feel that gender quotas result in tokenism or added value for firms? *Journal of Business Ethics, 182*, 679–697.

Rizzotti, D., & Frisenna, C. (2017). Caratteristiche dell'Audit Committee e Gestione del Rischio Bancario: Un'analisi empirica del contesto europeo. *Management Control, 2*(2017), 125–146.

Rubino, F. E., Tenuta, P., & Cambrea, D. R. (2016). Board characteristics effects on performance in family and non-family business: A multi-theoretical approach. *Journal of Management & Governance*, 1–36.

Srinidhi, B., Gul, F. A., & Tsui, J. (2011). Female directors and earnings quality. *Contemporary Accounting Research, 28*(5), 1610–1644.

Sultana, N., Cahan, S. F., & Rahman, A. (2020). Do gender diversity recommendations in corporate governance codes matter? Evidence from audit committees. *Auditing: A Journal of Practice & Theory, 39*(1), 173–197.

Sweeney, A. P. (1994). Debt-covenant violations and managers' accounting responses. *Journal of Accounting and Economics, 17*(3), 281–308.

Terjesen, S., Aguilera, R. V., & Lorenz, R. (2015). Legislating a woman's seat on the board: Institutional factors driving gender quotas for boards of directors. *Journal of Business Ethics, 128*(2), 233–251.

Terjesen, S., Couto, E. B., & Francisco, P. M. (2016). Does the presence of independent and female directors impact firm performance? A multi-country study of board diversity. *Journal of Management & Governance, 20*(3), 447–483.

Terjesen, S., Sealy, R., & Singh, V. (2009). Women directors on corporate boards: A review and research agenda. *Corporate Governance: An International Review, 17*(3), 320–337.

Wahid, A. S. (2019). The effects and the mechanisms of board gender diversity: Evidence from financial manipulation. *Journal of Business Ethics, 159*(3), 705–725.

Watts, R. L., & Zimmerman, J. L. (1990). Positive accounting theory: A ten year perspective. *Accounting Review*, 131–156.

World Economic Forum. (2016). *The global gender gap report 2016*. http://reports.weforum.org

Wysocki, P. D. (2004). Discussion of ultimate ownership, income management, and legal and extra-legal institutions. *Journal of Accounting Research, 42*, 463–474.

Part IV
Empirical Corporate Cases on Diversity and Equity

Equity and Inclusion from a Historical Organizational Perspective: The Case of the FIAT Group

Marisa Agostini and Elisa Truant

1 Introduction

The aim of the chapter is to analyze FIAT S.p.A. (Fabbrica Italiana Automobili Torino), hereafter FIAT, focusing on efforts on equity and inclusion involving employees at different organizational levels.

The chapter is based on a historical analysis of FIAT annual financial statements, publicly available on the online archive, so to depict the main initiatives on equity and inclusion disclosed.

FIAT had a pivotal role for the Italian economic development and was often scrutinized for the social policies implemented, especially in the last century. Given this premise, a historical perspective on this company could be of interest to advance the literature on diversity, equity, and inclusion.

Also, FIAT was chosen for its relevance both at a national and international level. Indeed, it can be considered an icon of the Italian, but also worldwide, automotive industry and one of the world's best-known and long-lasting brands.

Founded on July 11, 1899, in Turin by a group of visionary investors, FIAT has traced a history of innovation, engineering, and success throughout the course of its industrial activity. At the end of the nineteenth century, Italy was undergoing a major phase of industrialization, and the automotive sector was booming. In this context, Giovanni Agnelli and a group of daring entrepreneurs decided to create FIAT, with the aim of producing affordable cars for the Italian market. FIAT's first

M. Agostini (✉)
Sustainability Lab, Venice School of Management, Ca' Foscari University, Venice, Italy
e-mail: marisa.agostini@unive.it

E. Truant
Department of Management "Valter Cantino", University of Turin, Turin, Italy
e-mail: elisa.truant@unito.it

M. Agostini et al. (eds.), *Diversity and Equity in Accounting*, SIDREA Series in Accounting and Business Administration,
https://doi.org/10.1007/978-3-031-78247-3_16

factory, located on Corso Dante in Turin, with a workforce of just 30, quickly became a state-of-the-art production center, attracting talent and creative minds. However, the real turning point for FIAT came with Vittorio Valletta joining the company in 1921. Valletta, Managing Director of the company from 1939 and later elected President in 1946, introduced major innovations under the organizational and social perspective. Since the beginning of the last century, FIAT paid particular attention to the development of corporate welfare. Indeed, the company was already involved in the provision and development of various services and activities in favor of workers in those years—housing, schools, health management, assistance for retired workers, company canteens, and much more—precisely to strengthen proximity and inclusion.

The historical analysis of FIAT's reporting disclosure reveals clear signs of the company's focus on the social sphere and the sense of inclusion of employees.

These results came from the access to the online archive of the company and the analysis of available annual financial statements from the first decades of the last century until the 1990s, years in which social and environmental issues began to be clearly made explicit in the requests and decisional processes of various stakeholders and policymakers. In order to analyze the evolution of financial statement disclosure over the years, the researchers created a grid on Excel to better structure and formalize the investigation around the two themes of equity and inclusion. Then, evidences have been scrutinized in association with the main historical events so to provide a more integrated and complete interpretation.

The research contributes to the debate on equity and inclusion, providing a historical perspective to better understand the company's commitment and origins of such topics. This research can help to understand the evolutionary role of large companies in a community and can provide insights for managers on what has been done and what still needs to be done in terms of equity and inclusions so to better take decisions.

2 Equity and Inclusion: Meaning, Evolution, and Perspectives

Equity refers to the adoption by companies of actions aimed at removing obstacles and/or barriers that prevent equal opportunities to the detriment of social welfare. To achieve it, one seeks to discourage and eliminate behavior that would reinforce practices contrary to this logic. Equity could also be seen as a way to achieve equality (WBCSD, 2022).

The latter, in fact, is achieved by treating everyone equally, regardless of need or situation, as opposed to equity which "is about taking deliberate actions to remove systemic, group, and individual barriers and obstacles that hinder opportunities and disrupt well-being. Equity is achieved through the identification and elimination of policies, practices, attitudes, and cultural messages that create and reinforce unfair outcomes" (GDEIB, 2021, p. 5). In essence, with equality, the same opportunities would be offered to all, neglecting individual differences or needs, which are instead taken into account in the pursuit of equity. A further cardinal principle pursued by the aforementioned DEI (diversity, equity, and inclusion) policies is inclusion. Inclusion is the behavior whereby the company welcomes and understands diversity, making every employee feel an essential part of the organization "to create a fair, healthy, and high-performing organisation or community. An inclusive culture and environment ensure equitable access to resources and opportunities for all. It also enables individuals and groups to feel safe, respected, heard, engaged, motivated, and valued for who they are" (GDEIB, 2021, p. 5). Inclusion is a theme that began to develop as early as the 1960s in the United States, thanks to the many migratory currents that intervened in the country at that time. In Europe, the topic spread later, especially in the 1990s, but it was an issue that was not given much consideration and remained unresolved for many years. However, with the advance of time and the development of certain factors such as migratory currents, the issue began to emerge as a priority.

In the past, the main focus of companies has always been on profit maximization and economic growth, without adequate consideration of the other (e.g., social) impacts of their activities. In 1953, corporate social responsibility was introduced as a partly ethical concept, developed by Howard R. Bowen in his book *Social Responsibility of Businessmen*. In that writing, the author discusses the responsibilities of those who run a business toward the other components of the business. Corporate social responsibility (CSR) includes economic, legal, ethical, and philanthropic responsibilities of society that go far beyond the pure pursuit of corporate profit: "the social responsibility of business encompasses the economic, legal, ethical and discretionary (later referred to as philanthropic) expectations society has of organisations at a given point in time" (Carroll, 1991, p. 42). It includes business practices such as improving working conditions, ethics in business, and community engagement.

This emphasizes the importance of an intimate and voluntary relationship between business and society to be taken into account when setting and pursuing corporate objectives, according to a proactive and noncoercive process for the company itself. CSR should be considered not only in terms of a balance between different interests, but also as an integral part of long-term corporate strategy, seeking a close and direct connection between CSR and the economic-financial performance of companies. With this in mind, as early as 1971, the Committee for Economic Development (CED) defined social responsibility as a corporate function based on public consensus, the main purpose of which is to constructively serve the needs of society, thereby contributing to increasing the quality of life. This perspective emphasizes how companies can and should actively contribute to social welfare. From a vision initially limited to economic and legal aspects, CSR has evolved into a broader concept encompassing corporate social, ethical, and environmental responsibility. This evolution reflects a growing recognition of the interdependence between business and society and the need for companies to include a wide range of stakeholders in their decision-making processes. The more recent concept of "sustainable development" (Laine, 2005) aims to overcome poverty and maintain social equity both within the current community and between the community and different generations. Thus, the focus is on the necessary guarantee of fair access to resources and services, as well as the protection of human rights and cultural diversity in order to decrease social inequalities. This multidimensionality leads profit-maximizing companies to integrate sustainable and ethical practices into their daily operations, paying increasing attention to equity and inclusion as well. CSR aims to make a company responsible in the first place through self-regulation. Indeed, it is based on a voluntary approach of the company to include practices of economic, legal, ethical, and philanthropic responsibility, in addition to the pursuit of profit. Through this approach, companies have thus begun to include new responsible programs and activities within their usual business practices. In order to account for these initiatives, which gradually spread into business practices, the sustainability report was developed. The drafting of such reports was, initially, a voluntary choice of the company, but in the last years, it is becoming more and more widespread, thanks also to the legislative developments. Despite the increasing attention on social issues, and the studies that underline the need to focus on inclusion and equity as essential aspects of corporate governance (Lehman, 2019), it has been underlined that accounting practices and governance systems still require considerable progresses (Rumens, 2017) and discrimination nowadays still persists (Kokot-Blamey, 2021; Lassou et al., 2021). There is a clear need for more management practices and theories to develop inclusive practices and organizational culture, as these goals are difficult to achieve (Bernstein et al., 2020). However, businesses should place equal emphasis on creating ecosystems that support innovation and well-being as they do on profits. DEI initiatives, when truly embraced and carried out, have the potential to create a win-win cycle that strengthens performances. Indeed, diverse perspectives, backgrounds, and skill sets from a broad spectrum of people can help a company to discover new opportunities (Gross et al., 2023). The challenge is to integrate these elements in the management system and identify methods to assess DEI (Stamps & Foley, 2023; Vargas-Solar et al., 2022; Romansky et al., 2021), setting the right tools to implement these projects and to communicate results to internal and external stakeholders. Despite the relevance of these topics, there is the urgency for more researches in accounting and accountability to close the knowledge gap (Deore & Krishnan, 2024).

3 Methodology

The research is conducted through an archival analysis based on the information presented in FIAT's annual financial statements. Specifically, two researchers accessed the online archive of the company and downloaded the available financial statements from the early 1930s to the end of 1990s. At the end of the process, 70 years of reports were analyzed. The analysis was limited to the 1990s because from that years, there has started to be growing attention from different stakeholders and policymakers on social issues (Carroll, 1991; Atkinson, et al., 2004).

In order to analyze the evolution of financial statement disclosure over the years, the researchers created a grid on Excel to better structure and formalize the investigation around the following areas:

- General characteristics of the financial statements, as the comprising documents, charts, and stylistic changes in the disclosure comparing to the previous period
- Main economic and financial results and other key performance indicators
- Environmental, social, and governance (ESG) disclosure
- Specific DEI initiatives

The information extracted from financial statements were linked to the main historical events described, so to achieve a more holistic overview and interpretation. The analysis was conducted by two researchers separately, but a constant dialog between the authors was carried out to resolve any issues or misalignments and better investigate the financial statement evidences under a historical lens.

The results of the analysis were finally integrated to define the final outcome.

4 FIAT Corporate Case: Its Economic, Political, and Social Relevance

FIAT, Fabbrica Italiana Automobili Torino, is an icon of the Italian automotive industry and one of the best-known brands in the world. Founded on July 11, 1899, the first FIAT factory was opened in 1900 on Corso Dante in Turin. Initially counting only few workers, after some years (in 1915), the number of employees exceeded 10,000. In 1903, only 4 years after its foundation, FIAT's shares were listed on the stock exchange, consolidating the company's competitive position in the industrial market. One of the highlights of FIAT's early years was the launch of its first car model, the FIAT 4 HP. In the following years, the model range was expanded, offering a variety of options to meet the needs of different types of customers. At the end of its first decade of activity, FIAT had 14,000,000 lire of share capital, 1215 cars produced, and more than 2500 employees (Paravia, 1996). In 1916, the construction of the Lingotto production plant was started, which became the largest factory in Europe and the emblem of the Italian automobile industry. Moreover, in those years, FIAT developed its activities in diversified sectors, including steel, electronics, and public transport services. However, production growth slowed down with the outbreak of the First World War, which started a decade characterized by profound changes and tensions, such as the occupation of the company's plants by workers in September 1920. Over the next 2 years, the company tried to implement cost-cutting maneuvers, cutting the number of employees and reducing salaries. A turning point came with the entry of Vittorio Valletta into the company in 1921 (Castronovo, 2005) who was then appointed Managing Director from 1939 and President in

1946. During the 1920s and 1930s, Mussolini's autarkic policy forced the company to reduce its plans for international expansion, focusing instead on the domestic market. With a workforce of 22,000 workers, the new Mirafiori plant in Turin was inaugurated in 1939 on an area of 1,000,000 square meters, 300,000 of which were covered, thanks to which FIAT strengthened its position in the automobile production cycle but also in the production of agricultural, railway, aeronautical, and electromechanical machinery. Between the 1930s and 1940s, FIAT had 22 branches throughout Italy and 435 commission agents, authorized workshops, and spare parts dealers. Abroad, on the other hand, there were 800 dealers scattered across the major nations, with several affiliations in Argentina, Great Britain, Indonesia, Spain, and many other countries. At the beginning of the Second World War, FIAT's workforce exceeded 60,000: in order to make up for the physiological reduction in car production (down to a quarter of those manufactured in 1939) and to meet wartime requirements, the company concentrated on the production of military and industrial vehicles, becoming one of the main suppliers to the Italian armed forces. Both during and after the war, FIAT provided assistance services for its employees, including a supply of linen, shoes, and firewood, as well as canteen services where more than a hundred thousand meals a day were distributed.

In the postwar era, FIAT faced new challenges and opportunities. During this period, Italy experienced significant economic growth and an increase in demand for cars. The company also responded to this by introducing new car models, such as the FIAT 500, which, with record sales, became an icon of Italian design (FIAT, 1957). This growth also came about, thanks to funding from the Marshall Plan launched in 1947, which made it possible to complete the reconstruction and modernization of plants that had been badly damaged by bombing.

In this period from the 1940s to the end of the 1960s, the financial statements show a significant commitment of the company with regard to predominantly social aspects, with a particular focus on initiatives aimed at enhancing the well-being of employees. It appears, in fact, that the company in those years was committed to the provision and development of various services and activities in favor of workers: housing, schools, health management, assistance for retired workers, company catering outlets, and much more.

Starting from the mid-1960s, greater attention has been paid to environmental issues, with an increasing volume and detailed quality information. From those years until the 1990s, efforts have been addressed to encourage studies and improve training and professional advancement for the different levels of the organization, also collaborating with high schools and universities. The investments in knowledge and skills went hand in hand with an organizational decentralization and reduction of hierarchical levels.

The next section describes all the initiatives, especially of a social nature, undertaken by FIAT and reported in its financial statements, highlighting how this inclusive vision, reported in detail by the company, conflicts with what is reported in some of the literature.

5 Equity, Inclusion, and Social Issues: Divergent Perspectives

FIAT's financial statements highlight how it was one of the first companies in Italy to facilitate inclusive cooperation between capital and labor, primarily through the implementation of initiatives that helped managers and workers work together. In this particular area of its activity, FIAT seems to have been ahead of its time, providing services for both its employees and their relatives. Indeed, the company provided not only direct help in every contingency of the worker's life but also the education and moral and material assistance of their children and assisted the employee even after the end of the employment relationship, as highlighted in the following section. However, in this regard, the literature also points to a different approach, which, on the contrary, was not very inclusive, especially for employees.

5.1 Employee Initiatives: An Inclusive and Fair Approach Is Reflected in Corporate Reporting

FIAT's financial statements show an inclusive approach of the company from the earliest decades of the last century, paying particular attention to the working conditions of its employees and the social impacts of its actions and policies before this was taken into account by regulations. The promotion of inclusion and work ethics seems to emerge through the many services promoted by the company (Fig. 1), such as the after-work club, the employees' and workers' internal health insurance fund, the factory medical service, vocational schools, scholarships, the library, the villages, and the workers' homes. Below we briefly describe some of these initiatives to give an understanding of their scope.

First, the FIAT after-work club offered both sports and recreational activities. The sports grouping was aimed at direct physical education and consisted of 12 activities offered to employees such as mountaineering, athletics, cycling, and tennis. In contrast, the cultural-recreational grouping included, for example, the hiking group, the orchestral group, and the philharmonic group.

Second, founded in 1921, the Mutual Assistance Fund guaranteed medical (Fig. 2) and legal assistance to members, the granting of special subsidies, the admission of members' children to seaside camps, and the granting of interest-free loans for registered employees.

In addition, further forms of assistance such as cradle premiums, maternity allowances, and reimbursement of medicine costs were established for workers' families.

Third, the Mutua Interna Operai FIAT was founded in 1923. Its purpose was to pay daily subsidies to members during periods of illness, provide a free medical and pharmaceutical service, subsidize families on the death of the member, subsidize women members in the event of childbirth, and grant extraordinary subsidies in

Fig. 1 The many services promoted by the company for the benefit of employees and their families (Source: FIAT Historical Archives)

cases of special need. While the Mutua Interna Operai provided treatment for members in the event of illness or accident outside work, the Servizio Medico di Fabbrica (Factory Medical Service), organized directly by FIAT, supervised the health, hygiene, and physical integrity of the worker while at work. The service also included periodic examinations of workers engaged in work that was hazardous to their health, offering them special insurance for occupational diseases. In addition, the Service ensured the hygiene of the plants and facilities and medically examined every technical project. FIAT implemented special measures regarding the layout and operation of machinery and the ventilation of the departments, also studying, for each type of work, appropriate clothing and protective measures for the most dangerous places.

Fourth, the FIAT vocational schools, established since 1922, catered for two different categories of pupils: apprentices and adult workers. The school for apprentices, known as the Scuola Allievi FIAT (Fig. 3), was reserved for the children and relatives of FIAT employees aged between 14 and 17. It provided for the training of young people through a 3-year course, one of which was a specialization course. On the other hand, the Dopolavoro school was for adults and lasted 2 years: it was intended for those workers, aged between 20 and 30, who wished to improve their

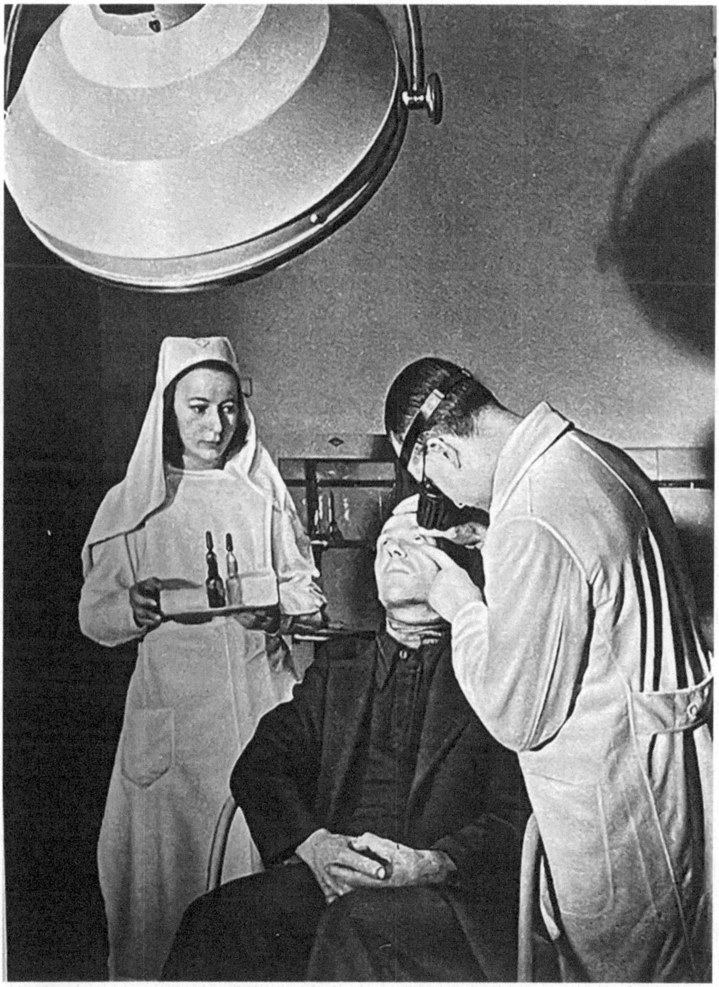

Fig. 2 The FIAT mutual company's healthcare for registered employees (Source: FIAT Historical Archives)

skills in order to obtain job promotions. Admission to the school was by application and included an oral test of general culture.

Fifth, in 1943, FIAT scholarships were established for the children of factory and white-collar workers who were praiseworthy in school, for the children of fallen employees, and also for employees who, facing great sacrifices, sought to improve their condition by aiming to obtain a license, diploma, or degree. Scholarships to the value of half a million lira were awarded in the 1945–1946 school year.

Sixth, within the framework of the provisions set up by FIAT for the cultural elevation of its workers and employees was also the FIAT library. Founded in 1925 at the suggestion of Giovanni Agnelli, the library offered free home loans of books

Fig. 3 The FIAT Allievi School for the training of young children and relatives of employees (Source: FIAT Historical Archives)

of all kinds to employees of FIAT and its subsidiaries. In addition to volumes for the technical education of personnel, the FIAT library also offered recreational reading for families. FIAT allocated a substantial annual sum to the operation and growth of the library.

Seventh, in 1972 in Marentino, in the province of Turin, the new headquarters of ISVOR (Institute for Organizational Development) came into operation, where specialization and refresher courses for managers were carried out (FIAT, 1973). Three years later, work also began on the "Southern Housing Project," which provided for the construction in the south of Italy of housing for the workers of the new factories, attempting to replicate the same service provided in the north as the "FIAT Houses" (Fig. 4): this was housing made available to office and factory workers in the area of the Turin factories to solve the postwar housing crisis.

Lastly, FIAT also provided assistance to former company workers, for example, through the Gruppo Anziani FIAT (FIAT Senior Citizens Group) for the purpose of receiving loyalty bonuses and pensions. The "Giovanni Agnelli Retirement Home"was also founded to accommodate retired senior citizens, and in 1969 the "Vittorio Valletta Retirement Home for the Elderly" was opened in Ospedaletti, Liguria, which could accommodate up to 200 people (FIAT, 1970).

All these initiatives recall the inclusive approach and seem to underpin a clear corporate behavior aimed at welcoming and making the employee and his or her family feel good.

There are a large number of services offered by the company in support of workers, including child-rearing, day-care services, healthcare, accident insurance services, and leisure activities such as library services or sports activity organizations. With reference to the interventions carried out in southern Italy, FIAT sought to increase, through investment plans, its presence by expanding its factories, thus reducing the emigration to the north of workers seeking better jobs and a better quality of life. FIAT also showed great commitment to public utility projects,

Fig. 4 The FIAT House Plan promoted for employees (Source: FIAT Historical Archives)

contributing to the improvement of transport infrastructure and the construction of works of public interest such as dams and aqueducts even outside Italy. All of this is accounted for in detail in the financial statements but is at odds with what is described in the next paragraph.

5.2 The Divergent Perspective Emerging in the Historical Literature

On the one hand, the social initiatives promoted by FIAT toward its employees and the southern regions are reported in detail and seem to be precursors of an inclusive approach aimed at ensuring equity. On the other hand, there is little information provided by the company regarding its governance. We note the fact that within the administrative bodies, such as the board of directors and board of auditors, no role and/or office held by a woman appears in the financial statements. This fact is reported and maintained in all the years and financial statements analyzed.

Moreover, in some documents outside the company, employee dissatisfaction concerning certain aspects of working life emerges. It is important to emphasize that this analysis does not deny or call into question the work carried out by FIAT, but it does highlight the presence of certain "weak points" within the company that would otherwise have been impossible to know about. In 1970, trade unionist Sergio Garavini wrote an article in the magazine *Politica ed. Economia* about the relationship between the working class and FIAT management in the late 1950s and early 1960s (Garavini, 1970). In particular, in this article, the author describes how FIAT in those years adopted a paternalistic policy linked to an attitude of repression toward its employees. Evidence of this is the fact that the management instituted the so-called "anti-strike bonus" of an annual sum of 7000 lire in 1954, rising to 50,000 lire in the early 1960s, in order to deter and discourage workers from participating in such protests, and also adopted a redundancy policy that led to the dismissal of more than 2,000 workers from the company between 1952 and 1959. This policy of repression also included intense surveillance of trade union and political activists, searches at factory entrances, permanent monitoring of supervisors, spying by guards disguised as workers, transfers to humiliating jobs, and even the delivery of letters to wives of workers, in which they threatened dismissal and starvation for the family. This threat was credible, as for many of those dismissed (in protest and retaliation) it proved difficult, for some impossible, to get any job, even if they had a good qualification.

In January 1988, a survey was proposed to the workers of FIAT Mirafiori in Turin, with the aim to understand and deepen the employees' opinions on certain topics, such as salary, job performance, professional skills, company canteen services, working hours, the condition of women, recruitment methods of ordinary workers, the trade, union and protest methods (Cerruti & Rieser, 1988). The sample consisted of 3100 workers from different sectors covering different shifts. Of the total number of questionnaires distributed, 2727 were returned completed (88% of respondents). One item that emerges as relevant (in third place, after salary increases and the introduction of a canteen with fresh produce) concerns the reduction of work rhythms and workloads. It shows a high degree of priority, at 34.9. This item appears to be a priority for 49.2% of workers at level 3, decreasing as the bands increase (29.8% for level 4 and 6.7% for level 5), since they enjoy greater professional and operational autonomy. The percentage of women who place this item at the top is 57.4%, which is far higher than that of men in general (30.3%) and of men at the same level. This may be attributable, to a large extent, to their specific working conditions. Improving environmental conditions and accident prevention (27.8%) is another important item. This item represents a high priority among blue collar workers at all levels, which is felt more strongly by the smaller groups, a symptom of the existence of widespread dissatisfaction and unease over the harmfulness and riskiness of working environments.

Another controversial element concerns FIAT's expansion into southern Italy, radically changing its business strategy, previously focused exclusively on the north. The reason behind this choice was the emergence of social tension in Turin, which had already been felt in the early 1960s, as the city was no longer able to absorb the workforce, leading to an increase in trade union protests. In the 5-year period 1955–1960, the number of southern immigrants in Turin was close to 85,000. This immigration process gradually amplified in the early 1960s: in 1962, the total number of immigrants was around 80,000, 44,000 of whom came from the south (Cersosimo, 1994). A further peak occurred in the 2-year period 1968–1969 in connection with the surge in international car demand. The sustained growth in demand induced the Turin-based automotive group to further expand its production capacity and employment base, both by upgrading existing plants and by building new ones. In the same years, more than 15,000 southern workers arrived in Turin. Turin thus reached its demographic peak, with a population of 1.2 million inhabitants, as opposed to 700,000 in 1951, 40% of whose residents were born in the south. As a result of this overcrowding, governing the city became increasingly difficult, conflicts grew, and strikes intensified. Moreover, poor environmental and working conditions fueled discontent among the workers, spreading insubordination and tension (Treves, 1994).

FIAT's top management made the decision to change course and relocate investments to the south due to ungovernable climate inside and outside the factory.

In this climate of ungovernability inside and outside the factory, FIAT's top management decided to reverse course, moving its investments to the south. The first massive settlement in the south, which started the southward migration of FIAT's capital, was launched in 1969 with an organic program for the 3-year period 1970–1972, which covered the Bari area, the large Cassino plant, Termoli, Lecce, Sulmona, and the expansion of Termini Imerese and San Salvo. A decisive reason behind this choice was the provision of public financial incentives, which in the 1960s also became available to large companies with Law 717 of 1965, enabling a second and more robust wave of industrial investment.

From what is reported in the literature, unlike the reporting in FIAT's financial statements, it seems clear that the reasons that led FIAT to contribute to the industrialization of the south, seeking to narrow the gap with the north, were not only inclusive and voluntary, but almost obligatory. Indeed, as argued by Cersosimo Dominico (1994) "for FIAT, the South of Italy is any 'South' of the world, the most suitable area in which to restart the capitalist game jammed in the north with reformed organisational and dimensional arrangements."

6 Concluding Remarks and Future Avenues of Research

The historical analysis of reporting disclosure reveals that themes such equity and inclusion of people working within organizations cannot be considered a novelty of recent years as can be identified in many corporate initiatives since the last century. FIAT, which dominated the national and international panorama from the beginning of the twentieth century, was clearly focused on the social sphere and the relevance of sense of inclusion of employees. Indeed, since the beginning of the last century, FIAT paid particular attention to the development of corporate welfare and was involved in the provision and development of various services and activities in favor of workers, such as housing, schools and professional training, health management, assistance for retired workers, company canteens, and other initiatives to strengthen proximity and inclusion, also involving workers' families. However, some initiatives have been also criticized in literature as some of those, apparently socially oriented, actually hid an opportunistic and in some cases paternalistic streak, aimed at resolving wrong strategies and policies, such as investments in Italian southern regions or incentives aimed at suppressing protests. From financial statement analysis, it also emerged limited gender policies, and, in the horizontal time analyzed, no information has been found on women covering high-level managerial or auditing roles.

Despite some criticalities, however, FIAT financial statements represent a positive example of comprehensive reporting disclosure as, since the first years of activities, it was possible to find a comprehensive set of information, beyond just the financial data.

The research contributes to the debate to equity and inclusion, providing a historical perspective to better understand the origins, the evolution of company's disclosure, and the commitment on such topics. Also, the study enhances to enrich the debate on large corporations and their pivotal role for a nation and many communities, able to influence and shape the culture, the behaviors, and the habits of thousands of workers and their families. Under a managerial perspective, the research can provide insights on what has been done and what still needs to be done in terms of equity and inclusions, also bringing to light best practices to take inspiration for today's company policies.

However, the study just focuses on financial reports of a single, but relevant, large corporation, providing evidences that may be complemented by additional information coming from other company's documents or external documents such as those of different stakeholders, local governments, and newspapers. Equity and inclusion could also benefit from an analysis integrated with other environmental or governance disclosure so to provide a holistic perspective about nonfinancial commitment.

Moreover, future avenues may be directed to investigate, under a historical lens, the evolutionary role of other large and significant companies, depicting DEI initiatives and disclosure, together with other sustainability issues.

References

Atkinson, A. B., Marlier, E., & Nolan, B. (2004). Indicators and targets for social inclusion in the European Union. *JCMS Journal of Common Market Studies, 42*(1), 47–75.

Bernstein, R. S., Bulger, M., Salipante, P., & Weisinger, J. Y. (2020). From diversity to inclusion to equity: A theory of generative interactions. *Journal of Business Ethics, 167*, 395–410.

Carroll, A. B. (1991). The pyramid of corporate social responsibility: Toward the moral management of organisational stakeholders. *Business Horizons, 34*(4), 39–48.

Castronovo, V. (2005). *FIAT. A history of Italian capitalism*. Rizzoli Storica.

Cerruti, G., & Rieser, V. (1988). What do the FIAT Mirafiori workers think. *Politics and Economics, 1*(4), 53–60.

Cersosimo, D. (1994). Da Torino a Melfi. Ragioni e percorsi della meridionalizzazione FIAT. *Meridian, 1*(21), 35–68.

Deore, A., & Krishnan, R. (2024). Diversity and firm performance: A management accounting and control systems perspective. In *Why diversity, equity, and inclusion matter: Challenges and solutions* (pp. 179–216).

FIAT. (1957). *52nd financial year*. Ordinary General Meeting of Shareholders, (30 April 1958).

FIAT. (30 April 1970). *Reports of the Board of Directors and Statutory Auditors*. Balance sheet and profit and loss account as of 31 December 1969.

FIAT. (27 April 1973). *Reports of the Board of Directors and Statutory Auditors*. Balance Sheet and Income Statement as of 31 December 1972.

Garavini, S. (1970). The 1950s at FIAT: A historical experience. *Politics and Economics, 1*(2), 44–55.

GDEIB. (2021). 'Global Diversity, Equity & Inclusion Benchmarks. Standards for Organisations around the World', *Center for Global Inclusion*. Retrieved at https://centreforglobalinclusion.org/wp-content/uploads/2021/06/GDEIB-APRIL-2021-1.pdf, March 2024.

Gross, C., Cissna, K., & Wickramasinghe, A. (2023). Diversity, equity, and inclusion: Strategic plans for start-ups. In *Global Encyclopedia of public administration, public policy, and governance* (pp. 3396–3404). Springer International Publishing.

Kokot-Blamey, P. (2021). Mothering in accounting: Feminism, motherhood, and making partnership in accountancy in Germany and the UK. *Accounting, Organizations and Society, 93*, 101255.

Laine, M. (2005). Meanings of the term 'sustainable development' in Finnish corporate disclosures. *Accounting Forum, 29*(4), 395–413. https://doi.org/10.1016/j.accfor.2005.04.001

Lassou, P. J., Hopper, T., & Ntim, C. (2021). Accounting and development in Africa. *Critical Perspectives on Accounting, 78*, 102280.

Lehman, C. R. (2019). Reflecting on now more than ever: Feminism in accounting. *Critical Perspectives on Accounting, 65*, 102080.

Paravia. (1996). *FIAT: le fasi della crescita. Tempi e cifre dello sviluppo aziendale*. G.B. Paravia & C. S.p.A., Archivio storico FIAT.

Romansky, L., Garrod, M., Brown, K., & Deo, K. (2021). How to measure inclusion in the workplace. *Harvard Business Review, 27*.

Rumens, N. (2017). Postfeminism, men, masculinities and work: A research agenda for gender and organization studies scholars. *Gender, Work and Organization, 24*(3), 245–259.

Stamps, D. C., & Foley, S. M. (2023). Strategies to implement diversity, equity, inclusion, and belonging in the workplace. *Nurse Leader, 21*(6), 675–680.

Treves, L. (1994). La FIAT nel Mezzogiorno: perchè Melfi. *Rivista economica del mezzogiorno, 8*(1), 261–268.

Vargas-Solar, G., Cerquitelli, T., Montorsi, A., Salvai, S., Sangineti, M. T., Darmont, J., & Favre, C. (2022). Promoting equity, diversity and inclusion: Policies, strategies and future directions in higher education, research communities and business. In *In 2022 IEEE international conference on big data (big data)* (pp. 4710–4718). IEEE.

WBCSD. (2022). *World Business Council for Sustainable Development and Korn Ferry, 'Diversity, Equity & Inclusion in the Workplace the journey to leading practice'*. GENEVA, 21 April 2022. Retrieved at https://www.google.com/url?sa=t&rct=j&q=&esrc=s&source=web&cd=&cad=rja&uact=8&ved=2ahUKEwj4g-m5jeWEAxU5Q_EDHdkcBvgQFnoECA4QAw&url=https%3A%2F%2Fwww.wbcsd.org%2FImperatives%2FEquity-Action%2FNews%2FWBCSD-and-Korn-Ferry-launch-report-exploring-key-dimensions-of-maturity-when-it-comes-to-Diversity-Equity-Inclusion-DEI&usg=AOvVaw1K_hRqY2-IFM5BWzgmn0oZ&opi=89978449, March 2024.

Drivers, Barriers, and Enablers of Gender Equality Certification Systems: Insights from a Case Study

Annalisa Sentuti, Federica Palazzi, and Francesca Maria Cesaroni

1 Introduction

Gender equality (GE) is one of the goals of the 2030 Agenda[1] (UN, 2015). Since its introduction, governments and institutions have been committed to creating the conditions to overcome discrimination and promote women's empowerment in all contexts, including the workplace. SDG 5 is the Sustainable Development Goal dedicated to achieving GE and women's empowerment. However, women's empowerment is crosscutting to other SDGs (Leal Filho et al., 2023). In fact, gender discrimination can lead to social, economic, and political inequalities that hinder development potential. Inequalities persist in developing and developed countries, influencing access to moral work, equal pay, education, healthcare, resources, and decision-making (Connor et al., 2020; Maheshwari & Nayak, 2020).

The growing attention to gender issues and their relevance for global and equal growth have recently led to some tools/standards aimed at promoting conscious and proactive behavior to overcome gender inequalities in organizations.

In Italy, the Gender Equality Certification System[2] has been introduced by the Italian National Recovery and Resilience Plan (NRRP)[3] and is based on the UNI/

[1] The 2030 Agenda is an action plan signed by all 193 UN member states in 2015 that identifies 17 Sustainable Development Goals (SDGs). All member countries are called upon to strive to promote economic prosperity, environmental protection, and human well-being globally.

[2] Source: https://certificazione.pariopportunita.gov.it/public/info

[3] Negotiated by Italy with the European Union in response to the pandemic crisis, the NRRP aims to repair the economic and social damages, contributing to tackling the structural weaknesses of

A. Sentuti (✉) · F. Palazzi · F. M. Cesaroni
Department of Economics, Society, Politics, University of Urbino Carlo Bo, Urbino, Italy
e-mail: annalisa.sentuti@uniurb.it; federica.palazzi@uniurb.it; francesca.cesaroni@uniurb.it

M. Agostini et al. (eds.), *Diversity and Equity in Accounting*, SIDREA Series in Accounting and Business Administration,
https://doi.org/10.1007/978-3-031-78247-3_17

PdR 125:2022 practice. This practice is a voluntary standard that defines guidelines for creating a management system for inclusive and gender-equal workplaces. It provides specific key performance indicators (KPIs) to measure, report, and evaluate the organization's GE policies in six assessment areas: culture and strategy, governance, human resources, opportunities for growth and inclusion of women in the company, pay equity by gender, protection of parenthood and work-life balance. The Italian government encourages the adoption of the UNI/PdR 125:2022 practice and the GE certification with specific incentives for companies that successfully conclude the certification process.

According to the Italian Department for Equal Opportunities, on February 22, 2024, 1480 companies obtained the GE certification according to the UNI/PdR 125:2022 practice. On October 18, 2023, there were 679 certified companies: the number has more than doubled in just 4 months, indicating an increasing trend and, probably, many other enterprises are striving in this direction. However, empirical research on this subject is still minimal, given the recent introduction of this certification system (Frey, 2023) and the focus of accounting research on traditional issues (Baker et al., 2023).

This research embraces a broad concept of accounting considered "neither a technical activity nor asocial" (Lehman, 2019, p. 8) since it is useful for measuring, reporting, and evaluating financial performance and also social aspects, including gender inequalities. To this end, new accounting tools are needed in organizations and should be the focus of accounting research. These tools can contribute to making the gender dimension visible in organizations and foster good practices on social justice (Velasco-Balmaseda et al., 2023). The UNI/PdR 125:2022 practice is an example. It can be considered a novel accounting system that allows organizations to measure, report, and evaluate gender data to bridge existing gaps, incorporate the GE paradigm into the organization, and produce a change toward inclusion and equity over time.

This chapter investigates the drivers, barriers, enablers, and benefits of adopting GE certification systems in enterprises according to the UNI/PdR 125:2022 practice. Based on insights from a case study, it presents theoretical and practical implications to guide the strategic implementation of GE certification in private organizations.

2 Theoretical Background

Certification has become popular in managing social problems (Brandén and Rönnblom 2019; Cacace et al., 2024). It is not only an assessing tool for the status quo but also indicates the direction of development (Daemen & Van der Krogt,

the Italian economy and reducing territorial, generational, and gender gaps. Source: https://www.mef.gov.it/en/focus/The-National-Recovery-and-Resilience-Plan-NRRP/

2008). However, certification is a conformity assessment that could create tension between emancipatory and control-based functions (Højlund, 2015). Thus, certification scheme ranges from control or accountability to quality improvement, emancipation, and development (Van der Krogt, 2006). Nevertheless, if the control function prevails, certification can be a "ticking the box" to satisfy accountability requirements without activating a change/transformation (Ahmed, 2007).

Several certifications or guidelines focus on people's working conditions and, more generally, corporate social responsibility (CSR). SA8000 is the leading social certification globally. It provides a holistic framework for fair treatment of workers. UNI EN ISO 26000:2020 is the guideline for CSR and a valuable tool for pursuing sustainable development goals (SDGs). UNI EN ISO 45001:2018 provides an international framework for managing occupational health and safety risks. UNI EN ISO 30415:2021 is an international standard dedicated to diversity and inclusion in organizations, including their governance body, leaders, workforce-recognized representatives, and other stakeholders.

An extensive literature analyzed the companies' approaches toward these certifications. Many authors focused on motivations or drivers for certification concerning people/workers (Table 1). Top management (TM) or entrepreneurs can begin the certification process to promote a new way of doing business that is more coherent with their values and beliefs. The certification focused on workers can improve the working environment and facilitate the hiring and retention of talents (Kanaka Latha, 2017; O'Donovan, 2018; Pavlíková & Basovníková, 2014). Additionally, these types of certifications create the opportunity for new partnerships, have a significant impact on customers and suppliers (Kanaka Latha, 2017; O'Donovan, 2018), and can determine a competitive advantage over competitors (Pavlíková & Basovníková, 2014). The demand for these certifications can also be derived from the market and the increasing sensitivity of consumers to human issues. Certifications improve the corporate image and reputation and enhance economic performance (Stigzelius & Mark-Herbert, 2009). According to Santos et al. (2018), incentives at

Table 1 Motivations and drivers

Motivations/drivers	References
To be promoters of a new way of doing business Competitive advantage over competitors Creation of new partnerships Improvement of the working environment	Pavlíková and Basovníková (2014)
More significant impact on customers and suppliers Facilitate hiring and winning the talent war	Kanaka Latha (2017); O'Donovan (2018)
Demand from the market Improvement of the image and reputation Achievement of economic benefits	Stigzelius and Mark-Herbert (2009)
Presence of incentives at the regional or local level Improvement of the efficiency of business management	Santos et al. (2018)
Enterprise risk management	Henkle (2005)

the regional or local level contribute to the spread of certification. Finally, certifications can be a tool to manage risks associated with workers management and could impact the efficiency of business management (Henkle, 2005; Santos et al., 2018).

Several authors investigated the expected benefits of the certification process. Improving the company's image and reputation and gaining a competitive advantage over its competitors (Santos et al., 2018) would lead to business growth through market expansion and a better understanding of the markets, with consequent economic benefits (Stigzelius & Mark-Herbert, 2009; de Andrade & Bizzo, 2019; Machado & Davim, 2018; O'Donovan, 2018). Workers certification is supposed to improve relationships with employees; reduce labor disputes, workplace risks, and absenteeism; and improve employee motivation (Stigzelius & Mark-Herbert, 2009; Henkle, 2005; Dhanesh, 2014; Machado & Davim, 2018; O'Donovan, 2018). This situation could, therefore, make leadership more effective (O'Donovan, 2018). In addition, workers certification would increase stakeholder transparency, improve customer loyalty, and help develop and consolidate partnerships (Prasad, 2009) (Table 2).

Previous analyses have pointed out that certifications may require investment, management and staff training, and change management (Stigzelius & Mark-Herbert, 2009; Arevalo & Aravind, 2011)—for example, internal health and safety monitoring be set up, working conditions adapted, disabled staff recruited, and equal opportunities promoted (Stigzelius & Mark-Herbert, 2009; Koster et al., 2019). Other barriers could include increased costs associated with certification, creating tensions, difficulty in managing change and complexity, lack of support

Table 2 Benefits

Benefits	References
Achievement of economic benefits Improvement of the relationship with employees	Stigzelius and Mark-Herbert (2009); de Andrade and Bizzo (2019); Machado and Davim (2018); O'Donovan (2018)
Reduction of risks at work	Stigzelius and Mark-Herbert (2009); Henkle (2005)
Reduction of labor conflicts Reduction in absenteeism Increase in staff motivation	Dhanesh (2014); Machado and Davim (2018); O'Donovan (2018)
Improvement of corporate image and reputation Achievement of a competitive advantage over competitors	Santos et al. (2018)
Increase in transparency toward stakeholders Improvement in customer loyalty Development and consolidation of partnerships	Prasad (2009)
More effective leadership	O'Donovan (2018)
Business growth (market expansion and better understanding)	O'Donovan (2018)

Table 3 Barriers

Barriers	References
Need of investments	Stigzelius and Mark-Herbert (2009); Arevalo and Aravind (2011)
Management training Staff training	Arevalo and Aravind (2011)
Reverse discrimination fears	Machado and Davim (2018)
Establishment of an internal health and security supervision Adaptation of working conditions Recruitment of staff with disabilities Promoting equal opportunities	Stigzelius and Mark-Herbert (2009); Koster et al. (2019)
Increased costs Tension Change and complexity Lack of senior management support Group agendas	O'Donovan (2018)

from senior management, the formation of groups whose members feel they need to be protected, and fears of reverse discrimination for people outside protected groups (Machado & Davim, 2018; O'Donovan, 2018) (Table 3).

The abovementioned studies offer an exciting framework about drivers, benefits, and barriers to adopting certifications or standards focused on people and, more generally, CSR. There are few specific studies on GE certification or standards (Tzanakou et al., 2021) mostly focused on certifying GE in research organizations (Cacace et al., 2024). For our research purpose, it is worth mentioning Velasco-Balmaseda et al. (2023), which investigated GE certifications and standards as a specific area of CSR. They mapped 36 initiatives worldwide and highlighted that for both public and private organizations, the main driver of GE standards seems to be commercial purposes, as the adoption is linked to improving their image more than their commitment to GE. Thus, the authors observed a "superficial and symbolic" use of the GE concept (Velasco-Balmaseda et al., 2023, p. 13). However, to promote real change in organizations, GE certification should introduce new accounting tools, involve both the operational and strategic level, have the TM support, and permeate the company DNA with the concepts of equity. For this reason, we believe it is essential to go beyond the existence of GE certification in the company and investigate what motivations, drivers, and factors may favor/hinder its adoption in organizations. The recent introduction of the Italian GE Certification System based on the UNI/PdR 125:2022 practice offers an interesting research opportunity in this regard to understand how companies approach this voluntary standard.

3 Method and Research Context

We adopted a qualitative research approach based on a single-case study (Yin, 2003; Eisenhardt & Graebner, 2007). This method enables researchers to investigate complex phenomena in which several variables, such as the main actors' decisions and behaviors, can significantly affect why and how organizational dynamics, processes, and practices unfold.

In single-case research design, cases can be chosen because they are unusually revelatory (Yin, 2003), valid for the investigation of a "transparently observable" phenomenon (Eisenhardt, 1989, p. 537) and primarily suitable for gaining new theoretical insights (Eisenhardt & Graebner, 2007).

The company involved was selected purposefully (Patton, 2002) using data from Atoka database. Specifically, we looked for a company that had obtained the UNI/PdR 125:2022 within the previous year (2022) and was willing to be involved in our research. Furthermore, we favored territorial proximity with the authors (located in the Marche region) to visit the company more readily and conduct in-person interviews.

Following these criteria, we selected the company Alpha SPA (fictitious name). Alpha SPA is one of the first private companies in the Marche region to have been awarded the UNI/PdR 125:2022, obtained in December 2022. We can consider it a pioneer company and still among the few certified ones since, as of the end of February 2024, only around 40 companies in the Marche region have certified GE. The company was founded in 1999, operates in the manufacturing industry, and produces heat exchangers for the plumbing and heating sectors. This is a male-dominated sector, which makes the company an even more interesting case for our research. Over the years, the business has grown. Currently, turnover exceeds 130 million euro, and the company employs 374 employees divided into 280 blue-collar workers (204 men, 76 women), 90 white-collar workers (69 men, 21 women), and 4 executives (all men). The Board of Directors involves five members, four men and one woman. For all these reasons, Alpha SPA can be considered an information-rich case from which we can learn much about our research topics (Patton, 2002).

In-depth semi-structured interviews with crucial actors are our primary source of data. Specifically, to gather the ownership, governance, and management perspectives, we interviewed the President of the Board of Directors (male, I1), the Vice-President (female, I2), the HR-Recruiting, Learning, and Development Manager (male, I3), and the HR-Administration and Payroll Manager (female, I4). The President and Vice-President of the Board of Directors also represent ownership as they are majority shareholders (75% of shares). Furthermore, we gathered secondary data from company website, press releases, articles in local newspapers, and company documents to accomplish triangulation. Additional data were added from field notes taken during interviews.

All interviews were carried out in November 2023 and then recorded (with the informants' permission) and transcribed. The interviews explored three aspects in-depth: the context (company profile and history, business priorities, approach to diversity, equity and inclusion issues before certification), the certification process (how and why it was initiated, which actors were involved, the main stages of the process, any critical issues or factors that hindered/favored its development, and main changes introduced), expected benefits, and an overall evaluation of the experience undertaken nearly 1 year after certification.

Data was analyzed using thematic analysis (Patton, 2002) following the six steps described by Braun and Clarke (2006). Manual coding was employed to identify key concepts and themes within our qualitative data. The factors that emerged as relevant from the literature about certifications and the themes that structured the interview checklist guided our thematic analysis and allowed us to explore the different underlying logic. The authors involved in the interviews undertook initial analysis and coding. A third author, not involved in the interviews, was appointed to check the coding. Then, the analysis was discussed among all authors to further increase the reliability of our findings (Eisenhardt, 1989). Collected secondary data was also used to integrate the analysis of the interviews.

Data analysis made it possible to identify the drivers, barriers, and benefits of adopting GE certification according to the UNI/PdR 125:2022 practice. Discussing barriers, some enablers also emerged, which we report below, along with the other results.

4 Findings

4.1 Drivers: Why Did the Company Embrace the UNI/PdR 125:2022 Practice?

The idea to undertake the certification process, according to UNI/PdR 125:2022, came from the Human Resources department, which learned about the GE certification through a periodic industry newsletter: "We realized immediately that this was an opportunity for us. Although we were aware that our TM team is all male and, as a metalworking company, our workforce is predominantly male, seeing the checklist and KPIs provided for the certification, we realized that we were on the right course […] We enquired and submitted a proposal to the TM and the Vice-President who immediately accepted" (I4).

Ownership and governance had long been sensitive to inclusion, equity, and workers' well-being issues. "We have always paid attention to these aspects, but the pandemic caused a major breakthrough. It changed working methods, certainly, there has been digitization and the use of new IT tools/methods, but it also brought out new values at the heart of the company, such as the workers' mental and physical health" (I2). Furthermore, combined with the constant growth of the business, the pandemic made it necessary to adopt "new, more targeted and sophisticated HR processes to make the company more attractive in the labor market, which has been turned upside down in the last five years, generating extreme difficulties in recruiting personnel" (I3). Shortly before the pandemic, the recruitment process had been internalized, and "the search for workers was carried out from the outset without prejudice and stereotypes, with a view to diversity and inclusion" (I3). But after the pandemic, "other HR processes, such as remuneration policies, also required updating to implement a 'fair pay system'" (I3). The company benchmarked its reference market and decided to award employees with better-than-market-average salaries. The company has also invested "in a more systematic and structured way in work-life balance and corporate welfare" and acknowledges that these "issues have become strategically important for us in attracting candidates and retaining employees" (I2). The company also introduced what they called "the 'welfare neighbourhood', that is, conventions with local shops offering discounts to employees, ticket restaurants, hourly flexibility and smart-working" (I4). More recently, based on the results of an internal survey on organizational well-being, the idea came about to implement a project called "I Take Care of You," which embraces the "mens sana in corpore sano" philosophy and aims to improve the employees' health and well-being, "benefiting both the individual and the company. The project includes prevention activities through cancer screenings, an on-site nutritionist available to workers and, in the long run, the establishment of a company fitness center. We are very proud of this idea" (I4).

While increasing the well-being of employees played a decisive role in initiating the gender certification process, the presence of national incentives was not a motivating factor: "Certifying GE only for the contributory advantage would have been an end in itself. Instead, we saw it as a way to formalize what we were already doing and have a working method to improve our behaviors" because "it's not all sunshine and roses: we had rooted habits and behaviors in the company that were fine thirty years ago but not anymore. Scheduling meetings late at night, having fixed times for lunch breaks … for those who have children and family, or want to go to the gym or have a hobby … these practices are not healthy. Yet, we struggle to eradicate them. Certification gives us one more tool to do so" (I2). The GE certification was "a starting point. We use it as leverage to improve our internal processes" (I3).

4.2 Barriers and Enablers: What Factors Favored/Hindered the Certification Process?

The barriers mentioned by the interviewees are operational and strategic in nature. "Certification, in itself, is a challenging path because it requires a lot of effort in terms of creating the data and preparing the documentation, and this can scare many companies and deter them from embarking on this path. There is a need for an operational structure and human resources who can devote part of their time to measuring, monitoring, and reporting data. But above all, certification demands commitment, i.e., it requires that the company make a real and ongoing effort to improve in terms of GE" (I2).

From these considerations, respondents recounted which factors enabled these barriers to be overcome. The presence of the majority owners, who are sensitive to the issues covered by the certification and have a strong involvement in the company's management, was a critical enabling factor at the strategic level: "When the HR department proposed applying for GE certification, I immediately said 'Yes! We must get it!' And I also said, 'Don't make a GE certification that is only on paper: it must become a reality, a tool for the company to evolve in a changing world'" (I1); "Ownership and management are very much present in the company, physically and mentally. To realize this path, it is essential that both owners and TM have GE founding principles as a core value […] a culture of equity is needed" (I2). The positive answer was not only formal but also substantive: ownership and TM promoted and supported the implementation of the project at all stages and actively contributed to communicating the project to all organizational levels. The Vice-President also worked with the HR department on the certification requirements and KPIs. "This behavior is not taken for granted. We made a proposal, but if we had not found fruitful ground, we could not have realized anything" (I4).

Furthermore, at the operational level, the company had the advantage of already having 11 certifications and a code of ethics as a result of the values that underpin the firm: "The health and safety of people, the quality of the products offered, as well as respect for the environment are essential values that have always been present in the Alpha SPA corporate policy and strategy" (company website). This was an essential enabler because "It was not necessary to create new procedures or new documents. In most cases, it was a matter of modifying, integrating or improving the ethical code, other documents or procedures already existing in the company, or formalizing actions we were already doing" (I2). Additionally, the company has long since adopted a management system to manage data and processes relating to HR that produces all employee-related analyses and reports. This was useful initially to quickly obtain the data required for certification and then to define a dedicated budget for GE actions and to measure KPIs over time.

4.3 Achieved Benefits: Is It Worth the Effort?

About a year after obtaining certification, it seems seamlessly integrated into the company and is gradually bringing concrete results: "Thanks to certification, we have got into the routine of writing down, and thus formalizing, all the procedures, actions and processes that deal with GE. Now they are an asset of the company: if tomorrow we are no longer in this department, those who come after us can easily be trained thanks to those we have formalized" (I3).

The certification also drew the attention of management and the HR department to some aspects that need to be improved, enabling a method to implement actions to overcome critical issues and monitor results. Finally, this tool has improved communication and transparency toward employees: "Certification is a further lever to achieve our strategic goals. It has helped us bring out things we knew and others of which we were less aware, it helps us to improve weaknesses. And then, in a working world where – especially in certain roles – there is a lot of turnover, companies steal professional figures from each other. This certification system can help attract and retain people, motivate them to stay or come to work here, and trigger positive word-of-mouth towards job seekers to communicate that people are well off in this company and that for this company, the well-being of people, women and men, really is a value" (I2). Furthermore, "Internal organizational well-being questionnaires tell us that we are moving in the right direction" (I3, I4).

The Vice-President still emphasizes that GE certification requires a significant effort, which mere economic incentives cannot justify. The effort, in terms of commitment, human resources, new accounting systems, and procedures, is rewarded by the company's increased ability to attract and retain talent and ensure employees' well-being. Furthermore, the company received considerable media attention and gained several awards, thanks to the obtaining of the GE certification. This certification thus increased the company's visibility, confirming its image as an active and people-oriented enterprise. To summarize, "Yes, it is worth it" (I2).

5 Discussion: Theoretical and Practical Implications

The analyzed case allowed us to identify the main drivers, i.e., motivating factors that led the company to adopt the GE certification; barriers as critical issues encountered in the implementation phase or factors that have hindered or slowed down the adoption of this standard or, on the contrary, factors that as enablers favored the development and adoption; and benefits obtained. The results confirmed some aspects that have emerged from the literature on CSR certifications, such as facilitating the hiring and retention of talents (Kanaka Latha, 2017; O'Donovan, 2018; Pavlíková & Basovníková, 2014) as a driver. Simultaneously, it made it possible to highlight other exciting highlights. The introduction of GE certification is not always driven by a desire to improve the company's image instrumentally (Velasco-Balmaseda et al., 2023). The company analyzed had long promoted a working environment and human resource management inspired by diversity, equity, and inclusion. Certification was the tool to enhance this culture, formalize the path undertaken, and be more transparent toward employees. Certification has also enabled the company to adopt a method for monitoring its actions and encouraging continuous improvement toward GE. The proactivity of the HR department and the support of the owners and the TM were decisive.

Furthermore, this study offered practical insights for entrepreneurs, managers, and business owners. Identifying drivers, barriers, enablers, and benefits will help them understand how best to develop and implement the GE certification based on the UNI/PdR 125:2022 practice in their companies. Specifically, the analyzed case showed that the HR department's proactivity could drive the TM team's attention toward the GE certification by providing information about related opportunities and challenges. The company's determination to remain appealing in the labor market may motivate it to apply for the GE certification to attract candidates, hire talents, and retain the best employees. Furthermore, the sensitiveness of the ownership and TM teams toward workers' well-being can promote the introduction of GE certification as a tool to formalize the company's commitment toward GE, foster good practices in this regard, and valorize the culture of diversity, equity, and inclusion. The study also highlighted that once a company chooses to apply for GE certification, two factors favor its adoption. First, having GE founding principles as core values for ownership and management gives to the certification process appropriate sponsorship, supporting its implementation and driving collective efforts. Second, having a well-developed management system, previous certifications about employees' health and safety and ethical codes enhance the company's ability to adopt the new accounting tool for gender dimension more efficiently and effectively. These factors prepare the organization's mindset toward the certification process and allow data to be produced without creating new processes. Finally, a company benefits from introducing the GE certification by institutionalizing a system for measuring, reporting, and evaluating gender data, acquiring greater awareness about gender diversity, equity, and inclusion and of what it is achieving or must strive to accomplish from this perspective. No less, a company can benefit from introducing the GE certification by gaining a competitive advantage in the labor market, improving employee loyalty and well-being, achieving greater external visibility, and reinforcing its image.

6 Conclusions

This study contributed to the academic debate about promoting GE culture in enterprises and related new accounting tools (Lehman, 2019)—namely, the UNI/PdR 125:2022 practice—for measuring, reporting, and evaluating gender dimension in organizations (Velasco-Balmaseda et al., 2023). Specifically, it addressed the research gap in empirical studies about GE certification systems and can be considered a pilot case (Yin, 2003), which lays the foundations for quantitative research to investigate drivers, barriers/enablers, and benefits in large samples of companies to confirm, extend, or refute the identified factors. In particular, we are aware that the analysis of a large company does not reflect the situation of SMEs, which cannot rely on the same organizational structures and resources. Future research should consider these aspects and pay attention to the specificities of SMEs. Finally, this research can also help policymakers formulate a robust strategy to encourage companies to adopt GE certification systems and thus foster the creation of economic and social contexts that are increasingly aware, attentive, and proactive toward equity between men and women in the workplace.

References

Ahmed, S. (2007). 'You end up doing the document rather than doing the doing': Diversity, race equality and the politics of documentation. *Ethnic and Racial Studies, 30*(4), 590–609.

Arevalo, J. A., & Aravind, D. (2011). Corporate social responsibility practices in India: Approach, drivers, and barriers. *Corporate Governance: The International Journal of Business in Society, 11*(4), 399–414.

Baker, H. K., Kumar, S., Pandey, N., & Kraus, S. (2023). Contemporary accounting research: A retrospective between 1984 and 2021 using bibliometric analysis. *Contemporary Accounting Research, 40*(1), 196–230.

Brandén, J., & Rönnblom, M. (2019). Selling the safe city? The politics of certification and the case of purple flag Sweden. *Scandinavian Journal of Public Administration, 23*(3/4), 23–41.

Braun, V., & Clarke, V. (2006). Using thematic analysis in psychology. *Qualitative Research in Psychology, 3*(2), 77–101.

Cacace, M., Pugliese, F., Tzanakou, C., Müller, J., Denis, A., & Sangiuliano, M. (2024). Certifying complexity? The case of a European gender equality certification scheme for research-performing organizations. *Science and Public Policy, 51*(2), 261–273.

Connor, J., Madhavan, S., Mokashi, M., Amanuel, H., Johnson, N. R., Pace, L. E., & Bartz, D. (2020). Health risks and outcomes that disproportionately affect women during the Covid-19 pandemic: A review. *Social Science & Medicine, 266*, 113364.

Daemen, H., & Van der Krogt, T. (2008). Four functions of international accreditation: The case of EAPAA and public Administration in The Netherlands. In G. Jenei & K. Mike (Eds.), *Public administration and public policy degree programmes in Europe: The road from Bologna* (pp. 23–38). NISPAcee.

de Andrade, V. F., & Bizzo, W. A. (2019). Corporate social responsibility in Brazil according to SA 8000: Case studies and the correlation with the supply chain. *Journal of Cleaner Production, 210*, 1022–1032.

Dhanesh, G. S. (2014). CSR as organization–employee relationship management strategy: A case study of socially responsible information technology companies in India. *Management Communication Quarterly, 28*(1), 130–149.

Eisenhardt, K. M. (1989). Building theories from case study research. *Academy of Management Review; 14*(4), 532–550.

Eisenhardt, K. M., & Graebner, M. E. (2007). Theory building from cases: Opportunities and challenges. *Academy of Management Journal, 50*(1), 25–32.

Frey, M. (2023). Il ritardo nel management della diversità in Italia e alcune rilevanti azioni in atto. *Impresa Progetto, 3*, 1–7.

Henkle, D. (2005). Gap Inc. sees supplier ownership of compliance with workplace standards as an essential element of socially responsible sourcing. *Journal of Organizational Excellence, 25*(1), 17–25.

Højlund, S. (2015). Evaluation in the European Commission: For accountability or learning? *European Journal of Risk Regulation, 6*(1), 35–46.

Kanaka Latha, V. (2017). Corporate social responsibility in India: Issues and challenges. *International Journal of Advance Research Ideas and Innovations in Technology, 3*(3), 1674–1679.

Koster, M., Vos, B., & van der Valk, W. (2019). Drivers and barriers for adoption of a leading social management standard (SA8000) in developing economies. *International Journal of Physical Distribution & Logistics Management, 49*(5), 534–551.

Leal Filho, W., Kovaleva, M., Tsani, S., et al. (2023). Promoting gender equality across the sustainable development goals. *Environment, Development and Sustainability, 25*, 14177–14198.

Lehman, C. R. (2019). Reflecting on now more than ever: Feminism in accounting. *Critical Perspectives on Accounting, 65*, 102080.

Machado, C., & Davim, J. P. (2018). *Organizational behaviour and human resource management*. Springer.

Maheshwari, G., & Nayak, R. (2020). Women leadership in Vietnamese higher education institutions: An exploratory study on barriers and enablers for career enhancement. *Educational Management Administration & Leadership, 50*(5), 758–775.

O'Donovan, D. (2018). Diversity and inclusion in the workplace. In C. Machado & J. Davim (Eds.), *Organizational behaviour and human resource management. Management and industrial engineering* (pp. 73–108). Springer.

Patton, M. Q. (2002). *Qualitative evaluation and research methods* (3rd ed.). Sage Publications, Inc.

Pavlíková, E. A., & Basovníková, M. (2014). Certification of corporate social responsibility. The case study of India. *Acta Universitatis Agriculturae et Silviculturae Mendelianae Brunensis, 62*(4), 605–611.

Prasad, V. V. S. K. (2009). *CSR initiatives of Indian companies-a study*. The Hindu College-MBA.

Santos, G., Murmura, F., & Bravi, L. (2018). SA 8000 as a tool for a sustainable development strategy. *Corporate Social Responsibility and Environmental Management, 25*(1), 95–105.

Stigzelius, I., & Mark-Herbert, C. (2009). Tailoring corporate responsibility to suppliers: Managing SA 8000 in Indian garment manufacturing. *Scandinavian Journal of Management, 25*(1), 46–56.

Tzanakou, C., Clayton-Hathway, K., & Humbert, A. L. (2021). Certifying gender equality in research: Lessons learnt from Athena Swan and total e-quality award schemes. *Frontiers in Sociology, 6*, 784446.

United Nations. (2015). *Transforming our world: the 2030 agenda for sustainable development*. Retrieved from https://sustainabledevelopment.un.org/content/documents/21252030%20Agenda%20for%20Sustainable%20Development%20web.pdf

Van der Krogt, T. (2006). *Quality Standards in Public Administration Education and Training*. Report issued by the IASIA/UNDESA Task Force on Standards of Excellence in Public Administration Education and Training. Mimeo, Warsaw.

Velasco-Balmaseda, E., de Celis, I.-R., & Izaguirre, N. E. (2023). Corporate social responsibility as a framework for gender equality: Mapping of gender equality standards for sustainable development. *Corporate Social Responsibility and Environmental Management*, 1–16. https://doi.org/10.1002/csr.2673

Yin, R. K. (2003). *Case study research: Design and methods* (3rd ed.). Sage.

The Integration of Diversity, Inclusion, and Equity in Management Control Systems: The Multiutility Experience

Laura Broccardo and Elisa Truant

1 Introduction

Diversity, equity, and inclusion (DEI) issues and projects aim at guaranteeing equitable treatment and equal opportunities for everyone. The main goal is to eliminate bias and unfair treatment that is rooted in the specific traits or attributes of a person or a group of individuals that are legally safeguarded. The initiative operates on the premise that everyone possesses the same abilities and capabilities and that they have equal access to advantages under identical circumstances. However, individuals exhibit diversity due to several factors, such as race, gender, geographical region, culture, and physical ability. Consequently, it is unfeasible to establish a universally applicable notion of a "person." Equity is a crucial factor that organizations must consider while aiming to comply with diversity and inclusion efforts (Vargas-Solar et al., 2022).

Despite studies and dedicated efforts from both organizational leaders and policymakers, issues of conflict and inequality around diversity and inclusion continue to exist in all types of organizations, industries, and sectors (Bernstein et al., 2020). Some of these conflicts arise from a dearth of productive relationships among varied individuals and organizations, and there is a clear need for more management alternatives and theories to guide efforts in developing inclusive practices and organizational cultures, as these goals are difficult to achieve and issues often arise (Bernstein et al., 2020).

Indeed, diversity, inclusion, and equity projects give organizations the chance to expedite the advancements made in addressing and rectifying substantial historical

L. Broccardo (✉) · E. Truant
Department of Management "Valter Cantino", University of Turin, Torino, Italy
e-mail: laura.broccardo@unito.it; elisa.truant@unito.it

M. Agostini et al. (eds.), *Diversity and Equity in Accounting*, SIDREA Series in Accounting and Business Administration,
https://doi.org/10.1007/978-3-031-78247-3_18

obstacles in this area. Companies must prioritize not only profitability but also the creation of ecosystems that are conducive to innovation, creativity, and well-being. When really adopted and genuinely implemented, diversity, inclusion, and equity projects may establish a mutually advantageous cycle that empowers high-performing teams and enhances productivity. By incorporating diverse viewpoints, experiences, and skill sets from a wide range of individuals, a firm may gain valuable insights and identify any overlooked possibilities (Gross et al., 2023).

DEI practices have been studied in management contexts to extensively minimize discrimination and improve performance, but the results are not homogeneous. This inconsistency makes it difficult to determine which policies to employ, how, why, and what results to expect (Nishii et al., 2018).

Consequently, considering the highlighted picture and gaps, the goal of this study is to evaluate the ways in which management control system (MCS) tools can be used and applied in companies to advance diversity, inclusion, and equity. In reaching the declared goal, the case study of an Italian multiutility firm was scrutinized.

In order to fulfil the goal of this study, a comprehensive qualitative case study (Yin, 1994) was carried out in 2023, and this method is particularly appropriate when it is necessary to examine internal dynamics. More specifically, the analysis was conducted at Multiutility SpA (the company name has been anonymized), a prominent Italian multiutility company, analyzing both primary and secondary data.

The results suggest that MCSs can play a crucial role in advancing DEI, hence cultivating long-term norms and cultures that further increase inclusion and equity. MCS and its associated key performance indicators (KPIs) were intentionally developed and utilized within established norms and cultures to advance the principles of inclusion and equity. Moreover, the utilization of MCS has a role in influencing norms and cultures that promote inclusivity and fairness through controlling and discussing the process of diffusion. It is evident that it is becoming more and more important for diversity, inclusion, and equity projects to use management control systems (MCSs). However, it is pointed out in the literature that not much is known about these parts of management control from this point of view, thus highlighting the need for additional research, filling the gap (Deore & Krishnan, 2024). Consequently, the main contribution of this study is providing and creating knowledge about MCS and DEI project implementation.

Moreover, this study emphasizes that MCS promotes diversity, inclusion, and equity, which continue to be unsolved matters in companies, while also offering relevant key performance indicators (KPIs) to push DEI in organizations.

This study is organized as follows: Section 2 illustrates the features of MCSs in implementing the main goals in organizations; the main arising issues of diversity, inclusion, and equity; and the role of MCS in effectively integrating them into a company's strategy. Section 3 presents the case study and the main findings, while Sect. 4 shows conclusions and future research.

2 Literature Overview

2.1 *Management Control Systems*

Management control systems (MCSs) refer to established processes and procedures that managers employ to effectively accomplish their desired objectives (Simons, 1995). MCS facilitates the monitoring and management of the entire organization's performance, enabling a precise and predictable allocation of responsibility for outcomes to individual members. It also supports the implementation of incentive plans to motivate employees to achieve multiple goal targets.

The use of a management control system enables adaptation to environmental changes, analysis of and feedback on performance, and advice on capital investment decisions (Kaplan & Norton, 2000). Additionally, its adoption aims to ease reporting to other parties and lower internal tensions and disputes (Cooper, 1984).

Recent research on MCS has focused primarily on a few primary topics, including the following: the various types of controls; the examination of MCS as a whole rather than as a collection of separate mechanisms; the investigation of the role and characteristics of MCS in various business and environmental settings; the investigation of the numerous factors that influence MCS, such as the degree of complexity of the business and environmental setting; and the investigation of the effects and results of MCS (Songini et al., 2018).

However, currently, businesses are encountering a highly dynamic and chaotic situation, as they strive to meet the complicated and different requirements of several stakeholders. Hence, it is imperative that the MCS remains adaptable and flexible rather than rigid. It should be designed to effectively execute the chosen strategy in dynamic and ever-changing circumstances (Becker, 2016). Nevertheless, several unresolved concerns and obstacles persist in the pursuit of establishing an optimal system, such as diversity, inclusion, and equity challenges.

Since MCS provides managers with information to plan, control, and make decisions linking strategies and business processes to achieve a competitive advantage, it is expected that this system will strongly support efforts to enhance DEI projects. These issues are increasingly important, and it is crucial for MCS, through appropriate adaptations of this system, to support organizations in including them in their business strategy and enhance good practices (Cheffi et al., 2023; Fähndrich, 2023; Bhimani, 2020).

Unquestionably, it is necessary to modify MCS in a challenging context. Also, researchers indicate that MCS needs to be revised when there is a change in strategy, such as in environmental, social, or other areas of concern (Riccaboni & Leone, 2010), in order to generate useful information for decision-making. Consequently, it is necessary that MCS identifies new and revised parameters, metrics, and indicators (Cinquini & Norreklit, 2015) to accurately assess a company's strategic goals, which include DEI aspects. Accordingly, it is crucial to correctly calibrate these systems, and failure to do so may result in delayed or inadequate measurements that lack the essential strategy implementation.

To include DEI aspects in MCS, it is necessary to clarify their meaning. In particular, the term "diversity" was initially defined by Cox (1993) as the presence of individuals with varied cultural connections within the same social structure. Molefi et al. (2021) define diversity as the range of similarities and differences among individuals, encompassing various dimensions such as "gender, sex, gender identity and expression, ethnicity, race, native or indigenous identity/origin, age, generation, disability, sexual orientation, culture, religion, belief system, marital status, parental status, pregnancy, socio-economic status/caste, appearance, language and accent, mental health, education, geography, nationality, work style, work experience, job role and function, thinking style, and personality type. The presence of different diversity dimensions in organizations might differ based on geographical location, time, or the organization itself" (Molefi et al., 2021, p. 22).

Although extensive research was conducted to investigate the impact of diversity among management practices to reduce discrimination, increase diversity, and enhance performance, the findings have been scant and contradictory (Nishii et al., 2018). This lack of consistency hinders our understanding of which diversity practices should be implemented, how they should be implemented, the purpose behind their implementation, and the expected outcomes. Researchers and practitioners face a challenge in integrating various study findings due to a lack of theoretical guidance on achieving desired outcomes (Nishii et al., 2018).

Inclusion differs from diversity in that it prioritizes the integration of each employee into the company's operations and culture, as well as their compositional mix. According to Mor-Barak and Cherin's (1998) definition, inclusion refers to the extent to which people believe they are involved in significant organizational activities, such as having access to information and resources, taking part in work groups, and having the power to influence decision-making. The Gartner Inclusion Index 4 employs a comprehensive and diverse definition of inclusion. It also considers the concept of diversity by including a category that focuses on how employees perceive representation, fair treatment, integration of differences, decision-making, psychological safety, trust, belonging, and diversity. Moreover, the Commission of the European Communities (2003, p. 10) provided a definition of social inclusion as "a process that ensures that those at risk of poverty and social exclusion gain the opportunities and resources necessary to participate fully in economic, social, political, and cultural life and to enjoy a standard of living that is considered normal in the society in which they live. It ensures that they have greater participation in decision-making that affects their lives and access to their fundamental rights." Inclusion is also a key concept of the 2030 Agenda and refers to individuals facing disadvantage due to several factors such as gender, race, or socioeconomic status.

Finally, equity was defined by Chin and Chien (2006, p. 79) as "the absence of systematic disparities…between groups with different levels of underlying social advantage/disadvantage—that is, wealth, power, or prestige." Unlike inclusion, equity prioritizes the results at the organizational or systemic level rather than at the level of the group or individual. Addressing systemic and structural imbalances is essential for achieving equity.

2.2 Management Control and Diversity, Inclusion, and Equity Integration

The promotion of diversity, equity, and inclusion is currently a top priority for businesses. Organizations are becoming aware that integrating diversity, equity, and inclusion into their culture and strategy leads to enhanced relationships, improved quality and employee retention, and increased profitability. Managers must do more than simply draw attention to a need or raise awareness of DEI ideas. Productive diversity efforts are nurtured by surroundings that foster inclusiveness and a culture that embraces and promotes differences. Indeed, a wise execution of diversity, equity, and inclusion strategy plan that takes into account structural dynamics and regards diversity education as a continuous endeavor to attain cultural humility is necessary (Stamps & Foley, 2023).

In line with the changing context, companies are moving to allocate greater focus and resources toward the advancement of diversity, equity, and inclusion. A total of over 1600 chief executive officers have committed to the CEO Action for Diversity & Inclusion pledge. In the second quarter of 2020, 40% of firms mentioned diversity and inclusion during their earnings calls, compared to just 4% in the same quarter of the previous year (Romansky et al., 2021), and there has been an over 800% surge in job advertisements specifically seeking diversity recruiters (Romansky et al., 2021).

While organizations have developed methods to measure and monitor diversity, they have not yet achieved the same level of success in measuring inclusion. In order to accurately monitor and assess inclusion, organizations must gauge employee mood using a well-defined understanding of inclusion, therefore enabling the organization to promptly respond to the findings (Vargas-Solar et al., 2022; Romansky et al., 2021).

Due to the highlighted picture, management control systems are essential for ensuring the alignment of individuals' behavior throughout the implementation of DEI programs and setting the right tools and measurements to implement diversity, inclusion, and equity strategic projects. According to Malmi and Brown (2008), management controls refer to the metrics and systems that managers apply to guarantee that their workers' behaviors and decisions align with the organization's objectives and strategy. Accordingly, it is important to create MCSs that effectively lead employees to align their actions with the objectives of the firm (Van der Stede, 2017). Despite this, different studies show that traditional management control systems may need to be changed in order to better meet the goals of diversity, inclusion, and equity, as well as the different expectations of stakeholders that businesses face (Ball & Milne, 2005; Durden, 2008; Hosoda, 2018; Riccaboni & Leone, 2010).

3 Methodology and Main Evidences on Diversity, Inclusion, and Equity in MCS

3.1 Company Overview and Its Commitment in Diversity, Inclusion, and Equity

To achieve the objective of this work, a qualitative case study (Yin, 1994) was carried out, with a specific focus on Multiutility SpA, a prominent Italian multiutility company. Multiutility SpA has a workforce of about 11,000 individuals and is involved in many industries, including electricity, gas, district heating, water, and waste management. In addition, the firm offers services such as public illumination, traffic light services, and facility management. These services are provided to a wide geographical area that includes the Piedmont, Liguria, and Emilia-Romagna regions (Multiutility website, 2024). The Multiutility group emerged as the winner in the 12th edition of the Top Utility Award in 2024. This prestigious award recognizes the outstanding performance of the top 100 Italian firms in the energy, environment, and water sectors. In addition, the Multiutility group was awarded the 2023 Financial Statement Oscar Award, which recognizes firms that excel in their reporting operations and in maintaining relationships with their stakeholders.

Multiutility SpA was formed in 2010 with the strategic objective of opposing multinational corporations. Multiutility operates as a holding company with separate divisions responsible for various services like electricity, gas, district heating, water, and waste management. The organization of Multiutility SpA is defined by the presence of local committees, which serve the purpose of facilitating communication between Multiutility and local stakeholders. Multiutility is publicly traded on the Italian Stock Exchange. In March 2024, Multiutility's shareholders consisted of several Italian towns (Turin, Genoa, Reggio Emilia, Parma, Piacenza, La Spezia), Compagnia di San Paolo, and free float, as stated on the Multiutility website in 2024. According to the Multiutility website in 2024, Multiutility has shown a favorable financial performance in recent years, with strong outcomes in terms of revenues, EBITDA, net profit, ROI, and ROE. In 2022, the company generated revenues of 7.863 million euros, achieved an EBITDA of 1.055 million euros, and had a net profit of 226 million euros. Moreover, there was a 55% surge in investment compared to the previous year, as reported on the Multiutility website in 2024.

Moreover, diversity and inclusion are fundamental principles and essential components of Multiutility culture. The company is dedicated, as demonstrated by its corporate purpose and values and the business plan, to enriching the variety within the company, promoting a harmonious work-life balance, and raising the quality of the working environment. The goal is to form a cohesive team that enhances the overall result of individual efforts and fosters a sense of unity, by establishing a common social, cultural, professional, and intellectual foundation. Due to this specific reason, Multiutility has made the decision to establish a "Diversity and Inclusion Policy" that specifically addresses four key areas: gender, generational, cultural, and ability diversity. In Multiutility SpA, diversity is a valuable asset that, when embraced inclusively, enhances the overall well-being of everyone. Multiutility's goal is to create a corporate community where each individual feels included and can contribute their unique perspectives. Moreover, the Multiutility group has accomplished a significant milestone with Bloomberg's Gender-Equality Index (GEI), which is an international index that assesses gender equity inside corporations.

3.2 Methodology

This research employed the case study method to conduct a thorough investigation of the conditions and internal dynamics within an organization that led to the adoption and implementation of DEI practices (Yin, 1994).

This method facilitates a thorough examination (Otley & Berry, 1994; Yin, 1994; Scapens, 1990) of the internal dynamics, in which inclusive and equitable policies are implemented. A qualitative methodology elucidates the intricacies around the acceptance and implementation of new management tools, as well as the necessary associated adjustments. According to Alsharari and Al-Shboul (2019), Baumgartner (2014), and Klettner et al. (2014), this approach examines the perspectives of the parties involved.

Primary and secondary data were analyzed. The collection of primary data involved conducting semi-structured interviews with managers who possess expertise in fostering inclusion and gender equity. Moreover, Multiutility (the company name has been anonymized) documents and website information were also scrutinized.

A total of eight semi-structured, face-to-face interviews were conducted with selected members of the company's Board of Directors (BoD) and executives. The respondents, listed in Table 1, were chosen based on their direct or indirect involvement in activities related to diversity, inclusion, and equity.

The participants were deliberately presented with comparable inquiries in order to identify any potential contradictions.

Table 1 Interview details

#	Interviewees	Date and length
I 1	Chairman of the BoD	December 11, 2023 (36 min)
I 2	Deputy Chairman	December 02, 2023 (38 min)
I 3	Independent Director	January 18, 2024 (42 min)
I 4	CSR Manager	December 20, 2023 (45 min)
I 5	Strategic Planning Manager	January 22, 2024 (50 min)
I 6	Chief Financial Officer (CFO) Manager	January 26, 2024 (58 min)
I 7	Communication Manager	February 05, 2024 (33 min)
I 8	Human Resources Manager	February 21, 2024 (61 min)

Source: own elaboration

The authors recorded and transcribed interviews that they conducted in Italian. The analysis of each interview transcript involved a careful examination of the respondents' remarks, with the specific objective of identifying any possible inconsistencies or distortions. Moreover, the authors independently read and examined all transcripts. Prior actions were implemented to resolve concerns regarding the appropriateness of the situation (Ryan, 2002).

Furthermore, a document analysis was conducted by gathering significant data from Multiutility's sustainability report 2022, the business plan at 2030 update, the code of ethics 2022, the remuneration plan 2022, and the policy on diversity and inclusion 2022, as well as from Multiutility's website.

3.3 Management Control System and Diversity, Inclusion, and Equity KPI

Analyzing Multiutility documents, it was possible to discover that the company is involved in some DEI initiatives. In particular, the main initiatives mentioned refer to gender, nationality, disability, and age.

Moreover, by analyzing both interview transcripts and Multiutility documents, it was possible to depict the main goals and KPIs that the company declares are connected to diversity, inclusion, and equity, presented in the next Table 2.

From document analysis and interviews, it emerges that Multiutility pays attention in favoring well-being in terms of diversity, inclusion, and equity. As explained by the Chairman of the BoD "It is with pride that for the third consecutive year, Multiutility has been included in Bloomberg's Gender-Equality Index (GEI), the international index that measures gender equality in companies. This important recognition highlights that the company is going in the right direction and that many efforts have been made."

However, from a deeper investigation, it emerged that efforts are mainly focused on gender diversity, more specifically in avoiding women's discrimination. The Human Resource Manager affirmed, "We pay a lot of attention in supporting gender equity, implementing internal policies for example, to facilitate working mothers, guarantee equal career opportunities for women and avoid salary gaps," and the Deputy Chairman confirmed that "Gender equity and inclusiveness are fundamental values for Multiutility. One of our goals is to have, by 2030, 30% of women in managerial positions."

Furthermore, from multiple sources, it emerged that KPIs are mainly monitored for sustainability purposes, in particular to prepare the sustainability report. As affirmed by the CFO, and confirmed by the CSR Manager "Currently, we assess diversity, inclusion and equity to prepare the Sustainability Report, but more could certainly be done to communicate these issues to the various internal and external stakeholders." The CSR Manager also underlined that within the sustainability

Table 2 Multiutility diversity, inclusion, and equity KPIs

Goals in diversity, inclusion, and equity	KPI
Women in Board of Directors (BoD)	% of women in BoD
Women in managerial position	% of women in managerial position (executive and middle management)
Women employed	% of women employed
Generational diversity	% of new hiring under 30
Cultural diversity	% of ethnic, linguistic, or other group
Disability	% of employees with disability or special needs
Flexible working	Number of employees participating in flexible working
Career progression free from all discrimination	Number of complaints survey ad hoc
Diversity and inclusion training	Number of training hours per organizational level
Violence, harassment, and bullying	Number of complaints surveyed ad hoc
Parenting protection	Number of new initiatives proposed/ number of adherences
Promotion of healthy lifestyle and well-being	Number of new project proposed Number of new projects realized
Selection, recruiting, training, management, development, and remuneration free from discrimination	Number of complaints surveyed ad hoc

Source: own elaboration

report, information on these themes needs to be more exhaustive as "especially on equity and inclusion I am not yet fully satisfied."

Moreover, from the Strategic Planning Manager interview, it emerged that "Nowadays the management control system, as well as the incentive and remuneration system don't include KPIs related to diversity equity and inclusion. And it is a pity because if we want to align the whole organization on these issues, we need to invest more in managerial systems." As affirmed by the Independent Director, "Strategic and operational systems have enormous potential that has not yet been fully exploited. In recent years, efforts have been made to include some sustainability goals and indicators, but much can still be done towards diversity, inclusion, and equity." This evidence shows as more efforts are still required to align strategy and MCS on these issues. Therefore, it is essential to align individuals' behavior in implementing DEI programs, enlarging and identifying more tailor-made KPI measurements.

Matching both documents and interview transcripts of Multiutility, it emerged an increasing attention and efforts to DEI issues, but fragmented approaches persist, both at organizational and documentary level. Some guidelines at corporate level exist, but each operative manager acts in autonomous way, and not always integrated. Indeed, there is a call for MCS system to integrate diversity, inclusion, and equity issues both at strategic and operative levels. "This path requires cultural changing and it requires open-mind and to accept to be evaluated on those challenging goals." The full implementation must be sponsored by top management, to achieve a strong commitment from the bottom line.

4 Conclusions and Future Development

The analysis revealed Multiutility's involvement in pushing diversity, inclusion, and equity at the strategic level implementation, also if improvements are required. Indeed, the company is mainly focused on gender diversity, thus neglecting inclusion and how to realize equity policies in the company. This evidence is proven by a good level of diversity KPI, but a lack of inclusion and equity measurement, as also highlighted in the literature (Romansky et al., 2021).

Organizations must prioritize equity while striving to meet diversity and inclusion goals (Vargas-Solar et al., 2022). When diversity, inclusion, and equity projects are fully embraced and effectively executed, they may create a mutually beneficial loop that empowers high-performing teams and boosts productivity. By integrating a variety of perspectives, backgrounds, and expertise from a broad spectrum of individuals, a company may get useful insights and detect any potential opportunities that may have been missed (Gross et al., 2023).

Moreover, analyzing the Multiutility' Report of Remuneration policy, there is no trace in the reward system (part of management control) of incentives to managers linked to diversity, inclusion, and equity initiatives. This document is still too focused on economic and financial metrics, and incentive plans, more diversity, inclusion, and equity orientations are necessary to motivate managers and employees.

The interviews offered some perspectives on how the management control system might effectively support the diversity, inclusion, and equity initiatives. In particular, MCS functions as an instrument to enhance communication and internal coordination among employees, operational managers, and senior management. This promotes the spread of a culture that values diversity, inclusion, and equity throughout a company, closing the gap between goals and real-world implementation. Unfortunately, there is still a long way to go.

The research linking diversity, inclusion, and equity issues to MCS contributes to expanding the still limited literature on these topics. From a managerial perspective, the book chapter contributes to underline that MCS enables widespread adoption of this organizational culture and enhances to monitor diversity, inclusion, and equity performances.

However, the research shows some limitations in focusing on a single business and involving managers covering top positions. In order to validate the findings, the study may be replicated at other levels within the organization, taking into account the perspective of employees and not only the managerial perspective. This will allow for an exploration of other positions within the organization. It is also important to examine management control practices and tools in various settings, taking into consideration variables like size, industry, and culture, because they might influence the types and content of tools. Concluding, the case study approach is important for conducting early research and analyzing a complicated collection of management practices and changes. It provides a valuable means of achieving a thorough knowledge and mapping the insights of firms. However, surveys and larger comparative research across many businesses might be valuable methodologies to broaden the evidence.

References

Alsharari, N. M., & Al-Shboul, M. (2019). Evaluating qualitative research in management accounting using the criteria of "convincingness". *Pacific Accounting Review, 31*(1), 43–62.

Ball, F., & Milne, R. K. (2005). Simple derivations of properties of counting processes associated with Markov renewal processes. *Journal of Applied Probability, 42*(4), 1031–1043.

Baumgartner, R. J. (2014). Managing corporate sustainability and CSR: A conceptual framework combining values, strategies and instruments contributing to sustainable development. *Corporate Social Responsibility and Environmental Management, 21*(5), 258–271.

Becker, S. D. (2016). Budgeting in times of economic crisis. *Contemporary Accounting Research, 33*(4), 1489–1517.

Bernstein, R. S., Bulger, M., Salipante, P., & Weisinger, J. Y. (2020). From diversity to inclusion to equity: A theory of generative interactions. *Journal of Business Ethics, 167*, 395–410.

Bhimani, A. (2020). Digital data and management accounting: Why we need to rethink research methods. *Journal of Management Control, 31*(1), 9–23.

Cheffi, W., Zahir-ul-Hassan, M. K., Farooq, M. O., Baqrain, A., & Mansour, M. M. H. (2023). Ethical leadership, management control systems and circular economy in SMEs in an emerging economy, the UAE. *Journal of Business Research, 156*, 113513.

Chin, M. H., & Chien, A. T. (2006). Reducing racial and ethnic disparities in health care: An integral part of quality improvement scholarship. *Quality and Safety in Health Care, 15*, 79–80.

Cinquini, L., & Norreklit, H. (2015). "Management Control" Special Issue: Research perspectives in Performance Management. *Management Control*. (2015/2).

Commission of the European Communities. (2003). *Report from the commission on European governance*. Office for Official Publications of the EC.

Cooper, R. G. (1984). The strategy-performance link in product innovation. *R&D Management, 14*(4), 247–259.

Cox, T. (1993). *Cultural diversity in organizations: Theory, research and practice*. Berrett-Koehler.

Deore, A., & Krishnan, R. (2024). Diversity and Firm Performance: A Management Accounting and Control Systems Perspective. In *Why Diversity, Equity, and Inclusion Matter: Challenges and Solutions* (pp. 179–216).

Durden, C. (2008). Towards a socially responsible management control system. *Accounting, Auditing & Accountability Journal, 21*(5), 671–694.

Fähndrich, J. (2023). A literature review on the impact of digitalisation on management control. *Journal of Management Control, 34*(1), 9–65.

Gross, C., Cissna, K., & Wickramasinghe, A. (2023). Diversity, equity, and inclusion: Strategic plans for start-ups. In *Global Encyclopedia of public administration, public policy, and governance* (pp. 3396–3404). Springer International Publishing.

Hosoda, M. (2018). Management control systems and corporate social responsibility: Perspectives from a Japanese small company. *Corporate Governance, 18*(1), 68–80.

Kaplan, R. S., & Norton, D. P. (2000). Having trouble with your strategy? Then map it. *Focusing Your Organization on Strategy—with the Balanced Scorecard, 49*(5), 167–176.

Klettner, A., Clarke, T., & Boersma, M. (2014). The governance of corporate sustainability: Empirical insights into the development, leadership and implementation of responsible business strategy. *Journal of Business Ethics, 122*, 145–165.

Malmi, T., & Brown, D. A. (2008). Management control systems as a package—Opportunities, challenges and research directions. *Management Accounting Research, 19*(4), 287–300.

Molefi, N., O'Mara, J., & Richter, A. (2021). *Global diversity, equity and inclusion benchmarks: Standards for organizations around the world*. Centre for Global Inclusion.

Mor-Barak, M. E., & Cherin, D. A. (1998). A tool to expand organizational understanding of workforce diversity: Exploring a measure of inclusion-exclusion. *Administration in Social Work, 22*(1), 47–64.

Nishii, L., Khattab, J., Shemla, M., & Paluch, R. (2018). A multi-level process model for understanding diversity practice effectiveness. *Academy of Management Annals, 12*(1), 37–82.

Otley, D. T., & Berry, A. J. (1994). Case study research in management accounting and control. *Management Accounting Research, 5*(1), 45–65.

Riccaboni, A., & Leone, E. L. (2010). Implementing strategies through management control systems: The case of sustainability. *International Journal of Productivity and Performance Management, 59*(2), 130–144.

Romansky, L., Garrod, M., Brown, K., & Deo, K. (2021). How to measure inclusion in the workplace. *Harvard Business Review, 27*.

Ryan, B. (2002). *Research methods and methodology in finance and accounting*. Cengage Learning EMEA.

Scapens, R. W. (1990). Researching management accounting practice: The role of case study methods. *The British Accounting Review, 22*(3), 259–281.

Simons, R. (1995). *Levers of control: How managers use innovative control systems to drive strategic renewal*. Harvard Business School.

Songini, L., Morelli, C., & Vola, P. (2018). *Managerial control systems in family business: State of the art* (pp. 193–220). Performance Measurement and Management Control: The Relevance of Performance Measurement and Management Control Research.

Stamps, D. C., & Foley, S. M. (2023). Strategies to implement diversity, equity, inclusion, and belonging in the workplace. *Nurse Leader, 21*(6), 675–680.

Van der Stede, W. A. (2017). "Global" management accounting research: Some reflections. *Journal of International Accounting Research, 16*(2), 1–8.

Vargas-Solar, G., Cerquitelli, T., Montorsi, A., Salvai, S., Sangineti, M. T., Darmont, J., & Favre, C. (2022). Promoting equity, diversity and inclusion: Policies, strategies and future directions in higher education, research communities and business. In *2022 IEEE international conference on big data (big data)* (pp. 4710–4718). IEEE.

Yin, R. K. (1994). *Case study research: Design and methods* (2nd ed.). Sage.

Part V
Diversity and Equity in University Governance and Education

Action and Perception of Gender Equality in Higher Education Institutions: The Case Study of the University of Trieste

Eleonora Masiero, Grazia Garlatti Costa, and Alessio Maria Musella

1 Introduction

Much of the literature on higher education institutions (from now on, HEIs) emphasizes the role of these organizations as catalysts for empowerment and social transformation. Universities play a pivotal role in advancing gender equality (from now on, GE), diversity, and inclusion topics (Rosa et al., 2020; Pulejo, 2013). Despite progress in recent years, universities continue to be characterized by inherent gender biases and perpetuate gender-based practices (Rosa et al., 2020).

GE studies are thus emerging with prominence in HEIs, as these institutions, and particularly universities, occupy a strategic position to influence the training of future leaders and promote GE (Madeira et al., 2011).

Yet, despite growing interest in the issue (Galizzi & Siboni, 2016) and the extensive research on corporate social reporting (Atkins et al., 2015), the attention paid by the accounting literature to themes of GE in HEIs in the European landscape remains scant, highlighting the need to intensify research, especially in the accounting sector (Mauro et al., 2020; Oppi et al., 2021).

Broadbent (2016) and Siboni et al. (2016) highlighted the need to broaden the focus on this theme, considering GE as a fundamental aspect of the value generated by organizations, both in the public and private sectors.

E. Masiero (✉) · G. Garlatti Costa
Università degli Studi di Trieste, Dipartimento di Scienze Economiche, Aziendali, Matematiche e Statistiche, Trieste, Italy
e-mail: eleonora.masiero@deams.units.it; grazia.garlatticosta@units.it

A. M. Musella
Università degli Studi di Napoli "Federico II", Dipartimento di Scienze Economiche e Statistiche, Naples, Italy
e-mail: alessiomaria.musella@unina.it

M. Agostini et al. (eds.), *Diversity and Equity in Accounting*, SIDREA Series in Accounting and Business Administration,
https://doi.org/10.1007/978-3-031-78247-3_19

The case of Italian universities is particularly relevant, as very few studies are dedicated to this topic (Oppi et al., 2021). Among these, Oppi et al. (2021) investigate the development of the gender balance (from now on, GB) process, related reporting practices, and their integration into the strategic policies of the University of Ferrara, while Colombis (2019) examines the objectives of GB as a tool for analysis, planning, and accounting at the University of Salerno.

In this chapter, we aim to enrich the existing literature on GE in Italian HEIs by specifically focusing on the role and evolution of the *Comitato Unico di Garanzia*—Guarantee Committee for Equal Opportunities (from now on, CUG)—at the University of Trieste. First, we analyze the breadth of actions undertaken over time by the university to address the issue of GE. This initial exploration is essential to establish a thorough understanding of the research context. Accordingly, we explore how the CUG's role has evolved, highlighting the current perceptions and expectations of CUG members, as well as the motivations behind their actions and dedication.

The chapter is structured as follows: First, it recalls the literature on GE in HEIs and the tools developed over time to tackle the topic. Later, it provides the methodology, and subsequently the findings. Finally, the chapter concludes by summarizing the main points and implications.

2 Literature Review

2.1 Gender Equality in Higher Education Institutions

The persistent gender imbalances, evident in the wage disparities across different academic levels, gender-based segregation in various fields and roles within academia, and the limited integration of gender perspectives in education and research, highlight how gender disparities continue to influence the distribution of labor and academic resources significantly (Caprile et al., 2012; European Commission, 2019; Hearn et al., 2020; Husu, 2020; Kachchaf et al., 2015; Paoletti et al., 2020).

Literature has highlighted the need for a strategic approach that mobilizes leadership and commitment at all organizational levels of these institutions to foster GE in HEIs (Pulejo, 2013). Over time, an increasing number of universities, both in Italy and internationally, begun adopting different tools to monitor and address the GE themes. Documents such as those concerning social, environmental, end-of-mandate issues and, more recently, the dissemination of sustainability (and social) reports and GB have been designed to outline and account for the outcomes achieved by HEIs, facilitating a thorough understanding of their peculiarities, particularly regarding GE (Fiorani & Di Gerio, 2022; Meneguzzo & Fiorani, 2009). Accordingly, in addressing gender disparities within higher education, adopting gender equality plans (GEPs) is becoming increasingly prevalent as a strategy promoted by the European Commission (2021). While numerous examples attest to the successful implementation of GEPs in European universities (Rosa et al., 2020), their ability to induce significant structural and cultural changes within academic institutions remains under scrutiny, particularly in Italy (Oppi et al., 2021). It has been observed that GEPs often adhere to an overly instrumental logic centered on efficiency as a justification for policy interventions and conservative approaches in formulating and applying GE strategies (Lätti, 2017). Questions arise about how GEPs can evolve and respond to the ongoing transformations in the higher education sector, influenced by dynamics such as corporatization, marketisation, and globalization. Nevertheless, GEPs can only achieve their full potential when integrated with sustainability (and social) reports and GB (i.e., gender-based assessments of budgets, which incorporate a gender perspective at all stages of the budgetary process, thus promoting GE) (Addabbo et al., 2022). Within this context, the CUG represents an essential tool for advancing GE in HEIs. The CUG, to which this chapter is mostly dedicated, is critical to the GEPs due to its holistic strategy in addressing discrimination and promoting GE through active monitoring, advising, and proactive measures.

2.2 GE's Tools in Italian HEIs: The Establishment of the CUG

The establishment of the CUG within the Italian public sector is described in Article 21 of Legislative Decree 150/2009, further strengthened by Law 183/2010, known as "Collegato Lavoro." Article 21 of Legislative Decree No. 150/2009 describes the establishment, objectives, and functions of the CUG within public administrations. This legislative framework emphasizes the CUG's role in promoting equal opportunities, combating discrimination, and fostering a culture of respect and well-being. The ensuing integration and reinforcement of these provisions by the 2010 "Collegato Lavoro" further underlines the commitment of the Italian state to these issues, especially within the public sector, including HEIs like universities. The establishment of the CUG marks a significant advancement in gender-sensitive policymaking. From a gender-sensitive standpoint, the CUG is crucial in advocating and overseeing GE measures within universities, including creating the gender report.

Concerning the existing literature on the CUG, one of the first scholarly contributions is a book chapter in which Zilli (2012) provides an in-depth examination of the innovations introduced by the "Collegato Lavoro" regarding the role of the CUG in promoting GE, organizational well-being, and antidiscrimination protection. A more focused examination of the role of the CUG in universities is provided by Manganaro's contribution (2019), in which the author delves into the issue of gender balance within the specific realm of public administrations and universities. More recently, Vimercati (2021) examined the role of CUGs in organizational innovation in public administrations, particularly regarding GE. The analysis considers the power dynamics between social groups, influenced by both organizational and legal constraints. GE is examined as a crucial aspect of organizational well-being, and it is integrated into strategic planning, as required by various norms and directives that public institutions must consider. This includes the functions assigned to CUGs and the preparation of gender budgets.

Other notable contributions are the collection of conference proceedings named "Diversity Management: nuove frontiere dell'inclusione e sfide per i CUG universitari"[1] curated by Galgano and Papillo (2020) and the "Quaderni del Comitato Unico di Garanzia dell'Università Ca' Foscari Venezia."[2] The latter is a peer-reviewed series dedicated to gender discrimination and equal opportunities in working and academic life. It features essays that analyze and reflect on issues such as violence against women, sexual harassment, and the rights of LGBTQ+ individuals. It also offers insights into well-being at work and support for disadvantaged groups.

While the body of work on the CUG is diverse and spans multiple disciplines, a significant research gap remains in examining its crucial role in advancing GE and addressing discrimination in Italian universities. This oversight highlights a vital area for future scholarly investigation. To this end, this chapter aims to enrich the existing literature on GE in Italian HEIs, exploring how the CUG has facilitated the development of GE over time.

3 Methodology

We adopt a case study research methodology (Yin, 2016) to explore how equality evolved within a university system. This research approach is selected because the "how" question "deals with optional links needing to be traced over time" (Yin, 2016, p. 10). We focus our exploration on the University of Trieste because, given that two of us are part of this institution, we could gather in-depth insight into the perception of GE within it.

In this regard, we collected and triangulated multiple evidence sources, listed in Table 1.

First, we explored the University of Trieste's website to select and collect the different tools for reporting or addressing the topic of GE. Overall, the documentation collected comprises the social integrated reports published in the years 2020 and 2021; the social reports published in the years 2008 and 2009; the sustainability report published in 2020; the strategic plan published between 2009 and 2019; the GEP 2022–2024; the webpages dedicated to the UN Objective 5 "Gender Equality," to the social indicators, to the "Gender Advisor," and last but not least to the webpages dedicated to describing the CUG activity. The study of these documents served understanding how the gender topic was addressed over time through the different tools and to develop the content of the interviews.

[1] English Translation: "Diversity Management: New Frontiers of Inclusion and Challenges for the C.U.G. of Universities".

[2] Available at the following link: https://edizionicafoscari.unive.it/it/edizioni4/collane/comitato-unico-di-garanzia/.

Table 1 List of sources of evidence

Source of evidence	Type of source	Description—available at
Documentation	"Bilancio Sociale Integrato 2020"	https://www.units.it/ateneo/bilancio-sociale-integrato https://www.units.it/ateneo/bilanci-stategie-e-relazioni
	"Bilancio Sociale Integrato 2021"	https://www.units.it/ateneo/bilancio-sociale-integrato https://www.units.it/ateneo/bilanci-stategie-e-relazioni
	"Bilancio Sociale 2009"	https://www.openstarts.units.it/collections/5ccaf9f3-ea0c-477f-8c35d3f1d09ca4a3 https://www.units.it/ateneo/bilanci-stategie-e-relazioni
	"Bilancio Sociale 2008"	https://www.units.it/ateneo/bilanci-stategie-e-relazioni
	"Bilancio di Sostenibilità 2020"	https://www.units.it/sites/default/files/media/documenti/ateneo/varie/bs_26_03_2021_provino_spread_page.pdf
	"Rapporto di Sostenibilità 2020"	https://www.units.it/sites/default/files/media/documenti/ateneo/bilanci/rapporto_sostenibilita_incontro_mr_10062021.pdf
	"Piano di Uguaglianza di Genere (GEP) 2022–2024"	https://www.units.it/ateneo/bilanci-stategie-e-relazioni
	"Piano Strategico 2019–2023"	https://www.units.it/ateneo/bilanci-stategie-e-relazioni
	"Piano Strategico 2016–2018"	https://www.units.it/ateneo/bilanci-stategie-e-relazioni
	"Piano Strategico 2013–2015"	https://www.units.it/ateneo/bilanci-stategie-e-relazioni
	"Documento di Programmazione Triennale 2010–2012"	https://www.units.it/ateneo/bilanci-stategie-e-relazioni https://www.units.it/ateneo/bilanci-stategie-e-relazioni
	"Documento di Programmazione Triennale 2007–2009"	https://www.units.it/ateneo/bilanci-stategie-e-relazioni
	"Obiettivi per lo sviluppo sostenibile: 5—Parità di Genere"	https://www.units.it/rapporto-sostenibilita/obiettivi-sviluppo-sostenibile https://www.units.it/rapporto-sostenibilita/obiettivo/raggiungere-luguaglianza-di-genere-ed-emancipare-tutte-le-donne-e
	"Indicatori di performance sociale"	https://bilanciosociale.units.it/pari-opportunita/tipo?t=All
	"CUG—Comitato Unico di Garanzia"	https://web.units.it/page/cug/
	"Art. 5: Consigliera di Fiducia"	https://web.units.it/node/21711

(continued)

Table 1 (continued)

Source of evidence	Type of source	Description—available at
Interviews	Structured interview	CUG—11 members Media: Google Form
	Semi-structured interview with the President of the CUG	Professor Maria Dolores Ferrara Media: TEAMS—face to face
Participant observation	CUG member at the University of Trieste	One of the author of the paper: Assistant Professor Grazia Garlatti Costa

Second, the data collected from these documentation sources was triangulated with a structured and semi-structured interview (Bryman & Bell, 2003). The structured interview was directed to the CUG members of the University of Trieste. Regarding the roles of the 11 interviewees, we attained a balanced representation that reflects the CUG's membership composition. The interviewees embody a broad array of positions within the CUG, including the president, both effective and substitute members from the public and trade union sectors, and a student representative, thus encapsulating the committee's diverse perspectives and viewpoints. The structured interview, conducted via a Google Form, was organized into 18 questions. By collecting, analyzing, and reporting (Findings—Section 4.3) the feedback obtained from the structured interview, we aimed to highlight the viewpoints and insights of CUG members, thereby amplifying the voices of university stakeholders who are actively engaged in the advocacy for GE. Once collecting and analyzing the 11 interviews, we conducted a follow-up interview with the President of the CUG.

Third, during the research period, one of us, currently a CUG member, had the opportunity to act as a Participant Observer (Yin, 2016, p. 114), gathering insight into interpersonal behavior within the CUG and consequently facilitating the data analysis.

4 Findings

4.1 GE at the University of Trieste

The University of Trieste was among the first in Italy to publish social reports in 2008 and 2009.[3] At that time, the committee preparing the social report included Professor Ondina Gabrovec Mei, President of the Scientific Committee of the GBS (*Gruppo di Studio per il Bilancio Sociale*). The social reports published in

[3] Reference: Bilancio Sociale Integrato 2020.

2008 and 2009 followed the GBS standards,[4] the public sector standards,[5] and Baccini's guidelines issued on March 16, 2006.[6] In these two reports, the focus on equal opportunities, within the university, is intended in its various aspects and addressed through the following activities: the Disability Desk (*Sportello Disabili*), the Equal Opportunities Committee (*Comitato Pari Opportunità*), and the Mobbing Committee (*Comitato Mobbing*). Concerning the Equal Opportunities and Mobbing Staff, this unit represented the administrative support structure to these committees, taking care of the management of the activities delegated by the committees, implementing collateral and supplementary activities, and managing courses.[7]

Accordingly, to promote access to and rebalance gender participation in technical-scientific degree courses, 117 attendance awards were distributed to deserving female students in the academic year 2007/2008.[8] The social report 2008 dedicates "Appendix I - *Le Pari Opportunità*" to describing strategies, policies, activities, and tools related to this topic, detailing the structure and role of the Equal Opportunity Committee, and providing a detailed numerical description of the personnel (distinguished by role) and students (distinguished by faculty) by gender. Following the Italian Law, the Equal Opportunity Committee was later substituted by the CUG, first mentioned in the strategic plan 2013–2015.[9] In this regard, the GEP 2022–2024 highlights how the CUG is expected to support the planned objectives. The role of the CUG is emphasized in relation to the promotion of equal opportunities for students, the improvement of internal decision-making processes, the development of knowledge and skills on gender issues through international workshops, the integration of a gender dimension in research content through departmental workshops and graduation awards, and the integration of a gender dimension within teaching content.[10]

---

[4] The reference document has been the GBS: "La rendicontazione sociale nelle Università, Doc. di Ricerca n° 7, Giuffrè Editore, 2008." Reference: Bilancio Sociale 2009; Bilancio Sociale Integrato 2020 - Note.

[5] More precisely: "Standard di base. La rendicontazione sociale nel settore pubblico-Gruppo di Studio per il Bilancio Sociale GBS, Giuffrè Editore, 2005." Reference: Bilancio Sociale 2009.

[6] More precisely: "Direttiva del Ministro della Funzione Pubblica sulla rendicontazione sociale nelle amministrazioni pubbliche." Reference: Bilancio Sociale 2009.

[7] Reference: Bilancio Sociale 2008, p. 65; Bilancio Sociale 2009, p. 63.

[8] Bilancio Sociale 2008, p. 125.

[9] Piano strategico 2013–2015 "1°Aggiornamento al Piano approvato con delibera del Consiglio di Amministrazione del 28 marzo 2014 (odg 9-a) approvato con delibera del Consiglio di Amministrazione del 25 luglio 2014 (ODG 9-A)" (p. 9).

[10] Reference: "Piano di Uguaglianza di Genere 2022–2024" - Area IV - Obiettivo IV.5 *Favorire l'integrazione di una dimensione di genere nei contenuti della didattica.* (pp. 27–28).

4.2 The CUG at the University of Trieste

The CUG is structured to ensure a comprehensive approach to its mandate of equal opportunities and antidiscrimination. Chaired by a President, the CUG includes members from both public and trade union sectors, with designated positions for effective (*componenti effettivi*) and substitute members (*componenti supplenti*) to ensure continuity and representation in cases of members' absences. The public sector representatives include members from both the faculty (including researchers) and the administrative staff. The committee includes two members: representatives of the student body and doctoral students. This diverse composition of the CUG reflects the Committee's commitment to safeguard the welfare and rights of all individuals within the University. The committee currently comprises 25 members,[11] distributed across the categories, hence reflecting a diverse and representative cohort.

The CUG has spearheaded notable initiatives to foster equal opportunities, inclusion, and well-being within the academic community. Recent initiatives encompass the "Paths to Female Empowerment" summer meeting on May 29, 2023, the family oriented "Where Mom and Dad Work" event on September 7, 2023, and a conference on workplace well-being on November 9, 2023. Moreover, the CUG organized a focus week named "Know, Educate, and Inform to Eliminate Violence Against Women," aimed at deepening the understanding of this issue from various perspectives and providing tools for awareness, education, and information.[12] Additionally, the CUG has launched a scholarship competition, offering four scholarships to facilitate participation in summer training schools.[13] These schools focus on critical issues such as the societal role of women, strategies to combat all forms of discrimination, and improving organizational and workplace well-being in public administration. Collectively, these initiatives underscore the CUG's commitment to creating a more equitable, informed, and healthy university environment.

For stakeholder engagement and activity promotion, the CUG operates through a specialized website[14] linked from the University's main page. This portal includes a "public" segment that disseminates crucial information like the list of the CUG members, their governing rules, roles, contact details, reports, notices, and various projects, ensuring clear communication and providing important information to the academic community. Moreover, a "private" section is designated for the archived minutes from CUG meetings and additional confidential materials accessible exclusively to the CUG members.[15]

[11] For further information, visit the web page of "CUG-component": https://web.units.it/page/cug/it/cug-componenti/15.

[12] For more information, visit the web page of "Eventi organizzati dal CUG": https://web.units.it/page/cug/it/eventi-organizzati-dal-cug/263.

[13] For further information, visit the web page of "Premi di laurea e borse di studio": https://web.units.it/page/cug/it/premi-di-laurea-e-borse-di-studio/266.

[14] Reference: https://web.units.it/page/cug/it.

[15] For further information: https://web.units.it/page/cug/it/cug-verbali/6.

4.3 The Voice of the CUG Members

The rationale of the narrative reporting follows the themes tackled during the interview. On average, the respondents have been members of the CUG for 4 years. Four of them have been involved for a period ranging from 7 to 9 years, demonstrating a significant tenure within the committee. Conversely, six members have been part of the CUG for just 1 year, appointed during the last nomination process to fulfill the 4-year term from January 2023 to December 2026. This mixture of long-standing and newly appointed members contributes to a blend of experience and fresh perspectives within the CUG.

Individuals expressed a variety of motivations for joining the CUG, highlighting a shared commitment to fostering a positive environment within the academic community. Many respondents were driven by a desire to actively contribute to improving the well-being of all members of the university, reflecting deep-seated altruism and sense of responsibility for the collective good. The alignment of CUG's goals with their personal and professional values was another important factor, with participants citing their passion for the committee's key issues and concerns as a central reason for their involvement.

Perspectives on the evolution of the CUG's role over time present a spectrum of sentiments among its members. While some laud a notable shift toward increased sensitivity and focus on pertinent issues, others remain skeptical about the committee's influence, pointing out a lack of substantial change in practice. Despite this, there is a shared recognition of the CUG's enhanced visibility within the academic sphere, considered a positive stride by many. Some members even observe a broadening in the committee's authority and reach.

When asked about the CUG's distinctiveness from other university initiatives, respondents highlighted its unique embodiment of collective representation that surpasses individual interests, ensuring comprehensive inclusivity within the university. Its multifaceted approach to awareness, through meetings, initiatives, and communications, distinguishes it as a proactively engaged entity. The CUG's advantage is notably rooted in its supervisory and advisory capabilities, which empower it to effectively monitor and recommend enhancements. As a body focused on specific issues, the CUG offers an authoritative and concentrated viewpoint. Furthermore, its collaborative nature fosters shared and participatory solutions, cultivating a community spirit and cooperation seldom seen in singular initiatives.

In terms of the CUG's primary stakeholders, there is a broad range that encompasses the entire university community, underscoring the CUG's central role at all levels of the university. Respondents acknowledge the involvement of internal stakeholders, including students, faculty, and administrative staff, who are directly engaged in the university's educational and administrative functions. Also, external stakeholders are recognized, including groups with diverse perspectives on the public mission of the university, the public, and other governmental agencies, underscoring the significant impact of the CUG on the broader community.

Respondents' views reveal a variety of communication channels used by the CUG to engage with its stakeholders, reflecting a mix of traditional and modern approaches. Participants acknowledge the importance of both monologic and dialogic forms of communication in fulfilling the CUG's role. Traditional channels such as print and broadcast media are mentioned alongside more dynamic platforms such as social media, indicating a multifaceted strategy to effectively reach different stakeholders. The mention of word of mouth underlines the value of personal networks and informal communication in disseminating information and fostering dialog. In addition, the university's official website is highlighted as an important monologic channel for disseminating official information and reports, serving as a reliable source for stakeholders seeking formal communication.

Regarding the relationship between the CUG and the social report of the University of Trieste, currently, only the President of the CUG contributes to its formulation. However, the composition of the drafting team is in the process of being defined. This situation is mirrored in the development of the university's strategic plan, which also involves only the President in the drafting process.

The responses regarding the representation of the CUG in the University of Trieste's social report reveal different perceptions of adequacy and visibility. Some respondents feel that the CUG's initiatives are not sufficiently highlighted and point to the need for the social report to capture the committee's efforts and achievements more comprehensively. The lack of detailed information in past reports has left some stakeholders uncertain about the CUG's impact and activities. While a few individuals express a sense of partial representation, others feel that the coverage is adequate.

The CUG's future actions, which stakeholders expect to be incorporated into the University's strategic plan, highlight a strong commitment to fostering an inclusive and equitable academic environment. Key areas of focus include promoting GE across disciplines and ensuring the elimination of all forms of discrimination within the university community. The call for improvements in the GEP and the use of gender-inclusive language reflect a nuanced approach to addressing gender issues, emphasizing the importance of language in shaping an inclusive culture. In addition, initiatives to improve work-life balance and raise awareness of gender issues represent a comprehensive strategy to enhance the well-being and engagement of all members of the university.

To assess participants' views on the proportion of CUG initiatives focused on gender issues, we asked them to quantify this proportion on a scale of 1 (none) to 7 (all) in relation to the total number of initiatives. The collective average score was 5, indicating that the CUG has a substantial commitment to gender issues, which reasonably meets the criterion and is therefore described as "enough."

We asked respondents to comment on the adequacy of funding for CUG activities and received different responses. Some participants acknowledged that while current funding supports basic operations, there is potential for growth that could be realized with increased funding, thereby increasing the committee's impact. Others emphasized that the adequacy of funding goes beyond mere quantity to include effective management, clear goals, and strategic planning. The prevailing view among some that funding is inadequate underscores concerns about current financial arrangements. In addition, there is consensus on the need not only for increased funding but also for its integration into a comprehensive strategy, underscoring the call for financial planning that is consistent with the CUG's overarching goals.

Regarding the role that the CUG should play in promoting GE in the future, respondents believe that the starting point is the implementation of education. They believe that the CUG should start its efforts at the school level, advocating for early awareness and shaping attitudes toward GE. The CUG is expected to focus on raising awareness, disseminating information, and conducting targeted training to address gender inequalities. However, some are concerned that the CUG's impact on GE may be diluted as it expands to cover a wider range of issues. Nevertheless, many see the CUG as an important reference and advisory body on gender issues, with a mandate to propose and monitor initiatives aimed at promoting a more equitable environment.

More specifically, to promote GE, several respondents emphasize the importance of specialized training for educators and administrators to raise awareness and develop skills relevant to gender issues. In addition, advocacy for gender-neutral language is emphasized, highlighting its importance in creating inclusive spaces. There is also a recommendation to establish an ongoing consultation mechanism with internal stakeholders, underscoring the value of ongoing interaction and feedback for sustainable progress. To engage students, one respondent recommends organizing educational workshops focused on gender issues, implementing data monitoring of student engagement based on gender, and hosting events dedicated to GE. Finally, other suggested initiatives include offering support to prevent gender discrimination and initiating a podcast with expert guests to increase institutional visibility and public engagement.

5 Conclusions

This chapter contributes to the literature on GE within Italian universities by specifically examining the role of the CUG as a pivotal academic body for addressing gender disparities and planning future actions in Italian HEIs. Despite the limitations associated with the single case study, this chapter offers an unusual perspective on the CUG because it gives voice to its members, hence shedding light on their perceptions and lived experiences rather than merely describing the CUG's role over time and its intervention policies. This approach allows for a deep exploration of the internal dynamics and challenges faced by the CUG, providing a more comprehensive and "humanized" picture of its impact on the academic environment. Accordingly, findings illustrate how the GE topic's perception evolved over the last decade among the CUG members and the significance of the CUG as an academic institution that not only addresses immediate GE issues but also plans for long-term strategic interventions. The insights gained from the perceptions and viewpoints of the CUG members enrich our understanding of the challenges and opportunities in advancing GE within the Italian university setting. Findings also highlight the crucial active role played by student representatives in enriching and contributing to this committee with a dynamic viewpoint and new perspectives.

Considering these findings, future studies could involve explorations of the CUG's evolving role in academia and its impact on GE in Italian HEIs from a broader perspective, hence considering the role and actions undertaken by the different stakeholders. Additionally, future comparative case studies could support discussions on internal and external factors influencing the effectiveness of CUG practices.

References

Addabbo, T., Badalassi, G., & Pusch, C. (2022). The connection between gender budgeting and academic housekeeping in RPOs. *International Conference on Gender Research, 5*(1), 1–10.

Atkins, J., Solomon, A., Joseph, N., & Norton, S. (2015). The emergence of integrated private reporting. *Meditari Accountancy Research, 23*(1), 28–61.

Broadbent, J. (2016). A gender agenda. *Meditari Accountancy Research, 24*(2), 169–181.

Bryman, A., & Bell, E. (2003). *Business research methods*. Oxford University Press.

Caprile, M., Addis, E., Castaño, C., Klinge, I., Larios, M., Meulders, D., Müller, J., O'Dorchao, S., Palasik, M., Plasman, R., & Roivas, S. (2012). *Meta-analysis of gender and science research*. European Union Publications Office.

Colombis, M. (2019). Il Bilancio di Genere nell'ottica della Responsabilità Sociale d'Impresa: Il caso dell'Università degli Studi di Salerno. In ICSR Mediterranean Knowledge (Ed.), *Working Papers Series*. ICSR Mediterranean Knowledge, Fisciano (SA).

European Commission. (2019). *SHE Figures 2018*. Publications Office of the European Union.

European Commission. (2021). *SHE Figures 2021. The path towards gender equality in research and innovation (R&I)*. Publications Office of the European Union.

Fiorani, G., & Di Gerio, C. (2022). Reporting university performance through the sustainable development goals of the 2030 agenda: Lessons learned from Italian case study. *Sustainability, 14*(15), 1–19.

Galgano, F., & Papillo, M. S. (2020). *Diversity management: nuove frontiere dell'inclusione e sfide per i CUG universitari* (Vol. 3). FedOA-Federico II University Press.

Galizzi, G., & Siboni, B. (2016). Positive action plans in Italian universities: Does gender really matter? *Meditari Accountancy Research, 24*(2), 246–268.

Hearn, J., Strid, S., Humbert, A., & Balkmar, D. (2020). From gender regimes to violence regimes. *Social Politics: International Studies in Gender, State & Society, 29*(2), 682–705.

Husu, L. (2020). What does not happen: Interrogating a tool for building a gender-sensitive university. In D. Eileen & S. Canavan (Eds.), *The gender-sensitive university. A contradiction in terms?* (pp. 52–66). Routledge.

Italian Law No. 150 of 2019.

Italian Law No. 183 of 2010.

Kachchaf, R., Ko, L., Hodari, A., & Ong, M. (2015). Career-life balance for women of color: Experiences in science and engineering academia. *Journal of Diversity in Higher Education, 8*(3), 175–191.

Lätti, J. (2017). Individualized sex equality in transforming Finnish academia. *European Educational Research Journal, 16*(2–3), 258–276.

Madeira, A. C., Carravilla, M. A., Oliveira, J. F., & Costa, C. A. V. (2011). A methodology for sustainability evaluation and reporting in higher education institutions. *Higher Education Policy, 24*(4), 459–479.

Manganaro, F. (2019). *L'eguaglianza di genere nelle pubbliche amministrazioni e nelle Università*. Editoriale Scientifica.

Mauro, S. G., Cinquini, L., Simonini, E., & Tenucci, A. (2020). Moving from social and sustainability reporting to integrated reporting: Exploring the potential of Italian public-funded universities' reports. *Sustainability, 12*(1), 1–19.

Meneguzzo, M. G., & Fiorani, G. (2009). Scelte di sviluppo, innovazione organizzativa e rendicontazione sociale: il bilancio di mandato dell'Università degli Studi di Roma Tor Vergata. *Rivista Italiana di Ragioneria ed Economia Aziendale, 109*(5–6), 347–359.

Oppi, C., Cavicchi, C., & Vagnoni, E. (2021). The journey to gender-responsive budgeting: Lessons learned from higher education. *Sustainability, 13*(1), 1–23.

Paoletti, M., Quintin, S., Gray-Sadran, J., & Squarcioni, L. (2020). Sexual violence on campus objectification, awareness-raising and response. In D. Eileen & S. Canavan (Eds.), *The gender-sensitive university. A contradiction in terms?* Routledge.

Pulejo, L. (2013). Il "bilancio di genere": Uno strumento di analisi e di programmazione per le Università nell'ottica della strategia di gender mainstreaming. *Annali della Facoltà di Economia, Università degli Studi di Messina, 3*(1), 119–130.

Quaderni del Comitato Unico di Garanzia dell'Università Ca' Foscari Venezia: https://edizionicafoscari.unive.it/en/edizioni4/collane/comitato-unico-di-garanzia/.

Rosa, R., Drew, E., & Canavan, S. (2020). An overview of gender inequality in EU universities. In D. Eileen & S. Canavan (Eds.), *The gender-sensitive university. A contradiction in terms?* Routledge.

Siboni, B., Sangiorgi, D., Farneti, F., & De Villiers, C. (2016). Gender (in) accounting: Insights, gaps and an agenda for future research. *Meditari Accountancy Research, 24*(1), 158–168.

Vimercati, A. A. (2021). L'azione dei CUG e l'innovazione organizzativa delle pubbliche amministrazioni tra conflitto e partecipazione. Il caso della parità di genere. In *Liber amicorum per Umberto Carabelli* (pp. 417–427). Cacucci Editore.

Yin, R. K. (2016). *Qualitative research from start to finish* (2nd ed.). Guilford.

Zilli, A. (2012). Il Comitato unico di garanzia nelle pubbliche amministrazioni: ancora sulla soglia? In S. Serafin & M. Brollo (Eds.), *Donne, politica e istituzioni: varcare la soglia?* Forum.

The Determinants of Gender Equality in the Academic World: An Empirical Analysis in International Universities

Nicola Raimo, Vitiana L'Abate, Arcangelo Marrone, and Filippo Vitolla

1 Introduction

Gender equality is a fundamental principle in the international context but is not yet a reality (García-Holgado et al., 2020). Indeed, although in recent years there has been a more active participation of women in all sectors of society, progress in gender equality has not been proportional and uniform (García-Holgado et al., 2020). According to the World Economic Forum (WEF) (2019) estimates, it will take around 100 years for women to achieve the same goals as their male colleagues. Specifically, gender inequalities continue to persist in the labor market, highlighting disparities in wages, access to career opportunities, and underrepresentation in leadership positions. In this regard, according to the WEF (2021), only 27.1% of senior managers were women in 2021. The advent of the COVID-19 pandemic has highlighted and accentuated gender inequalities in the labor market (Foley & Cooper, 2021). Indeed, the pandemic has led to significant job losses for women, as well as an increase in the unpaid workload related to domestic responsibilities, caused by the closure of schools and childcare services (Foley & Cooper, 2021).

Due to the significance of this issue, gender equality has emerged as a critical challenge that has attracted the attention of international institutions (Deiana et al., 2023). In this context, the United Nations (UN), in formulating the Sustainable Development Goals (SDGs) as part of the 2030 Agenda, has established a dedicated goal for gender equality, referred to as SDG 5 (UN, 2015). Furthermore, numerous regulatory measures have been envisaged aimed at fighting gender inequality issues such as the Lisbon Strategy 2000–2010 and the European Research Area Policy

N. Raimo (✉) · V. L'Abate · A. Marrone · F. Vitolla
Department of Management, Finance and Technology, LUM University, Casamassima, Italy
e-mail: raimo@lum.it; labate.phdstudent@lum.it; marrone@lum.it; vitolla@lum.it

M. Agostini et al. (eds.), *Diversity and Equity in Accounting*, SIDREA Series in Accounting and Business Administration,
https://doi.org/10.1007/978-3-031-78247-3_20

Agenda (European Parliament, 2010; European Commission, 2021; Deiana et al., 2023). Despite the commitment of the institutions, achieving gender equality in the labor market still represents an important challenge (European Parliament, 2010; European Commission, 2021). Indeed, SDG 5 has been identified as a goal that remains unfulfilled even today (Deiana et al., 2023).

An area where gender equality issues are particularly relevant, contributing to the enduring gender gap, is within the realm of higher education (Su et al., 2015). Indeed, the available data reveal a diminished visibility for women and a sparse representation of the latter among first-level professors and in top positions in universities with a high research rate (Su et al., 2015). Moreover, women have a reduced likelihood of securing promotions compared to men (Fox & Colatrella, 2006).

The gender equality issues in higher education have attracted the interest of academics. Most studies have aimed to explore its challenges and barriers (e.g., Tildesley et al., 2022), regulatory context (e.g., Verge, 2021), related disclosure (e.g., Galizzi & Siboni, 2016), and the gender gap in science, technology, engineering, and mathematics (STEM) fields (e.g., García-Holgado et al., 2020). However, an area still little explored in the literature is represented by the determinants of gender equality in universities (Su et al., 2015), thus highlighting the need to further explore this line of research.

The objective of this study therefore consists in bridging the knowledge gap in the academic literature, exploring the factors capable of affecting the level of gender equality in international universities. More in detail, among the different determinants, this study focuses attention on some characteristics of universities such as size, complexity, internationalization, and age.

The remainder of this work proceeds with a presentation of the background and hypotheses development (Sect. 2), followed by the research design (Sect. 3). Subsequently, the main results obtained in this study are presented and discussed (Sect. 4). Finally, conclusions are exposed (Sect. 5).

2 Background and Hypotheses Development

The academic literature has investigated gender equality in the university environment by considering different perspectives. Some authors have focused on challenges and barriers. In this context, David (2015) examined the transformations in higher education and women's experiences over the past 50 years. The author noted that while there has been a notable rise in women's enrolment in university studies, a corresponding increase in their participation in the academic job market has not been equally observed, largely due to factors such as patriarchy or hegemonic masculinity (David, 2015). The presence of barriers was also confirmed by Harford (2018). The author observed that universities continue to operate according to male definitions of merit. Furthermore, female professors choose not to accept senior management roles due to the presence of entrenched masculine norms and practices in the university context and believe that there is not enough space to manage caring responsibilities within the academic environment (Harford, 2018). Powell et al. (2018) discovered that gender equality initiatives are unable to bring about profound changes in the Swedish university context. According to the authors, real change requires specific solutions in this sense. Finally, Tildesley et al. (2022), examining Spanish higher education, observed the presence of some resistance to gender equality including refusing accountability, frequently coupled with the trivialization of gender equality policies, and rejecting the necessity for gender-based reform. According to the authors, these represent power dynamics that serve to uphold male privileges and undermine the work and roles of women within academic contexts.

Other authors have instead focused attention on the regulatory context regarding gender equality in the context of higher education. In this regard, Zippel et al. (2016) observed that gender equality was supported by compliance with international standards, self-regulation rules, the use of formal gender plans, and competition. Verge (2021) explored the important reforms introduced in the Spanish university context in terms of gender equality and revealed the opportunity structures and institutional settings that shape the micropolitical strategies implemented by the feminist strategic alliances which have spurred political changes within the context.

Other studies have explored gender equality from a disclosure perspective. In this context, Galizzi and Siboni (2016) investigated gender equality through positive action plans published by Italian universities. They discovered a predominance of information on establishing an enabling environment for women within universities, while the document overlooked the creation of gender awareness in teaching and research activities, as well as the support for female leadership.

Other studies have instead examined the gender gap in some particular sectors of higher education. In this context, García-Holgado et al. (2020) investigated the gender gap in STEM programs in Europe and Latin America. According to the authors, although the majority of enrolled students are women, there is a significant gender gap in STEM careers. The authors advocate for universities to actively promote strategies aimed at recruiting and retaining women in these careers, in order to continuously increase the presence of women in STEM disciplines.

Only a limited part of the literature has instead devoted attention to studying the determinants of gender diversity. In this context, Su et al. (2015) found that chairs' administrative power and their assessment influence the commitment and responsiveness of STEM departments in adopting gender equality strategies. Furthermore, the authors observed that women chairs seem less likely to pursue gender equality policies and that a higher number of female faculty members reduces the likelihood of adopting such strategies. Bertoletti et al. (2023) investigated the impact of COVID-19 school closures on the gender gap in the grade 8 students' performance, as well as the underlying factors contributing to this phenomenon, discovering that female students tend to perceive changes in their learning less positively compared to male students. The primary factors contributing to this gender disparity include the levels of physical activity and psychological distress experienced by students during the COVID-19 disruptions, as well as their perception of the family environment. Lastly, Johnson et al. (2023) observed that the stress induced by the pandemic in higher education is more pronounced among women than men and it is negatively affected by factors such as age, perceived organizational support, and perceived supervisory support.

The limited presence of contributions aimed at investigating the determinants of gender equality in the university context justifies this study. It aims to fill this gap through the analysis of the impact of some characteristics of universities such as size, complexity, internationalization, and age on the level of gender equality.

Size represents a first characteristic potentially capable of influencing the level of gender equality of universities. Large organizations, being more visible to the state, the media, and the community at large, are under greater pressure to conform to the societal expectations (Raimo et al., 2024). Recently, gender diversity has assumed fundamental relevance for society, establishing itself as a fundamental part of societal expectations (Saeed et al., 2016). Considering the greater sensitivity of larger organizations to public pressures and stakeholder expectations (Manes Rossi et al., 2018), they may be more inclined to commit to reducing the gender gap (Zahra & Pearce, 1990). Furthermore, larger organizations, having greater monetary and human resources than smaller ones (Nicolò et al., 2022; Raimo et al., 2024), could make greater efforts toward achieving gender equality. Such circumstances, which are applicable to various types of organizations, may also hold true for universities. Therefore, in light of this, it is possible to introduce the following hypothesis:

H1: The university's level of gender equality is positively influenced by its size.

Complexity represents a second characteristic potentially capable of influencing the level of gender equality of universities. More complex organizations present more articulated dynamics and tend to interface with a broader audience of stakeholders interested in learning about their activities and initiatives (Garzoni et al., 2023; L'Abate et al., 2023). This circumstance leads to greater pressure from different categories of stakeholders (Gallego-Álvarez et al. 2011). Having to manage a broader range of interests and perspectives (Gallego-Álvarez et al. 2011), they may be more likely to adopt policies and practices that promote gender equality in order to meet the needs and expectations of this diverse audience of stakeholders. Furthermore, more complex organizations can tend to count on a higher amount of monetary and human resources (Rella et al., 2022) which could allow the implementation of initiatives related to gender equality policies. Such circumstances, which are applicable to various types of organizations, may also hold true for universities. Therefore, in light of this, it is possible to introduce the following hypothesis:

H2: The university's level of gender equality is positively influenced by its complexity.

Internationalization represents a third characteristic potentially capable of influencing the level of gender equality of universities. Organizations with a greater international orientation often achieve a higher competitive advantage due to their better reputation (Kolk & Fortanier, 2013). Specifically, organizations that adopt internationalization strategies tend to develop and maintain a good image which contributes to determining a long-lasting and difficult to replicate competitive advantage (Gallego-Álvarez et al., 2011). By promoting gender equality policies, they could further improve their image and therefore increase their competitive advantage. However, greater internationalization also determines the need to consider the interests of a wider and more heterogeneous audience of stakeholders, including those of different nationalities, in order to maintain the competitive advantage they enjoy (Dyduch & Krasodomska, 2017). This could also lead to a greater propensity to adopt policies and practices that promote gender equality. Such circumstances, which are applicable to various types of organizations, may also hold true for universities. Therefore, in light of this, it is possible to introduce the following hypothesis:

H3: The university's level of gender equality is positively influenced by its degree of internationalization.

Age represents a fourth characteristic potentially capable of influencing the level of gender equality of universities. The older organizations, having more experience (Al-Gamrh & Al-Dhamari, 2016), have consolidated policies and practices compared to the younger ones (Garde Sanchez et al., 2021). These policies and practices could facilitate the implementation of strategies aimed at satisfying the needs of stakeholders (Roberts, 1992; De Iorio et al., 2022), also with respect to the promotion of gender equality. In addition, longer-lived organizations may have more experienced leadership capable of managing power dynamics and gender disparities within the organization, thus contributing to the mitigation of the gender gap. Such circumstances, which are applicable to various types of organizations, may also hold true for universities. Therefore, in light of this, it is possible to introduce the following hypothesis:

H4: The university's level of gender equality is positively influenced by its age.

3 Research Design

The sample of this study comprises 96 international universities, selected based on the "Impact Rankings 2022: Gender Equality" by Times Higher Education, a British weekly periodical headquartered in London. It develops the only global performance tables that measure universities' commitment to achieving the SDGs (Raimo et al., 2024). Starting from the "Impact Rankings 2022," only the SDG 5 was considered. It contained an initial list of 1,180 universities across 106 countries. Starting from this list, exclusively the top 100 universities were chosen. Subsequently, universities lacking data on independent and control variables were excluded, resulting in a final sample of 96 universities from 27 countries, including Argentina, Australia, Canada, Chile, Ecuador, Greece, India, Indonesia, Iran, Ireland, Israel, Italy, Latvia, Malaysia, Mexico, New Zealand, Portugal, Romania, Saudi Arabia, South Africa,

Spain, Thailand, the Netherlands, the United Arab Emirates, the United Kingdom, the United States, and Turkey.

The dependent variable in this study, *Gender_Equality_Score*, reflects the level of gender equality among the international universities in the sample. It was assessed using the scores from the "Impact Rankings 2022: Gender Equality," which evaluates universities' contributions to SDG 5. This ranking considers the research conducted on gender equality issues, the adoption of gender equality policies, and commitment to the recruitment and promotion of women (Times Higher Education, 2022). More in detail, this score considers six different metrics: (1) research on gender equality (27%), (2) proportion of first-generation female students (15.4%), (3) student access measures (15.4%), (4) proportion of senior female academics (15.4%), (5) proportion of women receiving degrees (11.5%), and (6) women's progress measures (15.3%) (Times Higher Education, 2022). The score obtained with respect to SDG 5 is scaled so that the highest score is 100 and the lowest score is 0 (Times Higher Education, 2022). Therefore, the dependent variable of this study can range from 0 to 100.

The independent variables of this study are represented by *Uni_Size*, *Uni_Complexity*, *Uni_Internationalization*, and *Uni_Age*. *Uni_Size* expresses the size of the university and is measured in terms of the natural logarithm of the number of full-time equivalent students (Manes Rossi et al., 2018). *Uni_Complexity* represents the complexity of the university and is measured in terms of the natural logarithm of the number of departments (Manes Rossi et al., 2018). *Uni_Internationalization* expresses the degree of internationalization of the university and is measured in terms of percentage of foreign students enrolled (Gallego-Álvarez et al., 2011). *Uni_Age* represents the longevity of the university and is measured in terms of number of years since its foundation (Manes Rossi et al., 2018; Vitolla et al., 2023).

The econometric model also includes the following control variables: *Uni_Public_Status*, *Female_Rector*, *BoD_Size*, *BoD_Independence*, *BoD_Gender_Diversity*, and *Leadership_Team*. *Uni_Public_Status* is a dichotomous variable that assumes a score of 1 for public universities and 0 for private ones (Raimo et al., 2024). *Female_Rector* is another dichotomous variable that takes on a score of 1 for universities led by a female rector, and 0 otherwise (Raimo et al., 2024). *BoD_Size* quantifies the size of the board of directors and is determined by the number of members comprising the university board (Ntim et al., 2017). *BoD_Independence* represents the independence of the board of directors and is measured in terms of the percentage of nonexecutive members included in the university board (Ntim et al., 2017). *BoD_Gender_Diversity* expresses the female presence on the board of directors and is measured in terms of percentage of women included on the university board (Vitolla et al., 2023). Finally, *Leadership_Team* represents the size of the university leadership team and is measured as the sum of the number of rector and vice rectors (Garde Sánchez et al., 2020).

To explore the factors influencing the level of gender equality in universities, a linear regression model was employed, as reflected in the following equation:

$$
\begin{aligned}
&Gender\_Equality\_Score_i = \beta_0 + \beta_1 Uni\_Size_i + \\
&\beta_2 Uni\_Complexity_i + \beta_3 Uni\_Internationalization_i \\
&+\beta_4 Uni\_Age_i + \beta_5 Uni\_Public\_Status_i \\
&+\beta_6 Female\_Rector_i + \beta_7 BoD\_Size_i \\
&+\beta_8 BoD\_Independence_i + \beta_9 BoD\_Gender\_Diversity_i \\
&+\beta_{10} Leadership\_Team_i + \varepsilon_i
\end{aligned}
$$

4 Results and Discussions

Table 1 offers descriptive statistics. The dependent variable, *Gender_Equality_Score*, has an average value of 70.989. This result reveals that the universities included in the sample show a fairly high commitment to achieving SDG 5, also justified by the high position that these institutions hold in the ranking used in this study. In relation to the independent variables, *Uni_Size* presents an average value of 10.006, while *Uni_Complexity* has an average value of 2.266. *Uni_Internationalization* takes on an average value of 19.075, showing that the universities included in the sample have a percentage of foreign students of approximately 19%. *Uni_Age* presents an average value equal to 140.281, showing that the universities included in the sample were founded on average 140 years ago.

Table 1 also offers the results of the correlation analysis. The highest correlation coefficient value is observed between *Uni_Complexity* and *Uni_Size* and is equal to 0.396. Following the literature (Tabachnick & Fidell, 2001), collinearity is not a problem as long as the correlation coefficient does not exceed the thresholds of ±0.7. Since in this case the highest correlation coefficient does not exceed these thresholds, it is possible to state that there are no multicollinearity problems.

The results of the regression analysis are presented in Table 2. The adjusted R^2 value is equal to 0.313, revealing that the regression model is able to explain 31.3% of the variability in the dependent variable. The research hypotheses are partially supported by the results.

Firstly, the results do not support H1. They show a nonsignificant relationship between *Uni_Size* and *Gender_Equality_Score*. This result reveals that the size of universities has no significant effects on the level of gender equality.

Secondly, the results support H2. They show a positive and significant relationship ($p = 0.026$) between *Uni_Complexity* and *Gender_Equality_Score*. This result reveals that the more complex universities have a greater propensity to adopt policies and strategies on gender equality, contributing more to the achievement of SDG 5. This result can be explained by the greater pressure from a large and diversified audience of stakeholders and the greater availability of resources enjoyed by more complex universities which can lead to a greater propensity to adopt gender equality initiatives.

Thirdly, the results do not support H3. They show a nonsignificant relationship between *Uni_Internationalization* and *Gender_Equality_Score*. This result reveals

Table 1 Descriptive statistics and correlation analysis

	Variable	Mean	SD	1	2	3	4	5	6	7	8	9	10	11
1	*Gender_Equality_Score*	70.989	3.772	1										
2	*Uni_Size*	10.006	0.726	0.134	1									
3	*Uni_Complexity*	2.266	0.637	0.281***	0.396***	1								
4	*Uni_ Internationalization*	19.075	17.442	−0.097	−0.266***	−0.284***	1							
5	*Uni_Age*	140.281	180.501	−0.145	0.279***	0.004	−0.119	1						
6	*Uni_Public_Status*	0.917	0.278	0.110	0.026	0.017	0.062	0.080	1					
7	*Female_Rector*	0.250	0.435	−0.058	−0.023	−0.119	0.102	0.145	−0.001	1				
8	*BoD_Size*	15.491	8.491	−0.212**	−0.026	−0.087	−0.080	0.003	−0.081	0.126	1			
9	*BoD_Independence*	32.441	25.219	0.258**	−0.001	0.035	0.241*	−0.025	−0.088	0.122	−0.046	1		
10	*BoD_Gender_Diversity*	35.784	17.729	0.185*	0.030	−0.057	0.101	−0.074	0.046	0.111	0.062	0.026	1	
11	*Leadership_Team*	5.427	3.976	0.153	0.078	−0.144	0.031	0.186*	0.099	0.236*	0.144	0.050	0.101	1

Notes: ***significant at the 1% level; **significant at the 5% level; *significant at the 10% level

Table 2 Regression model results

Variables	Coefficient	Standard error	*p*-value	Sign
Cons	*64.475*	*5.284*	*0.000*	***
Uni_Size	0.097	0.545	0.859	
Uni_Complexity	1.391	0.613	0.026	**
Uni_Internationalization	−0.034	0.022	0.122	
Uni_Age	−0.004	0.002	0.054	*
Uni_Public_Status	1.431	1.249	0.255	
Female_Rector	−0.580	0.826	0.484	
BoD_Size	−0.097	0.041	0.021	**
BoD_Independence	0.041	0.014	0.005	***
BoD_Gender_Diversity	0.039	0.019	0.047	**
Leadership_Team	0.218	0.092	0.019	**
N	96			
Adj. R^2	0.313			

Notes: ***significant at the 1% level; **significant at the 5% level; *significant at the 10% level

that the degree of internationalization of universities has no significant effects on their level of gender equality.

Finally, the results do not support H4. They show a negative and significant relationship ($p = 0.054$) between *Uni_Age* and *Gender_Equality_Score*, while a positive association was hypothesized. This result shows that more recently founded universities have a greater propensity to adopt policies and strategies on gender equality, contributing more to the achievement of SDG 5. This result, although unexpected, could be explained by the greater openness to change and the higher attention toward issues relating to sustainability aspects that characterize younger institutions.

5 Conclusions

The objective of this study was to investigate the determinants of the level of gender equality in international universities. More specifically, this study aimed to analyze the impact of some characteristics of universities including size, complexity, internationalization, and age. The main results revealed that more complex and younger universities exhibit a greater propensity to adopt policies and strategies for gender equality and contribute to the achievement of SDG 5.

This study contributes to enriching the academic literature in several ways. First of all, it expands knowledge relating to gender equality in the university context which represents a topic still little explored by existing literature. Furthermore, this study extends knowledge relating to the factors capable of influencing the level of gender equality of universities and the contribution that these institutions offer to the achievement of SDG 5. Finally, compared to previous studies, this study expands the geographical area of investigation through an analysis conducted at an international level.

This study offers important practical implications for universities and policymakers. In light of the importance of gender equality, it is imperative for universities to enhance their commitment by embracing policies and strategies aimed at its promotion. They should promote equality of opportunities for men and women in recruitment, selection, and promotion. Furthermore, universities should implement mentorship and support programs tailored for female students and researchers to assist them in navigating the specific challenges they may face in their academic and professional journeys. Alongside this, organizing training sessions on gender issues is crucial to fostering awareness and combating gender stereotypes and biases within the university community. Additionally, adopting policies that promote a better balance between work and personal life is essential, especially for female academics who frequently encounter the need to harmonize their academic pursuits with familial responsibilities. Finally, universities should collaborate with local and international organizations and institutions to share best practices and work together to address gender disparities more effectively. Policymakers should consider adopting legislative and regulatory measures aimed at promoting gender equality in universities. This could include introducing financial incentives for institutions that demonstrate significant commitment to gender equality, as well as establishing monitoring and evaluation mechanisms to ensure the respect and implementation of gender equality policies. Additionally, policymakers could collaborate with universities and civil society organizations to develop concrete strategies and programs to address gender disparities in the academic context.

This study is not without its limitations. A first limitation is the restricted sample size, while a second limitation is the time horizon considered. These limitations offer ideas for future research. Firstly, future research could extend the sample size by also considering universities with lower positions in the gender equality rankings. Secondly, future research could conduct the econometric analysis over a more extended time period in order to also consider trends in the adoption of gender equality policies and strategies by international universities. Finally, future studies could examine other determinants of the level of gender equality of universities such as the characteristics of the governance bodies.

References

Al-Gamrh, B., & Al-Dhamari, R. (2016). Firm characteristics and corporate social responsibility disclosure in Saudi Arabia. *International Business Management, 10*(18), 4283–4291.

Bertoletti, A., Biagi, F., Di Pietro, G., & Karpiński, Z. (2023). The effect of the COVID-19 disruption on the gender gap in students' performance: A cross-country analysis. *Large-Scale Assessments in Education, 11*(1), 6.

David, M. E. (2015). Women and gender equality in higher education? *Education Sciences, 5*(1), 10–25.

De Iorio, S., Zampone, G., & Piccolo, A. (2022). Determinant factors of SDG disclosure in the university context. *Administrative Sciences, 12*(1), 21.

Deiana, G., Dettori, M., Muresu, N., Puci, M. V., Saderi, L., Piga, M. L., Sias, V., Pisu, D., Foddai, M. A., Gazzolo, T., Fiorini, P. P., Milia, L., Mariotti, G., Sotgiu, G., Azara, A., & Piana, A. (2023). Gender equality in the Italian academic context. Results from the IGEA project. *Frontiers in Public Health, 11*, 1125496.

Dyduch, J., & Krasodomska, J. (2017). Determinants of corporate social responsibility disclosure: An empirical study of Polish listed companies. *Sustainability, 9*(11), 1934.

European Commission. (2021). *European Research Area Policy Agenda*. Overview of Actions for the Period 2022–2024. Available online at: https://apre.it/wp-content/uploads/2022/03/KI0121450ENN.en_.pdf

European Parliament. (2010). *The Lisbon Strategy 2000–2010. An Analysis and Evaluation of Methods Used and Results Achieved*. Available online at: https://www.europarl.europa.eu/thinktank/en/document/IPOL-EMPL_ET(2010)440285

Foley, M., & Cooper, R. (2021). Workplace gender equality in the post-pandemic era: Where to next? *Journal of Industrial Relations, 63*(4), 463–476.

Fox, M. F., & Colatrella, C. (2006). Participation, performance, and advancement of women in academic science and engineering: What is at issue and why. *The Journal of Technology Transfer, 31*, 377–386.

Galizzi, G., & Siboni, B. (2016). Positive action plans in Italian universities: Does gender really matter? *Meditari Accountancy Research, 24*(2), 246–268.

Gallego-Álvarez, I., Rodríguez-Domínguez, L., & García-Sánchez, I. M. (2011). Information disclosed online by Spanish universities: Content and explanatory factors. *Online Information Review, 35*(3), 360–385.

García-Holgado, A., Mena, J., García-Peñalvo, F. J., Pascual, J., Heikkinen, M., Harmoinen, S., García-Ramos, L., Peñabaena-Niebles, R., & Amores, L. (2020). Gender equality in STEM programs: A proposal to analyse the situation of a university about the gender gap. In *2020 IEEE Global Engineering Education Conference*, (pp 1824–1830). IEEE.

Garde Sanchez, R., Rodríguez Bolívar, M. P., & López Hernandez, A. M. (2021). Which are the main factors influencing corporate social responsibility information disclosures on universities' websites. *International Journal of Environmental Research and Public Health, 18*(2), 524.

Garzoni, A., L'Abate, V., Raimo, N., & Vitolla, F. (2023). Exploring online sustainability disclosure in the healthcare industry: Evidence from best international hospitals. *Business Strategy and the Environment.*

Harford, J. (2018). The perspectives of women professors on the professoriate: A missing piece in the narrative on gender equality in the university. *Education Sciences, 8*(2), 50–67.

Johnson, D. S., Johnson, A. D., Crossney, K. B., & Devereux, E. (2023). Women in higher education: A brief report on stress during COVID-19. *Management in Education, 37*(2), 93–100.

Kolk, A., & Fortanier, F. (2013). Internationalization and environmental disclosure: The role of home and host institutions. *Multinational Business Review, 21*(1), 87–114.

L'Abate, V., Vitolla, F., Esposito, P., & Raimo, N. (2023). The drivers of sustainability disclosure practices in the airport industry: A legitimacy theory perspective. *Corporate Social Responsibility and Environmental Management, 30*(4), 1903–1916.

Manes Rossi, F., Nicolò, G., & Tartaglia Polcini, P. (2018). New trends in intellectual capital reporting: Exploring online intellectual capital disclosure in Italian universities. *Journal of Intellectual Capital, 19*(4), 814–835.

Nicolò, G., Ricciardelli, A., Raimo, N., & Vitolla, F. (2022). Visual disclosure through integrated reporting. *Management Decision, 60*(4), 976–994.

Ntim, C. G., Soobaroyen, T., & Broad, M. J. (2017). Governance structures, voluntary disclosures and public accountability: The case of UK higher education institutions. *Accounting, Auditing & Accountability Journal, 30*(1), 65–118.

Powell, S., Ah-King, M., & Hussénius, A. (2018). 'Are we to become a gender university?' Facets of resistance to a gender equality project. *Gender, Work & Organization, 25*(2), 127–143.

Raimo, N., Nicolò, G., L'Abate, V., & Vitolla, F. (2024). Analyzing the factors affecting university contributions to achieving the sustainable development goals in European Union countries. *Sustainable Development.*

Rella, A., Marrone, A., Raimo, N., & Vitolla, F. (2022). The antecedents of transparency of Italian public entities: An empirical analysis in universities and public research institutes. *Administrative Sciences, 12*(1), 29.

Roberts, R. W. (1992). Determinants of corporate social responsibility disclosure: An application of stakeholder theory. *Accounting, Organizations and Society, 17*(6), 595–612.

Saeed, A., Belghitar, Y., & Yousaf, A. (2016). Firm-level determinants of gender diversity in the boardrooms: Evidence from some emerging markets. *International Business Review, 25*(5), 1076–1088.

Su, X., Johnson, J., & Bozeman, B. (2015). Gender diversity strategy in academic departments: Exploring organizational determinants. *Higher Education, 69*(5), 839–858.

Tabachnick, B. G., & Fidell, L. S. (2001). *Using multivariate statistics* (4th ed.). Allyn and Bacon.

Tildesley, R., Lombardo, E., & Verge, T. (2022). Power struggles in the implementation of gender equality policies: The politics of resistance and counter-resistance in universities. *Politics & Gender, 18*(4), 879–910.

Times Higher Education. (2022). *Impact Rankings Methodology 2022.* Available online at: https://www.timeshighereducation.com/world-university-rankings/impact-rankings-2022-methodology

UN. (2015). *Transforming our World: The 2030 Agenda for Sustainable Development.* Available online at: https://sustainabledevelopment.un.org/content/documents/21252030%20Agenda%20for%20Sustainable%20Development%20web.pdf

Verge, T. (2021). Gender equality policy and universities: Feminist strategic alliances to re-gender the curriculum. *Journal of Women, Politics & Policy, 42*(3), 191–206.

Vitolla, F., Raimo, N., Nicolò, G., & Ricciardelli, A. (2023). Exploring intellectual capital disclosure and its determinants in knowledge-based institutions: Empirical evidence from international universities. *Measuring Business Excellence, 27*(2), 227–245.

WEF. (2019). *The Global Competiteviness Report 2019.* Available online at: https://www.weforum.org/publications/how-to-end-a-decade-of-lost-productivity-growth/

WEF. (2021). *Global Gender Gap Report 2021.* Available online at: https://www.weforum.org/publications/global-gender-gap-report-2021/

Zahra, S. A., & Pearce, J. A. (1990). Research evidence on the miles-snow typology. *Journal of Management, 16*(4), 751–768.

Zippel, K., Ferree, M. M., & Zimmermann, K. (2016). Gender equality in German universities: Vernacularising the battle for the best brains. *Gender and Education, 28*(7), 867–885.

Gender Equality as Public Value: An Empirical Analysis of Gender Equality Plans in Italian Higher Education Institutions

C. Oppi and G. Galizzi

1 Introduction

Women's participation in academia is increasing globally, yet barriers persist in their career progression (EC 2021). To harness female talent and leadership, the European Union has initiated various efforts to promote gender equality (GE) in academia since the early 2000s (European Commission - EC 2012).

The EU has mandated the adoption of gender equality plans (GEPs) for accessing Horizon Europe funding, leading HEIs to embark on developing, implementing, and publishing these plans (EC 2020). GEPs serve as strategic instruments delineating clear priorities, objectives, and measures aimed at enhancing GE within HEIs and research institutions. They encompass diverse thematic areas including recruitment, career advancement, work-life balance, leadership, gender integration in research and education, and addressing gender violence and harassment.

The EU aims to empower HEIs to drive structural change toward GE, a core EU value (Galizzi and Siboni 2016). Consequently, integrating GE as a public value (PV) across all EU activities is imperative. Yet, the public sector accounting literature overlooks accounting's role in PV creation from a social perspective (Bracci et al. 2021). Moreover, scant attention has been paid to GE within organizations and their commitment to it, particularly regarding the nexus between GE and PV creation (Oppi and Galizzi 2024; Wittbom and Häyrén 2021).

This study investigates how HEIs have formulated strategies to promote GE and assesses their contribution to PV creation. The study presents a content analysis (Krippendorff 2018) of GEPs published by public Italian HEIs, focusing on GE outlined objectives and actions. Specifically, the study focuses on two crucial areas:

C. Oppi (✉) · G. Galizzi
Department of Management, University of Bergamo, Bergamo, Italy
e-mail: chiara.oppi@unibg.it; giovanna.galizzi@unibg.it

M. Agostini et al. (eds.), *Diversity and Equity in Accounting*, SIDREA Series in Accounting and Business Administration,
https://doi.org/10.1007/978-3-031-78247-3_21

achieving gender balance in leadership and decision-making processes and promoting GE in recruitment and career progression. These areas are deemed pivotal for advancing GE within HEIs, as they underscore the importance of equal representation of academics and technical/administrative staff (TAS) in leadership roles and decision-making bodies, as well as ensuring fairness in recruitment and career advancement processes. This cultural transformation aligns with the EU's advocacy for GE in HEIs.

2 GE in Academia

In recent decades, a growing body of literature has focused on gender issues in academia, traditionally focusing on the academic profession, including women's entry, career advancement, and empowerment (e.g., Broadbent 2016; Haynes and Fearfull 2008; Galizzi et al. 2023). These studies illuminate how barriers and discrimination in male-dominated fields shape women's professional identity (Galizzi et al. 2023), often resulting in "horizontal segregation," wherein women are disproportionately represented in teaching, pastoral, and administrative roles (Haynes and Fearfull 2008). Moreover, research indicates the underrepresentation of women in top-level positions, illustrating the "glass ceiling" phenomenon (Broadbent and Kirkham 2008).

Despite academia being idealized as a realm of meritocracy and equality, the academic literature portrays a workplace dominated by a masculine mindset, prioritizing research and international networking over student and administrative duties. This bias toward masculine norms shapes work dynamics and career trajectories for both academics and TAS (Haynes and Fearfull 2008).

Recent studies have delved into strategies and actions for promoting GE within organizations, including HEIs (e.g., Galizzi and Siboni 2016; Steinþórsdóttir et al. 2019; Oppi and Galizzi 2024). Galizzi and Siboni (2016) observed that Italian HEIs predominantly focus on establishing a supportive environment for women, with services catering to maternity and parenting needs, but initiatives aimed at supporting career advancement and women's leadership remain limited. Steinþórsdóttir et al. (2019) explored the potential of gender-responsive budgeting in HEIs to foster equality, while Oppi and Galizzi (2024) highlighted its role in legitimizing and reinforcing GE as a PV. Examining GEPs adopted by European HEIs, recent studies (Diaz et al. 2023; Naciti et al. 2024; Picardi et al. 2023; Rosa and Clavero 2022) have raised concerns about their efficacy in driving cultural change within HEIs. Regarding Italy and focusing on GEPs published by 58 HEIs, Diaz et al. (2023) identified a lack of operationalization in addressing GE goals, with several universities failing to allocate resources and personnel for implementation. In terms of integrating gender perspectives into research and teaching, Picardi et al. (2023) found GEPs to be lacking transformative actions in this area, planning few core actions in this sense. Additionally, the notion of a universal "one-size-fits-all" model for GE policies and practices is challenged, as tailored approaches are necessary based on contextual factors (Ní Laoire et al. 2021).

HEIs are pivotal agents of cultural transformation, necessitating the internal promotion of GE and its dissemination across society, facilitated by strategic PV accounting practices (Oppi and Galizzi 2024). However, exploration of GE within organizations and their commitment to it, particularly regarding its relationship with PV creation, remains limited. HEIs require tools to formulate policies and allocate resources to legitimize and support PV creation, institutionalizing strategic processes toward GE (Wittbom and Häyrén 2021).

3 Design of the Study

3.1 The Study Context

The proliferation of GE policies within the public sector, driven by EU directives, has heightened scrutiny on HEIs, particularly regarding gender-based horizontal and vertical segregation in scientific fields and careers (EC 2012).

To align with gender mainstreaming strategies, the EU introduced gender-responsive budgeting and mandated GEPs for research organizations to access Horizon Europe funding.

A GEP is "a set of actions which start by conducting audits of procedures and practices to identify gender bias; move on to identifying and implementing strategies to address bias; and also set targets and monitor progress via specific indicators" (European Institute for Gender Equality – EIGE 2016p. 8). GEPs are comprehensive frameworks encompassing five strategic areas: (i) work-life balance and organizational culture; (ii) gender balance in leadership and decision-making processes; (iii) gender equality in recruitment and career progression; (iv) gender mainstreaming in research and teaching content; and (v) measures against gender-based violence, including sexual harassment.

A well-structured GEP delineates objectives and actions for each strategic area, clarifies responsibilities, outlines governance and leadership structures for implementation, and tracks progress and outcomes (EC 2020). It is informed by gender-disaggregated personnel data, incorporates dedicated resources and expertise, sets timelines for action, defines indicators for monitoring progress, and is publicly endorsed and disseminated within the organization (EC 2020).

3.2 Methodology

This study conducts a content analysis (Krippendorff 2018) of GEPs published by public Italian HEIs. Public HEIs represent more than 60% of the sector (Ministry of University Research 2024), leveraging a diverse sample in terms of geography and size. Relevance of public institutions is also emphasized by EU Directive 2006/54, stating that these must "lead by example" for private ones in promoting and implementing GE (consistent with Galizzi and Siboni 2016).

Initially, a list of 61 public HEIs was obtained from the Italian Ministry of University Research (2023) website. Secondly, the most recent GEPs were downloaded from each institution's website, resulting in 58 documents after excluding three HEIs (4.9% of the sample) that did not publish GEPs. In the third step, GEPs were scrutinized and only those structured based on EU guidelines were selected, thus eliminating 11 GEPs (18.0%) and leading to a final sample of 47 documents to be analyzed (77.1% of total).

Researchers analyzed objectives and corresponding actions from Areas 2 and 3 in each document separately. The researchers assessed (i) the coherence of objectives with respective areas and (ii) the coherence of the actions with identified objectives. Categories for objectives and actions were inductively coded; inductive coding was deemed appropriate due to the limited research on the phenomenon, aligning with Krippendorf's approach (2018). To ensure validity, the researchers independently conducted the analysis and then discussed the results, collaboratively reaching consensus on results and continually refining the coding list to ensure reliability. Table 1 presents a synthesis of the coding structure adopted for each area.

4 Results

The final sample consists of 47 HEIs classified based on CENSIS (Italian center for social investment studies classification): 10 mega (21.3%), 13 large (27.7%), 12 medium (25.5%), and 8 small (17.0%) HEIs, along with 4 polytechnics (8.5% of the sample). These HEIs are evenly distributed between the north and south of Italy, with 18 institutions in each region, constituting 38.3% of the sample each, while 11 HEIs (23.4% of the sample) are situated in the central region.

Table 2 provides a breakdown of coherent and noncoherent objectives identified for each area. Area 2 centers on gender balance in leadership and decision-making. HEIs outline a total of 90 objectives in this domain, with 65 of them (72.2%) aligning with the area's goals. The majority of these objectives are broad, aiming to ensure gender balance in governance, constituting 53.3% of the total. Some objectives are more specific, such as providing training for individuals in leadership roles (5.6%), establishing dedicated governance structures for GE (e.g., Deputy Rector for Equal Opportunities), or revising regulations to ensure GE in leadership and decision-making bodies (4.4% each). Noncoherent objectives include promoting

Table 1 The coding structure adopted

University name	Objective (as reported in the GEP)	Objective coded	Objective coherence with the area (1 = yes; 0 = no)	Action (as reported in the GEP)	Action coded	Action coherence with the objective (1 = yes; 0 = no)

Table 2 Objectives, coherence with their area, frequencies, and percentages of the total area

Area	Coherence with area	Objectives (description and coding, if coherent)	Frequency	%
Area 2—Gender balance in leadership and decision-making	Yes	Gender balance in academic and administrative governance (2.A)	48	53.3%
		Training on GE in decision-making processes (2.B)	5	5.6%
		Establishment of governance structures for GE (2.C)	4	4.4%
		Revision of regulations to facilitate GE in leadership and decision-making bodies (2.D)	4	4.4%
		Incentives for candidacies (2.E)	2	2.2%
		Monitoring of gender balance in leadership and decision-making bodies (2.F)	2	2.2%
		Total of coherent objectives	*65*	*72.2%*
	No	Promotion of culture, activities, and structures on GE	14	15.6%
		Integration of GEP in university strategic documents	4	4.4%
		Monitoring gender data	4	4.4%
		Gender balance of students in decision-making bodies	1	1.1%
		Training on career progressions	1	1.1%
		GE in recruitment and career progression	1	1.1%
		Total of noncoherent objectives	*25*	*27.8%*
	Total		*90*	*100%*

(continued)

Table 2 (continued)

Area	Coherence with area	Objectives (description and coding, if coherent)	Frequency	%
Area 3—GE in recruitment and career progression	Yes	Combating vertical segregation of staff (3.A)	22	20.6%
		Combating horizontal segregation among students (3.B)	12	11.2%
		Training on bias and empowerment (3.C)	12	11.2%
		Combating vertical segregation of academics (3.D)	10	9.3%
		Support for research for career progression (3.E)	9	8.4%
		Gender balance in recruitment (3.F)	7	6.5%
		Combating vertical and horizontal segregation of staff and students (3.G)	6	5.6%
		Gender balance in the composition of competition selection boards (3.H)	5	4.7%
		Monitoring data on career progressions (3.I)	4	3.7%
		Combating horizontal segregation of academics (3.J)	2	1.9%
		Support for maternity (3.K)	2	1.9%
		Combating vertical segregation of academics and TAS (3.L)	1	0.9%
		Combating vertical segregation of TAS (3.M)	1	0.9%
		Combating vertical and horizontal segregation of staff (3.N)	1	0.9%
		Total of coherent objectives	*94*	*87.9%*
	No	Objectives related to leadership and participation in bodies	4	3.7%
		GE in scientific events	3	2.8%
		Reporting on GE	2	1.9%
		Integration of GEP in university strategic documents	1	0.9%
		Monitoring gender balance data	1	0.9%
		Gender dimension into research	1	0.9%
		Promotion of GE culture	1	0.9%
		Total of noncoherent objectives	*13*	*12.1%*
	Total		*107*	*100%*

cultural initiatives against stereotypes or establishing collaborative platforms with institutional or private entities, with limited emphasis on leadership and governance. They also involve integrating GEPs into strategic documents and collecting and analyzing gender-disaggregated data.

Moving to Area 3, which addresses recruitment and career paths, 87.9% of the total 107 objectives were deemed coherent. This area encompasses a wider array of objectives. Many target vertical segregation, addressing HEIs overall (20.6%), academics alone (9.3%), TAS alone (0.9%), or both (0.9%). Horizontal segregation is also tackled, particularly concerning students (11.2%) or academics alone (1.9%), while certain objectives address both vertical and horizontal segregation concurrently. Additionally, several objectives focus on combating selection bias, empowering female professionals through training (11.2%), and supporting research activities (8.4%). Noncoherent objectives were identified, such as those discussing topics related to Area 2 or emphasizing the importance of ensuring GE in the organization of scientific events.

The following paragraph reports the actions identified in the GEPs, focusing specifically on objectives coherent with their respective area.

Regarding Area 2, a total of 126 actions were identified. However, upon coding, only 99 were deemed coherent with their respective objectives. Noncoherent actions encompassed endeavors such as integrating GEPs into strategic documents, revising regulations for academics' career progressions, ensuring gender balance in the composition of competition selection boards, and promoting research centers on GE. Table 3 presents the frequencies of coherent actions corresponding to coherent objectives in Area 2, categorized into eight main areas. Nearly half of the actions (n = 48) pertains to regulations for accessing and composing decision-making bodies, considering gender balance. Other actions include data collection and monitoring on gender representation in leadership and decision-making (16.2%), mentoring programs to support candidacies for leadership roles (14.1%), and identifying specific roles of responsibility concerning GE issues to ensure a stronger strategic orientation in this regard (10.1%).

Actions have been observed to intersect with multiple objectives, primarily because HEIs tend to formulate broad objectives that encompass various actions.

Table 3 Coherent actions identified within coherent objectives for Area 2

Coherent actions (coding)	Coherent actions (coding description)	Frequency	%
2.1	Analysis and review of regulations regarding access to and composition of decision-making bodies and structures, commissions, and top roles	48	48.5%
2.2	Data collection and analysis on gender composition in leadership positions and decision-making bodies	16	16.2%
2.3	Training activities to support candidacies (mentoring)	14	14.1%
2.4	Identification of specific roles of responsibility regarding GE	10	10.1%
2.5	Training activities for personnel in leadership positions	6	6.1%
2.6	Training initiatives on gender balance and related practices	3	3.0%
2.7	Acquisition of information to encourage candidacies	1	1.0%
2.8	Gender pay gap analysis	1	1.0%
	Total	*99*	*100%*

For instance, objective 2.A, aiming to ensure gender balance in governance, encompasses 78 out of 99 actions. Consequently, more specific objectives are operationalized in fewer actions (e.g., 2.D, 2.E, 2.F). Table 4 presents a summary of the distribution of actions across objectives.

In Area 3, a total of 201 actions have been identified among the objectives coherent with the area. However, only 180 can be considered coherent with the objectives they reference. Noncoherent actions include efforts such as ensuring the gender balance of speakers in scientific events or promoting a non-stereotyped culture among all HEI staff to impact their daily lives.

The landscape of coherent actions in this area is more fragmented compared to that of the previous area (refer to Table 5). Three actions have been the most reported: establishing award criteria for evaluating research activity and project participation by considering parental leaves and gender balance in research groups (12.8%), implementing mechanisms directed at departments to incentivize GE in academic careers (11.7%), and collecting data and monitoring career progressions among academics and TAS (11.7%). Additionally, attention has been paid to actions aimed at addressing horizontal segregation among students (9.4%) and establishing

Table 4 Distribution of coherent actions across coherent objectives in Area 2

Coded objectives	Coherent actions (coded)	Frequency	% of the objective
2.A	2.1	42	53.8%
	2.2	12	15.4%
	2.3	11	14.1%
	2.4	7	9.0%
	2.5	3	3.8%
	2.6	2	2.6%
	2.8	1	1.3%
	Total	*78*	*100.0%*
2.D	2.1	6	100.0%
	Total	*6*	*100.0%*
2.C	2.4	3	60.0%
	2.3	1	20.0%
	2.2	1	20.0%
	Total	*5*	*100.0%*
2.B	2.5	3	60.0%
	2.6	1	20.0%
	2.2	1	20.0%
	Total	*5*	*100.0%*
2.E	2.3	2	66.7%
	2.7	1	33.3%
	Total	*3*	*100.0%*
2.F	2.2	2	100.0%
	Total	2	*100.0%*

Table 5 Coherent actions identified within coherent objectives for Area 3

Coherent actions (coding)	Coherent actions (coding description)	Frequency	%
3.1	Award criteria related to GE in project participation and research activity evaluation	23	12.8%
3.2	Mechanisms for incentivizing departments to promote equitable career paths for academics	21	11.7%
3.3	Collection and analysis of data on recruitment and career progressions of academics and TAS	21	11.7%
3.4	Student orientation activities	17	9.4%
3.5	Mechanisms for promoting of gender balance in the composition of competition selection boards	17	9.4%
3.6	Combatting dropout rates and supporting parenthood	12	6.7%
3.7	Empowerment, encouragement of candidacies, communication of opportunities, and scouting	11	6.1%
3.8	Training to counter gender bias in selection procedures	11	6.1%
3.9	Mentoring	10	5.6%
3.10	Introduction of measures to rebalance gender presence among academics and TAS	7	3.9%
3.11	Monitoring of data related to research projects	5	2.8%
3.12	Student orientation activities and scholarships for STEM disciplines	4	2.2%
3.13	Scholarships for undergraduate and doctoral courses for the underrepresented gender	4	2.2%
3.14	Scholarships for STEM disciplines	4	2.2%
3.15	Research training	3	1.7%
3.16	Incentive mechanisms to promote equitable career paths of TAS	3	1.7%
3.17	Data collection and analysis of participation in academic assignments and coordination positions	3	1.7%
3.18	Monitoring of student distribution and applications (for limited enrolment courses or PhD programs)	2	1.1%
3.19	Scientific outreach against stereotypes	1	0.6%
3.20	Monitoring of best practices at national and international levels for career progression	1	0.6%
	Total	*180*	*100.0%*

appropriate mechanisms to enhance gender balance in the composition of competition selection boards (9.4%).

In Area 3, actions also span across various objectives (see Table 6). Several actions support different objectives aimed at tackling vertical segregation among staff, particularly academics (e.g., 3.A, 3.D, 3.L). Objectives 3.E (support for research for career progression) and 3.C (training on bias and empowerment) received considerable attention, each with 21 actions. Close behind is objective 3.B, which focuses on addressing horizontal segregation among students, with 19 reported actions.

Table 6 Distribution of coherent actions across coherent objectives in Area 3

Coded objectives	Coherent actions (coded)	Frequency	% of the objective
3.A	3.2	12	24.5%
	3.1	8	16.3%
	3.3	8	16.3%
	3.6	7	14.3%
	3.5	6	12.2%
	3.8	3	6.1%
	3.7	2	4.1%
	3.9	2	4.1%
	3.10	1	2.0%
	Total	*49*	*100.0%*
3.E	3.1	8	38.1%
	3.11	5	23.8%
	3.15	3	14.3%
	3.2	2	9.5%
	3.19	1	4.8%
	3.9	1	4.8%
	3.20	1	4.8%
	Total	*21*	*100.0%*
3.C	3.7	6	28.6%
	3.8	5	23.8%
	3.9	5	23.8%
	3.4	3	14.3%
	3.3	2	9.5%
	Total	*21*	*100.0%*
3.B	3.4	12	63.2%
	3.14	3	15.8%
	3.12	2	10.5%
	3.18	2	10.5%
	Total	*19*	*100.0%*
3.G	3.4	2	11.8%
	3.12	2	11.8%
	3.6	2	11.8%
	3.1	2	11.8%
	3.10	2	11.8%
	3.17	2	11.8%
	3.13	1	5.9%
	3.14	1	5.9%
	3.16	1	5.9%
	3.5	1	5.9%
	3.3	1	5.9%
	Total	*17*	*100.0%*

(continued)

Table 6 (continued)

Coded objectives	Coherent actions (coded)	Frequency	% of the objective
3.F	3.3	5	29.4%
	3.13	3	17.6%
	3.5	3	17.6%
	3.10	2	11.8%
	3.2	2	11.8%
	3.8	1	5.9%
	3.16	1	5.9%
	Total	*17*	*100.0%*
3.D	3.2	4	30.8%
	3.1	3	23.1%
	3.9	2	15.4%
	3.3	2	15.4%
	3.6	1	7.7%
	3.7	1	7.7%
	Total	*13*	*100.0%*
3.H	3.5	7	87.5%
	3.10	1	12.5%
	Total	*8*	*100.0%*
3.J	3.7	2	25.0%
	3.8	1	12.5%
	3.10	1	12.5%
	3.2	1	12.5%
	Total	*5*	*100.0%*
3.I	3.3	3	75.0%
	3.17	1	25.0%
	Total	*4*	*100.0%*
3.K	3.6	2	66.7%
	3.1	1	33.3%
	Total	*3*	*100.0%*
3.L	3.1	1	100.0%
	Total	*1*	*100.0%*
3.M	3.16	1	100.0%
	Total	*1*	*100.0%*
3.N	3.8	1	100.0%
	Total	*1*	*100.0%*

5 Discussion and Conclusions

This chapter presented an analysis of GEPs published by 47 Italian HEIs, focusing on Areas 2 and 3, crucial for GE advancement in academia.

Area 2, addressing gender balance in leadership and decision-making, features fewer objectives compared to Area 3, resulting in fewer actions. Cross-referencing the most frequent objective (2.A—gender balance in academic and administrative governance) with its predominant action (2.1) reveals a necessity for well-established regulations to promote GE. This action underscores the need for a cultural shift within HEIs and society at large (Broadbent 2016). Moreover, the second most frequent action (2.2), concerning data collection and analysis on gender composition in leadership positions and decision-making bodies, suggests a lack of routine management of gender-disaggregated data within HEIs. Lastly, only three out of eight actions are person-oriented, focusing on training to support future or current leadership roles.

Area 3 focuses on GE in recruitment and career progression, displaying a higher degree of action fragmentation compared to Area 2. Cross-referencing the most cited objective (3.A—combating vertical segregation of staff) with its predominant actions (3.2, 3.1, 3.3) elucidates that countering vertical segregation primarily targets academic staff. Notably, action 3.2, involving mechanisms to incentivize departments for promoting equitable career paths, may benefit from national legislative intervention to enhance its effectiveness. Conversely, action 3.1, concerning the definition of award criteria related to GE in project participation and research activity evaluation, falls within HEIs' jurisdiction, warranting ongoing monitoring of its progress over time.

The last action, focused on data collection and analysis regarding staff recruitment and career progressions (3.3), akin to Area 2, underscores the necessity for an internally maintained database to be regularly updated. Interestingly, the second most cited objective pertains to actions toward students, highlighting HEIs' pivotal role in cultural change where GE is recognized as PV (Oppi and Galizzi 2024).

Considering the total 47 GEPs analyzed, several general insights emerge. Some HEIs have incorporated an additional area, sometimes referred to as Area 0, dedicated to promoting cultural and educational initiatives supporting GE, or combating stereotypes, thus recognizing the importance of fostering a gender-inclusive cultural background. This need also emerges from those objectives that were considered noncoherent with the areas analyzed, particularly those advocating for cultural actions that should be a prerequisite to GE strategizing, especially in the academic context. Similarly, the integration of GEPs into HEIs' overall strategic processes and documents is essential. This is a crucial issue for the integration of GE into HEIs' planning and performance measurement systems, also in a PV perspective (Oppi and Galizzi 2024), but it also serves as a prerequisite for GEP implementation. Furthermore, the substantial number of objectives not coherent with Areas 2 and 3, along with actions not aligning with objectives, indicates that some HEIs encounter challenges in integrating GE issues within their processes.

In summary, this contribution presents some suggestions both for policy and decision-makers. Firstly, there is a need to foster cross-institutional gender culture and awareness (Picardi et al. 2023). In this sense, targeted training on GE may be needed for those leading these processes; otherwise, the number of noncoherent objectives and actions within only two of the five areas comprising the GEP would remain unexplained. In fact, the development of effective GEPs is crucial for HEIs to fulfill their role as change agents. Proper strategic and accounting logics can facilitate the creation of PV from a GE perspective (Wittbom and Häyrén 2021). PV is shaped by actors who devise GE strategies (Bracci et al. 2021) and endeavor to operationalize the PV concept to align organizational objectives with stakeholders' needs. Therefore, enhancing GE culture within HEI, especially among those responsible for GE processes, is pivotal. Consequently, expertise in strategic planning should be provided to support the working groups tasked with formulating GEPs (Naciti et al. 2024).

However, the successful implementation of GEPs hinges not only on established structures of governance, legislation, resources, and external rewards but also on the personal initiative and activism of passionate individuals within institutions, often "with no collective force or voice to systematically challenge the *status quo*" (Rosa and Clavero 2022, p. 3). The suggestions provided may offer the necessary "force or voice" required to propel Italian HEIs forward on the path of GE.

The study has some limitations. It does not analyze the GEPs as a whole document, as it focuses only on two out of five areas. Additionally, it exclusively examines public universities, while there are several private entities in Italy dedicated to tertiary education. Therefore, further developments should involve analyzing GEPs implemented by private universities and delving into the patterns of GEPs to understand how universities define strategies, objectives, and actions.

References

Bracci, E., Saliterer, I., Sicilia, M., & Steccolini, I. (2021). Accounting for (public) value (s): reconsidering publicness in accounting research and practice. *Account Audit Accountabil J, 34*(7), 1513–1526.

Broadbent, J. (2016). A gender agenda. *Meditari Account Res, 24*(2), 169–181.

Broadbent, J., & Kirkham, L. (2008). Glass ceilings, glass cliffs or new worlds? Revisiting gender and accounting. *Account Audit Accountabil J, 21*(4), 465–473.

Diaz, G. D. C., Palazzi, F., Sentuti, A., & Sgrò, F. (2023). Gender equality plan: an explorative analysis of Italian Academia. *Int Conf Gend Res, 6*(1), 82–91.

European Commission. (2012). *Structural change in research institutions: enhancing excellence, gender equality and efficiency in research and innovation*. Publications Office of the European Union.

European Commission. (2020). *A Union of equality: gender equality strategy 2020–2025*. Publications Office of the European Union.

European Commission. (2021). *She Figures 2021*. Publications Office of the European Union.

European Institute for Gender Equality. (2016). *Gender equality in academia and research. GEAR tool*. Publications Office of the European Union.

Galizzi, G., & Siboni, B. (2016). Positive action plans in Italian universities: does gender really matter? *Meditari Account Res, 24*(2), 246–268.

Galizzi, G., McBride, K., & Siboni, B. (2023). Patriarchy persists: experiences of barriers to women's career progression in Italian accounting academia. *Crit Perspect Account, 102625*.

Haynes, K., & Fearfull, A. (2008). Exploring ourselves: exploiting and resisting gendered identities of women academics in accounting and management. *Pac Account Rev, 20*(2), 185–204.

Krippendorff, K. (2018). *Content analysis: an introduction to its methodology*. Sage Publications.
Ministry of University Research. (2023). Università statali. Available at: https://www.mur.gov.it/it/aree-tematiche/universita/le-universita/universita-statali. Accessed: 21st November 2023
Ministry of University Research (2024) Le Università. Available at: https://www.mur.gov.it/it/aree-tematiche/universita/le-universita. Accessed 23rd April 2024
Naciti, V., Noto, G., Pulejo, L., & Vermiglio, C. (2024). Gender equality plan development in universities: a strategic management perspective. *Eur J Volunt Commun-Based Projects, 1*(1), 34–57.
Ní Laoire, C., Linehan, C., Archibong, U., Picardi, I., & Udén, M. (2021). Context matters: problematizing the policy-practice interface in the enactment of gender equality action plans in universities. *Gender Work Org, 28*(2), 575–593.
Oppi, C., & Galizzi, G. (2024). Gender-responsive budgeting for public value creation: insights from higher education. *Financ Accountabil Manage, 40*(1), 85–104.
Picardi, I., Addabbo, T., & Cois, E. (2023) Lost in translation: integrating the gender dimension in research and teaching in Universities through gender equality plans. AG About Gender-Int J Gend Stud 12(24)
Rosa, R., & Clavero, S. (2022). Gender equality in higher education and research. *J Gend Stud, 31*(1), 1–7.
Steinþórsdóttir, F. S., Brorsen Smidt, T., Pétursdóttir, G. M., Einarsdóttir, Þ., & Le Feuvre, N. (2019). New managerialism in the academy: gender bias and precarity. *Gend Work Org, 26*(2), 124–139.
Wittbom, E. E., & Häyrén, A. I. (2021). Post-NPM gender accounting—can public value management enhance gender mainstreaming? *Public Money Manage, 41*(7), 507–515.

Disability Disclosure in the Sustainability Reports of Universities: An Exploratory Study in Italy

Carmela Gulluscio, Sara Giovanna Mauro, and Pina Puntillo

1 Introduction

Over the last few decades, growing attention has been paid to nonfinancial disclosure and specifically to sustainability reporting, recognizing it as a tool suitable for addressing stakeholders' multiple requests, strengthening accountability, and improving transparency.

According to Carnegie et al. (2021, p. 69), accounting can be redefined as "a technical, social and moral practice concerned with the sustainable utilisation of resources and proper accountability to stakeholders to enable the flourishing of organisations, people and nature." This new definition of accounting refers to organizational and social contexts in which accounting operates and focuses on the importance of broadening the boundaries of accounting from the historical technical function of bookkeeping and balancing of the books to a more composite activity that combines the *technical* function with a *social* and a *moral* function of accounting. These considerations support the development of sustainability accounting and reporting. In this context, diversity and equity issues are recently developing as crucial social issues to account for, due to their relevance for organizations and their multiple stakeholders.

C. Gulluscio (✉)
"UnitelmaSapienza" University, Rome, Italy
e-mail: carmela.gulluscio@unitelmasapienza.it

S. G. Mauro
University of Modena and Reggio Emilia, Modena, Italy
e-mail: saragiovanna.mauro@unimore.it

P. Puntillo
Università della Calabria, Arcavacata, Italy
e-mail: pina.puntillo@unical.it

M. Agostini et al. (eds.), *Diversity and Equity in Accounting*, SIDREA Series in Accounting and Business Administration,
https://doi.org/10.1007/978-3-031-78247-3_22

Sustainability reporting is expected to be the reporting tool to be used also to account for the activities implemented to have an impact on society and pursue social goals, taking into account diversity and equity. Despite the growing strand of research about corporate social responsibility and diversity in the workplace (Cucari et al., 2018; Fernandez-Feijoo et al., 2014; Khan et al., 2019; Taylor et al., 2018), the reporting on diversity and equity is still underdeveloped.

A topic still little explored in this context is the disclosure of disability. People with disabilities are conceived as the world's largest minority stakeholder group (Khan et al., 2019). According to the World Health Organization, almost 15% of humanity lives with a disability. The disability condition is increasing worldwide. More than one billion people live with "long-term physical, mental, intellectual or sensory impairments which, in interaction with various barriers, may hinder their full and effective participation in society on an equal basis with others" (Iriarte et al., 2016). They face not only relevant barriers to labor market entry and corporate inclusion but also to attending school and university. Their rights are often not respected and they are frequently victims of discrimination (Bickenbach et al., 2017; Luo & Wang, 2017; Quinn 2009). Disabled people are more subject to discrimination at a young age and have a high risk of dropping out of school or university (OECD, 2012; Weedon, 2017).

In light of these considerations, there emerges the need for explicitly focusing on disability, devoting attention to the actions implemented for taking care of and accounting for it. As universities are expected to be an inclusive place and guide and inspire developments that impact people, the planet, and organizations, influencing future leaders and generations (Adams 2013), they have been chosen as a research context. Indeed, universities' research, education, and knowledge transfer activities, as also the accounting practices adopted to manage and account for their performance, can play a crucial role in educating future leaders toward inclusiveness and acting as an example for other organizations, by being inclusive concerning both external (e.g., students) and internal stakeholders (e.g., employees).

The current research is thus designed to investigate whether and how universities report their commitment toward disability in the context of sustainability reporting. This chapter aims to fill a research gap, as disability disclosure in universities' sustainability reporting is a very little explored area of investigation. In addition to the low number of universities and higher education institutions publishing sustainability reports, sustainability reporting in higher education and specifically diversity and disability disclosure are limited areas of investigation (Azizi et al., 2018; Ceulemans et al., 2015; Fonseca et al., 2011; Wolbring & Lillywhite, 2021). This chapter will then contribute to the stream of literature on sustainability and disability disclosure in the higher education field by exploring whether and how universities in Italy report on disability in their sustainability reports.

For this purpose, we analyze the most recent sustainability reports published by the Italian universities belonging to the *Rete delle Università per lo Sviluppo Sostenibile*—RUS—(Network of Universities for Sustainable Development), which is the first case of coordination and sharing among Italian universities committed to promoting the themes of social responsibility and sustainability.

The remainder of the chapter is as follows: §2 briefly contextualizes the research by referring to guidelines and requirements on disability disclosure, §3 focuses on the relevant literature about disability reporting, §4 describes the research methodology, §5 presents the main results emerging from the analysis, and §6 reports discussion and conclusions.

2 Research Background

Disability disclosure can be guided and enhanced by rules, guidelines, principles, and widely shared goals, which can act as drivers for disability reporting.

Starting from the foundation of the Global Reporting Initiative (GRI) at the beginning of the 2000s, nonfinancial information requirements have gradually grown, moving from voluntary disclosure to increasing mandatory disclosures, especially following the issuing of Directive 2014/95/EU on nonfinancial and diversity information (so-called NFRD Directive). It requires large undertakings exceeding certain parameters to disclose information about environmental and social aspects and also about employees, human rights, anti-corruption, and bribery. The NFRD Directive mentions the concept of diversity related to gender, age, education, professional background, etc., without explicitly mentioning disability. Notwithstanding, disability is widely recognized as an aspect included in the diversity concept. Based on the NFRD Directive, in 2017 the European Commission guidelines on nonfinancial reporting introduced references to disabled people.

The most relevant GRI standard in this area is GRI 405 entitled "Diversity and Equal Opportunity 2016," intended for any type of organization, without distinction of size, type, geographical area, economic sector, etc., which calls for reporting information relating to the impact of the organization's activity on diversity and equal opportunity at work. This principle does not explicitly refer to a disability but implicitly mentions it, as it requires that the reporting organization shall report (among others) other relevant indicators of diversity (e.g., minority or vulnerable groups). Still, on the subject of diversity, we may also recall GRI 404 "Training and Education 2016" on the impacts of teaching and n. 406 "Nondiscrimination."

Relevant and explicit rules about disability reporting can be found in the Guide on Disability in Sustainability Reporting issued in 2015 by GRI and Fundación ONCE, explaining how to disclose actions promoted to support disabled people. Other references to disability in nonfinancial reporting can be found in the EU Disability Rights Agenda 2021–2030.

Also the 2030 Agenda focuses on disability: five SDGs (n. 4 "Quality Education; n. 8 "Decent Work and Economic Growth"; n. 10 "Reduced Inequalities"; n. 11 "Sustainable Cities and Communities"; and n. 17 "Partnerships for the Goals") explicitly mention disability. GRI and the SDGs are, therefore, relevant sources for disability disclosure.

It is worth recalling also normative references that may influence disability reporting, taking into account actions implemented for employees. University's commitment to disability concerns both students and university workers, from an external and internal perspective. Concerning the latter, the placement of disabled people is regulated in Italy by Law No. 68 of 1999, containing "Regulations for the Right to Work of Disabled People" and subsequent amendments and additions. The 1999 law introduces the concept of "targeted placement," aimed at promoting the meeting between the company's needs and the worker's disability. In the international context, the protection of disabled workers is contained in the United Nations Convention on the Rights of Persons with Disabilities approved by the European Community by Council Decision 2010/48/EC. At the European level, the regulation of this topic is contained in Directive 2000/78/EC of the European Council. The existing normative framework is designed to guarantee the inclusion of the disabled in the workplace and may influence the reporting of data on the number of disabled workers employed, while reporting other actions promoted to support an inclusive environment is less regulated.

3 Literature Review

Recent research highlights the importance of diversity and disability disclosure and reporting as efforts to promote equity and inclusion. Universities are becoming increasingly aware of the importance of collecting detailed and accurate data on student and staff diversity, including disability information, to assess and improve their performance in terms of inclusion (Wolbring & Lillywhite, 2021), although attention is then mainly paid to diversity in general and the disability disclosure is still limited analyzed in the accounting and management field.

Several key factors influencing diversity disclosure and reporting in universities have been identified. These include institutional policies and practices, organizational culture, individual perceptions of safety and privacy, and broader sociocultural factors. For instance, institutional policies promoting transparency and inclusion may encourage disclosure, while an organizational culture stigmatizing disabilities may discourage it (Shore et al., 2011).

Common barriers to diversity disclosure and reporting in universities have been identified. These include a lack of trust in data use, concerns about privacy and security of personal information, and a lack of awareness and training on diversity and disability issues.

Finally, the literature emphasizes the importance of collaboration among various stakeholders, including students, staff, administrators, and external organizations, in promoting effective disclosure and reporting of diversity in universities. This collaboration can help overcome existing barriers and promote a welcoming and inclusive environment for all members of the university community.

The studies highlight also the benefits of accurate disclosure and reporting of diversity in universities, including increased transparency and accountability, a better understanding of the needs of differently abled students and staff, and the opportunity to develop more inclusive policies and practices.

Previous studies have also paid attention to the financial side of the reporting on diversity. Sandra et al. present an intervention aimed at providing leadership with a report card containing metrics related to diversity efforts within an institution, such as diversity expenditures, and participation in clerkship programs targeting diverse candidates. The study found a significant relationship between some of these metrics and the representation of underrepresented minority (URM) groups within a department, in addition to other potential benefits of diversity metrics.

Unangst et al. (2022) utilize quantitative textual analysis to examine a specific subset of institutional statements: diversity statements from American higher education institutions (HEIs) with chief diversity officers (CDOs). The process of crafting a diversity statement or revisiting an existing one can be viewed as transformative practical labor and results of knowledge building around diversity and related concepts, including systemic oppression. Diversity statements are considered the initial step in operationalizing institutional commitments to social justice and dismantling systemic oppression. While the mere existence of a diversity statement does not guarantee operationalization, the paper argues that such statements are essential for comprehensive diversity, equity, and inclusion programs or policies that allocate resources and ensure transparency of relevant data across the institution.

Despite the growth in the studies on diversity disclosure in higher education, to the best of our knowledge, there are currently no studies on reporting in Italian higher education that specifically incorporate disabilities, and overall the academic debate on disability disclosure is limited.

4 Research Methodology

The research analyzes the content of sustainability reports by carrying out a manual content analysis. Content analysis has long been adopted to systematically and rigorously collect, codify, and analyze textual information (Guthrie & Parker, 1990; Milne & Adler, 1999). This methodology has been widely used in accounting research designed to investigate the extent of adoption and development of sustainability reports (e.g., Landrum & Ohsowski, 2018; Torelli et al., 2020), even in the higher education field (Azizi et al., 2018). Since it has proven to be relevant in investigating nonfinancial disclosure, it is expected to be useful in analyzing and interpreting the extent and type of disclosure about disability in the sustainability reports.

Content analysis is a type of text analysis based on the identification and analysis of concepts, such as words or phrases. As the focus of the current research is the analysis of what has been disclosed in the sustainability reports with reference to disability, a keyword search has been performed to find out the frequency of words such as disability-disabil*, ability-abil*, or the acronym DSA (Italian acronym standing for *Disturbi Specifici dell'Apprendimento*, equivalent to the English acronym *specific learning disabilities*—SLD) used to refer to people with a disability or learning difficulty and the meaning of the words in use.

Once the key words have been identified in the text of the reports, they have been analyzed in the context where they were cited to interpret their meaning. Each of the researchers has analyzed a subset of the reports to classify the information identified. Doubts or divergences during this process have been discussed among the researchers, and at the end, one of the researchers cross-checked the analysis performed by the other two, to minimize the discrepancies that could be resulted from the diverging interpretation, guarantee coherence, and avoid subjectivity as much as possible.

The codification has been doubled.

First, to codify the purpose of why such words were used in the text, a framework of analysis has been elaborated. According to it, the pieces of information identified were codified based on whether they referred to the following:

- *Declaration of intent*, which refers to strategy and objectives concerning disability (e.g., statements concerning aims to achieve such as guaranteeing equality in study and working conditions)
- *Governance structure* of the university (e.g., offices and experts devoted to managing activities supporting the disabled)
- *Curricular activities* performed to support disabled students (e.g., tutoring, teaching materials, teaching digital tools)
- *Extracurricular activities* performed to support the disabled (e.g., mobility, accommodation, job search, leisure activities)
- *Training activities* performed to train professors and tutors to manage disabled students' needs (e.g., training courses and guidelines)
- *Contextual data* (e.g., number of students/workers with disability)
- *Generic reporting* (without numbers and examples) of actions implemented for the disabled and those with SLD
- *Reference to specific SDGs* (i.e., 4, 8, 10, 11, and 17) or *SDGs in general* reference to the GRI Standard 405 "Diversity and Equal Opportunity"
- *Others*, i.e., a residual category

The last category was included to allow us to take notes in case of pieces of information not easily classifiable in the previous categories.

For each of these categories, it has been taken note of whether the information was narrative (description) or quantitative to classify the type of information reported on disability and whether information reported was on results achieved or to be achieved, on strategic objectives, or on actions. This classification has been performed by the researchers through in-depth readings of the sections identified through the key word search, and for each category, there was an indication of the presence or lack of information.

Second, the framework used by Fundación ONCE and KPMG for the Spanish IBEX 35 constituents (including 235 company reports) was adapted to our case to analyze the disability disclosure. This framework has been selected as it has paid specific attention to analyzing the disclosure of disability in the context of sustainability reports.

Fundación ONCE is co-funded by the European Social Fund and has activated a relevant initiative on the subject of disability, called Disability Hub Europe. The framework proposed by Fundación ONCE and KPMG is particularly well suited to the current analysis since it was built to analyze the Spanish reality, which is a pioneer in nonfinancial reporting legislation relating to people with disabilities. While many European countries have transposed Directive 2014/95/EU in a rather generic way, without making explicit reference to the concepts of disability and accessibility, Spain (and also France) has transposed it by inserting specific and measurable parameters to analyze the protection of disability and the achievement of accessibility. IBEX 35 is an index of the Madrid Stock Exchange including the 35 stocks with the largest capitalization. This framework analyzes Spanish companies operating in different economic sectors according to the information displayed in their nonfinancial reports and identifies seven major blocks of information, as follows:

A. *Number of employees with disabilities*: It requires disclosing information about the total number of employees with disabilities in the workforce, with the possibility to include further information about the scope of information provided (e.g., the group level observed) and the level of disaggregation (e.g., by gender, age, professional category). Compared to our inductive framework of analysis described above, this indicator block is a specific point of attention entirely devoted to the disclosure of information relating to staff with disabilities, not limited to the simple count of the number of employees with disabilities;
B. *Universal accessibility*: It includes measures to guarantee the digital and physical accessibility of employees. Compared to the abovementioned inductive framework, this indicator block is a specific point of attention entirely devoted to the disclosure of information relating to physical and digital accessibility only of employees.
C. *Commitment to disability*: It refers to an explicit commitment to disability within the report. Here we refer to an explicit and clear commitment to disability, less generic than the *declaration of intent* proposed in our inductive framework.
D. *Benefits and actions for employees*: It includes actions and measures to guarantee the integration of employees with disabilities (e.g., home working or flexitime) or for their direct relatives with disabilities.
E. *Social initiatives and corporate volunteering for disability*: It includes cooperation with external organizations, nongovernmental organizations, and associations for the protection of disability and to ensure accessibility
F. *Products and services*: It refers to the production of products and services having a "design for all," i.e., usable also by people with disabilities.
G. *Extension of the disability inclusion commitment to the supply chain*: It refers to the use of suppliers chosen based on their disability performance.

We adapted this framework to the characteristics of universities, including the following indicator blocks:

A1. Number of students with disabilities
A2. Number of students with specific learning disorders (SLD)
A3. Number of students with specific learning disorders (SLD) and/or disability
A4. Number of graduates with disabilities

A5. Number of graduates with learning difficulties/specific learning disorders (SLD)
B1. Universal accessibility (specific measures to ensure the digital and physical accessibility of students)
D1. Benefits and actions for students

For each dimension, we took note of its presence or absence in the reports analyzed. The use of this framework complements the results obtained from the previous one, with a focus on more detailed pieces of information. As the two frameworks have common points, the discussion of the results will analyze and interpret the results in an integrated and comprehensive manner.

This content analysis has been performed to analyze all the last editions of the sustainability reports published by the Italian university members of the RUS. This network has been promoted by CRUI (*Conferenza dei Rettori delle Università Italiane*—Conference of the Italian University Rectors) since 2016 and can be considered "the first experience of information sharing and coordination among all Italian Universities committed to the topic of environmental sustainability and social responsibility," as stated in their official website (https://reterus.it/en/goals-and-objectives/). The network aims at spreading the culture of sustainability and contributing to the achievement of the SDGs.

The last edition of the sustainability reports (published in 2023) of the RUS member universities, as available on the official website of the network, was downloaded. In total, 14 reports have been downloaded and analyzed. The full list of universities involved in the analysis (n. 13) is available in the Appendix 1. To achieve a more in-depth understanding of the scenario, the geographical location and the dimension of the universities have been analyzed, classifying the higher education institutions as located in the north, center, or south of Italy and according to their size (number of students). The integrated consideration of university location, dimension, extent, and type of disability disclosure can allow the development of deeper reflections on the state-of-the-art.

Since this is an initial and explorative analysis of the state of disclosure on disability in the sustainability reports of the Italian universities belonging to the RUS, it was decided not to build a disclosure index, but to limit this first analysis to a mapping of whether and how Italian higher education organizations report their commitment toward disability in their sustainability reports.

5 Results

This section illustrates the results emerging from the analysis of the sustainability reports of the Italian universities using the two different interpretation frameworks described in the previous section. Section 5.1 focuses on the first interpretation framework, while Sect. 5.2 focuses on the latter.

In total, 14 reports published by 13 universities have been analyzed. The universities are publicly funded in the majority of the cases (77%)—in one case, it is a private university (8%), and two are polytechnics (15%). Among the 14 reports analyzed, three were published by two different polytechnics since one of them, the Polytechnic of Milan, published in 2023 on the RUS website both a sustainability report and an SDG report.

In most cases, the universities here analyzed have published on the RUS website sustainability reports covering several years. Only four universities (31%) have published sustainability reports relating to the year 2022 alone. This means that the majority of universities publishing sustainability reports on the RUS website have at least 2 years of experience with this kind of nonfinancial disclosure. Indeed, their belonging to the RUS network suggests their strong commitment to sustainability and contributes to explaining their experiences with sustainability reporting.

The time horizon covered by the reports analyzed (all published on the RUS website in 2023) is not homogeneous: in most cases (71%), they refer to the year 2022, but there are also two reports (14%) relating to the academic year (a.y.) 2021–2022, as well as a university that has published data relating to the a.y. 2020–2021, and a university that has published data relating to three years from 2020 to 2022. This can be considered an evident sign of the voluntary nature of this form of reporting and consequently of the variety of approaches that can be used by universities to elaborate the sustainability reports.

Further, if we analyze the geographical setting of the institutions (Fig. 1), five of the universities analyzed are located in the geographical area of central Italy, while the eight remaining universities are located in northern Italy. No university in southern Italy and the islands have published sustainability reports on the RUS website in 2023. In the years before 2023, there were rare cases of universities in southern Italy and the islands that have published sustainability reports (e.g., universities of Cagliari, Napoli Vanvitelli, and Bari Aldo Moro), but without continuity over the years.

Table 1 focuses on the size of the universities whose sustainability reports were analyzed, based on the CENSIS (*Centro Studi Investimenti Sociali*—Social Investment Study Center) classification. The universities that have published the

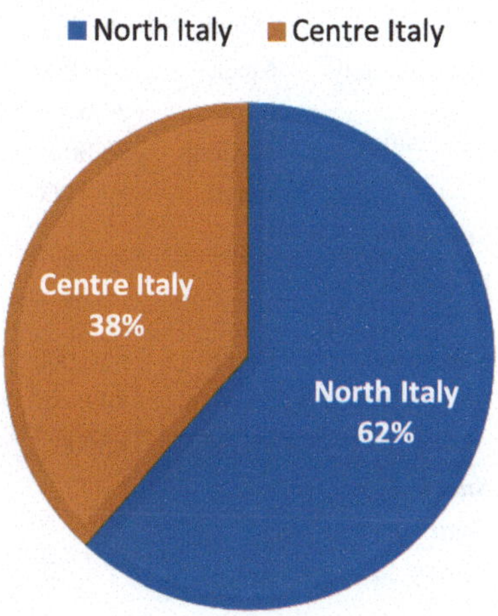

Fig. 1 Geographical setting. *Source: own elaboration*

sustainability reports under scrutiny are mainly public or state universities, predominantly mega and large.

Concerning the key words searched in the documents, the one that occurs most frequently and more significantly in the analyzed reports is "disabil*." This occurs from a minimum of 2 times to a maximum of 25 times in the various reports analyzed. In general, we found that the greater number of times the key words used appear in the reports corresponds to a greater variety of information relating to the actions to protect disability promoted by the various universities.

5.1 First Interpretation Framework

We analyzed the reports, inductively identifying the main information emerging from them and classifying them according to the framework reported above.

First, overall, there are mainly *generic declarations of intent by universities to remove disadvantageous conditions and guarantee equal conditions of access to study and work*, often not detailed in content, without specifying how the university intends to achieve these intentions.

Concerning *governance and university structures responsible for dealing with disabilities/SLD*, we found information relating to the university bodies institutionally responsible for dealing with disabilities/SLD. Among these bodies, the reports often mention the CUG (*Comitato Unico di Garanzia*—Single Guarantee Committee), which is aimed at promoting a work and study environment based on principles of equal opportunities, organizational well-being, and absence of discrimination relating to gender, age, disability, language, ethnic origins, sexual

Table 1 Size of the universities whose sustainability reports were analyzed

Type of university	Dimension	N. of students enrolled	N. of reports	% of reports over the total of reports per type of university	% of reports over the total of the reports collected
State/publicly funded universities	Mega	>40,000	5	50%	36%
	Large	20,000–40,000	3	30%	21%
	Medium	10,000–20,000	1	10%	7%
	Small	≤10,000	1	10%	7%
Subtotal			***10***	***100%***	***71%***
Polytechnics			3	100%	21%
			3	***100%***	***21%***
Non-state universities	Large	>10,000	1	100%	7%
	Medium	5000–10,000	0	0%	0%
	Small	<5000	0	0%	0%
Subtotal			***1***	***100%***	***7%***
Total			***14***		***100%***

Source: own elaboration

orientation, political opinions, etc. Other structures often mentioned are service offices for the inclusion of students with disabilities, which take on different names in the various universities but have the common objective of removing the obstacles that stand between students with disabilities and university life, promoting their participation in the various university activities. Many reports also mention the Rector's delegates for the protection of vulnerable groups and students with disabilities/SLD. Among the various universities that mentioned this specific point in their report, the Bocconi University of Milan stands out, which has a particularly rich governance of institutional bodies and positions falling within the scope to protect disabled people and individuals with SLD.

Concerning *curricular initiatives*, there is often mention (sometimes with detailed explanations and numbers relating to students who have benefited from it) of tutoring for students with disabilities/SLD. Other times, there is mention of training products and educational initiatives within the degree courses (bachelor and master degrees) on disability. Some universities have mentioned training for the acquisition of a correct study method. Overall, it is recurrent to refer to curricular activities implemented to support students during the courses and their learning processes.

In the field of *extracurricular initiatives*, there is often information about the need to prepare entrance tests suitable for students with disabilities/SLD, the need to assist these students in entrance tests, and the need to help undergraduates and graduates find a job. There were various initiatives for the benefit of students and employees with disabilities/SLD and their caregivers, including visits to the botanical garden, organization of theatrical performances focused on the theme of disability, and participation in events to raise awareness of disability and SLD conditions. In this regard, reports also refer to initiatives implemented for improving mobility and accommodation for disabled students.

On the contrary, in very few cases, the analyzed reports mentioned *training activities aimed at teachers and tutors to help them correctly manage students with disabilities and SLD*.

Contextual data have been inserted, for example, indicating the number of students with disabilities/SLD, often compared, in tables, with the total number of students enrolled. This item is analyzed more in-depth in the next section.

In the reports, there are also general pieces of information—*generic reporting (without numbers and examples) of actions implemented for disabled students and those with SLD*, e.g., mention of not specified actions to integrate disabled students into academic life.

The reports include *reference to specific SDGs* or *SDGs in general*. Considering the importance of disability in SDGs, Table 2 shows, per typology, whether there was a specific mention of SDGs n. 4, 8, 10, 11, and 17 or SDGs in general (with 0 indicating the lack of mention and otherwise the number of reports referring to it) and whether aspects linked to disability were identified or not (indicating 0 if no correlation between SDG/SDGs and disability is mentioned in the report, otherwise the number of reports mentioning not only the SDG/SDGs, but also its/their relevance for disability). In most cases, the reports mention the specific SDGs n. 4, 8,

10, 11, and 17 (as well as the SDGs in general), but only in rare cases do they explicitly mention them in correlation with disability issues.

Six of the analyzed reports mention the *GRI Standard 405* titled "Diversity and Equal Opportunity," but no one of them develops the reporting according to this standard to disability.

Finally, there is the residual category *other*, in which information that cannot be classified into well-defined and recurring categories has been placed. This is the case, for example, of references to materiality matrix about topics of disability and SLD, to the reticence of many students, who tend not to self-report their disability and SLD condition, or to various projects to protect disabilities that are difficult to fit into the previous categories.

Overall, in most cases, the information found concerns students. There are few cases in which the reports refer to actions undertaken in favor of disabled workers.

In the majority of the cases, the information reported are narrative, aimed at illustrating activities carried out without supporting the narration with specific indicators and results achieved expressed in quantitative terms. The numerical pieces of information reported are usually contextual data, such as the number of students with SLD, the number of tutors, etc. Nonfinancial information about activities and initiatives is predominant compared to financial information about resources allocated and spent to support such initiatives.

5.2 Second Interpretation Framework

As shown in Table 3, the details and types of information reported vary across universities.

The analyzed reports detail the numbers of disabled students according to different criteria. In only one case, numbers are detailed according to gender. Only one university distinguishes between students with a disability greater than 66% and a disability less than 66%, and one university distinguishes between students with total and partial disabilities. Only one university distinguishes among the different types of disabilities identifying motor, neurological, mental, auditory, and visual disabilities, due to temporary injury, with illness or not declared by the student. This indicates a different extent of details concerning the illustration of the context.

Information relating to graduates with disabilities and/or SLD is even more scarce as only one report includes this data.

In most cases, universities report on the number of students with disabilities in different years (three), while others report only on the numbers related to the last year, using the academic year or the calendar year as a reference. This last aspect makes it impossible to use for comparison the data reported in the reports published in 2023, but also relating to previous years. For this reason, we analyzed only the data relating to the year to which the report refers.

Furthermore, the lack of quantitative information on employees with disabilities and/or SLD emerges.

Table 2 SDGs and disability within the analyzed reports

			SDG 4 "Quality education"		SDG 8 "Decent work and economic growth"		SDG 10 "Reduced inequalities"		SDG 11 "Sustainable cities and communities"		SDG 17 "Partnership for the goals"		Generic reference to SDGs	
Type of university	Size	N. of reports	Generic reference	Specific reference to disability/SLD	Generic reference	Specific reference to disability/SLD	Generic reference	Specific reference to disability/SLD	Generic reference	Specific reference to disability/SLD	Generic reference	Specific reference to disability/SLD	Generic reference	Specific reference to disability/SLD
State/publicly funded university	Mega	5	4 (80%)	1 (20%)	5 (100%)	0	4 (80%)	1 (20%)	5 (100%)	0	4 (80%)	0	5 (100%)	0
	Large	3	3 (100%)	1 (33%)	3 (100%)	0	2 (67%)	1 (33%)	1 (33%)	1 (33%)	2 (67%)	0	3 (100%)	1 (33%)
	Medium	1	0	0	1 (100%)	0	0	0	0	0	0	0	1 (100%)	0
	Small	1	1 (100%	0	1 (100%)	0	1 (100%)	0	1 (100%)	0	1 (100%)	0	1 (100%)	0
Polytechnic		3	3 (100%)	1 (33%)	3 (100%)	0	3 (100%)	3 (100%)	3 (100%)	1 (33%)	3 (100%)	0	3 (100%)	1 (33%)
Non-state university	Large	1	1 (100%)	0	1 (100%)	0	1 (100%)	1 (100%)	1 (100%)	0	1 (100%)	0	1 (100%)	0
Total		***14***	***12 (86%)***	***3 (21%)***	***14 (100%)***	***0***	***11 (79%)***	***11 (79%)***	***11 (79%)***	***2 (14%)***	***11. (79%)***	***0***	***14 (100%)***	***2 (14%)***

Source: own elaboration

Note: Percentages (%) are calculated over the total of the respective category, per row

Table 3 Number of sustainability reports including references to specific disability aspects

	Academic year 2022/2023	
Type of reference to disability	N. of reports	%
A. Employees with disabilities	0	0%
A1. Students with disabilities	9	64.29
A2. Students with specific learning disorders (SLD)	9	64.29
A3. Students with specific learning disorders (SLD) and/or disability	8	57.14
A4. Graduates with disabilities	1	7.14
A5. Graduates with learning difficulties/SLD	1	7.14
B. Universal accessibility for employees	5	35.71
B1. Universal accessibility for students	7	50.00
C. Commitment to disability	14	100.00
D. Benefits and actions for employees	5	35.71
D1. Benefits and actions for students	8	57.14
E. Social initiatives and corporate volunteering	4	28.57
F. Products and services	1	7.14
G. Extension of the disability inclusion commitment to the supply chain	0	0%

Source: own elaboration

Coming to the part of the framework devoted to the benefits and actions taken, few reports discuss "Benefits and actions for employees" referring to specific actions in favor of workers with disabilities or who assist disabled people. By way of example, this category includes points in sustainability reports in which it is specified that agile working must be assigned as a priority to workers with disabled children or description of tools to protect disabled workers, e.g., the use of interpreting service with Italian sign language (LIS), the use of audio supports for blind workers, and the creation of a system with radio beacons for people with visual disabilities.

"Benefits and actions for students" includes actions in favor of students as well as benefits concerning only disabled/SLD students, e.g., reserved beds in student residences and digitization of texts for use by students with disabilities or specific learning disorders with authorization from the Ministry of Culture. A greater number of reports include these data compared to the previous category.

Finally, in rare cases, "social initiatives and corporate volunteering" including, for example, volunteer initiatives for the physical accompaniment of disabled students, are discussed, and only in one report, information on "products and services" is included referring to a subtitling and transcription service for lessons which can be useful not only for students with disabilities but for all students.

6 Discussion and Conclusions

The topic of disability is particularly relevant in nonfinancial reporting first because people with disabilities constitute the world's largest minority stakeholder group and disability affects people who need particular care and protection.

Sustainability reporting is among the ideal tools for providing information regarding the objectives, actions, and results achieved by organizations (including universities) to protect staff and other people with disabilities. However, sustainability reporting in general and specifically disclosure on disability in universities are growing but still seem to be at an initial stage of development, because of both the limited number of reporting universities and the fragmented academic literature on sustainability and disclosure reporting in higher education (Lozano 2011; Ceulemans et al., 2015; Wolbring & Lillywhite, 2021). This research thus contributes to this stream of literature from an accounting and management perspective, by exploring the Italian context. This lens enriches our understanding of the broader trends and challenges shaping reporting practices across different contexts. The findings also provide a foundation for future research, policy development, and institutional interventions aimed at promoting equity, diversity, and inclusion within Italian universities.

By analyzing the content of the sustainability reports published in 2023 by Italian universities belonging to the RUS, which are mainly publicly funded, large or mega, and located in the center or north of Italy, it emerges the presence of the term "disability" within all the reports analyzed, signaling quite widespread attention paid by universities to this topic probably because of institutional policies and their cultural orientation (Wolbring & Lillywhite, 2021). However, there is a variation in the depth and detail of reporting among different universities. Overall, the sustainability reporting on the subject of disability appears to be still at an initial stage of development. This may be considered a consequence of the still limitedly developed regulations on this specific disclosure, which on the contrary would be useful for encouraging disability reporting and facilitating the comparability of these data, setting common basic standards on the type and degree of detail of the information to be reported regarding people with disabilities and/or SLD. Guidelines from the RUS and the GRI, as well as the establishment of a working group within the RUS, can support disability disclosure.

The analyzed reports focus mainly on narrative data, sometimes with mere declarations of intent regarding an unspecified commitment of the universities to deal with disability, and more rarely they include quantitative data. The latter mainly refers to, for instance, the number of students with disabilities and/or SLD, the number of tutoring hours carried out for students with disabilities/SLD, the number of entrance tests calibrated for students with disabilities/SLD, and the amount of public funds received to prepare actions aimed at protecting this category of students. Concerning the latter, the financial information on disability-related issues is less reported, unlike previous evidence. The lack of detailed quantitative information and the variation in reported information among universities suggest the existence of potential challenges in data collection and disclosure, as the literature points out (Shore et al., 2011).

The information most frequently reported concerns generic declarations of intent regarding the universities' commitment to protecting students with disabilities/SLD, the curricular and extracurricular initiatives prepared for their protection, and the mention of the academic bodies and governance structures responsible for dealing with disability/SLD. Cases in which the analyzed reports contain data relating to disabled university staff are very rare.

Overall, while the sustainability reports demonstrate universities' commitment to disability inclusion, there is a need for more comprehensive reporting practices, including detailed quantitative information and a focus on outcomes and impact assessment. Further, in light of the previous considerations, additional information should be included in the reports on the following issues:

- *Employees with disabilities*, for whom information should be provided in terms of the number of disabled, types of disabilities, particular needs that distinguish them, actions implemented to protect them, and results achieved, to overcome the current limited availability of data on employees. The latter should come not only from data processed by the universities that draw up the sustainability report but also from anonymous questionnaires to be administered to employees, to identify outstanding needs, perceived strengths, and weaknesses of the protection system provided by the universities.
- *Newly enrolled students with disabilities/SLD, students with disabilities/SLD enrolled for at least 1 year, and graduates with disabilities/SLD*. For them the universities shoud provide information on their number, types of disability/SLD, particular needs that distinguish them. Also, actions implemented to protect them, results actually achieved, average academic performance data of these students, and for graduated, change in their employment status after graduation are potentially relevant information. Further, in this case, it would be particularly useful to administer an anonymous questionnaire, through which to verify what type of needs these students feel, which of these needs were not satisfied during their previous school career and the actual degree of satisfaction of their needs compared to the expectations they had at the time of enrollment in the university.
- *Periodic reports from the university office in charge of disability/SLD inclusion and protection services*, in which data, observations, and needs to be satisfied should be reported. These data differ from the information provided by students and graduates since they are analyzed from the point of view of university staff experts.
- *Inclusion of students with disabilities/SLD's feedback and proposals in the report*, for instance, by engaging them in the *Commissione Paritetica Docenti-Studenti* (Joint Teacher-Student Commission).

These suggested pieces of information would allow a more complete picture of the needs of employees and students with disabilities/SLD, their current level of satisfaction, and the actions necessary to improve it, by engaging the different stakeholders in the reporting process.

The study provides valuable insights for management and standard setters in several ways. Higher education managers can benchmark their reporting practices against those of peer institutions and evaluate how to improve their own institution's disclosure practices, identifying areas for improvement or alignment with the context. The variety of the reporting practices and the predominance of large and mega public universities in north or central Italy could then prompt standard setters to consider initiatives aimed at encouraging more comprehensive reporting across all regions, fostering a more balanced approach to sustainability initiatives nationwide.

The study has several limitations, which may constitute at the same time ideas for future analyses. Since this was initial exploratory research, it focused only on the last edition (2023) of sustainability reports of the Italian universities belonging to the RUS, without searching on the websites of other Italian universities for further sustainability reports. In the future, it would be useful to broaden the analysis, including other universities in the analysis and enlarging the reference time horizon, to also analyze the evolution over time of the type, quantity, and quality of the information reported therein.

Most of the pieces of information found are narrative and have been codified manually by the researchers, with the risk of a certain level of subjectivity. In the next step of the research, it would be interesting to combine the analysis presented here with scales to analyze the level of depth of the reports' content and construct a disclosure index based on the analysis frameworks.

Appendix 1 List of Universities

1. Alma Mater Studiorum Università di Bologna
2. Bocconi
3. Politecnico di Milano
4. Politecnico di Torino
5. Sant'Anna Scuola Universitaria Superiore di Pisa
6. Sapienza Università di Roma
7. Tor Vergata Università degli Studi di Roma
8. Università degli Studi di Brescia
9. Università degli Studi di Firenze
10. Università Ca' Foscari Venezia
11. Università degli Studi di Padova
12. Università di Parma
13. Università di Pisa

References

Adams, C. A. (2013). Sustainability reporting and performance management in universities: Challenges and benefits. *Sustainability Accounting, Management and Policy Journal, 4*(3), 384–392.

Azizi, L., Bien, C., & Sassen, R. (2018). Recent trends in sustainability reporting by German universities. *Sustainability Management Forum, 26*(1/4), 1–19.

Bickenbach, J., Rubinelli, S., & Stucki, G. (2017). Being a person with disabilities or experiencing disability: Two perspectives on the social response to disability. *Journal of Rehabilitation Medicine, 49*(7), 543–549.

Carnegie, G., Parker, L., & Tsahuridu, E. (2021). It's 2020: What is accounting today? *Australian Accounting Review, 31*(1), 65–73.

Ceulemans, K., Molderez, I., & Van Liedekerke, L. (2015). Sustainability reporting in higher education: A comprehensive review of the recent literature and paths for further research. *Journal of Cleaner Production, 106*, 127–143.
Cucari, N., Esposito De Falco, S., & Orlando, B. (2018). Diversity of board of directors and environmental social governance: Evidence from Italian listed companies. *Corporate Social Responsibility and Environmental Management, 25*(3), 250–266.
Fernandez-Feijoo, B., Romero, S., & Ruiz-Blanco, S. (2014). Women on boards: Do they affect sustainability reporting? *Corporate Social Responsibility and Environmental Management, 21*(6), 351–364.
Fonseca, A., Macdonald, A., Dandy, E., & Valenti, P. (2011). The state of sustainability reporting at Canadian universities. *International Journal of Sustainability in Higher Education, 12*(1), 22–40.
Guthrie, J., & Parker, L. D. (1990). Corporate social disclosure practice: A comparative international analysis. *Advances in Public Interest Accounting, 3*, 159–175.
Iriarte, E. G., Mcconkey, R., & Gilligan, R. H. (2016). *Disability and human rights: Global perspectives* (pp. 1–9). Macmillan Education.
Khan, N., Korac-Kakabadse, N., Skouloudis, A., & Dimopoulos, A. (2019). Diversity in the workplace: An overview of disability employment disclosures among UK firms. *Corporate Social Responsibility and Environmental Management, 26*(1), 170–185.
Landrum, N. E., & Ohsowski, B. (2018). Identifying worldviews on corporate sustainability: A content analysis of corporate sustainability reports. *Business Strategy and the Environment, 27*(1), 128–151.
Lozano, R. (2011). The state of sustainability reporting in universities. *International Journal of Sustainability in Higher Education, 12*(1), 67–78.
Luo, L., & Wang, W. (2017). Disability discrimination in employment: Three countries comparison. *Journal of Law, Policy and Globalization, 65*, 14.
Milne, M. J., & Adler, R. W. (1999). Exploring the reliability of social and environmental disclosures content analysis. *Accounting, Auditing and Accountability Journal, 12*(2), 237–256.
OECD - Organization for Economic Cooperation and Development. (2012). *Equity and quality in education: Supporting disadvantaged students and schools*. OECD Publishing.
Quinn, J. (2009). Rethinking 'failed transitions' to higher education. *In Transitions and learning through the lifecourse*. (pp. 142–153). Routledge.
Shore, L. M., Randel, A. E., Chung, B. G., Dean, M. A., Holcombe Ehrhart, K., & Singh, G. (2011). Inclusion and diversity in work groups: A review and model for future research. *Journal of Management, 37*(4), 1262–1289.
Taylor, J., Vithayathil, J., & Yim, D. (2018). Are corporate social responsibility (CSR) initiatives such as sustainable development and environmental policies value enhancing or window dressing? *Corporate Social Responsibility and Environmental Management, 25*(5), 971–980.
Torelli, R., Balluchi, F., & Furlotti, K. (2020). The materiality assessment and stakeholder engagement: A content analysis of sustainability reports. *Corporate Social Responsibility and Environmental Management, 27*(2), 470–484.
Unangst, L., Borg, N., Casellas Connors, I., & Barone, N. (2022). Diversities at US Colleges and Universities: Online diversity statements at institutions employing chief diversity officers. *Journal of Higher Education Policy and Leadership Studies, 3*(3), 16–36.
Weedon, E. (2017). The construction of under-representation in UK and Swedish higher education: Implications for disabled students. *Education, Citizenship and Social Justice, 12*(1), 75–88.
Wolbring, G., & Lillywhite, A. (2021). Equity/equality, diversity, and inclusion (EDI) in universities: The case of disabled people. *Societies, 11*(2), 49.

Diversity in Sustainability Accounting Education: The Role of Formative Assessment to Promote Inclusion

Ericka Costa, Anna Serbati, and Federica Picasso

1 Introduction

This chapter aims to promote a reflection on inclusive teaching and learning strategies in sustainability accounting education through a case study. Sustainability accounting education has, to date, focused on the importance of new pedagogies (Thomson & Bebbington, 2005; Contrafatto, 2013) that can promote a participatory and inclusive classroom. Different authors highlighted the *transformative role of education* by forming future generations with new approaches and methods to manage sustainability issues. The pedagogies proposed by Thomson and Bebbington (2005) and other authors reflected a dialogic approach to education, which is based upon the idea that students can build their own knowledge based on interaction with both educators and peers (Clements & Battista, 1990). Previous studies have explored the processes of sustainability accounting education, with a focus on the design of interdisciplinary curriculum (Cho et al., 2022; Powell & McGuigan, 2023) and the inclusion of new pedagogies in the teaching methods (Alm et al., 2021).

However, the education process also includes the final assessment, which has received scant attention in the sustainability accounting literature. To the best of our knowledge, a focus on the role of assessment in constructing an inclusive learning process is missing in this field of research. Therefore, this chapter is framed within the universal design for assessment (UDA, hereafter) as a key framework for developing equitable and inclusive learning through assessment methods that promote learning. Our contribution focuses on the power of assessment for learning (AfL, hereafter) as an authentic assessment strategy (Sambell et al., 2012) to support

E. Costa (✉) · A. Serbati · F. Picasso
University of Trento, Trento, Italy
e-mail: ericka.costa@unitn.it; anna.serbati@unitn.it; federica.picasso@unitn.it

M. Agostini et al. (eds.), *Diversity and Equity in Accounting*, SIDREA Series in Accounting and Business Administration,
https://doi.org/10.1007/978-3-031-78247-3_23

inclusive teaching and learning experiences in the sustainability accounting context. With students as essential, engaged, and active participants in the teaching, learning, and assessment process, AfL is a design assessment approach that aims to build a more robust and an engaging relationship between the assessment practice and students (Sambell et al., 2012).

Through the analysis of a case study on the design of AfL strategies in a master's course in sustainability accounting at an Italian university, the chapter shows the process of implementing a renewed approach to formative assessment and feedback to scaffold inclusive learners' engagement.

The results showed that, thanks to AfL experience, students could apply their knowledge to real-life tasks and open problems, allowing them to improve their work, thanks to a co-creation process of the assessment criteria and the introduction of peer review activity before final submission, the design proposed also following the principles of sustainable assessment (SA, hereafter) (Boud & Soler, 2016). In the specific sustainability accounting course, students had the opportunity to better understand the complexity of sustainability accounting in society, with the stakeholder identification and analyses of stakeholder engagement policies.

The chapter contributes to the sustainability accounting education literature (Thomson & Bebbington, 2005; Contrafatto, 2013; Gray, 2013) by highlighting the role of assessment as a formative tool through the involvement of students in tasks that foster their agency. Moreover, the paper also contributes to the debate about diversity and inclusion in universities, and it supports the idea that students do not need different assessment systems but somewhat different tools for an assessment approach that accompanies and orientates the whole process, preventing hindering actions (Nicol, 2014).

The remainder of the chapter is structured as follows: Section 2 introduces the field of sustainability accounting education, focusing on different pedagogies that have been approached in the learning process. Section 3 focuses on UDA and AfL, while Sect. 4 introduces the methodology and case development in the master course in sustainability accounting education. Section 5 discusses the results and draws some final remarks.

2 Diversity in Sustainability Accounting Education

Sustainability accounting has recently highlighted the urgency to open accounting to diversity (Alawattage et al., 2021), thanks to an urgent need to enrich and enlarge the accounting curriculum, thus including greater attention to ecological systems, business ethics, values, diversity, gender, equality, poverty, and many other marginalized issue. The "Open Accounting Manifesto" (Alawattage et al., 2021) has been specifically addressed to the accounting community with the desire "to expand its focus to issues of significant importance, recognising inequities and our complacency, or worse, our perpetuation of said oppression" (p. 228).

Beyond the calls for expanding the focus of accounting studies and, therefore, including multiple diversities, there has also been attention to being more inclusive in accounting education. In detail, studies on sustainability accounting education (Thomson & Bebbington, 2005; Contrafatto, 2013) have supported Freire's pedagogical approach (1996) that promotes a constructivist approach to teaching and learning. A constructivist approach to teaching is dialogical and process-oriented and aimed at co-creating knowledge with the students. It relies on education practices rich in conversation and engagement between peers (students) than at teacher-student and student-teacher levels (Gray, 1997; Clements & Battista, 1990). Researchers have echoed the importance of advancing pedagogical innovations that allow for interactive, experiential, transformative, and real-world learning experiences (Alm et al., 2021). Sustainability accounting education has therefore promoted a process-oriented approach to teaching and knowledge-building that can foster critical awareness and impact on society.

While a traditional accounting classroom is based on the "banking approach" (Freire, 1996), according to which, students passively "absorb" accounting notions and standards defined by authoritative (regulatory) bodies. Teaching involves transmitting facts, skills, and concepts to students (Clements & Battista, 1990). A constructive perspective of learning and teaching contrasts this view sharply. Based on Piagetian (1977) view of learning, Clements and Battista (1990) set constructive learning as a process in which students actively create knowledge about their own interpretations of the world and the interplay with the teacher and peers. This constructivist perspective of learning is inclusive and open to diversity, suggesting that there may be many ways of interpreting or understanding the world. This inclusiveness should be handled by the educator in the educational environment. While in a "banking approach," the educator is seen as an expert who knows all the possible answers and "fills the brain" of students with content, issues, formulas, notions, frameworks, and theory, instead, in a constructivist approach to teaching, the educator acts as a "facilitator" (Othman, 2020), which can help students to construct their own meanings (Gray, 1997; Clements & Battista, 1990).

However, this innovation should not be explored only in the content design and delivery, but it should also be engaged in the assessment. To the best of our knowledge, previous studies have not focused on inclusive assessment and the inclusion of diversity into the assessment of tasks. Therefore, this chapter is inspired by the universal design for learning approach and explores a case of technology-enhanced assessment.

3 Inclusive Approaches to Assessment

3.1 Universal Design for Assessment (UDA)

Within the universal design for learning (UDL[1]) perspective, the UDA approach has been developed, intended as "an integrated system with a broad spectrum of possible supports so as to provide the best environment in which to capture student knowledge and skills [...] UDA allows for greater flexibility in the design of assessment tasks to support the wide range of student needs within the general education setting" (Ketterlin-Geller, 2005, p. 5). This statement highlights the importance of the assessment design process in guaranteeing a complete and rich overview of the student's learning progress.

The UDA approach challenges the purpose and function of assessment. It invites us to look ahead and anticipate how the assessment will include many ways of involvement, representation, and evidence of learning. Through UDA, students should understand why they are being assessed and the abilities and competencies they are working on throughout assessments. Explaining how assessment aligns with learning outcomes and objectives is crucial for engaging students and promoting goal-setting (Zhang et al., 2021).

Within the UDA approach, a powerful tool to enhance the accessibility of the assessment process is represented by digital technologies which could have the potential to improve assessment possibilities and practices, including a broader range of concepts, skills, and means of expression, and this expands the scope of evidence-collection opportunities (Dolan et al., 2013).

3.2 Assessment for Learning (AfL)

Inspired by Sambell et al. (2012), Grion and Serbati (2019) define AfL as an essential moment of the educational experience, characterized by situations in which students are enabled to analyze and understand the processes in which they are involved and can thus participate in decisions about their learning objectives by becoming increasingly aware of their own progress. Assessment is, therefore, conceptualized as a support for improving learning, a set of assessment activities, designs, or practices prioritizing promoting student learning (Sambell et al., 2012). We can, therefore, understand it as an approach that breaks the traditional concept

[1] Universal design for learning (UDL) takes a proactive approach to inclusive education by recognizing student variety and providing flexibility and choice in learning activities. The framework is based on a set of three principles which affirm that students (i) have numerous methods to engage/be engaged in learning; (ii) have several options for accessing their material through various modes of representation; and (iii) have many options for demonstrating and sharing their learning, allowing for flexibility and choice (Bray et al., 2023).

of assessment as a summative measurement of results, and on the contrary, it proposes a new vision in which, through assessment, students can understand what and how to improve their learning.

The AfL model developed by Sambell et al. (2012) proposed six elements that characterize assessment processes in higher education, as follows:

1. The assessment action should be considered as an activity that provides students with opportunities to assess and reflect on their own learning level, progress, and acquired skills, experimenting it before facing summative assessment.
2. Sharing, interacting, and collaborating in the classroom represent a space where dialog creates dynamic flows of informal feedback between students and the class community (i.e., through peer review activities).
3. The formal use of feedback should support learning enhancement, thus making students aware of their learning.
4. Assessment activities should allow students to develop self-assessment skills practical for lifelong learning. The student, therefore, is an active and autonomous subject in the learning process.
5. Establishing a balance between the summative and formative functions of assessment is important to promote learning.
6. Assessment should propose authentic, challenging, and complex reality tasks through which students can experience actual involvement and consequently effective and profound learning.

In sum, AfL should promote full integration of teaching, learning, and assessment where assessment is part of the learning experience. Therefore, academics should actively involve students as participants in the assessment process, by creating a space for negotiating evaluation criteria, adopting self-assessment and peer assessment practices, providing feedback for student improvement, and using authentic tasks.

3.3 Sustainable Assessment (SA)

An AfL approach envisages the lifelong dimension of assessment skills, as defined in the SA perspective. SA is defined as a process that accompanies students in their growth as lifelong learners, preparing them for the assessment tasks they will encounter in life (Boud & Soler, 2016). SA refers to the lifelong learning process, which is connected to an assessment process that does not remain the exclusive domain of assessors/lecturers but passes into the hands of learners (Boud & Soler, 2016; Grion & Serbati, 2019). SA, therefore, is a new process that focuses on learners' ability to develop an evaluative judgement capability that will guide them in future professional and life contexts. Assessment is no longer understood as a unilateral act but as a choral process established between teacher and student directed toward the formulation of informed judgements and, therefore, the student as an active protagonist of the assessment process, be it formative or summative (Boud & Falchikov, 2007).

SA also includes the possibility for students to be involved in direct and authentic assessment experiences, supporting them in acquiring the concept of quality and accustoming them to making complex judgements according to a multiplicity of criteria (Sadler, 1989). Boud and Falchikov (2007) propose nine applicable principles for reflecting on and designing SA processes, as follows:

- Sharing clear assessment criteria for students
- Considering students as individuals who can achieve success
- Separating feedback processes from the awarding of grades
- Keeping a focus on learning during the assessment process rather than a focus on performance
- Supporting the development of self-assessment competencies
- Encouraging the use of reflective peer assessment practices
- Completing the feedback loop as a tool for reviewing student work
- Introducing formative assessment processes as learning experiences
- Adopting a peer review process and a well-founded and weighted judgement based on agreed and shared assessment criteria

Based on these premises, this chapter aims to present a case study of an inclusive experience of AfL implemented in two master's courses in management at Italian Northern University.

4 Methodology: A Case for Sustainable Assessment for Learning Experience

From September to December 2023, an authentic assessment activity was designed and implemented in two master's courses at a public Northern Italian university. The courses "Social Accounting and Reporting" (19 students) and "Social and Environmental Reporting" (20 students) were chosen to improve the ability of students to perform a stakeholder analysis of a specific company case. The student sample was therefore purposefully selected (Suri, 2011) and specifically related to these courses to introduce a process of scholarship of teaching and learning (Boyer, 1990): in fact, we aimed at exploring students' perceptions when these new learning and assessment experiences are introduced. In order to answer this question, we adopted a case study (Yin, 2009) in terms of design and implementation in an actual classroom setting.

One of the purposes of the courses was to make students capable of conducting a stakeholder analysis (based on the stakeholders' salience and stakeholder engagement criteria) on a specific company case that the students selected. To do so, students were asked to deliver a short company report (no longer than ten pages) with the required analysis. The activity has been designed at the group level to help students develop soft skills related to teamwork and intra- and inter-group activities.

The AfL approach was implemented through three main steps:

- (i) *First*, students were engaged in the assessment, thanks to an activity of co-construction of assessment criteria (Grion & Serbati, 2019) designed with the help of technology (Wooclap software[2]).
- (ii) *Second*, an intermediate formative assessment was implemented using a peer review activity, to scaffold the enhancement of the report, before the final delivery.
- (iii) *Third*, a reflective questionnaire was created and delivered to students to collect their perception and their satisfaction about the activity.

Step1: Co-construction of Assessment Criteria
To support the development of evaluation skills in the students and to scaffold the planned project activity in small groups, an activity of co-construction of assessment criteria was designed with the help of Wooclap. Creating and sharing standard assessment criteria was necessary to design and implement the report group activity efficiently to guide students in their collaborative activity and make them aware of the quality concept connected to the report production process (Grion & Serbati, 2019).

The process was structured as follows:

- *Structuring the Wooclap activity through the "brainstorming mode"*: Creating sharing boards, one for each criterion. The students were asked to discuss in the small group what the descriptors characterizing the criteria areas could be. During the small group's reflection process, each group member wrote the descriptors from the discussion on each criterion board using Wooclap.
- *Discussion in the large group with the educator*: Thanks to the plenary sharing and the support and guidance of the educator, the criteria were then synthesized to arrive at a set of shared descriptors (related to each criterion).
- *Sharing the criteria and final descriptors*: After the brainstorming session, the educator shared with the students the final grid resulting from the work carried out in class, a valuable grid as support for activating self-assessment processes and generally supporting the planning activity in the small group (report group development and peer review process).

Step 2: Formative Assessment and Peer Review
As previously mentioned, the co-construction criteria activity was preparatory to the group work that required the delivery of the final output (then-pages company report on stakeholder analysis), which underwent a peer review process (Grion et al., 2017; Li & Grion, 2019), following the co-constructed evaluation grid with a 1–5 scale.

---

[2] Wooclap is an instant polling valuable platform for engaging students during different class activities. Due to the University's license agreement with Wooclap, this tool is freely accessible to all academic staff and students at the institution and complies with GDPR requirements; for these reasons, it was decided to adopt this specific resource for the activity.

The peer review activity was structured as follows and was proposed asynchronously. Once all groups had delivered their company report, the educators created online folders dedicated to sets of groups (two collaborating and revising groups) where the company reports were made available. Students were asked to provide feedback individually on the other group's work using the shared assessment grid uploaded on Wooclap. Therefore, specific Wooclap resources dedicated to each group have been created so that feedback is collected. Each group, therefore, received at least one grid of feedback and provided feedback to one group. This allowed trigger comparison processes that stimulated self-feedback and self-assessment processes within the group, which were then supported in their product redesign and improvement processes (Nicol, 2019).

Step 3: Reflective Questionnaire
After implementing both activities, a reflective questionnaire was delivered to students to better understand the students' perception of the proposed activities, both in terms of inclusiveness and participation in the learning process. The instrument was designed for the purposes of exploring students' perceptions about the use of formative assessment methods and the impact on the quality of learning and active participation.

The results and discussion of the analysis are presented in the subsequent section.

5 Results and Discussion

The authentic assessment experience design on the basis of AfL (Sambell et al., 2012) and SA (Boud & Soler, 2016) provided in the two master's courses happened in groups (between peers), on real-life tasks and open problems (stakeholder analysis of a case company), with the possibility for students to continuously improve their work before final submission (intermediate formative assessment). The design of these features in our case study allowed for diversity and inclusion in the sustainability education field. Indeed, as highlighted by many authors (Cho et al., 2022; Powell & McGuigan, 2023), sustainability accounting needs a transformation not only in terms of content and curricula but also in terms of pedagogy. According to the UDA approach, the assessment moves from being a "selection instrument" to a more democratic, inclusive, open tool for continuous improvement and learning for every student to achieve his/her own best performance. In fact, students had the chance to contribute to criteria construction and to receive feedback, improving their work before submitting it for final evaluation.

The results of our analysis are presented in Table 1. Twenty students replied to the questionnaire aimed at comprehending different types of areas and related items to deeply understand the student's perception of the proposed activities (see Table 1).

Generally, students seem satisfied with the assessment activities implemented (Item 2, $M = 4.4$; SD = 0.6); they appreciated how the educator interacted with them during the proposed assessment activities (Item 3, $M = 4.5$; SD = 0.5) and how the

Table 1 Student's satisfaction with the proposed activities (multiple choice questions on a Likert scale of 1–5)

Area	Item	Mean	Std. dev.
Satisfaction with the organization of the teaching experience	1. The aim of the proposed assessment activities through the use of technology in teaching was clearly shared by the teacher	4.6	0.5
	2. The assessment activities proposed through the use of technology were interesting	4.4	0.6
	3. I am satisfied with how the educator interacted with the students during the proposed assessment activities using technology	4.5	0.5
Impact of tools and methods on the quality of learning and active participation	4. Through the assessment activities proposed by the educator through the use of technology, I was able to learn more profitably	4.1	0.8
	5. The digital resources used (e.g., Feedback, Quiz, Diary, Workshop, Task, Wooclap) encouraged active participation	4.6	0.6
	6. The use of technology has facilitated peer interaction	4.5	0.6
Satisfaction with formative assessment activities	7. I consider having taken an intermediate assignment with formative assessment a more comprehensive form of assessment compared to a single final test	4.2	1.0
	8. Receiving feedback from the educator and my peers on the work done, including through technological tools, during teaching was helpful in my learning	4.6	0.6
	9. Conducting nongraded formative tests (e.g., self-assessment quizzes, discussions, formative assessment tests, etc.) during teaching helped me to keep up with the professor's understanding of the content	4.6	0.8
Impact of teaching activities	10. The assessment activities proposed through the use of technology increased my level of motivation toward participation and study	4.2	1.2
	11. The assessment activities proposed through the use of technology made teaching enjoyable and interesting	4.3	0.8
	12. Being able to converse with the educator when she supported us in the proposed assessment activities through the use of technology fostered a deeper understanding of the topics covered	4.3	0.9
General satisfaction	13. Overall, I found the assessment activities proposed through the use of technology in this teaching satisfactory	4.4	0.7
	14. The assessment activities proposed through the use of technology carried out in this teaching fostered the development of transversal skills (critical thinking, communication, collaboration, problem-solving, creativity)	4.4	0.7
	15. I would recommend a classmate to participate in this course next year for the proposed technology-based assessment activities	4.3	0.9

activity was explained from the very beginning of the course (Item 1, $M = 4.6$; SD = 0.5).

Beyond the general evaluation, three main areas have been investigated: (i) the impact of tools and methods on the quality of learning and active participation, (ii) the students' satisfaction with formative assessment activities, and (iii) the impact of teaching activities on motivation, engagement, and learning.

In terms of impact on the quality of learning and active participation, students felt involved in the learning process, also thanks to the empowerment of peer interaction during the group work (Item 6, $M = 4.5$; SD = 0.6). They confirm that receiving intermediate informative feedback from the educator and their peers on the company report developed was helpful in their learning (Item 5, $M = 4.6$; SD = 0.6). This data highlights the power of the AfL design (Grion & Serbati, 2019) to enhance students' learning.

In terms of students' satisfaction, students consider formative assessment experiences during the course a more comprehensive form of assessment than a standard final test (Item 7, $M = 4.2$; SD = 1.0). Also, conducting nongraded formative activities during teaching helped students to keep up with the educator's understanding of the content (Item 9, $M = 4.6$; SD = 0.8).

Finally, regarding the impact of teaching activities on motivation, engagement, and learning, students appreciated the possibility of discussing with the educator during the proposed assessment activities because this fostered a deeper understanding of the topics covered (Item 12, $M = 4.3$; SD = 0.9). Moreover, regarding transversal skills development, most students found the formative assessment activities strategic to foster the development of critical thinking, communication, collaboration, problem-solving, and creativity (Item 14, $M = 4.4$; SD = 0.7).

As the literature points out, students were introduced to an authentic UDA process because students were put in a proactive position, understanding why and how they were being assessed and collaborating directly in the *assessment for the learning* process (Grion & Serbati, 2019). Specifically, the peer review process required critical thinking, observation, and good communication, enhancing assessment strategies, and in the light of the UDL framework, it allows embracing learner diversity to gain a more comprehensive understanding of learning and support learners to whom is given more responsibility for monitoring and reflecting on their own and peers' learning (Sambell et al., 2012; Nicol, 2019; Zhang et al., 2021).

6 Conclusion

Sustainability accounting has to date reflected on the need of new pedagogical approaches to include multiple and diverse voices (Thomson & Bebbington, 2005; Gray, 2013; Powell & McGuigan, 2023; Cho et al., 2022). Different studies have focused on the agenda to develop in the classes or the process of acquiring knowledge (Contrafatto, 2013; Thomson & Bebbington; 2005).

However, to date, there has been scant attention to the assessment process and the way in which this process could be formative, i.e., it could help to improve and facilitate the learning process of the students, in a more inclusive and democratic form of approach to the teaching experience. Therefore, this chapter would contribute in this direction.

Starting from the UDA theoretical framework, an assessment design following the AfL model has been implemented in two master's courses "Social Accounting and Reporting" and "Social and Environmental Reporting" (overall 39 students). The formative assessment was enriched by the introduction of specific activities, designed following the SA nine principles of Boud and Falchikov (2007), which have seen students as active and central protagonists of the learning and SA processes developed in class.

First, the design of assessment criteria co-creation activity through the use of Wooclap allowed students to creatively share their vision, discussing how to collaboratively build a common framework of elements crucial for the development and the assessment of the group report itself.

Second, peer review activity was crucial for the adoption of the assessment criteria by students themselves, with a vision of enhancing assessment skills through collaboration and comparison with peers. As the literature previously highlighted, peer review is defined as an activity of making a well-founded and weighted judgement based on agreed and/or shared assessment criteria, a learning experience structured in such a way that students have the opportunity to evaluate, make judgements, and elaborate written comments on the work of peers (Nicol, 2014).

After the implementation of these activities, we collected some questionnaires from the students to understand if these initiatives allowed a more inclusive and sustainable way of learning. The result of the analysis highlighted that students were very satisfied about the assessment activities proposed by the educator and they perceived formative assessment and feedback as relevant learning experiences.

Criteria co-construction made them clear, transparent, and concrete; everyone could contribute to this exercise, thanks to the use of Wooclap. Moreover, peer feedback and teacher feedback represented great opportunities to improve their performance before the final submission of the report.

This represents a quite unique experience of using an inclusive approach to assessment, by enhancing students' agency in the assessment process and therefore fostering students' engagement and learning.

Although the number of students of this exploratory research is limited, we hope this case study can open up the debate and future research on this topic in the field of sustainability accounting education. Research implications envisage the opportunity to replicate and scale up the use of an inclusive approach to assessment in this field, by broadening the research in innovative teaching and students' agency in learning. Educational implications can also be very wide, by modeling new strategies and tools for an assessment approach in sustainability accounting education that accompanies and orientates the whole learning process, fostering deeper students' learning, motivation, and engagement.

References

Alawattage, C., Arjaliès, D.-L., Barrett, M., Bernard, J., Casa Nova, S. P. C., Cho, C. H., Cooper, C., Denedo, M., Drujon D'Astros, C., Evans, R., Ejiogu, A., Frieden, L., Ghio, A., McGuigan, N., Luo, Y., Pimentel, E., Powell, L., Navarro Pérez, P. A., Quattrone, P., Romi, A. M., Smyth, S., Sopt, J., & Sorola, M. (2021). Opening accounting: A Manifesto. *Accounting Forum, 45*(3), 227–246.

Alm, K., Melén, M., & Aggestam-Pontoppidan, C. (2021). Advancing SDG competencies in higher education: Exploring an interdisciplinary pedagogical approach. *International Journal of Sustainability in Higher Education, 22*(6), 1450–1466.

Boud, D., & Falchikov, N. (2007). *Rethinking assessment in higher education* (pp. 191–207). Routledge.

Boud, D., & Soler, R. (2016). Sustainable assessment revisited. *Assessment & Evaluation in Higher Education, 41*(3), 400–413.

Boyer, E. L. (1990). *Scholarship reconsidered: Priorities of the professoriate*. Princeton University Press. 3175 Princeton Pike, Lawrenceville, NJ 08648.

Bray, A., Devitt, A., Banks, J., Sanchez Fuentes, S., Sandoval, M., Riviou, K., Byrne, D., Flood, M., Reale, J., & Terrenzio, S. (2023). What next for universal design for learning? A systematic literature review of technology in UDL implementations at second level. *British Journal of Educational Technology*, 113–138.

Cho, C. H., Senn, J., & Sobkowiak, M. (2022). Sustainability at stake during COVID-19: Exploring the role of accounting in addressing environmental crises. *Critical Perspectives on Accounting, 82*, 102327.

Clements, D. H., & Battista, M. T. (1990). Constructivist learning and teaching. *The Arithmetic Teacher, 38*(1), 34–35.

Contrafatto, M. (2013). Utopia and Passion': A commentary on sustainability and accounting education: The elephant in the classroom. *Accounting Education, 22*(4), 336–339.

Dolan, R. P., Burling, K., Harms, M., Strain-Seymour, E., Way, W. D., & Rose, D. H. (2013). *A universal design for learning-based framework for designing accessible technology-enhanced assessments*. Research Report: Universal Design for Learning.

Freire, P. (1996). *Pedagogy of the oppressed (Revised)*. Continuum.

Gray, A.J. (1997). *Constructivist teaching and learning*. SSTA Research Centre Report 97(7).

Gray, R. (2013). Sustainability + accounting education: The elephant in the classroom. *Accounting Education, 22*(4), 308–332.

Grion, V., & Serbati, A. (2019). *Valutazione sostenibile e feedback nei contesti universitari. Prospettive emergenti, rubriche e pratiche*. PensaMultimedia.

Grion, V., Serbati, A., Tino, C., & Nicol, D. (2017). Ripensare la teoria della valutazione e dell'apprendimento all'università: un modello per implementare pratiche di peer review. *Italian Journal of Educational Research, 19*, 209–226.

Ketterlin-Geller, L. R. (2005). Knowing what all students know: Procedures for developing universal design for assessment. *Journal of Technology, Learning, and Assessment, 4*(2) Available from http://www.jtla.org

Li, L., & Grion, V. (2019). The power of giving feedback and receiving feedback in peer assessment. *AISHE-J, 11*(2), 1–17.

Nicol, D. (2014). Guiding principles for peer review: Unlocking learners' evaluative skills. In C. Kreber, C. Anderson, N. Entwistle, & J. McArthur (Eds.), *Advances and innovations in university assessment and feedback* (pp. 197–224). Edinburgh University Press.

Nicol, D. (2019). Reconceptualising feedback as an internal not an external process. *Italian Journal of Educational Research*, 71–84.

Othman, R. (2020), Managing student and faculty expectations and the unexpected during the COVID-19 lockdown: role transformation. *Accounting Research Journal, 34*(2), 217–228.

Piaget, J. (1977). *The development of thought: Equilibration of cognitive structures*. (A. Rosin, Trans),. The Viking Press.

Powell, L., & McGuigan, N. (2023). Responding to crises: Rewilding accounting education for the Anthropocene. *Meditari Accountancy Research, 31*(1), 101–120.

Sadler, D. R. (1989). Formative assessment and the design of instructional systems. *Instructional science, 18*(2), 119–144.

Sambell, K., McDowell, L., & Montgomery, C. (2012). *Assessment for learning in higher education*. Routledge.

Suri, H. (2011). Purposeful sampling in qualitative research synthesis. *Qualitative Research Journal, 11*(2), 63–75. https://doi.org/10.3316/QRJ1102063

Thomson, I. H., & Bebbington, J. (2005). Social and environmental reporting in the UK: A pedagogic evaluation. *Critical Perspectives on Accounting, 16*(5), 507–533.

Yin, R. K. (2009). How to do better case studies. *The SAGE Handbook of Applied Social Research Methods*, 2(254–282).

Zhang, J., Takacs, S., Truong L., Smulders, D., & Lee, H. (2021). Assessment design: Perspectives and examples informed by universal design for learning. Centre for Teaching, Learning, and Innovation. Justice Institute of British Columbia, 1–25.

Concluding Remarks

Alessandro Ghio

This concluding chapter reflects on the key insights from the discussions of diversity and equity in accounting in the preceding chapters. It also provides a critical appreciation of the approaches used by the authors throughout the book. Finally, the chapter outlines several promising directions for future research aimed at deepening our understanding of diversity and equity in accounting.

What We Can Learn from Reading This Book

This book represents an impressive collection of work exploring and advancing our understanding of diversity and equity in accounting. The five parts begin with an important analysis of the state of the art through different perspectives (Part I). The focus then shifts to reporting on diversity (Part II) and the organizational challenges (Part III) involved in addressing diversity and equity. Empirical case studies complement these conceptual analyses (Part IV). The final section provides relevant insights into diversity and equity within accounting education and higher education (Part V).

This work is groundbreaking in many dimensions. Its richness and depth of insights signal that questions of diversity and equity are core to accounting. This is particularly crucial in accounting, where technical aspects often dominate the field (Gendron, 2015; Gendron & Rodrigue, 2021; Humphrey & Gendron, 2015). Ontologically, examining diversity collides with the traditional reluctance to deviate from the norm characterizing the accounting field (Burrell, 1987). The mainstream

A. Ghio
ESCP Business School, Paris, France
e-mail: aghio@escp.edu

M. Agostini et al. (eds.), *Diversity and Equity in Accounting*, SIDREA Series in Accounting and Business Administration,
https://doi.org/10.1007/978-3-031-78247-3

approach to diversity in accounting has largely focused on gender and its potential to improve organizational performance (Ghio et al., 2024). The well-known 2015 McKinsey article reinforced this view by connecting organizational diversity to firm financial performance, emphasizing the business case for diversity. This book effectively debunks this myth, adopting an approach grounded in social justice. This perspective has the potential to advance a society that welcomes diversity in all its forms without the underlying pressure to maximize financial performance.

These contributions also further demonstrate how accounting continues to shape our society (Burchell et al., 1980; Hines, 1988; Hopwood, 1987). The book highlights that accounting impacts our understanding and view of diversity through management control practices, reporting methods, and even the types of assessments we require from accounting students. Recognizing the pervasiveness of accounting is a vital step toward identifying and dismantling power structures that hinder diversity and equity.

This book then addresses the call for research on grand challenges and how accounting research can contribute to the United Nations Sustainable Development Goals (UN SDGs) (Bebbington & Unerman, 2018, 2020). The contributions are relevant for achieving UN SDG 3 (Good health and well-being), UN SDG 4 (Quality education), UN SDG 5 (Gender equality), UN SDG 10 (Reduced inequalities), and UN SDG 11 (Sustainable cities and communities). Additionally, they contribute to the burgeoning discussions on ESG (environmental, social, and governance) practices. Diversity and equity primarily fall under the "S" (social) category but have clear connections to both "G" (governance) and "E" (environment). The "S" has often suffered from the "middle child" syndrome (Neilan et al., 2020), overshadowed by governance and environmental concerns. As such, these contributions on diversity and equity in accounting are most welcome to avoid the widespread of diversity washing (Baker et al., 2024; Brown-Liburd et al., 2024).

I commend the authors, many of whom are junior, untenured scholars or PhD students in Italian universities, for their courage in undertaking this type of research. While the context is sometimes evolving, Galizzi et al. (2023) show how patriarchy, heteronormativity, and sexism still characterize this context. Universities are also facing claims of wokeism and their social relevance is questioned. This book on diversity and equity in accounting, the 2023 conference on Diversity in Accounting at "Università degli Studi Internazionali di Roma," and the creation of a research group on diversity and equity in accounting within the Italian Accounting Association are all positive and encouraging signs. The hope is that more accounting scholars will join these conversations because diversity and equity concern everyone.

Future Avenues

Future research on diversity and equity in accounting can be developed from this book. I encourage studies that further explore these topics from a historical perspective. The case study on the Fiat group is an excellent example of examining the evolution of organizational practices and control systems related to diversity (Agostini & Truant, 2024). Understanding past experiences helps us comprehend why certain diversity practices and measurements are in place (or not) in today's organizations.

Another area that deserves further attention is accounting education (Ghio et al., 2023). Costa et al. (2024) provide an innovative approach to combining diversity questions with sustainability topics in their accounting course. These reflections are also connected to the institutional context and the perception of diversity in higher education institutions (Masiero et al., 2024; Oppi & Galizzi, 2024; Raimo et al., 2024). Connecting and exploring macro and/or meso to micro levels in terms of diversity and accounting education is particularly important as universities and business schools increasingly make diversity claims. This would also be relevant in terms of providing further insight into whether these claims of diversity in our workplace are substantiated by actions, or whether they are merely symbolic in order to attract highly paid students and ensure accreditation.

There also emerges a need for more conceptual papers that advance our understanding of diversity and equity in accounting and for the mobilization of new theories and paradigms. The chapters in the first section show the complexity of the current state of diversity and equity in accounting (Berardi et al., 2024; Beretta et al., 2024; Garcia-Sanchez et al., 2024; Occhipinti et al., 2024; Tommaso, 2024). What emerges is a form of isomorphism and stagnation in conceptual development. Southern contexts or theories drawn from diversity studies, such as queer theory, can provide more nuanced understandings of diversity and equity in accounting (Gómez-Villegas & Larrinaga, 2023; Rumens, 2016).

The book also provides insights into social identities such as queerness (Giusepponi, 2024) and disability (Gulluscio et al., 2024; Raucci & Paolini, 2024) that have been underexplored in accounting research (Ghio et al., 2024). More work is needed to understand the implications of accounting for numerous marginalized communities (e.g., Indigenous, queer, mental and physical disabilities) and from an intersectional perspective (Janssens & Zanoni, 2021). Past research has often focused on one social dimension at a time, but these dimensions can intersect, creating unique experiences that should not be assimilated into a single category. Oral histories and ethnographies can be particularly valuable for gathering in-depth insights from unique life experiences in accounting (Hammond, 2018; Vollmer, 2023).

This book has also started to advance our understanding that diversity and equity in accounting vary across organization types. While large multinationals and Big4 accounting firms often attract attention due to their media relevance and data availability, the organizational world is much broader. This book innovatively gathers insights on the public sector and higher education institutions (Masiero et al., 2024; Oppi & Galizzi, 2024; Raimo et al., 2024), local governments (Cardillo et al., 2024), and B-Corps (Aureli et al., 2024). Other fields that could be explored include cooperatives, informal organizations, small and medium-sized companies, and accounting firms. These organizations may have fewer resources for developing formal diversity practices, but they may have informal mechanisms that support or hinder their diverse workforce.

Reporting and disclosure about diversity and governance appear to be the most developed fields of research (Agostini, 2024; Demartini & Soriano, 2024; Frisenna & Rizzotti, 2024; Magnanelli & Raoli, 2024; Marrone et al., 2024). However, control systems and audit procedures also contribute to power imbalances regarding diversity and equity (Broccardo & Truant, 2024; Sentuti et al., 2024). The increasing external pressure to improve diversity performance will likely affect how diversity key performance indicators are developed and perceived by stakeholders. While diversity reporting has mostly been voluntary and unaudited, stakeholders now expect high-quality, verified information. Auditors are beginning to approach social data, including diversity. It is important to understand how these processes unfold.

Diversity should also be integrated into the broader business ecosystem, which is rapidly evolving (McGee, 2023; Motoki et al., 2023). Artificial intelligence (AI) is likely to be a game-changer for how we approach diversity (Ghio, 2024). There are growing concerns about the disparities AI may generate in the business world and society at large (Fornsari & Bannò, 2024). Ethical reflections on how accounting practices may enhance these power imbalances are crucial. Both academic and regulatory perspectives must further understand the effects of AI on diversity in accounting and suggest actions to avoid fostering inequities.

To conclude, this book has been an incredible journey and represents a starting point toward a better future. Researchers from all epistemological and methodological backgrounds are invited to join these discussions, as diversity and equity in accounting concern everyone. These discussions should not remain on the fringes of academia or in the hands of a few experts. Diverse perspectives are encouraged so that society can draw on our work to make the world a better place for everyone.

References

Agostini, M. (2024). Diversity and equity disclosure in corporate reporting. In M. Agostini, V. Beretta, C. Demartini, A. Ghio, & S. Trucco (Eds.), *Diversity and equity in accounting*. Springer.

Agostini, M., & Truant, E. (2024). Equity and inclusion: A historical perspective in the Fiat group. In M. Agostini, V. Beretta, C. Demartini, A. Ghio, & S. Trucco (Eds.), *Diversity and equity in accounting*. Springer.

Aureli, S., Bartolini, M., & Moschini, G. (2024). Assessing Italian B-Corps commitment on diversity and inclusion and its linkage with financial performance. In M. Agostini, V. Beretta, C. Demartini, A. Ghio, & S. Trucco (Eds.), *Diversity and equity in accounting*. Springer.

Baker, A., Larcker, D. F., McClure, C., Saraph, D., & Watts, E. (2024). Diversity washing. *Journal of Accounting Research. 62*(5), 1661–1709.

Bebbington, J., & Unerman, J. (2018). Achieving the United Nations Sustainable Development goals: An enabling role for accounting research. *Accounting, Auditing & Accountability Journal, 31*(1), 2–24.

Bebbington, J., & Unerman, J. (2020). Advancing research into accounting and the UN sustainable development goals. *Accounting, Auditing & Accountability Journal, 33*(7), 1657–1670.

Berardi, L., Mook, L., & Monaco, M. L. (2024). The reporting of diversity, equity, and inclusion by nonprofit organizations. First evidence from the literature. In M. Agostini, V. Beretta, C. Demartini, A. Ghio, & S. Trucco (Eds.), *Diversity and equity in accounting*. Springer.

Beretta, V., Demartini, C., & Trucco, S. (2024). Diversity, equity and inclusion: A bibliometric literature review. In M. Agostini, V. Beretta, C. Demartini, A. Ghio, & S. Trucco (Eds.), *Diversity and equity in accounting*. Springer.

Broccardo, L., & Truant, E. (2024). The integration of diversity, inclusion and equity in management control systems: The Iren experience. In M. Agostini, V. Beretta, C. Demartini, A. Ghio, & S. Trucco (Eds.), *Diversity and equity in accounting*. Springer.

Brown-Liburd, H. L., Ghio, A., & Roberts, A. A. (2024). Diversity, equity, inclusion and belonging: Practice problems of real consequence. *Accounting Horizons, 38*(1), 1–5.

Burchell, S., Clubb, C., Hopwood, A., Hughes, J., & Nahapiet, J. (1980). The roles of accounting in organizations and society. *Accounting, Organizations and Society, 5*(1), 5–27.

Burrell, G. (1987). No accounting for sexuality. *Accounting, Organizations and Society, 12*(1), 89–101.

Cardillo, E., Leotta, A., Rizza, C., & Ruggeri, D. (2024). Social equity reporting and practices in local governments. Findings from a pilot case study. In M. Agostini, V. Beretta, C. Demartini, A. Ghio, & S. Trucco (Eds.), *Diversity and equity in accounting*. Springer.

M. Agostini et al. (eds.), *Diversity and Equity in Accounting*, SIDREA Series in Accounting and Business Administration,
https://doi.org/10.1007/978-3-031-78247-3

Costa, E., Serbati, A., & Picasso, F. (2024). Diversity in sustainability accounting education: The role of formative assessment to promote inclusion. In M. Agostini, V. Beretta, C. Demartini, A. Ghio, & S. Trucco (Eds.), *Diversity and equity in accounting*. Springer.

Demartini, P., & Soriano, S. (2024). Are the European sustainability reporting standards effective to fight modern slavery risk? In M. Agostini, V. Beretta, C. Demartini, A. Ghio, & S. Trucco (Eds.), *Diversity and equity in accounting*. Springer.

Fornsari, T., & Bannò, M. (2024). Exploring gender disparities in the era of AI. In M. Agostini, V. Beretta, C. Demartini, A. Ghio, & S. Trucco (Eds.), *Diversity and equity in accounting*. Springer.

Frisenna, C., & Rizzotti, D. (2024). Do women behave more ethically than men? Evidence from the impact of female CEO on the level of earnings management. In M. Agostini, V. Beretta, C. Demartini, A. Ghio, & S. Trucco (Eds.), *Diversity and equity in accounting*. Springer.

Galizzi, G., McBride, K., & Siboni, B. (2023). Patriarchy persists: Experiences of barriers to women's career progression in Italian accounting academia. *Critical Perspectives on Accounting, 102625*.

Garcia-Sanchez, I. M., Minutiello, V., & Tettamanzi, P. (2024). Diversity, equity and inclusion practices in family firms: A review of the literature. In M. Agostini, V. Beretta, C. Demartini, A. Ghio, & S. Trucco (Eds.), *Diversity and equity in accounting*. Springer.

Gendron, Y. (2015). Accounting academia and the threat of the paying-off mentality. *Critical Perspectives on Accounting, 26*, 168–176.

Gendron, Y., & Rodrigue, M. (2021). On the centrality of peripheral research and the dangers of tight boundary gatekeeping. *Critical Perspectives on Accounting, 76*, 102076.

Ghio, A. (2024). Democratizing academic research with artificial intelligence: The misleading case of language. *Critical Perspectives on Accounting, 98*, 102687.

Ghio, A., McGuigan, N., Stewart, O. J., Tharapos, M., & Wood, L. I. (2023). Diversity, equity, and social justice in accounting education. *Issues in Accounting Education, 38*(1), 1–5.

Ghio, A., Occhipinti, Z., & Verona, R. (2024). The consideration of diversity in the accounting literature: A systematic literature review. *European Accounting Review*. forthcoming.

Giusepponi, K. (2024). Queer dimensions and other diversities. Valorization and positive language within organizations. In M. Agostini, V. Beretta, C. Demartini, A. Ghio, & S. Trucco (Eds.), *Diversity and equity in accounting*. Springer.

Gómez-Villegas, M., & Larrinaga, C. (2023). A critical accounting project for Latin America? Objects of knowledge or ways of knowing. *Critical Perspectives on Accounting, 93*, 102508.

Gulluscio, C., Maura, S. G., & Puntillo, P. (2024). Disability disclosure in the sustainability reports of RUS member universities: An exploratory study in Italy. In M. Agostini, V. Beretta, C. Demartini, A. Ghio, & S. Trucco (Eds.), *Diversity and equity in accounting*. Springer.

Hammond, T. (2018). LGBTQ+ accountants: A call for oral history research. *Sustainability Accounting Management and Policy Journal, 9*(5), 615–624.

Hines, R. D. (1988). Financial accounting: In communicating reality, we construct reality. *Accounting, Organizations and Society, 13*(3), 251–261.

Hopwood, A. G. (1987). Accounting and gender: An introduction. *Accounting, Organizations and Society, 12*(1), 65–69.

Humphrey, C., & Gendron, Y. (2015). What is going on? The sustainability of accounting academia. *Critical Perspectives on Accounting, 26*(C), 47–66.

Janssens, M., & Zanoni, P. (2021). Making diversity research matter for social change: New conversations beyond the firm. *Organization Theory, 2*(2), 26317877211004603.

Magnanelli, B. S., & Raoli, E. (2024). Female leadership. In M. Agostini, V. Beretta, C. Demartini, A. Ghio, & S. Trucco (Eds.), *Diversity and equity in accounting*. Springer.

Marrone, A., Pontrelli, V., & Oliva, L. (2024). Diversity, equity and inclusion in environmental social and governance disclosure: An empirical analysis of governance determinants. In M. Agostini, V. Beretta, C. Demartini, A. Ghio, & S. Trucco (Eds.), *Diversity and equity in accounting*. Springer.

Masiero, E., Garlatti Costa, G., & Musella, A. M. (2024). Action and perception of gender equality in the higher education institutions: The case study of the University of Trieste. In M. Agostini, V. Beretta, C. Demartini, A. Ghio, & S. Trucco (Eds.), *Diversity and equity in accounting*. Springer.

McGee, R. W. (2023). *What will the United States look like in 2050? A ChatGPT short story*. Fayetteville State University working paper.

Motoki, F., Neto, V. N., & Rodrigues, V. (2023). More human than human: Measuring ChatGPT political bias. *Public Choice*. forthcoming.

Neilan, J., Reilly, P., & Fitzpatrick, G. (2020). *Time to rethink the S in ESG*. Harvard Law School Forum on Corporate Governance woking paper.

Occhipinti, Z., Tallarico, S., & Verona, R. (2024). Diversity in accounting: Implications for environmental sustainability. In M. Agostini, V. Beretta, C. Demartini, A. Ghio, & S. Trucco (Eds.), *Diversity and equity in accounting*. Springer.

Oppi, C., & Galizzi, G. (2024). Gender equality as public value: An empirical analysis of gender equality plans in italian higher education institutions. In M. Agostini, V. Beretta, C. Demartini, A. Ghio, & S. Trucco (Eds.), *Diversity and equity in accounting*. Springer.

Raimo, N., L'Abate, V., Marrone, A., & Vitolla, F. (2024). The determinants of gender equality in the academic world: An empirical analysis in international universities. In M. Agostini, V. Beretta, C. Demartini, A. Ghio, & S. Trucco (Eds.), *Diversity and equity in accounting*. Springer.

Raucci, D., & Paolini, M. (2024). How cultural and personnel controls influence inclusive workplace climate for people with disabilities? Insights from the Italian context. In M. Agostini, V. Beretta, C. Demartini, A. Ghio, & S. Trucco (Eds.), *Diversity and equity in accounting*. Springer.

Rumens, N. (2016). Sexualities and accounting: A queer theory perspective. *Critical Perspectives on Accounting, 35*(C), 111–120.

Sentuti, A., Palazzi, F., & Cesaroni, F. M. (2024). Drivers, barriers and enablers of gender equality certification system. Insights from a case study. In M. Agostini, V. Beretta, C. Demartini, A. Ghio, & S. Trucco (Eds.), *Diversity and equity in accounting*. Springer.

Tommaso, S. (2024). Diversity as determinant of firm performance: A literature review. In M. Agostini, V. Beretta, C. Demartini, A. Ghio, & S. Trucco (Eds.), *Diversity and equity in accounting*. Springer.

Vollmer, H. (2023). Accounting theory, ethnography, and the silence of the social. *Qualitative Research in Accounting & Management*. forthcoming.

The manufacturer's authorised representative in the EU is Springer Nature Customer Service Centre GmbH, Europaplatz 3, 69115 Heidelberg, Germany. If you have any concerns regarding our products, please contact ProductSafety@springernature.com

Printed and bound by CPI Group (UK) Ltd, Croydon, CR0 4YY
30/09/2026
02225568-0012